Windows 98

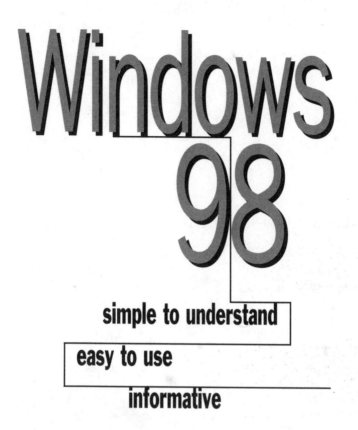

Windows 98

simple to understand
easy to use
informative

First published in Great Britain in 1999 by
Michael O'Mara Books Limited
9 Lion Yard
Tremadoc Road
London SW4 7NQ

First published in Germany by Mixing, 74172
Neckarsulm

A CIP catalogue record for this book is available from the British Library

ISBN 1-85479-430-2

1 3 5 7 9 10 8 6 4 2

Printed in Germany

Contents

Chapter 1:
Introduction to Windows 98

Chapter 2:
Windows Help

Chapter 3:
Programs and Documents

Chapter 4:
Desktop, Taskbar and *Start* Menu

Chapter 5:
My Computer and Explorer

Chapter 6:
The Recycle Bin

Chapter 7:
Windows 98 Search

Chapter 8:
Control Panel

Chapter 9:
System Tools

Chapter 10:
Multimedia Applications

Chapter 11:
Online Features

Chapter 12:
Paint

Chapter 13:
Word processing with Windows 98 and Office 97

Glossary

1. Introduction to Windows 98

In the first chapter, you will learn the basics of the graphical operating system *Windows 98*. We begin with the starting and closing operations of Windows, also taking into consideration the *MS-DOS Mode*, which is needed for DOS-based games. You will read about how to configure the startup and the MS-DOS prompt to suit your personal needs. You will also learn how to configure your mouse with *Windows 98* and which functions to execute with the right mouse button.

Starting Windows 98

Windows 98 is a powerful 32-bit operating system which does not require the earlier MS-DOS (Microsoft Disk Operating System) to function. For this reason, no command is needed to call up the graphic interface.

In order to start *Windows 98* you simply have to switch on your computer. We really cannot help you with that, but you should be able to find the power switch on your PC and that of the monitor by yourself.

BIOS
Directly after you have switched on the computer, all the systems will be verified. The BIOS (Basic Input Output System) makes sure that all available components like hard disk, floppy disk and CD-ROM drive, as well as the main memory and the graphics card, are recognized and working. On most computers, you can follow this process by reading the messages on your screen.

Once the diagnostics have been completed, you will see the *Windows 98* splash screen consisting of the *Windows 98* logo floating between clouds. At the bottom of this screen, an animated bar displays the ongoing process of loading all the necessary files. Right now your computer is working overtime, loading hundreds of system files, script files and drivers, as well as starting up the first programs.

Fig. 1.1: Windows 98 desktop after switching on the computer

Welcome to Windows 98 dialog

After the loading process, the *Windows 98* desktop is displayed on a stand-alone PC showing the *Welcome to Windows 98* dialog box. If this dialog box is not displayed, your dealer might have already disabled this function (See Tip below).

Windows 98-network

On a *Windows 98* network, the *Enter Network Password* dialog box is displayed (Figure 1.2). Type your name in the *User name* box and your password, which you will get from the system operator, into the *Password* box. Press ↵ or click the *OK* button.

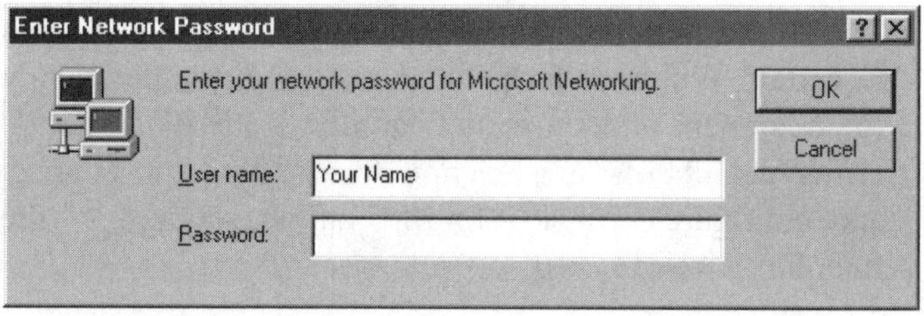

Fig. 1.2:   *Enter Network Password* dialog box

If the *Welcome to Windows 98* dialog box is displayed, press *Enter* ⏎ or click on the *Close* button ⊠ in the title bar. After this, a desktop similar to Figure 1.1 will be displayed.

Tip! In order to avoid the *Welcome to Windows 98* dialog box being displayed every time you start *Windows 98*, uncheck the *Show this screen each time Windows 98 starts* option and choose *Close* ⊠.

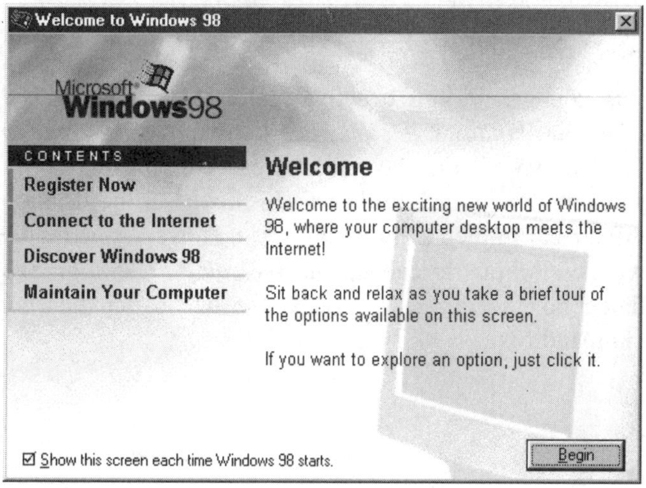

Fig. 1.3:   *Welcome to Windows 98* dialog box

Welcome to Windows 98 dialog box

The *Welcome to Windows 98* dialog box gives you access to certain Windows Help functions designed specifically for beginners and those not familiar with *Windows 98*. Using the *Internet Connection Wizard* you can connect and configure your PC for the online services of the Internet.

Online-Registration

You can register your user information with the *Registration Wizard* in the Internet, via an installed modem and telephone line.

Discover Windows 98 option

Discover Windows 98 is a useful tutorial teaching you how to work with *Windows 98*. Call up this function by inserting the setup CD-ROM and choosing *Discover Windows 98*.

Call up the *Welcome to Windows 98* Dialog Box Again

By default, the *Welcome to Windows 98* dialog box appears automatically on your screen after every startup. You can close this window by clicking on the *Close* button ⊠ in the title bar.

This changes if you deactivated the *Show this screen each time Windows 98 starts* checkbox in the *Welcome to Windows 98* dialog box and closed the window by choosing *Close* in the title bar. In this case, the desktop will appear immediately after startup. However, you have two possibilities to call up the *Welcome to Windows 98* dialog box again. Let's look at the one using the *Run* command first.

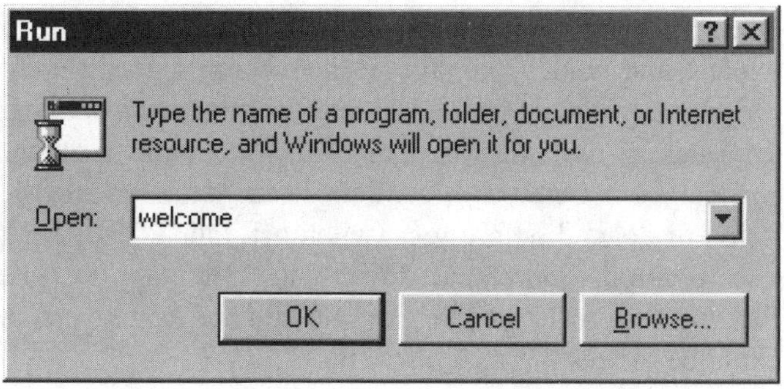

Fig. 1.4: Call up the *Welcome* screen again

The first method of recalling the *Welcome to Windows 98* screen uses the *Run* command in the *Start* menu. Type 'welcome' in the open box and click the *OK* button. The *Welcome to Windows 98* screen will be displayed.

Alternatively, you can click on the *Start* button and point the mouse cursor to *Programs*. Choose *Accessories* from the overlapping menu and the *System Tools* item from the options after that. To display the *Welcome to Windows 98* screen again, click on *Welcome To Windows* in the submenu which will then be displayed on your screen. You can close the box by choosing *Close* ☒ in the title bar, or call up information by selecting one of the options.

Close Windows 98

After having finished your work on the computer using *Windows 98*, you will probably want to switch off your computer again. Follow all the steps given below from beginning to end every time you end your work session.

Tip! During the startup hundreds of files have already been loaded, and while you have been working with different programs, your computer has been continuously loading information onto the hard disk and the main memory without your being aware of it. These data have to be saved or deleted before you switch off your PC. Bearing this in mind, don't shut down your computer by just flipping the power switch. Loss of data and system errors could be the result of such an action.

Shutting down
Windows 98

Shutting down *Windows 98* is straightforward. Since the *Start* menu functions as the coordinator of the graphic operating system, you need to go back to the *Start* button in order to close *Windows 98*.

Click the *Start* button and select the *Shut Down* command from the *Start* menu which appears.

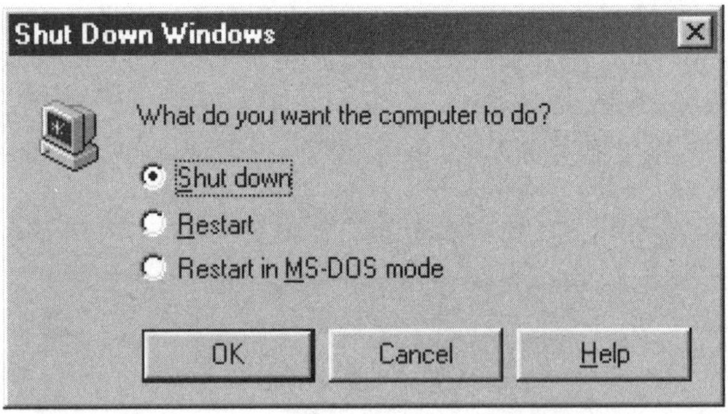

Fig. 1.5: The *Shut Down Windows* dialog box

What happens now depends on whether you have already saved all the documents which are open. If this is the case then the desktop gets dark and the *Shut Down Windows* dialog box appears. Choose the *Shut down* option and press Enter ⏎ or click the *OK* button.

If there are documents still open in any Windows application, a message will appear when you choose the *Shut Down* command asking if you want to save those data. If you don't, choose *No* in the message box.

Following this, *Windows 98* automatically closes all open applications and shuts down the computer. On the screen you see a graphic display of clouds with the message 'Windows is shutting down'. Shortly after that, the screen blacks out and a message appears in the center saying 'It is now safe to turn off your computer'. Only at this point should you switch off your computer.

Handling the Mouse with Windows 98

If you have never worked with a graphic operating system before, you might feel a bit uncomfortable in the beginning while handling this electronic rodent called a mouse. Especially beginners often feel that the mouse pointer has a life of its own rather than following the instructions of its user.

This unease, however, will soon be forgotten. You will experience for yourself how quickly you get used to the mouse and soon you won't want to be without it. Apart from some basic tips concerning the handling and movement of the mouse, you should also know the most important mouse commands.

In this book we constantly talk about the things that can be done using the mouse. In fact, precisely this is the enormous advantage of a graphic interface. Almost any step in *Windows 98* can be executed using the mouse. Rest your hand lightly on the mouse with the palm of your hand touching the mouse pad. Your index finger should be placed on the left mouse button without putting any pressure on it. We need clear commands for the most important mouse actions for everybody to understand and execute the same thing.

After the Windows startup, a small arrow will appear somewhere on the desktop. This is the mouse pointer, sometimes called a cursor or just pointer. If you cannot see the mouse pointer just move the mouse a bit on the mouse pad.

As you can see, the pointer of this little fellow is very obedient. If you move the mouse, the cursor on the screen follows your movement exactly. This means that as soon as you move the mouse up, the little arrow follows suit. Move your mouse to the left and the cursor will also move left.

Fig. 1.6:   Mouse actions: Pointing, clicking and dragging

While doing this, remember that the faster you move the mouse, the longer will be the distance which the mouse pointer moves on the screen. If you move the mouse slowly, the pointer will follow faithfully and cover only a short distance.

This ballistic consideration is very important. Before you execute a command or an action using the mouse, you should first of all place the mouse pointer in a specific position.

The Mouse Action *Pointing*

This process is called pointing. Try now to move the mouse so that the mouse arrow exactly points onto the icon labelled *Recycle Bin* on the desktop. Just pointing will not cause the computer to react in any way.

To make something happen, you have to press on one of the mouse buttons rapidly once or a few times, depending on the task.

The Mouse Action *Clicking*

If you press the left mouse button once, the *Recycle Bin* icon will be highlighted. This is called 'clicking'. For most mouse actions you will use the left mouse button. The right mouse button calls up a context menu. There-fore, as long as we don't specifically ask you to use the right mouse button, we always refer to the left one.

The Mouse Action D*ragging*

Put the mouse pointer on the highlighted *Recycle Bin*, press and hold the left mouse button and move the mouse to the right. This mouse action is called 'dragging'.

As you can see, the icon appears to be 'glued' to the mouse pointer (see the right side of Figure 1.6). If you release the mouse button, the icon will remain in that spot. This combination is called Drag-and-Drop.

You will need to drag the mouse in text fields of dialog boxes or while doing word processing, with *WordPad* for example. You can use dragging in cases when you are highlighting some text or an entire passage you want to format, overwrite, delete or copy. To do this, position the cursor in front of the first letter you wish to highlight and while holding down the button, drag the cursor along to the last letter you want to highlight.

The Mouse Action *Double-clicking*

Now place the cursor once again on the *Recycle Bin* icon. The following action will require some concentration from beginners. Press the left mouse button twice in quick succession. This is called double-clicking, and by using it you can open folders and files, start programs or even use it as a shortcut to some commands.

If the window shown in Figure 1.7 appears on your screen, you did everything right. If nothing happened the interval between the two clicks was too long. Just try it again, you will see that after a short while you will get the hang of it.

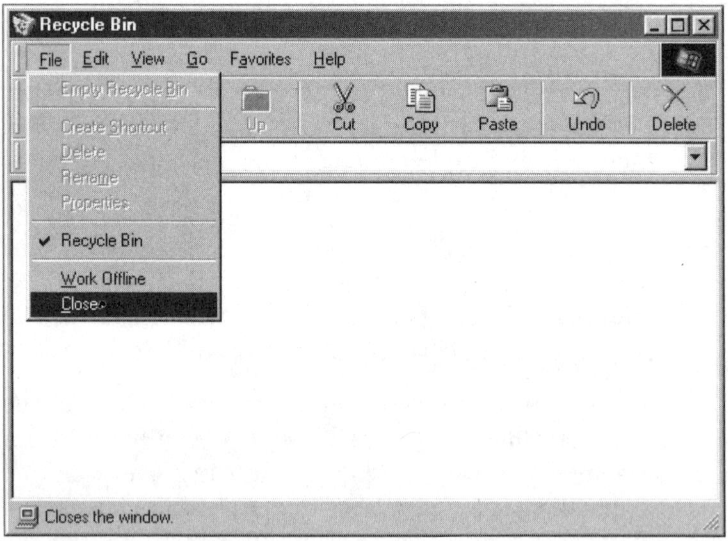

Fig. 1.7:   Open the menu with a single click, put the pointer on a command and execute with a single click.

22

To sum it all up let's repeat the most important mouse commands. Point at the *File* menu and click to open it. Point at the *Close* command and click to close the window. Then drag the icon back to its previous position.

Functions of the Right Mouse Button

If you have already worked with one of the previous Windows versions like *Windows 3.11*, you may have wondered about the second button on your mouse. This feature was quite unnecessary since only a few programs made use of it. All of this has completely changed with *Windows 98* and especially with *Windows 98* applications.

In *Windows 98* and all the latest *Windows 98* applications, the right mouse button has been assigned a function. You can call up context menus related to almost all parts or areas of your screen using the right mouse button. These little menus are called context menus because what they contain is related to the area where the pointer is positioned.

Try out some of these context menus right away. If you click on an open space on the desktop with the right mouse button, a context menu will appear with shortcut commands relating to arranging icons or creating new folders.

These are just the commands which will be used over and over again in connection with the desktop. Since the desktop does not have a menu bar, the context menu is the fastest and sometimes the only way to execute certain commands.

A click on the left mouse button executes the selected command. Click anywhere outside the menu area or press Esc to close the context menu.

Windows 98 will display other context menus if you put the cursor icons on the desktop, the taskbar or on the *Start* button.

Fig. 1.8:   Various context menus with Windows 98

Tip!

Windows 98 allows you to change the properties of the mouse with the *Control Panel*. If you are left-handed and you have changed the standard setting of the mouse button from right-handed to left-handed, the mouse buttons will be reversed. In that case you have to press the left mouse button to get the context menu. In our description, however, we always assume the standard setting for a right-handed user. You will find further information related to mouse configuration in Chapter 8.

Working with Menus.

Windows 98 arranges commands in menus. In both the *Folder* and *File* windows, you will see a menu bar with the menu items displayed below the title bar. Each menu contains a list of commands arranged by topic to carry out specific tasks.

The *System* menu is a specific menu containing commands to change the size and location of windows. This menu is accessible in folders and programs through the *System* menu icon in the form of file or folder (▣), in the upper left-hand corner of the title bar.

All file windows in which the contents of folders are displayed, as well as the program group window of the *Start* menu, are set up in the same way. You always find the menus *File, Edit, View, Go, Favorites* and *Help*. The number and meaning of the commands that can be called up with them depends on the object that is highlighted and the activity.

| File   Edit   View   Go   Favorites   Help |

| File   Edit   View   Insert   Format   Tools   Table   Window   Help |

Fig. 1.9:   Menu bar of folder window (above) and application window

The menu bar

The menu bar of all programs contains program-specific menus with related commands. However, the controls are handled the same way, independent of the menu or the commands contained therein. This also includes the command selection method.

Using the Menus with the Mouse

To open a menu, using the mouse, put the cursor on the name of the menu and click on it. The menu opens and displays a number of entries. If a menu is already open, you simply have to put the cursor on another menu name in order to open an adjacent menu.

Overlapping menus

In the case of overlapping menus, putting the cursor on a specific command is enough to open the submenu. Overlapping menus are always indicated by a small black triangle to the right of the menu item name.

Selecting commands

To select one of the commands shown in a menu, simply click on it. Whether the command will be executed immediately, or whether *Windows 98* or rather one of its programs has to open more controls for the configuration of this command, can be recognized by the menu convention. You will find out more about that later on.

Program and document windows have the additional *System* Menu. To open it, simply click on the *System* menu icon which is always displayed in the upper left-hand corner of the title bar. It is represented by the icon of the program, the folder ( ) or the program group.

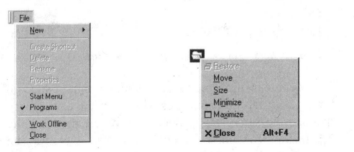

Fig. 1.10:   A menu (left) and the *System* menu of a document window.

The five *System* menu commands (Figure 1.10 right) are always the same and are used exclusively to change either the size or the location of a window.

Close command

The *Close* command will close a document or folder window as well as a program.

Tip!

A menu that was opened by mistake can be closed again by clicking on the menu name. Commands that were executed by mistake can usually, but not always, be undone by clicking on *Edit/Undo*.

Using Menus with the Keyboard

The mouse is not the only means of selecting menus and commands with *Windows 98*, although it is the method most people prefer. The reason for this is simply the principle of a graphic interface. You will now learn how to manipulate menus and commands using the keyboard.

Alt and F10
keys

By using the Alt or F10 key on the keyboard, the menu bar is activated. *Windows 98* indicates an activated menu by highlighting the first menu bar item, the *File* menu.

Press the right arrow key → to move to the menu on the right. Using the left arrow key ←, you can move back to the menu on the left. To open an activated menu, press *Enter* ↵ or the down arrow key ↓. Move to the command by using the up and down arrows ↓ ↑ and press *Enter* ↵.

If overlapping menus are available, use the left ← and right → cursor keys to change to the submenu or to go back to the parent menu.

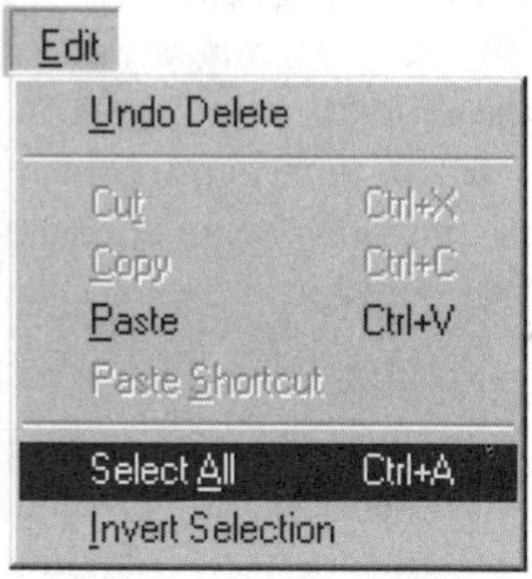

Edit	
Undo Delete	
Cut	Ctrl+X
Copy	Ctrl+C
Paste	Ctrl+V
Paste Shortcut	
Select All	Ctrl+A
Invert Selection	

Fig. 1.11:   Menu with a highlighted command

Underlined letters in the menu name indicate a key combinaton to open the menu. Press the [Alt] key and hold it down while typing the letter underlined in the menu name. To open the *Edit* menu of a folder window, for example, press [Alt]+[E]. To call up other menus press the [Alt] key followed by the letter underlined in the menu item.

Alternatively, with an open menu, you can also move to another menu using the left [←] or right [→] cursor keys. To close a menu using the keyboard press [Alt] or [F10].

Alternative

Another way to close a menu is to press the [Esc] key. The menu bar, however, will remain activated. You can now select once again. The last menu selected will be indicated by a three-dimensional border around the menu item, e.g. [Edit].

The Meaning of Menu Conventions

Every document and program window has a menu bar. The kind and number of menus available depends on the type of window or program you are running. Under every menu name is a different menu which contains entries specifically relating to the window or document you are working with. Most of the entries in a menu are commands, although sometimes there may also be an attribute which can be used in a text or a graphic drawing, like *Bold* or *Center*.

Not every menu command will be executed by a mouse click. Some commands will, without apparent change, close the menu, while others will open overlapping menus or call up a dialog box. You can tell what happens after a command is selected by the way the command is designed.

A small black triangle ▶ beside a command, for example, indicates an overlapping menu in which more commands are listed.

There are other menu actions which can be recognized by the menu entries. A little check mark in front of a menu entry, for instance, indicates that the command is activated, the program window is visible, or that an attribute is activated. These check marks are used in situations when more than one command can be executed at the same time, for example, the items in the *Toolbars* submenu or the *Status bar* item in the *View* menu of a folder window.

Entries marked with a dot (●), on the other hand, indicate that only one of several options can be selected. (e.g., *View* menu with the selection for the active view style, for example *Large Icons*).

		● Large Icons	
		Small Icons	
Toolbars	▶	List	
✔ Status Bar		Details	
Explorer Bar	▶		

Fig. 1.12:   Menu conventions

Commands that are followed by an ellipsis (...) will call up a dialog box in which you will find further options which need to be selected in order to execute the command (e.g. *File/Print...*). Independent of the menu design, the fastest way to select a menu command is by clicking on the mouse. If you point to a menu command, it will be highlighted with a coloured bar.

Alternatives

To choose menu commands using the keyboard, press ⌨Alt⌨ and then use the direction cursors ⌨↓⌨, ⌨←⌨, ⌨→⌨ or ⌨↑⌨ until you reach the selected item. Then press *Enter*

⌐⏎⌐. Another possibility would be to press the letter underlined in the selected command.

Overview

In the following overview you will find a summary of the most important menu designs used in *Windows 98*.

Menu Convention	Description
AutoText ►	*Triangle*: Overlapping menu with additional commands.
Date and Time...	*Ellipsis*: Calls up a dialog box with further options to be selected
Hyperlink... Ctrl+K	*Keyboard combination*: Shortcut for a command
Open	*Bold*: Default command executed with a double click
✓ Ruler	*Check mark*: Indicates an active command, document window or attribute. Several commands can be selected at the same time.
• Details	*Dot*: Active options out of a list of unique options
Footnotes	*Inactive* or *not available*: Option is not active or cannot be selected.

Fig. 1.13: Menu conventions under Windows 98

Working with Dialog Boxes

Windows 98 distinguishes between several different types of windows. In application windows a program might be running or a document window might be displayed which gives information. Folder windows are also document windows. A dialog box, on the other hand, is used to further specify a command selected in a program or document window. Because of this, dialog boxes have fixed control settings which we will discuss in this section.

Dialog box

You can always recognize a dialog box by the missing menu bar. Neither the toolbar nor the status bar are displayed. The size of a dialog box cannot be changed, only its position on the screen can be altered.

If *Windows* or a program needs further information in order to execute a command, a dialog box will be called up automatically. In a menu you can recognize this by the three dots (...) appearing next to the command in question.

Font   ? ☒

Fig. 1.14:   Title bar of a dialog box

If a command contains many possible settings, the different options are separated by topic on several pages or tabs. A particular page can be activated by clicking on the tab located at the top of it. In order to select options for a command, different controls are needed.

Rectangular buttons with a label are called command buttons. The function of a command button always corresponds to the contents of its label. The most important command buttons are [OK] and [Cancel]. Using *OK* you confirm all changes in a dialog box and execute the selected command with your settings. *Cancel*, on the other hand, cancels all changes and closes the dialog box. By pressing *Enter* ⏎ you activate the default button which can always be recognized by its thick border. Press *Escape* Esc to close a dialog box without making any changes.

By clicking on a command button with three dots marked beside the button (Ex. [Settings...]) you will call up another dialog box. If the label of a command button is dimmed, it means that this specific command cannot be executed and it is for this very reason that the label is greyed. Those letters which are underlined in the command button can be used to activate the command using the keyboard by pressing the underlined letter in conjunction with the Alt key.

In cases when only one out of several options can be selected at any time, small circles called radio buttons or option buttons are used. Deselected buttons can be recognized by this symbol: ○. The button is selected when it is marked by a black dot ◉. Underlined letters in the option description indicate the letter which can be used in conjunction with the Alt key to activate the command using the keyboard.

When several choices can be made within a single option, *Windows 98* uses check boxes inside a dialog box. These are small square boxes ☐ placed in front of each option. Selected check boxes are marked with a check mark ☑. To select one or more check boxes, simply click on the ☐ box in front of the description.

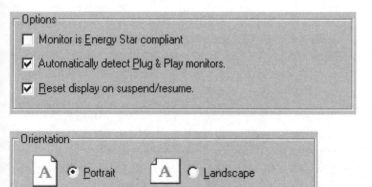

Fig. 1.15: Check box (above) and radio button

Text boxes

Text boxes are used to enter alphanumerical values with the keyboard. This can be a file name or a numerical value `Left: 250` necessary for setting the margins of a document, for example. The cursor is displayed as a blinking vertical line in a text box and marks the current position in the text.

With the *Backspace* key `←`, the character to the left and with the `Del` key the character to the right of the cursor can be deleted. If text boxes contain default values, sometimes spin buttons are displayed to the right of the box `1`. You can change the values step by step by clicking on these buttons.

Drop-down box

A box containing a triangle pointing downward is called a drop-down box `Times New Roman ▼`. It will display a list if you click on the drop-down button `▼`. You can select an item from the list by clicking it with the mouse button. After selection the list will close automatically and the selected item will appear in the text box. If the list is long, use the scroll bar which appears to the right of the list.

When more than one item is displayed in a box, it is called a list box. You can select an item with a mouse click, and it will appear in the text box placed above the list. If there are many entries, the scroll bar will appear automatically.

Scroll bar

A scroll bar ◄ ► consists of a sliding grey box with arrow buttons at both ends. Using the arrow buttons you can scroll up and down in the text a line or a column at a time. If you click in the open area above or below the scroll box the list will move up and down a screen at a time.

The scroll bar box can be moved with the mouse by clicking on it and holding down the mouse button. The size of the scroll box indicates the relationship between the size of the text which is displayed and the size of the text which does not appear.

Changing the Size of Windows

Windows 98 has different types of windows. Apart from the document windows which include all folder windows, you will meet application windows which can display document windows as well as running applications. Changing the size of a document or program window can be achieved in several ways.

However, in this section we only deal with the window size and how to change it.

Fig. 1.16: The title bar of document and application windows.

To change the size of a window you have to first select the window. *Windows 98* allows only one window at a time to be active. All entries and commands will take place in this window.

Document and application window

To activate a document or an application window you have to click on the title bar which will then be displayed in a different color. If the title bar is not visible, click on the button representing this window in the taskbar.

Buttons to Change the Size of a Window

Dialog boxes and message boxes are not equipped with buttons to change their size. This would simply make no sense with this type of window.

Close button

However, you will always find the *Close* button ⊠ in the right-hand corner of the title bar of all types of windows. Any window can be closed using this button.

Maximize-button

To the left of this button is the *Maximize* button ⬜. By clicking on this button, the active window can be maximized so that it fills the entire screen.

In a maximized window, the *Maximize* button will be replaced by the *Restore* button ⧉, with the help of which the window size can be restored to its former size again.

Minimize button

With the *Minimize* button ▬, an open window will shrink and be placed in the taskbar at the bottom of the screen in the form of a button.

Minimized windows remain loaded in the background. Click on the button in the taskbar to restore them to their previous size.

Changing the Size of Windows Using the Border

Windows 98 contains different types of windows. Apart from the document windows which include all file windows you will meet application windows which can display document windows as well as running applications. Other types of windows are dialog boxes and message boxes, which you will encounter when executing commands. Only document windows and application windows can be resized, however. Dialog boxes and messages boxes can only be moved to different locations, since changing their size would not make sense anyhow.

There are several ways to change the size of a document window or a program window. In this section we discuss how to use the borders and corners of a window to accomplish this.

To change the size of a window, you first have to select the window and thereby activate it. *Windows 98* allows only one window at a time to be active. All entries and commands will take place in this window. To select a document or a program window, you have to click in the window's title bar which will then be displayed in a different color. If the title bar is not visible, click on the button representing this window in the taskbar.

Document and appliction window

Document and application windows are always enclosed by a border. The point at which the horizontal and the vertical borders meet is called the window corner. With this part of the window you can, using the mouse, change the width and the height of the window. To do this, point the mouse cursor on a window edge. The shape of the mouse pointer will change from an arrow to a double-pointed arrow ←→ .

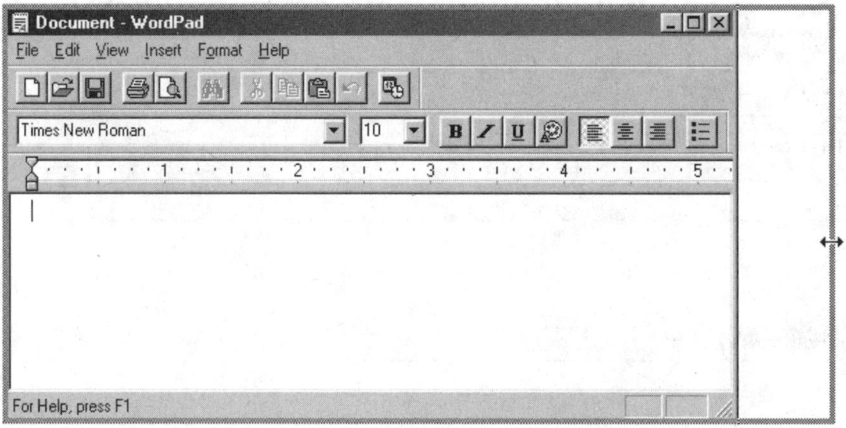

Fig. 1.17:   Changing the width of a window using the edge.

While holding down the mouse button, you can drag the window edge and thereby increase or reduce the size of the window by moving the mouse to the right or the left. While resizing the window, its new position is indicated by a dotted frame. To fix the new size, simply release the mouse button.

Changing a window height

To change the height of a window, position the mouse cursor so that it touches a horizontal window border. Once again the cursor will change, this time into a vertical double-arrow $\updownarrow$. With this you can 'grab' the edge and, while holding down the mouse button, increase the height of the window.

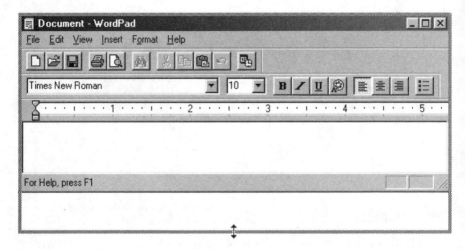

Fig. 1.18: Changing the height of the window using the edge

To change the height and the width of a window simultaneously, you can use any of the four corners. The cursor will change into a diagonal double-arrow ↖ or ↗. While holding down the mouse button, you can change the height as well as the width of the window in one go. An dotted frame indicates the future dimensions of the window currently being resized. To fix the new window's size, release the mouse button.

Changing the size of a window using the edge will not work on windows that are already maximized. A maximized window can be reduced to its original size using the *Restore* button 🗗.

Closing a Window

Windows 98 uses different types of windows. There is a difference, for example, between a document window and an application window. An application, for example *WordPad*, *Paint* or *Editor*, runs in a program window. A document window, on the other hand, will display information. This can be in the form of a text in the window of a word processor, or, on the other hand, folders or subfolders. Every opened folder is also a document window, for example *My Computer*. We will deal with this type of window in the following section.

Often, after working with Windows for only a short while, the screen can become cluttered with different windows. At one point you might want to close some of them.

You can close *Windows 98* document windows using any one of the following methods:

- the *Close* command in the *File* menu

- the Alt + F4 keyboard combination

- the *Close* command in the *System* menu

- a double-click on the *System* menu icon

- the *Close* button ☒ in the title bar

- the *Close* command in the context menu of a window button on the taskbar.

All of the above methods will close a document window. Please note the difference between an application window, in which a program is running and in which one or more document windows are displayed, and a document window. To close a program window use the *Exit* command. This will be discussed in Chapter 3.

System menu

The *System* menu can be called up by clicking on the *System* menu icon in the left-hand corner of the title bar of a document window. For folder windows, the *System* menu button appears with the icon of an open folder 📂, and for applications, it is shown as the program icon.

Changing and Arranging the Position of Windows on the Desktop.

Windows 98 allows many different windows to be open at the same time. The windows are then displayed in different layers, one on top of the other.

To change the position of a window you first have to select the window and thereby activate it.

Only one active
window

Windows 98 allows only one window at a time to be active, which means that all entries and commands will take place in this window. To select a document or an application window you have to click in the title bar, which will then be displayed in a different color. If the title bar is not visible, click on the button representing this window on the taskbar.

Although you cannot change the size of dialog boxes and message boxes, you can change their position anytime. Furthermore, you can arrange this type of window on your desktop using the following commands:

Moving a window

Moving a window on your desktop is always done for only one reason. With *Windows 98* your desktop can never be big enough. You move a window in order to see information contained in the window behind it, to get an overview of running applications or information in windows, or to exchange data between one window and another.

To move any window on the desktop, point on the title bar with the cursor. While holding down the mouse button, you can move the window. The new position is marked by a dotted frame. If you release the mouse button, the window will be moved to its new location.

System menu

Likewise, you can move a window by clicking on the *System* menu in the left corner of the title bar. Click on the *Move* command and change the window's position using the ⬆, ⬇, ⬅ or ➡ arrow keys on the keyboard. This command is not available when a window is maximized.

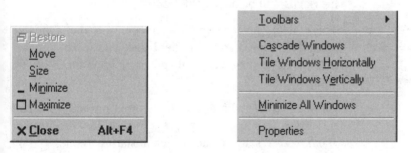

Fig. 1.19: *System* menu (left) and context menu of the taskbar

Automatic
arranging

To arrange all the windows on your desktop automatically, click on an empty space anywhere in the taskbar using the right mouse button. Choose one of the following commands: *Cascade Windows*, *Tile Windows Vertically*, or *Tile Windows Horizontally* from the context menu which appears in order to arrange all windows the way you want.

Automatically Interrupting Windows 98 Startup

The 32-bit graphic operating system *Windows 98* will automatically be started when you switch on your computer, without you having to enter any special commands. Sometimes it becomes necessary to interrupt the startup, for example, if you want to start Windows in *Safe Mode* to fix problems that occur in *Normal Mode*, or to start *Windows 98* in *MS-DOS mode* which emulates the earlier MS-DOS (Microsoft Disk Operation System).

In order to interrupt the automatic *Windows 98* startup procedure, you have to closely watch the messages on the screen. After initialising the system controls the first messages will be displayed.

These deal, for example, with counting the available memory or initializing the hard disk and in some cases displaying a summary of all the important system components.

As soon as your hard disk light turns on and you hard disk starts to sound active, press the F8 key to interrupt *Windows 98* startup and select a startup mode. If you press the F8 key, *Windows 98* will not be started and the Microsoft *Windows 98 Start* menu (Figure 1.20) will appear on your screen. The options displayed will depend on the installation of your computer.

```
Microsoft Windows 98 Startup Menu

  1. Normal
  2. Logged (\BOOTLOG.TXT)
  3. Safe mode
  4. Step-by-step confirmation
  5. Command prompt only
  6. Safe mode command prompt
  7. Pervious version of MS-DOS

Enter a choice: 1



F5=Safe mode  Shift+F5=Command prompt  Shift+F8=Step-by-step confirmation [N]
```

Fig. 1.20:   The Startup menu after interrupting the *Windows 98* Startup.

The first six options will be available in any case. Other options such as the previous MS-DOS version will depend on whether you have installed *Windows 98* on top of the previous *Windows 95* version. If this is the case, while installing *Windows 98*, a directory of the old system files will be kept. These should not be deleted while executing the installation program.

Select a mode

To call up one of the displayed options on the *Microsoft Windows 98 Startup menu*, simply press the respective number and confirm by pressing *Enter* ⏎. If you want to start in *Normal Start,* use the ① key and confirm the entry by pressing ⏎.

Normal or

Standard-mode

Windows 98 will now start in the so-called *Normal or Standard* mode, which is the normal and most powerful mode of operation. We will deal with the other options on the *Startup menu* in a different section of this book.

If problems or error messages occur during the automatic *Windows 98* startup the cause of which is not immediately apparent, interrupt the next startup using the [F8] key and choose the *2. Logged (\BOOTLOG.TXT)* option in the *Microsoft Windows 98 Startup* menu.

Windows will now create a text file in the root directory of the hard disk called *BOOTLOG.TXT*, which records the loading process of every file. The file *BOOTLOG.TXT* can be copied onto a floppy disk and accessed with any text editor. Experts can recognize which programs or components may be causing the startup difficulties by these entries.

Starting Windows 98 in Safe mode

Normally the graphic interface of the 32-bit operating system will appear automatically after switching on the computer. In rare cases a problem might occur during the automatic *Normal mode* startup of *Windows 98* which interrupts the startup in the most powerful operating mode.

Cause of these problems

These problems are usually caused by a faulty network or hardware setting of the computer. In other cases, programs that overwrite important drivers with incorrect versions are responsible.

Safe mode

If this is the case, you have the possibility of starting up *Windows 98* in the *Safe mode*. Now Windows will bypass the loading of all drivers and load only a minimal driver configuration and the system will always work. However, in *Safe mode* many expanded Windows options like multitasking or the use of CD-ROM drives and sound cards will not be available. In any case, this was not the intention since *Safe mode* is meant primarily for problem solving.

To call up *Safe mode*, you have to reboot your computer. After the system dianostics, as soon as the hard disk light comes on, press the [F8] key to interrupt the automatic starting process and display the *Microsoft Windows 98 Start menu*. On a stand-alone PC now press the [3] key and confirm with [↵], to start up in *Safe mode*. In a *Windows 98* network press the [4] key followed by [↵] to start up in *Safe Mode with Network Support*.

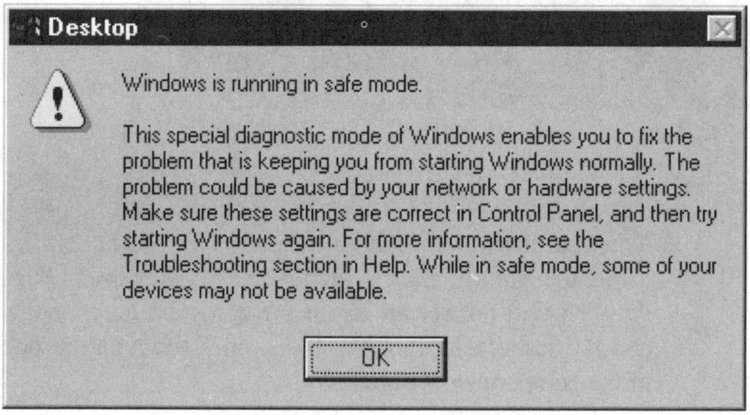

Fig. 1.21: Message box after starting in Safe mode

After the start of the graphic interface confirm the message box which appears in figure 1.22 with the [↵] key or by clicking on the *OK* button. In *Safe Mode*, *Windows 98* uses the VGA-resolution of 640 x 480 pixels with 16 colors to avoid conflicts.

Safe mode

The term *Safe mode* is displayed in all corners of the screen (Figure 1.22). Networks will display *Safe Mode With Network Support* if the computer was able to initialize the network.

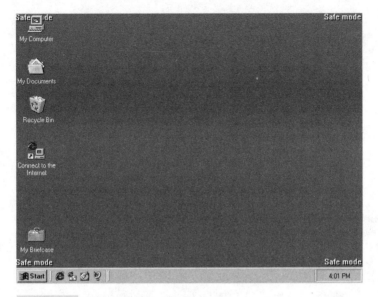

Fig. 1.22: Windows 98 in Safe mode

You can now try to correct the faulty hardware settings using the control panel. In *Safe mode*, however, *Windows 98* will not recognize all the hardware components and the resources available. Sometimes deactivating one of the components will help.

Normal mode

After you have made your changes, try restarting *Windows 98* in *Normal mode*. Now you can manually set the components needed by the hardware and restart the computer.

Safe mode can also be called up without displaying the Startup menu. To do this, press the F5 key as soon as the hard disk light comes on, after the system diagnostics is completed.

Starting the Computer in MS-DOS Mode

Basically *Windows 98* is a fully self-supporting graphic operating system, which executes all the functions of the earlier *MS-DOS* (*Microsoft Disk Operation System*). For reasons of compatibility with existing DOS applications or computer games, the *MS-DOS-Mode* has been integrated into *Windows 98*. In this mode the earlier operating system is emulated.

MS-DOS window

Unlike the MS-DOS Window, the *MS-DOS Mode* can only be used outside of the graphic interface of *Windows 98*. Before starting in *MS-DOS Mode*, try to start your MS-DOS application in the MS-DOS window in *Windows 98*. Jump to the section below on how to use the MS-DOS Window in *Windows 98*.

MS-DOS Mode

There are only two cases when it makes sense to directly call up *MS-DOS Mode* after starting the PC:

▪ MS-DOS applications or DOS games cannot be run in the MS-DOS window, or loading results in conflicts or slow execution.

▪ You only want to work with previous MS-DOS applications or with DOS games and not with *Windows 98*.

There are two ways to call up the *MS-DOS Mode*. If you are already in *Windows 98*, and want to call up an MS-DOS application or a DOS game, close all Windows applications and click the *Start* button in the taskbar. Now choose the *Shut Down* command and in the *Shut Down Windows* dialog box (Figure 1.23), choose the *Restart in MS-DOS Mode* option. Confirm by clicking *OK* or pressing *Enter* ⏎.

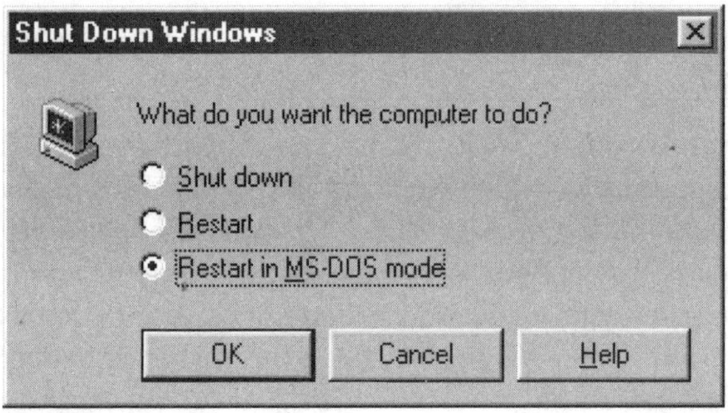

Fig. 1.23 Starting in MS-DOS Mode after shutting down Windows 98

MS-DOS Prompt

Windows 98 will shut down and several messages will appear on your screen. Among these will be the *MS-DOS Prompt*, which usually consists of the following four symbols:

```
C:\>
```

Enter a command

In the *MS-DOS Mode* you now have to enter a command. Change to the directory of your DOS application and start the program by typing in the necessary command and pressing ⏎.

Interrupting the automatic Windows 98 startup

The second way of starting *MS-DOS Mode* is to interrupt the automatic *Windows 98* startup by pressing the ⇧+F5 keys as soon as *Windows 98* starts to load. In this case the *CONFIG.SYS* and *AUTOEXEC.BAT* files and their drivers will be loaded and the programs and commands executed.

The *MS-DOS Prompt* is now awaiting your command. Change to the directory of your DOS application or the MS-DOS game and start the program by typing in the respective command and pressing the ⏎ key.

Tip!

After you have finished with your MS-DOS application in the *MS-DOS Mode* you can immediately switch off your computer. If you want to restart *Windows 98*, enter the command *EXIT* and press ⏎ or, if you have not started *Windows 98* yet, type *WIN* followed by ⏎. In both cases *Windows 98* will be loaded. You can also press the `Ctrl`+`Alt`+`Del` key combination to restart your computer.

Configuring the *MS-DOS Mode* Startup

If you interrupt the startup of the *Windows 98* graphic operating system with the `⇧`+`F5` keys as soon as *Windows 98* starts to load, the startup menu will appear. If you change to the *MS-DOS Mode* the *CONFIG. SYS* and *AUTOEXEC.BAT* system files will automatically be loaded and executed.

Updating
Windows 98

Because of this, after updating *Windows 98* from an earlier Windows version and then installing new hardware, problems may occur which prevent the *MS-DOS Mode* from starting. Even if the *MS-DOS Mode* does start, important drivers or program commands may be missing. As a result you may not be able to use your CD-ROM drive or your sound card in the *MS-DOS-Mode*. However, MS-DOS games often use graphics and are very memory intensive and can only be loaded in *MS-DOS Mode* and not in the *MS-DOS* window of *Windows 98*. For these, you will definitely need your CD-ROM-drive or the sound card.

Windows 98 offers several different ways to configure the startup of the *MS-DOS Mode* and to remove problems that occur during startup. The different ways of changing to the *MS-DOS Mode* should be taken into consideration.

```
Microsoft Windows 98 Startup Menu

   1.  Normal
   2.  Logged (\BOOTLOG.TXT)
   3.  Safe mode
   4.  Step-by-step confirmation
   5.  Command prompt only
   6.  Safe mode command prompt
   7.  Pervious version of MS-DOS

Enter a choice: 1






F5=Safe mode   Shift+F5=Command prompt   Shift+F8=Step-by-step confirmation [N]
```

Fig. 1.24:   With this menu you determine the startup of MS-DOS Mode

Startup Mode: Safe Mode Command Prompt

To begin with, we deal with calling up *MS-DOS Mode* after switching on your computer. To interrupt the start-up, press the ⌑F8⌑ key as soon as *Windows 98* begins to load. The *Microsoft Windows 98 Startup menu* will appear. If you want to interrupt the loading of drivers in the *CONFIG.SYS* file and the execution of commands in the *AUTOEXEC.BAT* file, choose the option *Safe Mode Command Prompt.* Press the number in front of the option, or use the ⌑↓⌑ key to highlight the option. After that confirm by pressing ⌑↵⌑.

This way, you bypass all entries in *CONFIG.SYS* and *AUTOEXEC.BAT*, which could lead to starting problems. You won't be able to use the CD-ROM drive or the sound card in the *MS-DOS Safe Mode*

Step by Step Confirmation Startup Mode

In order to locate a faulty driver or command, start the *MS-DOS-Mode* by choosing the option *Step by Step confirmation* or use the keyboard by pressing the ⌂ + F8 keys. Press the number in front of the option or use the ⬇ key to highlight the option and confirm by pressing *Enter* ↵.

CONFIG.SYS step
by step

To begin with, all entries of *CONFIG.SYS* will be displayed one by one. Every entry has to be confirmed with the Ⓨ key. The Ⓝ key will skip the command. After that all entries in *AUTOEXEC.BAT* will be displayed. To confirm a command press the Ⓨ key.

Faulty drivers

Faulty drivers or commands will lead to an error message in most cases. In this case, remember the command or the line number.

The entries in the startup files *CONFIG.SYS* and *AUTO-EXEC.BAT* can be added to, corrected or, by using *REM*, disabled using the *EDIT* text editor in *MS-DOS-Mode*, or by using *Notepad* in *Windows 98*, accessible through *Start/Programs/Accessories*.

Tip!

If you start the *MS-DOS-Mode* using the *Shut Down Windows* dialog box, Windows uses entries in the *DOSSTART.BAT* file, which is saved in the *Windows* directory and replaces the *AUTOEXEC.BAT* file.

Calling up the MS-DOS Prompt in Windows 98

For reasons of compatibility with previous MS-DOS applications or games, *Windows 98* contains a program which allows you to call up one or more DOS programs in the Windows graphic interface.

Start programs

This is called the *MS-DOS Prompt*. To start the program, open the *Start* menu on the taskbar and point to the *Programs* item. In the overlapping menu, click on the *MS-DOS Prompt* entry. What happens then depends on your system configuration.

For instance, the *MS-DOS Window* might appear in the upper left-hand corner of the desktop. Or the screen might go black and only display a few characters.

MS-DOS *Prompt*

In both cases the *MS-DOS Prompt* has started, in one case in the *Window* mode (Figure 1.25), and in the other in the *Full-screen* mode. Both modes work the same way.

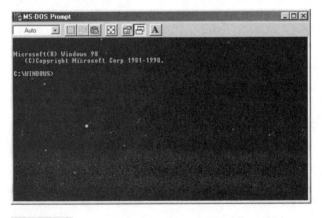

Fig. 1.25:   The MS-DOS Prompt under Windows 98

The *MS-DOS Prompt* emulates the previous MS-DOS (*Microsoft Disk Operation System*) operating system. In the upper left-hand corner the version number is shown; below that the system prompt cursor is blinking *C:\WINDOWS>_*. Using the *CD* MS-DOS command, change to the directory of your DOS application and start the program by typing in the specific command required.

Tip! To change from the *Full-screen* mode of the *MS-DOS Prompt* to the *Window* mode or vice versa, press the ⌈Alt⌋+⌈↵⌋ key combination. To leave the prompt, type the *EXIT* command and confirm by pressing ⌈↵⌋. This will close the window.

Setting *MS-DOS Prompt* Properties

According to *Microsoft*, almost all applications for MS-DOS can be started without any problem in the *MS-DOS* window directly in *Windows 98*. In most cases, this works quite well, but it's not exactly as simple as the theory says it should be.

More than one
DOS session

With *Windows 98*, you can run more than one DOS session simultaneously. These will run at the same time in protected memory areas. The only condition is that the *MS-DOS Prompt* has to run in *Windows* mode. In the *Full Screen* mode only one *MS-DOS Prompt* can be active. In the *Windows* mode, however, you can call up more DOS windows by using *Start/Programs/MS-DOS Prompt*.

Difficulties

However, simply calling up an MS-DOS window is just the first step. The tricky part starts when you want to call up a DOS application, even when only one *MS-DOS Prompt* has been started.

In the case of DOS applications which cannot be called up in the graphic mode (*MS-DOS Prompt* in a window), *Windows 98* will automatically switch to the *Full-screen* mode.

If a serious problem occurs after entering your command, the DOS application will not start. Ideally, an error message will appear, informing you to restart the computer in *MS-DOS Mode* without loading *Windows*.

Starting difficulties   If the starting difficulties are less problematic, you will usually get a corresponding error message, informing you of the nature of the error, like *The program will not work under windows* or *not enough memory*, etc. In cases like this the program will start without problems after configuring the settings for *MS-DOS Prompt*.

Configuring the Command Line and the Working Folder

Shortcut key   For the normal configuration of the *MS-DOS Prompt* change to the *Window* mode using the Alt+↵ keys and click the *Properties* button.

On the *Program* tab page, you can read the *Cmd Line* (or *Command Line*) and the *Working*, (or *Working directory*) of the command line interpreter, as well as fix a shortcut to call up the *MS-DOS Prompt* in the *Shortcut Key* text box.

Properties   Using the *Run* drop-down list box, you can set the start properties of the *MS-DOS Prompt*. You can choose between the *Normal window; minimized* or *maximized*. The *maximized* mode is recommended for 'difficult' programs.

Batch file   If a *batch file* is needed to run the DOS program, enter the name of the file in the *Batch file* text box. Check the

Close on exit check box if the DOS window should be closed after you are finished with the DOS application.

Setting the Fonts for MS-DOS Prompt

If you are using previous DOS applications in *Windows 98*, you cannot avoid dealing with the *MS-DOS prompt*. It is easiest to work in the *Window* mode of the *MS-DOS Prompt*. *Windows 98* treats the MS-DOS window almost the same way as any other window.

Standard font

Many users feel that the font is too small. The font is responsible for the size of the window of the *MS-DOS Prompt*, since the MS-DOS text and command-oriented operating system displays the screen contents with characters and lines. However, you can change this without difficulty.

Call up *MS-DOS Prompt* using *Start/Programs* and change to the window mode. There are two ways to change the font. One is by using the *font* `T 8 x 14` list in the toolbar; the other is by using the *Font* tab page in the *MS-DOS Properties* dialog box, which you can call up with the *Properties* button.

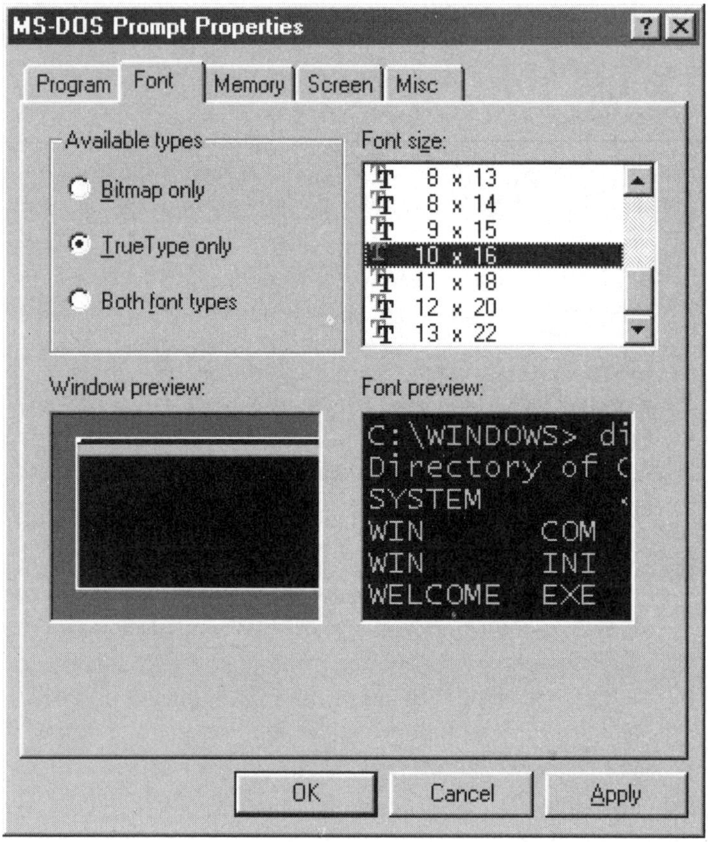

Fig. 1.26: The *Font* tab page

Font list box

Open the *Font* drop-down box in the toolbar and click on the selected font. *Windows 98* will simultaneously change the size of the *MS-DOS Prompt* window. On the *Font* tab page in the *Properties* window, you can follow the changes in two preview windows. On the left side below the window mode preview, the approximate size of the DOS window on the screen is shown; on the right under the font preview, a sample of the selected font is displayed. You have a choice of two fonts.

Either the fixed *Bitmap* fonts, or the flexible Windows-*TrueType* fonts. In the *Font* drop-down box on the toolbar of the *MS-DOS Window*, you can recognize the *TrueType* fonts by the **T** icon. In the *Properties* dialog box, you can determine the fonts in the *Available types* option group. Possible choices are: *Bitmap only*, *True Type only* or *Both font types*.

Tip!

Information is displayed in text mode under MS-DOS. Every character is defined by its height and width. And these are exactly the values that you will find in the *Font* list box. The font '8 x 14', for example, indicates that every symbol in the *MS-DOS Prompt* is exactly 8 pixels high and 14 pixels wide. This directly determines the height of the DOS window. The standard font setting of *MS-DOS Prompt* is 25 lines with 80 characters per line.

Auto option

The *Auto* option on top of the *Font* list is particularly handy, since it adjusts the font in the DOS window to the size of the actual window. The only way to increase the size of a DOS window is by using the *Auto* option. Minimizing is no problem even without the option, since you can reach entries that are not displayed in the window with the help of scroll bars.

Tip!

Changing the fonts in the *MS-DOS Prompt* can only be done in programs that use graphics. If this is not the case, it changes automatically to *Full screen mode*.

Changing Properties of MS-DOS Prompt for Single DOS Applications

To change the properties of the *MS-DOS Prompt* for particular DOS applications, point to the corresponding program file in *Explorer* or in a *My Computer* window. Point to the icon and press the right mouse button. In the context menu, select the *Properties* item.

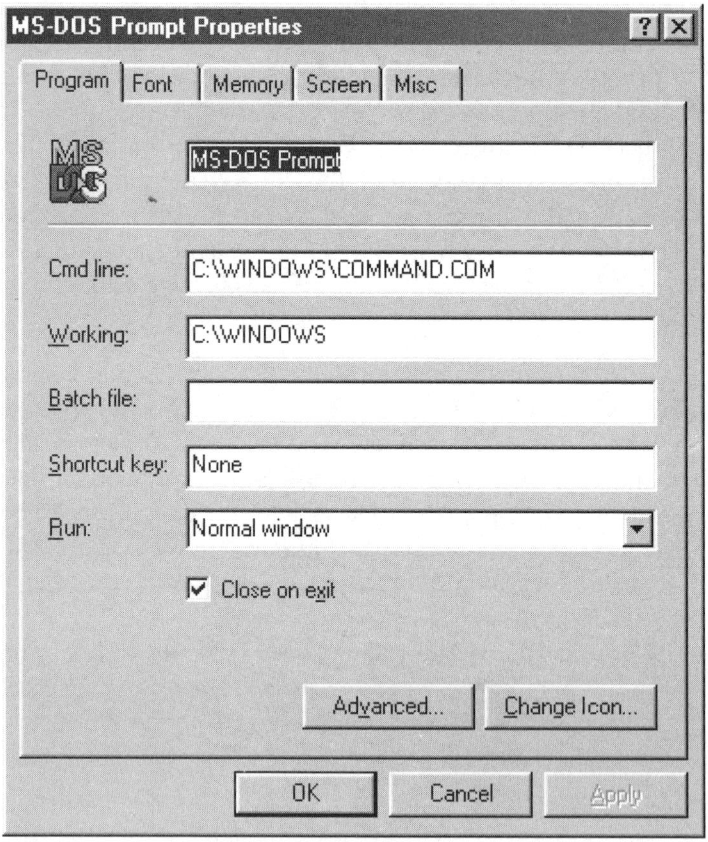

MS-DOS Prompt Properties ? ✕

Program | Font | Memory | Screen | Misc

MS-DOS Prompt

Cmd line: C:\WINDOWS\COMMAND.COM

Working: C:\WINDOWS

Batch file:

Shortcut key: None

Run: Normal window ▼

☑ Close on exit

Advanced... | Change Icon...

OK | Cancel | Apply

Fig. 1. 27:   Set properties for the MS-DOS Prompt

For programs that display the error message indicating that the program does not run under *Windows*, choose the

Advanced button on the *Program* tab page in the *Properties* dialog box. In the dialog box which now appears, select the *Prevent MS-DOS-based programs from detecting Windows* check box.

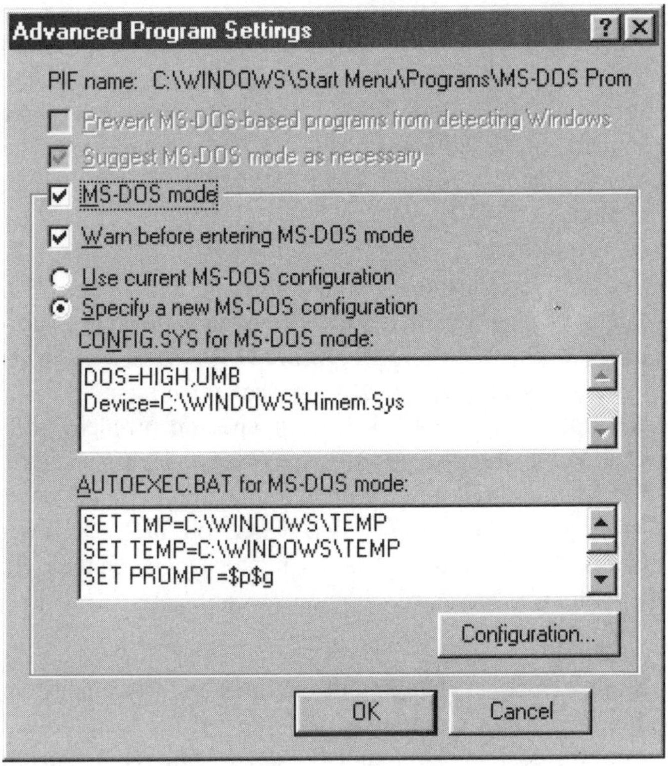

Advanced Program Settings

PIF name: C:\WINDOWS\Start Menu\Programs\MS-DOS Prom

☐ Prevent MS-DOS-based programs from detecting Windows

☑ Suggest MS-DOS mode as necessary

☑ MS-DOS mode

☑ Warn before entering MS-DOS mode

○ Use current MS-DOS configuration

⦿ Specify a new MS-DOS configuration

CONFIG.SYS for MS-DOS mode:

```
DOS=HIGH,UMB
Device=C:\WINDOWS\Himem.Sys
```

AUTOEXEC.BAT for MS-DOS mode:

```
SET TMP=C:\WINDOWS\TEMP
SET TEMP=C:\WINDOWS\TEMP
SET PROMPT=$p$g
```

Configuration...

OK   Cancel

Fig. 1.28:   Changing the startup files for MS-DOS Mode

Special
configuration

In the case of DOS applications which require special configurations in the startup files, select the *MS-DOS-mode* check box. Then click on the *Specify new MS-DOS-configuration* radio button, and change the entries in the *CONFIG.SYS* and *AUTOEXEC.BAT* files.

These changes should be made only by experienced users. Confirm the dialog box and start the DOS application again. *Windows 98* will shut down and the *MS-DOS Mode* will be called up. This step will only be neccessary in very rare cases.

Most DOS applications can be used without any problem by making some changes on the other tab pages in the *Properties* dialog box. If the message *not enough memory* appears after calling up the DOS program, use the *Memory* tab page and enter the required memory in kilobytes.

 MS-DOS applications, with preconfigured *Properties*, should be opened with a double click on the icon in *Explorer* or in the *My Computer* window. You can also place icons of a program group on the *Start* menu. If our description does not cover your specific problem with your MS-DOS application, start Windows Help. Open the *Windows 98* book *Troubleshooting* and point on the book *Windows 98 Troubleshooters*. Click on *MS-DOS Programs*. After that, follow the instructions given on the right side of the window.

Restarting in MS-DOS-mode

If all attempts at changing the settings on the tab pages in the *Properties* window of the *MS-DOS Prompt* don't yield the desired result, quit *Windows* using the *Restart in MS-DOS-Mode* option and open the DOS program or game in this mode. Many games require the installation of a memory manager before they will run.

Copying Contents from the MS-DOS Prompt

To be compatible with older MS-DOS programs, the *MS-DOS Prompt* has been integrated into *Windows 98*. As you know, the *Prompt* can be displayed in the *Full-screen* mode as well as in the *Window* mode. In the *Window* mode you can highlight window contents by character and, using the clipboard, copy them into other programs.

Copying text

To copy text from an *MS-DOS* window under *Windows 98*, click on the *MS-DOS* icon in the *MS-DOS Prompt* window on the left side of the title bar. Point to the *Edit* command and click on *Mark* in the overlapping menu.

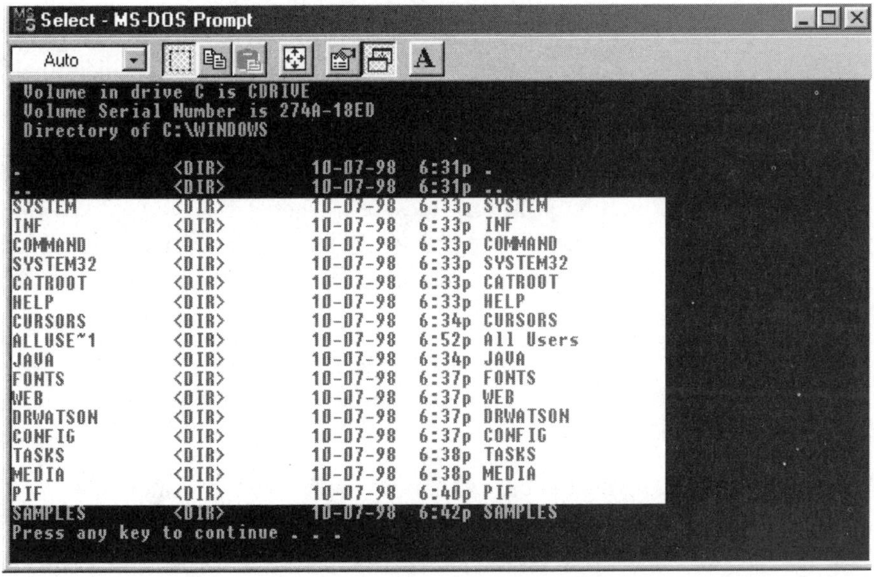

Fig. 1.29:   Highlighting window contents in the MS-DOS Prompt

Highlighting text

After that, click on the beginning of the text you want to copy. Press the ⬚, key and while continuing to hold down the button, click on the end of the text that you wish to copy. The area is now highlighted. Click the *System* menu icon again and choose *Edit/Copy*.

Paste command

Now point the cursor to the place in the MS-DOS program where you wish to insert the text, or change to a Windows program. In an MS-DOS program click on *Edit* in the *System* menu and choose *Insert* to insert the highlighted area. In a Windows program, choose the *Paste* command in the *Edit* menu, use the key combination [Ctrl]+[V] or click the *Paste* button in the toolbar of the program.

The *Mark* button

You can copy the contents of MS-DOS windows even more quickly by using the *Mark* button ⬚ in the toolbar of the *MS-DOS Prompt* window. Click on the button, and highlight the text area.

Using the keyboard

You can also use the keyboard: Move the cursor using the up and down arrows [↑] and [↓] to the beginning of the text you want to select. Then press the ⬚ key and continue to hold it down, while extending the highlighted area to the right with the [→] key and down with the [↓] key.

Copy the highlighted area

To copy the highlighted area press the [↵] key. Now you can insert the contents anywhere in MS-DOS or in a window in *Windows 98*.

Display toolbar.

If the toolbar of the *MS-DOS Prompt* is not displayed, choose the *Properties* command in the *System* menu. Select the *Screen* tab page and, in *Windows*, select the *Display toolbar* check box, and close the *Properties* window by pressing *OK*.

QuickEdit

You can also highlight contents in the *MS-DOS Prompt* by dragging the cursor across the selection. Open the *Properties* window of *MS-DOS Prompt* using the *System* menu and the command *Properties*. Change to the *Misc.* tab card and check the *QuickEdit* check box in the *Mouse* options group. Close the *Properties* window by clicking *OK*.

Tip!

You cannot paste text into an MS-DOS window or an MS-DOS-based program if it is displayed in the *Full screen* mode. Not all the contents of a DOS window will be displayed the same way as in a Window application. To close a DOS window, click the *Close* button and confirm the message which appears with *Yes*.

Tip!

To copy the entire window of the *MS-DOS Prompt* as a bitmap for *Windows* applications, press Alt+PrtScr. To insert the copy into a Windows application, use the *Edit/Paste* command, the Ctrl+V key combination or the *Paste* button .

2. Windows Help

Read on to learn more about how *Windows 98* can be of use to you in your daily work. Let's start with *Discover Windows 98*, an interactive learning program called the *Windows 98* tutorial. After that, we will look at the Help functions which will be of use to anyone who has already worked with a previous version of *Windows*, before going into a detailed discussion of the general Help functions of *Windows 98*. Then we will tell you about additional help for the programs of the *Microsoft Office Suite* and the *Office-Assistant*, an interactive and animated helper that closely follows your work and offers context-sensitive help.

Let's begin with the interactive learning program *Windows 98* tutorial for beginners. In *Discover Windows 98*, animated instructions will present you with problems which you can either solve yourself or which are already solved for you with the solution displayed. The program expects you to find the solution right there on the *Windows 98* screen. If you make mistakes, this part of the Windows Help shows you how to correctly solve the problem. To do this, the program uses short videos that can be activated by clicking on the *Show Me* button.

Calling up the Discover Windows 98 tutorial

The *Discover Windows 98* tutorial can only run when the *Windows 98* CD-ROM has been loaded, since it is not copied onto the hard disk. If you want to have a look at this excellent program, place the setup CD in the CD-drive. There are several methods of calling up the *Discover Windows 98* program.

Welcome to
Windows 98

Right after the Windows startup, the *Welcome to Windows 98* dialog box appears. By clicking on the *Discover*

Windows 98 link, the interactive learning program will start. If you have already closed the *Welcome* window or permanently deactivated it, choose *Start/Run* and enter the command *WELCOME* in the *Open* text box. After that press ⏎, or click on *OK* to start the *Windows-Tour*. You can also call up the *Welcome* window using *Start/Programs/Accessories/System Tools* and choosing the *Welcome To Windows 98* command.

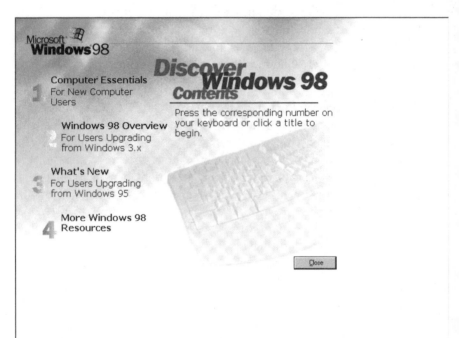

Fig. 2.1: Discover Windows 98, an animated tutorial

After loading the *Discover Windows 98* tutorial, click on the button or the text of the topic you want to know about in the first window. The shape of the mouse pointer will change from an arrow to that of a small hand. Ideally, you proceed step by step starting from the top. The first

Computer essentials

introduction, *1 Computer Essentials*, familiarizes you with the computer, the keyboard and the mouse and is particularly useful for new users. To begin, press the `→` key.

Choosing a topic

On the left hand side of the screen, a list of topics is displayed. To proceed step by step, press the `→` key. However, you can also click on one of the links on the left hand side of the screen to jump straight to the topic you want to see.

Simply follow the audio directions (soundcard and speakers are necessary for this, of course). If you need further help, click the *Getting Help* link. The tutorial will then display the corresponding explanation. As soon as you have finished one topic, the program will respond and display the next step. To get back to the contents list, click the *Contents* button.

At the end of a series of tasks you can move on to the next topic. If you want to close *Discover Windows 98*, press the `Esc` key and click the *Close* button in the *Contents* window. Confirm with *Yes* in the dialog box . This way you will find yourself back on the Windows desktop.

Tip!

The core of the tutorial *TOUR98.EXE* is in the *Windows* folder and can also be started using *Explorer*, if the CD is loaded.

Activate the Tutorial for Users of Earlier Windows Versions

Windows 98 has a special help function designed for users of previous Windows versions. Those familiar with older versions like *Windows 3.1* or *Windows 3.11* will find *Windows 98 Overview* tutorial designed to meet their needs, since it answers all the questions most often asked by users of the previous Windows versions.

Those familiar with the previous version, *Windows 95*, should click the *What's New* link in the *Windows 98 Overview*. After that, simply click on the topics which interest you, represented by links. To get back to *Contents* use the ⊠ button.

There are no demos of functions for users who are upgrading, but you will find an interactive tutorial instead. The tasks are performed on the *Windows 98* user interface. For this purpose, the tutorial window will be reduced to the size of the *Windows 98 Overview* after clicking the *Lessons* button and selecting one of the lessons displayed, to enable you to see the desktop (Figure 2.2.). Click the *Next* button to start the program.

The tutorial window

Read the information displayed for this topic or click on the *Next* button. If you have been given a task, try to execute it right then and there. If you are unable to do so, click on the *Show Me* button 🖭. The tutorial will start a video in which the required step or function is clearly shown to you.

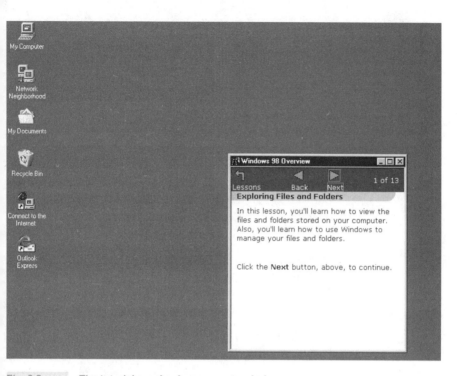

Fig. 2.2:   The tutorial running in a separate window.

Windows 98
Overview

Click anywhere in the demo window to close it. After that click the *Next* button in the *Windows 98 Overview* window to move on to the next task. Carry on in this way until the end of the lesson.

Close the tutorial

At the end of a lesson you will be taken back to the lesson overview, and you can start the next lesson from there. If you want to close the tutorial before that, choose the *Lessons* button and in the *Contents* window, the *Close* button. Confirm the next message with *Yes*, after which you will be taken back to the Windows desktop.

A completed lesson will be marked with a check mark in the overview. The *Welcome to Windows 98* dialog box can always be closed using the *Close* button ❎ in the title bar.

Calling up General Windows-Help

Do you need help at some point while working with *Windows 98*? You will, of course, find instructions on the most important points in *Windows 98* in this book, but the operating system itself will not leave you on your own to deal with its manifold functions either.

In this section we will deal with how to call up the internal *Windows Help*. How to use the different help functions will be explained below. You will be surprised at how much information can be found in *Help*.

Interactive

Some help functions are in a multimedia format, complete with graphics and videos; while others like the *Troubleshooter* are interactive and require a response from the user. To begin with, let's see how to get *Windows Help* onto the screen. You've probably already guessed that there are several possibilities to choose from.

Let's start with the conventional method. Using the *Start* button, open the *Start* menu and select the *Help* item. The *Windows Help* dialog box will be displayed with three tab pages, *Contents*, *Index*, and *Search*.

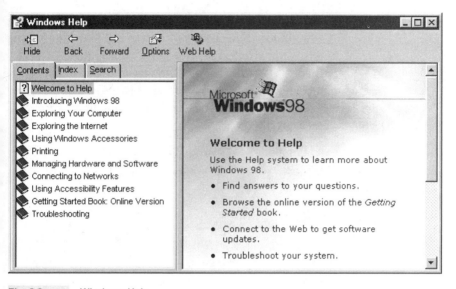

Windows-Help
dialog box

However, you can also access the *Windows Help* dialog box by using a keyboard shortcut: Close the *Windows Help* dialog box and press the ⌊F1⌋ key. But be careful: At least one file needs to be shown on the desktop as a window, or one of the Windows icons (*My Computer*, *Recycle Bin* etc.) has to be highlighted. If an active window has been minimized as an icon in the taskbar, the ⌊F1⌋ key will not start *Help*.

Tip!

Attention: While calling up *Windows Help* using the ⌊F1⌋ key, no application window should be open, otherwise the *Help* for this particular application will be displayed instead. We will talk more about this at the end of this chapter. Once the application is minimized in the taskbar and a file window has been opened, start *Windows Help* again using the ⌊F1⌋ key.

Help menu

You can call up the the *Windows Help* dialog box in a folder window by choosing the *Help Topics* item on the *Help* menu. Here, too, the same rule applies: In folder windows *Windows Help* will always start, while in application windows it will start help specific to that application. (More details on that will be found at the end of the chapter).

Three tab cards

The functions of *Windows Help* are separated on three tab pages which we will describe in the following paragraphs.

The Windows Help *Contents* Tab Page.

After calling up *Windows Help*, the *Windows Help* dialog box will display the tab page which was last used. When the *Windows Help* dialog box is displayed for the first time, the *Contents* tab page will be displayed. We will now discuss the help functions on this tab page.

The entries in the list box of the *Contents* tab page can be opened with a click on the *Topics* (📖) button in the left frame or with a click on *Welcome to Help* (?). The available help text will always appear in the frame on the right or, in some cases, more than one window will be displayed.

Welcome to Help

After starting Help, the first entry you will see is *Welcome to Help*. In the right frame, you will receive a short introduction to the help functions of *Windows 98*.

With a click on the second entry, *Introducing Windows 98*, the contents of this topic will be displayed. To go into more detail click on the *How to Use Help* topic. You will now see pages containing information explaining how to use *Windows Help*.

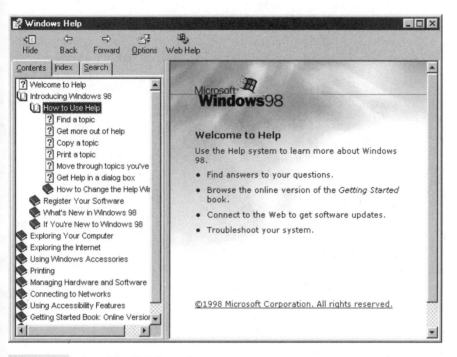

Fig. 2.4:   Searching Help by topic

Hierarchical organisation	We now move on to the hierarchical organisation of the entries in the left tab card, *Contents. Windows Help* is organized in the form of books, which are easily recognizable by the ● icon. The list box on the left acts like a shelf. A book can be opened with a single click.
Book	After that, the contents of the current book ▣ are displayed in the form of chapters, which are again displayed with ● icons.
Help entries	A book that is open ▣ can also contain certain help entries already. These are identified by the ? icon. The chapters of a book that's already open can be brought to the fore with a mouse click.

Basically, the whole thing works in much the same way as the files in the tree view of *Explorer*, except that the book icon is used instead of the folder icon and here you only need to click once.

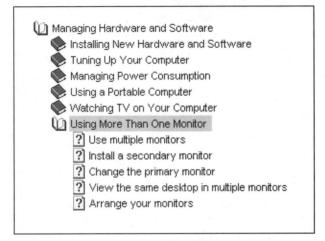

Managing Hardware and Software
   Installing New Hardware and Software
   Tuning Up Your Computer
   Managing Power Consumption
   Using a Portable Computer
   Watching TV on Your Computer
   Using More Than One Monitor
     [?] Use multiple monitors
     [?] Install a secondary monitor
     [?] Change the primary monitor
     [?] View the same desktop in multiple monitors
     [?] Arrange your monitors

Fig. 2.5:   Hierarchical structure of Windows-Help

Open book

An open book 📖 can be closed with a click, which will reduce the amount of information displayed in the left list box. If many books are open at the same time, use the scroll bar to reach the books or Help entries that are not displayed. A Help topic with the [?] icon on the left side can be opened by clicking on its name (Figure 2.4).

Displayed information

Read the information displayed. Help topics will display a toolbar with buttons which allow you to move around within the topic (*Back* and *Forward*).

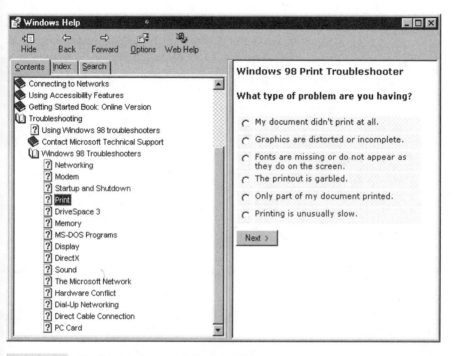

Fig. 2.6: The Troubleshooter of Windows Help

Displayed Help topic

You can change the Help topic displayed by clicking on a book ● or on another help entry ? in the list of topics shown on the left hand side. If displayed Help topics contain more than one page, you can display the next page by clicking on the ⇨ *Forward* button Using the *Back* button ⇦ you can move backwards page by page through the topics you have already accessed.

Options button

Using the *Options* button you can change the way Help is displayed. You can change the highlighting mode, switch to the Web Help (this requires a modem and Web access) and move backwards and forwards. Using the *Print* command, you can print out the information given in a Help topic, provided that your printer is installed and connected.

Additional information

To call up additional information, click on the text passages which are underlined in the right window, known as links. If you are in one of the *Troubleshooters*, first answer the question by selecting the correct option button ◌ and then clicking the *Next* button [Next >]. Go on like this until the solution to the problem is displayed.

Links to program help

Be careful: Some links call up program-specific help, like, for example, the *Microsoft Internet Explorer*. If you do not work with the mouse, you can use keyboard combinations to open Help topics. Using the up and down arrows [↓] and [↑], move the highlighted bar to the selected book and press the [↵] key to open the book. Highlight a topic and use the [↵] key to open the topic.

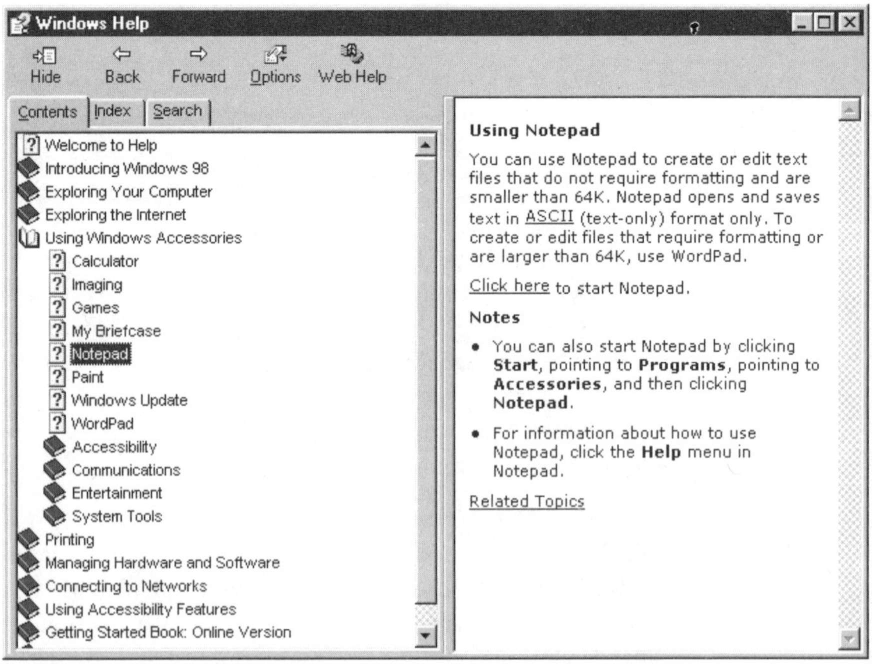

Fig. 2.7:   Link to the program start in a Help topic

Link to the
program start

In some help topics you can start the program being discussed by clicking the _Click here_ link. You can close Help anytime in any window using the _Close_ button ☒.

The Windows Help _Index_ Tab Page

In this section we focus on the alphabetical index of _Windows Help_, which can be called up using the _Index_ tab page in the _Windows Help_ dialog box.

Index tab page,

To begin with, call up _Windows Help_ through _Start/Help_, and select the _Index_ tab page. You may have to wait a little while until _Windows 98_ has loaded the search index. This depends on the system you are using and the available memory.

The left part of the _Index_ tab page is divided in half. The top part is a text box which allows you to enter a keyword. The list below displays all available index entries in _Windows Help_, in alphabetical order. Enter the first letter of the word in the text box and specify the keyword letter by letter. Sometimes it is even enough to enter just the first letter of the keyword.

Entering your key
word

The list below will adjust its contents following the entry of your keyword. If you enter a letter, you will see that the first entry in the list begins with that letter, too. Enter, for example, 'E' and observe how the list changes. Complete the entry by typing in 'Explorer'.

The first matching entry will be displayed. Select _Explorer, Internet_ in the list of index entries and click the _Display_ button. Double-click the _Channels_ item in the _Topics Found_ dialog box. Read the information in the right frame.

Click on the *E-mail* link after the ▣ button. Read the text displayed and when you are done, click the *Back* button ⬅ Back .

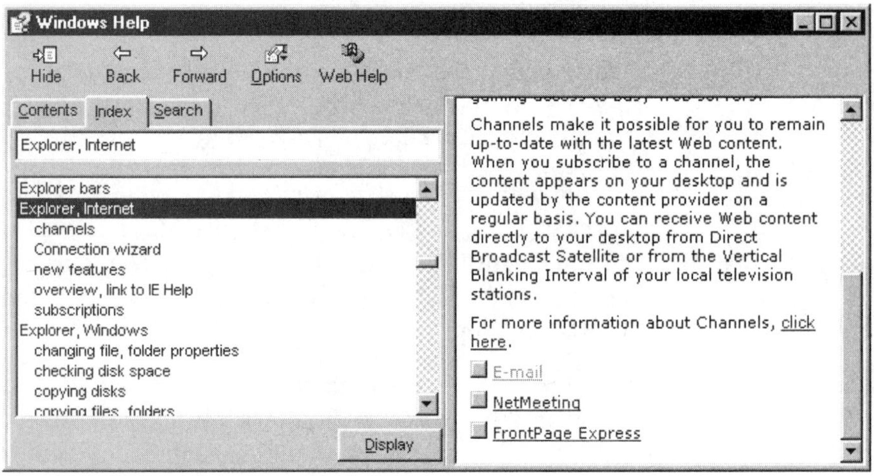

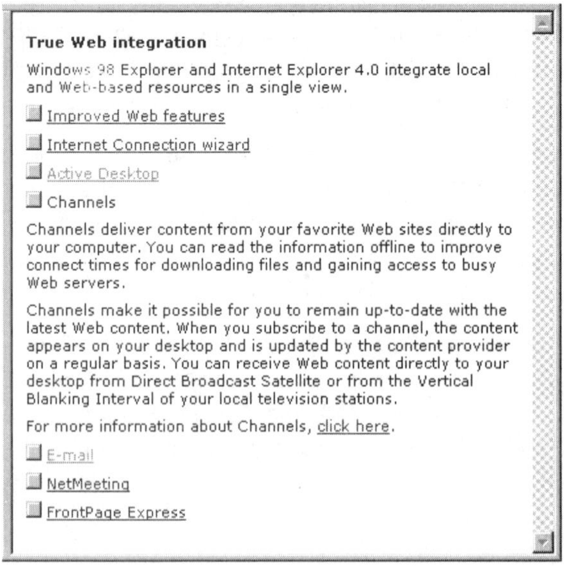

Fig. 2.8: The *Index* tab page (above) and the Help topic of a link

Double-click the *Explorer bars* entry in the left frame of *Windows Help*, and in the right window click the <u>Click here</u> link. The program-specific help of *Internet Explorer* will start. Open some books ❧ and point to some Help topics ? and close the *Internet Explorer Help* with ☒.

Tip!

In the example above, we started the external Help for the *Internet Explorer* Web browser program, which is shipped with *Windows 98*. This application's Help can be used just like the *Windows Help*. By the way, when entering a keyword it is not necessary to make a distinction between upper case and lower case.

Display the text of a topic

The *Topics Found* dialog box will be displayed for certain topics. To display the text of a topic, select the description from the list and click *Display*. A faster way is to double-click on the topic description itself

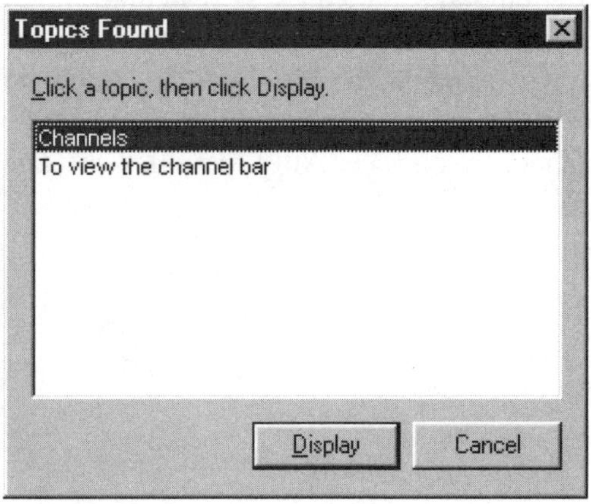

Fig. 2.9:   Dialog box with more than one topic

The *Search* Tab Page in Windows Help

After calling up *Windows Help*, the *Windows Help* dialog box will always display the tab page last accessed. The *Contents* tab page contains the topics sorted hierarchically by subject or by book. The *Index* tab page will display the alphabetically sorted index. If you were unable to find the topic you were looking for, the *Search* tab page offers yet another possibility.

Search text

Using *Search*, you can search the actual text of all the topics available. The number of matching words can be narrowed down by using search criteria. The end result will be a list displaying all Help entries which contain the keyword and fit the topic.

Loading a list
of words

To begin with, start *Windows Help* from *Start/Help*. After that, select the *Search* tab page. When calling up the *Search* tab page for the first time, *Windows 98* has first to load the list of words. This list functions as a kind of data bank which is used in the full text search mode.

Compound words

Using the *Search* tab page you can now search all topics looking for specific words or expressions. Enter the keyword or compound word in the text box. A compound word can be two unconnected words. In this case, enter the words separated by a space. After that click the *List Topics* button .

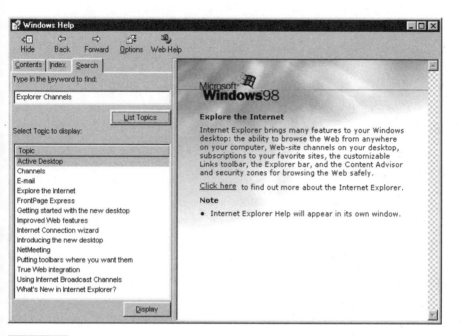

Fig. 2.10: Entry of compound words

List of topics

Be careful: *Windows Help* will not react to every keystroke, unlike the list of topics in the previous version, *Windows 95*.

The list of topics in the lower list box of the left window frame will be displayed after clicking on the *List Topics*  button. Try it out, using the expression *Explorer Channels*.

Reducing the search criteria

You can reduce the search criteria by selecting one of the topics in the lower list, which corresponds most closely to the topic or term you are looking for. To try it out highlight the entry *Channels*. To display the topic click the *Display* button ⌞ Display ⌟.

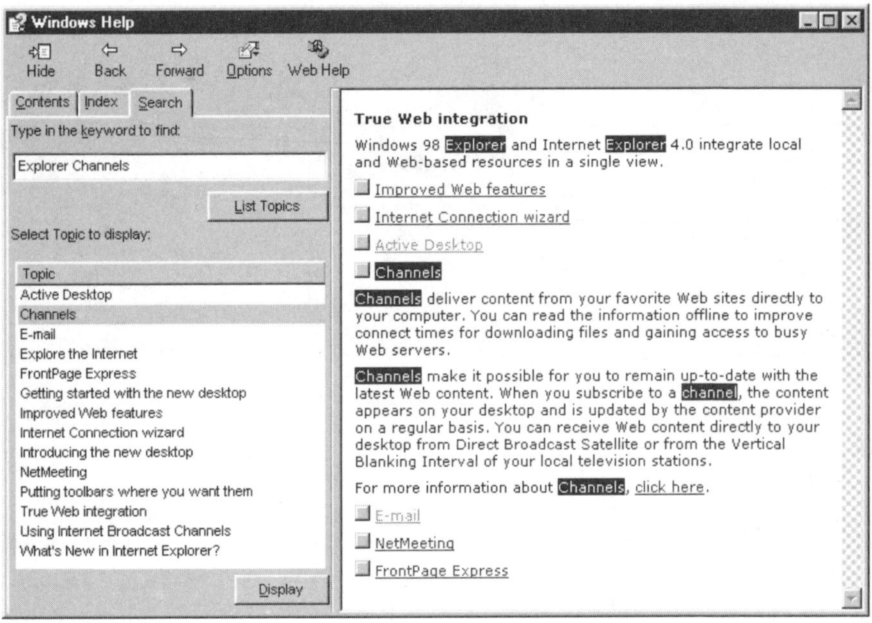

Fig 2.11: The requested search topic is displayed

Double-click the topic

The right window frame displays the corresponding text. To display the text you can also double-click on the topic in the left window frame.

Links display further details

Everything that corresponds to the keyword or phrase, will be displayed highlighted in the list of topics. Using the links which are displayed in blue and underlined in the text you can get more details displayed. Links that you have read (clicked with the mouse) will be highlighted in gray. This technology is the same as the one on the World Wide Web, an online information service of the Internet. Close the *Windows Help* using the *Close* button.

Windows Context-Sensitive Help Elements

Apart from the standard *Windows Help*, *Windows 98* also offers additional Help. This context-sensitive Help can be called up in almost every dialog box and in many applications. It will display information on unknown screen elements in *ScreenTips*.

Before you can try out this form of help, you have to open a dialog box. Start the *WordPad* word processor for example, and select the *File/Print* command. In the *Print* dialog box you will see the Help button [?] in the title bar to the left of the *Close* button.

 Help button

Now click on the *Help* button and move the mouse pointer in the dialog box. The tip of the mouse pointer now has a question mark ⟨?⟩. Click with the *Help Select* cursor on the part of the dialog box where you need help.

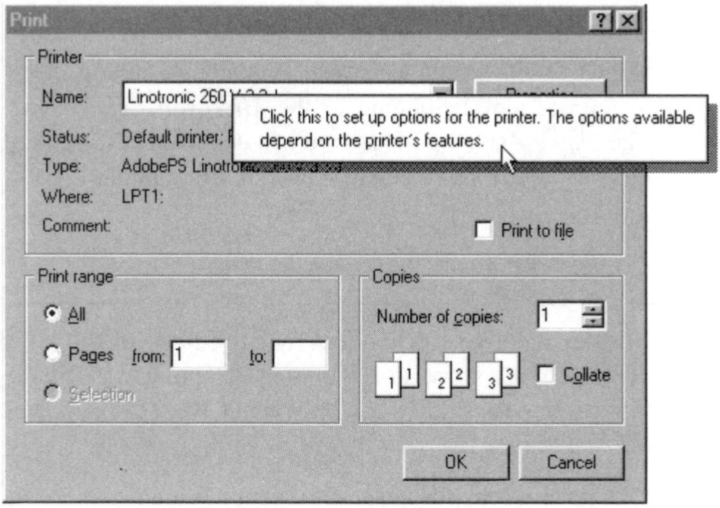

Fig. 2.12: Calling up context-sensitive Help in dialog boxes.

ScreenTips

If a Help description is available, *Windows* will display a *ScreenTip* with an explanatory text describing the function or the control element that you have selected. If no information is available, the question mark cursor will simply disappear. Repeat the process of calling up the context-sensitive Help in another part of the dialog box. The displayed *ScreenTip* can be closed with a mouse click.

Another way to get Help for an unknown screen element is to click with the right mouse button on the area where you need Help. Then select the the *What's This?* command.

If a dialog box does not have context-sensitive Help, choose the *Help* button or press F1. If you want to print or copy the information found in a *ScreenTip*, click with the right mouse button in the *ScreenTip* window and select the *Print* command in the shortcut menu.

Microsoft Office
Suite

Context-sensitive Help is also available in dialog boxes of applications belonging to the *Microsoft Office Suite*. The *Office-Assistant*, which we will deal with at the end of this chapter, is also a handy source of information.

Calling up and Using Help in Windows Applications

Even experts have difficulties keeping track of the large number of functions in a *Windows 98* application. Statistics say that most of us use only about 10 % of the potential of a program.

This need not be the case, since every Windows program has application-specific Help.

Online Help

In the multimedia age, many software manufactures do not bother to have user manuals printed and put all the information about the program and its functions in online Help. In this section we will tell you how to get Help with any Windows program.

Start the application

Before you can get Help with a program, the application first has to be started. Use the *Start* menu, point on *Programs*, and select the program, or open the program group first and then select the desired program.

Program window should be active

To give you some practice, call up the *WordPad* word processor now. We will deal with Help for *Word* and the other applictions of the *Microsoft Office Suite* later on. To get Help in *WordPad* or in some other Windows program press the F1 key. First make sure that the program window is active.

If a folder window is open and active on the desktop, you will get *Windows Help*. If programs are minimized as a button on the taskbar, however, the F1 key will not work to call up program-specific help.

The *Help* menu

This problem with the shortcut key can easily be avoided: All you have to do is use the *Help* menu. In the *Help* menu of applications you will always find the *Help Topics* command.

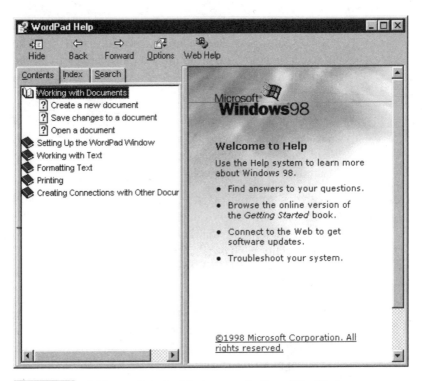

Calling up Help for Windows applications (WordPad)

This command will call up the (*Name of Application*) *Help* window, the contents of which is tailored to the active program, but resembles *Windows Help* in all other respects. Since every program offers its own Help topics, we will confine ourselves here to a description of the use of the general Help.

Identical to
Windows Help

In all applications the Help is used in essentially the same way. The left window frame displays the Help topics while the right window frame shows the text. The functions of the tab pages in the *Help* window of any application has already been dealt with above.

Tip!

The programs contained in the *Microsoft Office 97 Suite* have a new Help function called the *Office Assistant* (see the next section). The general Help topics can be called up in this program by opening the *Help* menu and selecting the *Contents and Index* command.

The Office Assistant in Microsoft Office 97 Programs

All *Office* applications have a new Help function in the form of the *Office Assistant*, which is displayed in a separate window after the program starts. It looks like the figure below. Click on the icon in the window of the *Office Assistant*, enter your question in the text box and click the *Search* button.

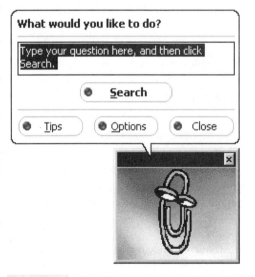

What would you like to do?

Type your question here, and then click Search.

● **Search**

● Tips   ● Options   ● Close

Fig. 2.14:   The Office Assistant of Word, Excel or PowerPoint

Context sensitive

The dialog box of the *Office Assistant* will be displayed every time *Office 97* programs start. The new *Office Assistant* can answer questions, offer tips and tricks and give context-sensitive help on exactly those functions you are working with at the moment. Further, the *Office Assistant* can start the *Contents and Index* of Help automatically.

Context information

The new *Office Assistant* can do more than just give tips. However, whenever you see a yellow bulb displayed in the assistant's window, a tip with useful information about the work you are doing right at that moment is at your fingertips. Click on the bulb to view this tip.

If the assistant is not displayed when a relevant tip is available, the *Office Assistant* button will display a bulb. Click on this button and then on the bulb to display the tip. The *Close* command will also close the tip.

Disable some functions

If you want to disable some of the *Office Assistant* functions, click the dialog box with the animated paper clip 'Clippit'. Choose *Options* and deselect the corresponding options in the dialog box.

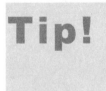

You will find the *Office Assistant* in all *Office 97* programs. Any changes which have been made in the options dialog, like for example what kind of tips should be displayed, will be working in all *Office* programs using the assistant.

To activate or deactivate the text balloon of the assistant, click the *Office Assistant* button in the *Standard* toolbar or choose the *Microsoft [name of the application] Help* item in the *Help* menu. The keyboard allows you to do this even more quickly. To call up the assistant simply press F1.

Two sizes

The *Office Assistant* can be displayed in two sizes. To increase or decrease the size of the assistant, point the mouse pointer on one of the borders, so that it assumes the shape of a two-headed arrow and, while holding down the mouse button, drag the mouse. If you release the mouse button the new size of the assistant will be fixed.

The Context-Sensitive Help in Microsoft Office Programs

Choose the *What's This?* command from the *Help* menu in *Microsoft Word 97* and point with the *Help Select* cursor ⓀⓅ at the program element you are having difficulty with. Read the information in the *ScreenTip*, and click to close.

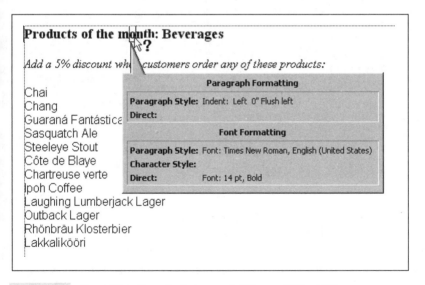

Fig. 2.15: Formatting the actual paragraph (Microsoft Word 97)

In *Microsoft Word*, clicking with the *Help Select* cursor ☟? on some text will call up a text bubble containing information regarding the character and paragraph style formatting of your current paragraph. Press ⎡Esc⎤, to close the context-sensitive Help.

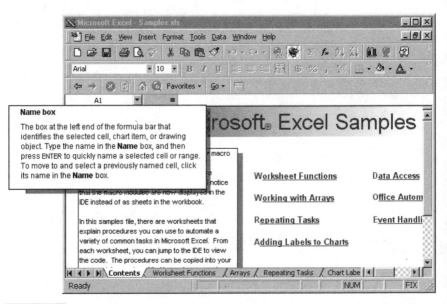

Fig. 2.16: The standard context-sensitive Help of a program, in this case, Excel 97

3. Programs and Documents

In this chapter, we will be working with programs and their files, called documents. To begin with, you will learn the different ways of starting and ending applications under *Windows 98*, and after that we will discuss the saving and loading of documents and how to organize them.

Starting Programs

Windows 98 is very flexible, and as the old saying goes, in Windows, too, 'all roads lead to Rome'. This applies particularly to the starting of programs.

To begin with, we will deal with the calling up of applications using the *Start* menu of *Windows 98*. This is the easiest method to follow for beginners. After some time, however, you will notice that using the *Start* menu can also be the most time-consuming way to start a program.

Starting Programs with the *Start* Menu

The *Start* menu represents the control center of *Windows 98* and can be called up by clicking the *Start* button on the left side of the taskbar. On this menu, you will find everything you need under Windows. All *Windows 98* applications can be called up using the *Start* menu's *Programs* item and its overlapping menus.

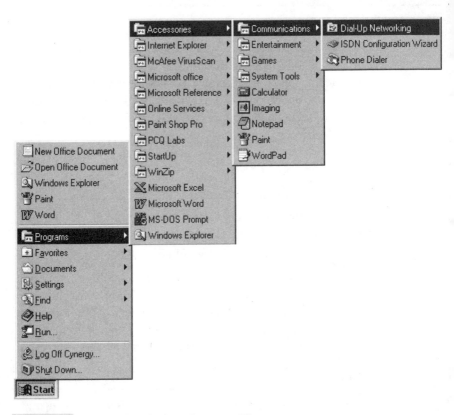

Fig. 3.1:   Applications in the submenus of Programs

Programs

To start a program, point on the *Programs* entry in the *Start* menu. The overlapping menu will open automatically. The first overlapping menu displays the *Windows Explorer* and *MS-DOS Prompt* programs, as well as all installed applications of the *Microsoft Office Suite*, such as *Microsoft Word*, *Microsoft Excel*, *Microsoft Power-Point* or *Microsoft Outlook*.

You will find more programs in the *Accessories* program group, such as a *Calculator*, a *Windows 98* scaled-down word processor called *WordPad* and the *Paint* graphics editor. If you point to a program group 🗔, the overlapping menu will open automatically. To start a program, simply click on the selected item, for example *WordPad*, to start the word processor.

Close automatically

Once a program is started, the *Start* menu closes automatically. You may understand now why we said it can be the most time-consuming way to begin. Try starting up two system programs in the *Start/Program/Accessories/System Tools* program group. The number of available programs in the *Start* menu depends on the system components selected during the installation of Windows, and of course on which other applications were also installed on your computer.

Sorted alphabetically

The *Programs* menu is sorted alphabetically. From the top down the program groups, sorted by name, are listed. Program entries appear below that. The program groups (🗔) are special files that do not contain the actual program files, but in fact only contain shortcuts to the program. Program groups are used to sort various applications according to topic. You can change the name of program groups, delete program groups or create program groups, into which you can subsequently place program commands.

Tip!

After installing a *Windows 98* program, the *Start* menu will automatically display the corresponding entry. Most programs create a new program group with overlapping menus in which their commands are displayed. If a newly installed program does not display its icon in the *Start* menu, this can be rectified manually later on.

Windows 98 offers many ways to start a program. We will now discuss the method which uses the *My Computer* folder in *Windows 98*.

My Computer is a Windows folder in which all the available drives of the computer are displayed as icons. You will also find the icons for *Printer* and *Control Panel* in *My Computer*, and if *Dial-Up Networking* is installed, this, too, will be displayed there.

Calling up Programs Using the *My Computer* System Folder

To open the folder, double-click on the *My Computer* icon on the desktop. In the opened folder, double-click the icon of the drive in which the program is placed, to open up the drive folder in a new window. Double-click the folder or subfolder in which the program you are looking for is stored.

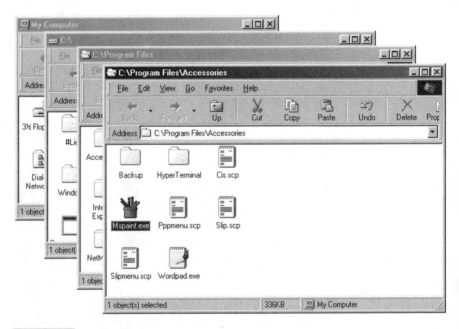

Fig. 3.2   Using *My Computer* to search for folders

Program files

Try it out by first opening the folder *(C:)*, then *Programs Files*, and finally *Accessories*. The program icons of *Paint* (*MSPAINT*) and *WordPad* (*WORDPAD*) are stored there. The shortcuts to start programs in the *Microsoft Office Suite* can be found in the folder *\Program Files\Microsoft Office*.

Program icon.

To start an application, double-click the program icon. Instead of a double click you can also select the folder or icon and choose the *Open* command from the context menu or the *File* menu. In order to use this method to start a program, you need to know the name of and the location where the program file is saved, or the shortcut to start the program, for example (*MSPAINT*).

Tip!

In order to stop a new window from appearing every time you open a folder in *My Computer*, choose the *Folder Options* item on the *View* menu. On the *General* tab page, select the *Custom* radio button and click on the *Settings* button. Select the *Open each folder in the same window* radio button in the *Browse folders as follows* option group and confirm by clicking *OK* and *Close*. From then on you will work in only one window, the contents of which will change every time you open a different folder.

Opening Programs Using the Windows Explorer

The *Windows Explorer* is useful for organizing and maintaining your folders and files. *Explorer* displays the folders in a way that allows you to get a comprehensive structural overview. Of course, it will do a lot more than just display the structure and contents of folders. You can also start any application from the *Windows Explorer*.

To begin with, start *Explorer*. Open the *Start* menu and choose the *Windows Explorer* entry in the *Programs* menu. The fastest alternative is to use the context menu of the *Start* button on the taskbar. Press the right mouse button and select the *Explore* item from the context menu.

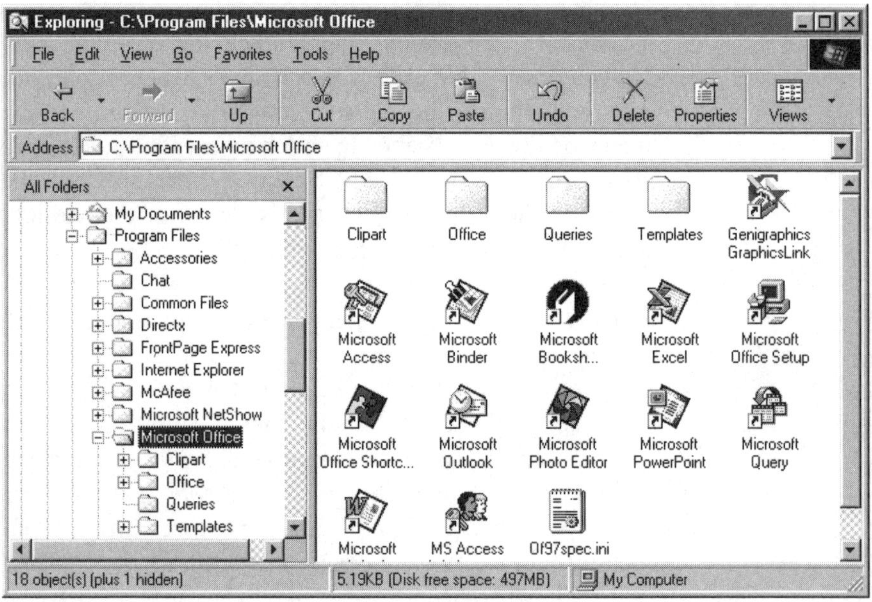

Fig. 3.3: Double-clicking a program icon will start the application

Folder structure

In order to start a program in *Explorer*, you need to know the name and the place where the program or shortcut is stored. Expand the folder structure by clicking on the ⊞ symbol in front of the drive icon and continue to expand it until you arrive at the folder of the program you wish to start. Display the contents by clicking on the name of the folder.

Double click

To start a program, double-click on the program file displayed in the right window pane. The *Windows Calculator*, for example, can be started by double-clicking the *CALC. EXE* file in the *C:\Windows* folder. It is easier to use shortcuts since then you do not have to know the name of the program file. For instance, the shortcut to start components of *Microsoft Office Suite* can be found in the folder *C:\Programs Files\Microsoft Office*.

Open command

Instead of a double click you can also highlight a program folder and open it by choosing the *Open* command in the context or *File* menu.

Structure of the *Start* menu

You can display the structure of the *Start* menu in *Explorer*. To do this, click on the ⊞ plus symbol in front of the *Windows* folder and then of the *Start Menu* folder. The structure of the subfolders corresponds exactly to your *Start* menu. However, the objects displayed in the right window pane of *Explorer* are only shortcuts to the actual location of the program files.

Starting Programs Using the *Run* Command

Windows 98 is very flexible as far as starting programs is concerned. If you would prefer a straightforward approach, or have worked a lot with the old *MS-DOS* operating system, the method using the *Run* dialog box that we will discuss in this section might just be the right one for you.

File location

Using this method, you have to know not only the file location, but also the correct file name. You also need to know the syntax to use when entering the file path in the command line. As you can see this is not for the pure *Windows* user, but rather something for the *DOSonians* among us.

To use *Run*, proceed as follows: Open the *Start* menu and click on the *Run* command to call up the *Run* dialog box. Enter the file path and file name of the application to run in the *Open* text box. Our example in Figure 3.4 will start the *Paint* graphics program, with its program file called *MSPAINT.EXE*. The *Run* command has got the following structure:

```
Drive Letter:\Path\File Name
```

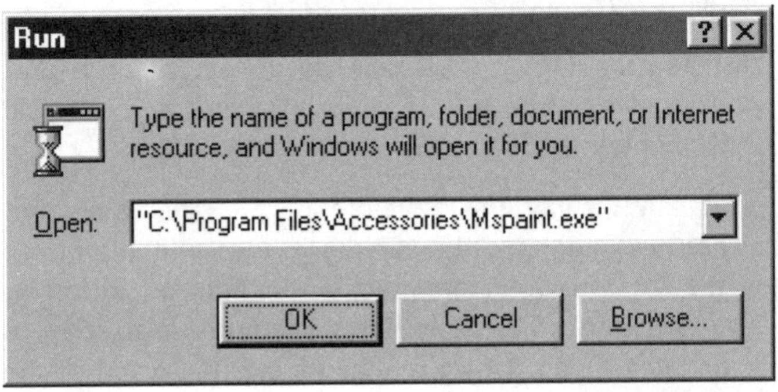

Run ? X

Type the name of a program, folder, document, or Internet resource, and Windows will open it for you.

O̲pen: "C:\Program Files\Accessories\Mspaint.exe"

[OK] [Cancel] [B̲rowse...]

Fig. 3.4:   The *Run* command needs the complete file path.

After that, press ⏎ or click *OK*. If you receive an error message, it means that the path or file name does not exist. Click on the *Browse* button and try to find the file location using the *Browse* dialog box. You will find the shortcut to start components of the *Microsoft Office Suite* in the folder *\Program Files\Microsoft Office*. The actual program files, however, are to be found in the folder *\Program Files\Microsoft Office\Office*. Take note of the fact that the *Word 97* program file is called *WINWORD. EXE*.

Select the program file

Select the program file once you have found it and click the *Open* button. The file path will be displayed in the *Open* command line in the *Run* dialog box. Click *OK* to start the application.

Calling up Programs with the Microsoft Office Shortcut-Bar

If the *Microsoft Office 97 Suite* has been installed, the programs *Microsoft Word, Excel, PowerPoint, Outlook* and, in the *Professional* version also *Microsoft Access*, can be started in yet another way. To do this, you first have to activate the shortcuts for the *Microsoft Office* components with the *Microsoft Office Shortcut Bar*.

Fig. 3.5:   The Microsoft Office Shortcut Bar with its program icons

Customize

The *Microsoft Office Shortcut Bar* should be started via *Start/Programs/Microsoft Office*. If you connot find it there, open *Explorer* and change to *C:\Program Files\ Microsoft Office\Microsoft Office* and double-click on the *Microsoft Office Shortcut Bar* shortcut. Click on the *System* menu icon of the *Microsoft Office Shortcut Bar* and choose the command *Customize*. Select the *Buttons* tab page and scroll through the *Show these files as Buttons* list box. Select *Microsoft Word, Excel, Power-Point, Outlook, Access*, etc by checking the corresponding check boxes in front of the entries. Confirm your changes by clicking *OK*.

Program start

To start one of the *Office* components, click the button representing the program on the *Microsoft Office Shortcut Bar*.

Tip! The *Microsoft Office Shortcut Bar* can also display buttons for other Windows applications. Click the system menu of the *Microsoft Office Shortcut Bar* and choose the *Customize* command. Select the *Buttons* tab page and click on the *Add File* button. Change to the drive and folder of the application, select the program file and click *Add* followed by *OK*.

Tip! The sequence of the buttons on the *Microsoft Office Shortcut Bar* can be changed. Click the *System* menu of the *Microsoft Office Shortcut Bar* and choose the command *Customize*. Change to the *Buttons* tab page. Select the entry of the button to be changed in the *Show these files as Buttons* list box. Then use the arrow buttons to move an entry up or down. A free space can be inserted above a selected entry by clicking on the *Add Space* button. Confirm your settings by clicking *OK*.

Opening Programs and Documents with Windows 98

If you work exclusively with one program under *Windows 98* such as a word processor like *Word 97*, it would be practical to start the program automatically after Windows starts. The same is true for documents that you work with over a longer period, like a thesis or something similar. In this case, you could save two steps if you could have the document opened automatically, since normally you first have to start the program and then open the file in the program.

It is exactly for cases like this that *Windows 98* has a special folder in which you can save all files that you would like to work with right after Windows starts. This folder, which is called the *StartUp* folder, can be found in the *Program* menu of the *Start* menu. If you have not yet installed additional Windows applications, the *StartUp* folder will probably be empty.

Open the *Start* menu and point at *Programs/StartUp*. If the folder is empty, the overlapping menu will display (*Empty*). If you have installed the *Microsoft Office Suite*, the *StartUp* folder will already contain some program icons, for example the icon of the *Microsoft Office Shortcut Bar*, which will automatically be displayed after Windows starts.

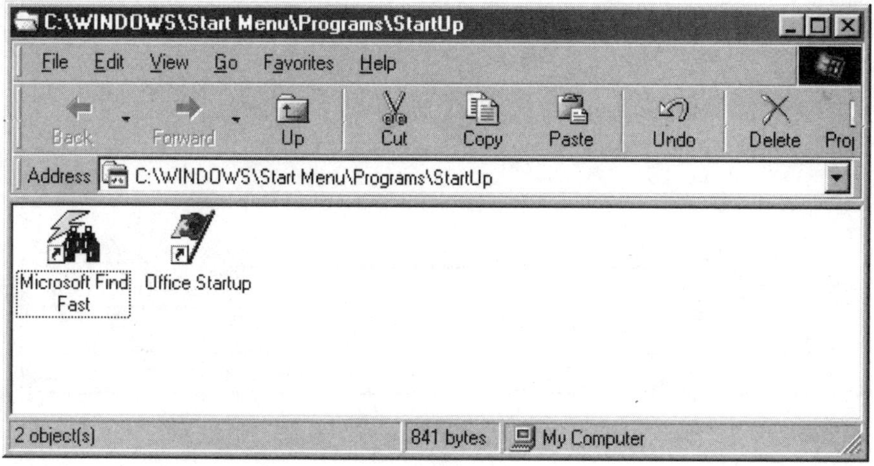

Fig. 3.6: The *StartUp* folder with program icons

To start a program every time you start *Windows 98*, you have to establish a shortcut to the program icon in the *StartUp* folder. To do this, you can use several methods. To begin with, we will tell you about how to add entries to the *Start* menu using the *Properties* window of the taskbar.

Click on the *Start* button and point to *Settings*. After that click on the entry *Taskbar & Start Menu* and change to the *Start Menu Programs* tab page. Now click on *Add* and, in the *Create Shortcut* dialog box, click on the *Browse* button. At this point you should know the location of the program file or its shortcut. Let's use the *WordPad* Windows word processor as an example.

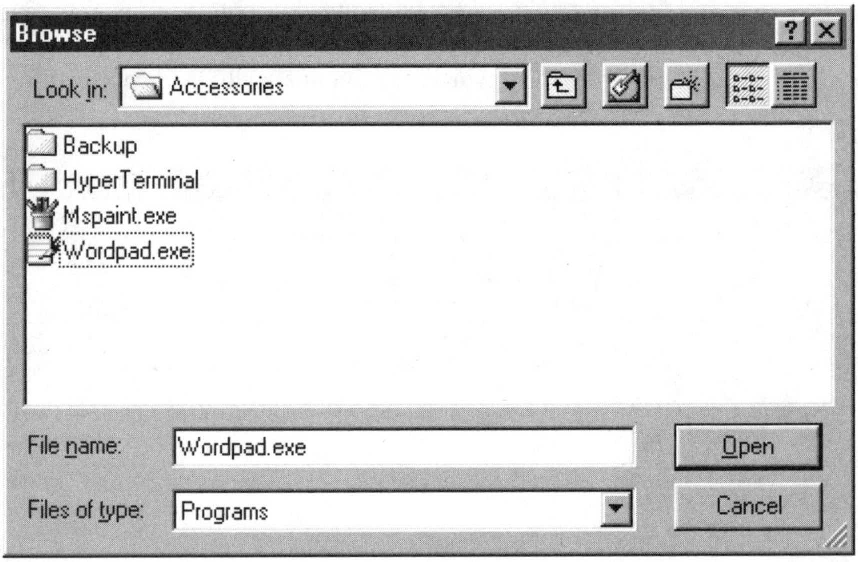

Fig. 3.7: Finding the path of a program file

The program file of *WordPad* is called *WORDPAD.EXE* and is saved in the folder *C:\Program Files\Accessories*. If you would rather have *Word 97* or another component of the *Office Suite* included in the *StartUp* folder instead, use one of the shortcuts for the *Microsoft Office* components from the *\Program Files\Microsoft Office* folder.

Highlight the selected program file and click on *Open*. In the *Create Shortcuts* dialog box click *Next* and double-click on the *StartUp* folder in the *Select Program Folder* dialog box.

Selecting a program group.

In the *Select a Title for the Program* dialog box you can now enter the name that will represent the program on the *StartUp* menu. After that click the *Finish* button.

Close the *Taskbar Properties* window by clicking *OK* and verify the contents of the *StartUp* program group on the *Start* menu.

These changes will come into effect only after the next system start. In the example used, the *WordPad* program will be started along with *Windows 98*. You should only put the most important applications in the *StartUp* folder, since otherwise the system start will be unnecessarily delayed and the load on the main memory will be increased. For this reason it is not advisable to call up *Microsoft Word*, *Microsoft Excel* and *Microsoft Power-Point* at the same time using the *StartUp* folder, since this would put an enormous load on your computer and unnecessarily delay the Windows start.

You can also add documents to the *StartUp* folder instead of programs. In this case the relevant application will start and open the document.

Tip!

It is easy just to copy existing shortcuts from the *Start* menu into the *StartUp* folder. Open the *Start* menu and the program group with the existing shortcut. For example the group *Programs/Accessories*. Highlight the program command which you want to copy into the *StartUp* program group.

While holding down the `Ctrl` key, drag a copy of the icon into the *StartUp* folder on the already open *Start* menu. If the `Ctrl` key is not held down, the program icon will be moved instead of copied. You can also remove shortcuts from the *Start* menu by using the *Delete* command on the context menu.

Closing Programs

After starting a program, and having worked with it to create a document for example, you will want to close the program after having saved your work.

Methods

The following methods can be used to do this:

- the *Close* command on the *File* menu

- the key combination [Alt]+[F4]

- the *Close* command on the *System* menu

- a double click on the *System* menu icon

- the *Close* button [X] in the title bar

- the *Close* command in the context menu of the program button on the task bar.

Save message

All the above methods will close an application. If a document in an application has not been saved, a message will be displayed prompting you to do so (Figure 3.9).

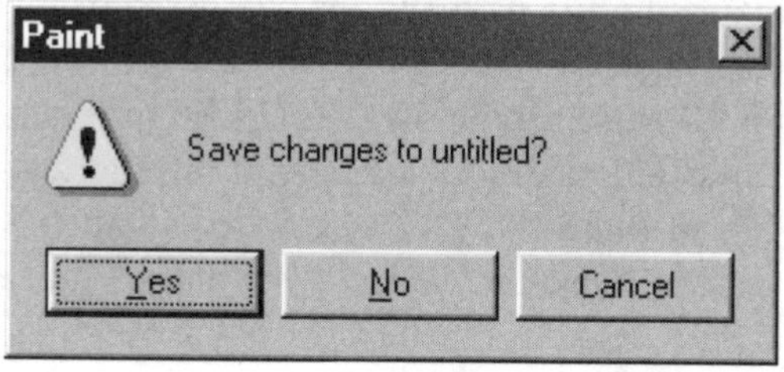

Fig. 3.9: Save message appears when data is not saved

If you click on the *Yes* button the *Save As* dialog box will be displayed. If you choose *No*, the application will close. *Cancel* will take you back to the program without closing down.

Tip! The *System* menu can be called up by clicking the *System* menu icon in the left side of the title bar of a program window. The *System* menu icon represents the program icon of the application. For the *Office* components you here will see the same icons which are used as shortcuts to the program on the *Start* menu and in *Explorer*.

Changing a Program Icon

Shortcuts

At the very beginning of this section, we have to modify the heading somewhat. Program icons under *Windows 98* reside in the executable program file *(EXE)* of an application and can only be changed with the help of special editing programs. When we say program icon we mean the shortcut icon which links to the program file. These shortcut icons are what you encounter on the *Start* menu that displays programs sorted by topic. For many of you, there may not be an obvious difference between a program and a shortcut icon.

Shortcut icon

A shortcut icon is simply a copy of the program icon, which also contains the file path and the file name of the program. The shortcut for the *Calculator* on the *Start* menu contains information about the *CALC.EXE* program in the *C:\Windows* folder. Concealed behind the shortcut for *Microsoft Word* is the *WINWORD.EXE* program file in the *\Program Files\Microsoft Office\Office* folder. Shortcut icons can always be recognized by the [icon] icon which appears in the lower left corner of the program icon.

Tip! To change the icon of any shortcut, select the icon in a folder window of *My Computer* or in *Windows Explorer*. The shortcuts on the *Start* menu can be reached more quickly using the context menu of the *Start* button. If you select the *Open* command, the *Start* menu folder will be displayed. Double-clicking on the *Programs* icon will open the program groups section.

We can use the example of the *WordPad* icon to describe how to change a shortcut icon. Change to the *Windows/ Start Menu/Programs/Accessories* folder. After that, select the *WordPad* icon and choose *File/Properties*. This command is also available in the context menu. Activate the *Shortcut* tab page. (Figure 3.10).

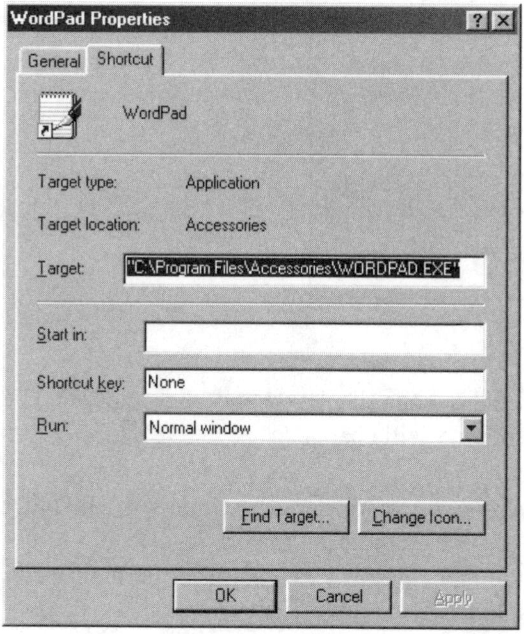

Fig. 3.10: The *Shortcut* tab page

Click the *Change Icon* button on the *Shortcut* tab page. In the *Change Icon* dialog box the icon currently being used is highlighted in the *Current icon* list. Other icons are displayed below it. Use the scroll bar to look at all the available icons.

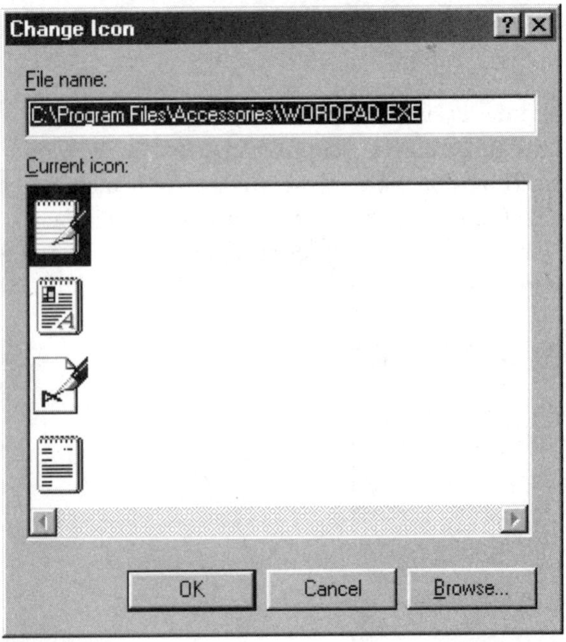

Fig. 3.11:   Select another icon

Select one of the icons displayed and click on *OK*. The icon of the shortcut will change.

Tip! If the *Change Icon* dialog box does not display other icons, click on the *Browse* button, change to the folder containing the icon file or icon library in the dialog box which is displayed, and click *Open*.

Opening Documents

Windows 98 is flexible not only when it comes to starting programs, but also when it comes to opening documents. There are many ways to call up a document. We begin with the easiest method of opening a document that has already been saved using the *Start* menu.

Opening Document Using the *Start* Menu

The *Start* menu provides the possibility to open programs as well as documents. In the *Documents* menu *Windows 98* keeps track of the 15 documents that have most recently been used, regardless of the application.

The only condition is that the file extension of those documents has to be registered in *Windows 98*.

15 last documents

To call up one of the last 15 documents that you have recently used, click on the *Start* button of the taskbar. Select the *Documents* item to open the overlapping menu.

Program icon

The program icon of the application is displayed in front of the file name of the document. To open a document, click on its file name in the overlapping menu (Figure 3.12).

The associated application will then start and automatically open the selected file.

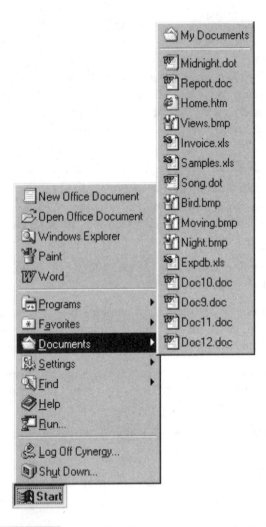

List of the 15 documents most recently used

If you have moved a document listed in the *Document* menu to a different folder since you last used it, *Windows 98* will automatically search your hard disk for the file. Once the file is found, *Windows 98* will automatically start the associated program and open the file. If the file is not found, a message similar to the one in Figure 3.13 will be displayed.

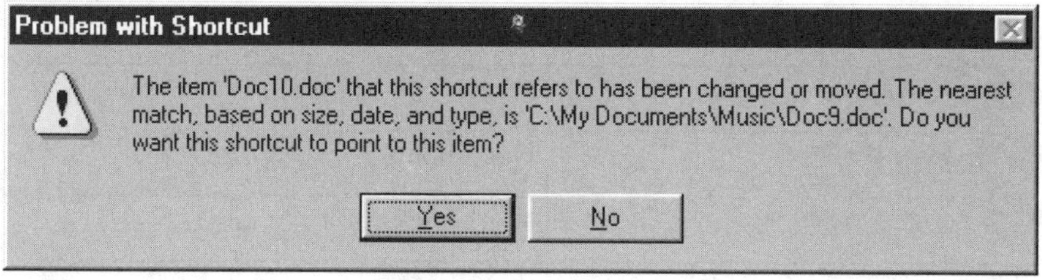

Problem with Shortcut

⚠ The item 'Doc10.doc' that this shortcut refers to has been changed or moved. The nearest match, based on size, date, and type, is 'C:\My Documents\Music\Doc9.doc'. Do you want this shortcut to point to this item?

[Yes]   No

Fig. 3.13:   Search for a similar file name

Alternative

If the name displayed is not the same, which happens when for example the file has already been deleted, then click on *No*, since otherwise the wrong file with a similar name will be opened.

We will now discuss another alternative method of opening a document.

Organization and administration

The *My Computer* window is used for the organization and administration of the drives and their contents. Further, using *My Computer* gives you quick access to the *Control Panel*, the *Printer* folder, *Scheduled Tasks*, and *Dial-Up Networking*. However, *My Computer* can do a lot more than just display the contents of drives and folders. In the next section, we will discuss how to open documents under *Windows 98* using *My Computer*.

Opening *Office* Documents Using the *Start* Menu

If you have installed the *Microsoft Office Suite*, the *Start* menu offers another way to open *Office* documents. Click on the *Start* button and choose the *Open Office Document* item above *Programs*.

In the *Open Office Documents* dialog box which appears, all file types of *Microsoft Office* components are displayed in the *My Documents* folder. If necessary, change the drive and the folder and select the desired file. Confirm by clicking the *Open* button.

Office-Program	File type	Extension
Microsoft Word	Documents	*.DOC*
Microsoft Excel	Workbooks	*.XLS*
Microsoft PowerPoint	Presentations	*.PPT*
Microsoft Access	Databases	*.MDB*
Microsoft Binder	Binders	*.OBD*

Fig. 3.14:   The file types of the Microsoft Office Suite

If you only want to open particular *Office* files such as documents, presentations, or databases, open the *List of Files* drop-down box and select the required file type.

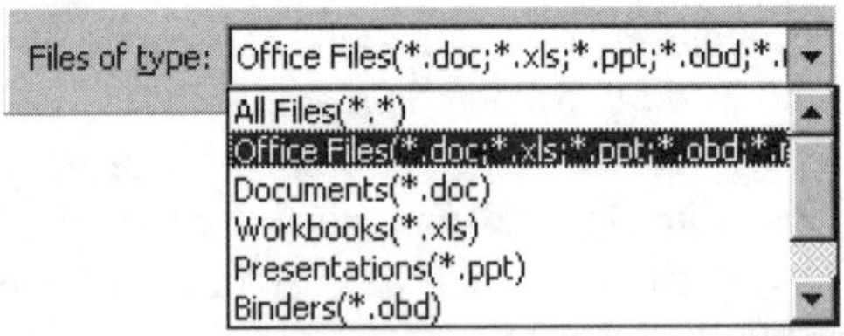

Files of type: | Office Files(*.doc;*.xls;*.ppt;*.obd;*. ▼

All Files(*.*)
Office Files(*.doc;*.xls;*.ppt;*.obd;*.
Documents(*.doc)
Workbooks(*.xls)
Presentations(*.ppt)
Binders(*.obd)

Fig. 3.15:   The *Files of type* list contains all *Office* file types.

Opening *Office* Documents Using the Microsoft Office Shortcut-Bar

The *Open Office Document* command is also available as a button 🖉 on the *Microsoft Office Shortcut Bar*. In the *Open Office Document* dialog box which appears, all file types of the *Microsoft Office* components in the *My Docu-*

ments folder are listed. If necessary, change the drive and the folder and select the required file. Load the document by clicking the *Open* button.

Opening Documents Using the *My Computer* System Folder

To begin with, open the *My Computer* window with a double click on its icon on the desktop. To open a document using *My Computer*, you have to know the name and location of the file or the shortcut. Double-click on the icon of the drive in which your document is saved. Change to the folder of the document. Files created by the the *Microsoft Office Suite* programs are usually stored in the *C:\My documents* folder.

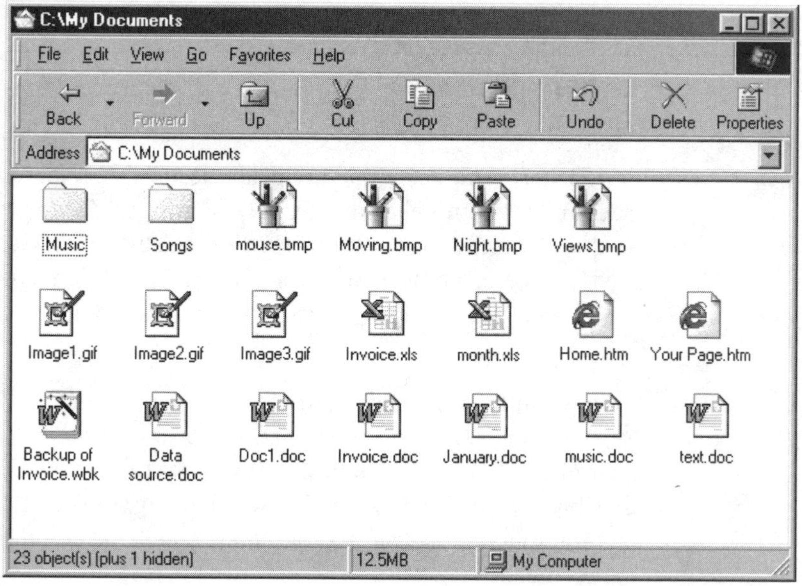

Fig. 3.16: Displaying contents of folders using My Computer

Double click

To open a document, all you have to do is double-click on the document icon. The associated application will start and automatically open the selected document. Alternatively, you can also select the document icon and open the document by choosing the *Open* command in the context menu or the *File* menu.

Tip!

Double-clicking on a program icon only works with registered file types. *Windows 98* first needs to know which program is associated with the extension in order to start it. All correctly installed programs like those of the *Microsoft Office Suite*, have registered file types. If the selected file type has no associated program, the *Open With* dialog box will appear, allowing you to select the application with which to open it.

Opening Documents Using the Windows Explorer

The *Windows Explorer* is useful for the advanced administration and organization of your files and folders.

Comprehensive
display

Use *Explorer* to get a hierarchical view of the folder structure in a comprehensive display. However, *Explorer* can do a lot more than just display the structure and contents of folders. You can also, for example, start all documents from registered applications using the *Windows Explorer*.

The fastest
alternative

To begin with, you should start up *Explorer*: Select *Start/Programs* and click on the *Windows Explorer* item. A faster alternative to that is to use the context menu of the *Start* button on the taskbar. To do this, right-click the *Start* button and select the *Explore* command in the context menu.

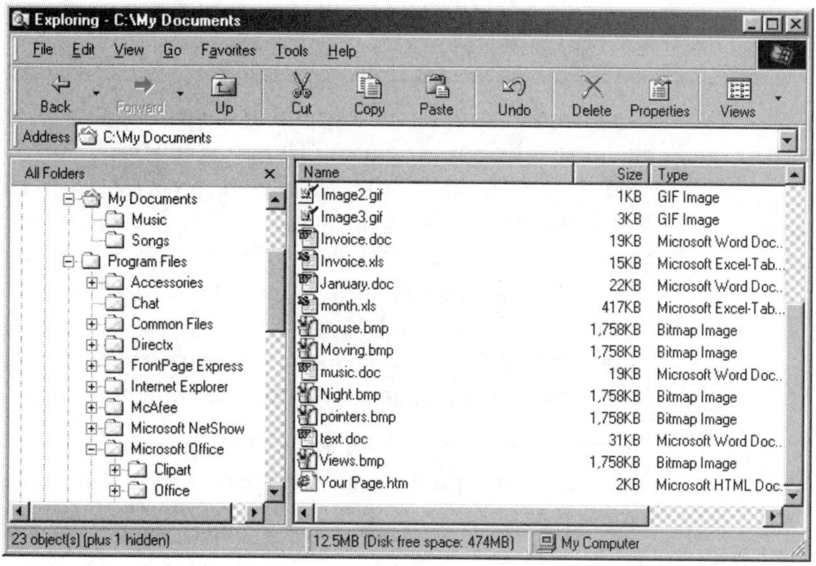

Fig. 3.17: A double click on a document icon in the Explorer will open the file

Open a document

To open a document in *Explorer*, you should know the name and the location of the file or the shortcut. Double-click on the icon of the drive in which your documents are saved. Expand the folder structure by clicking on the ⊞ plus sign in front of the folder icons and change to the folder containing the required document.

Microsoft Office Suite

Display the contents of a folder by clicking on the folder name. Document files of the *Microsoft Office Suite* are usually stored in the folder *C:\My documents*.

Double click

To open a document, all you have to do is double-click on one of the files displayed in the right window pane. The source application will start and open the document. Alternatively, you can also select the document icon and open it by displaying the context menu or the *File* menu and choosing the *Open* command.

Opening Documents Outside a Program

Windows 98 is a graphic operating system made for all kinds of different programs. These applications can be used to execute specific tasks. A word processor such as *Word* can be used to write letters, while the *Paint* graphics program that is shipped with *Windows 98* can be used for drawing graphics. You will need *Microsoft Excel*, on the other hand, to solve your spreadsheet calculations. *PowerPoint* allows you to create presentations and *Microsoft Access* prepares custom database applications.

The documents created with the different programs are saved in the specific format of this application, also called the file type.

Because of this, you can only open specific files types within an application. Normally this is the file type which the program uses while saving, and which *Windows 98* recognizes by the file extension. The file type is an abbreviation consisting of three letters. A *Word* document has the *DOC* file extension, which is short for *DOCument*, while a drawing in *Paint* has the *BMP* extension, short for *BitMaP*. To open a document using the program it was made with, first start the application.

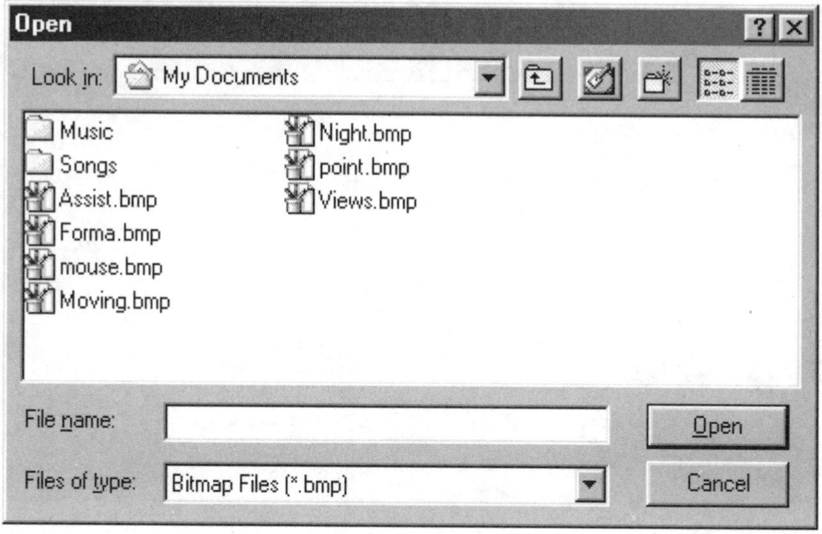

Fig. 3.18:   The *Open* dialog box (in Paint

Select the *File* menu in the program and choose the *Open* command. If the program possesses a toolbar, you can also click on the *Open* button 🖻. All programs will display the *Open* dialog box at this point, similar to the dialog box shown in Figure 3.18.

Certain elements of the *Open* dialog box are identical in all *Windows 98* applications, at least in all *Microsoft Office* components.

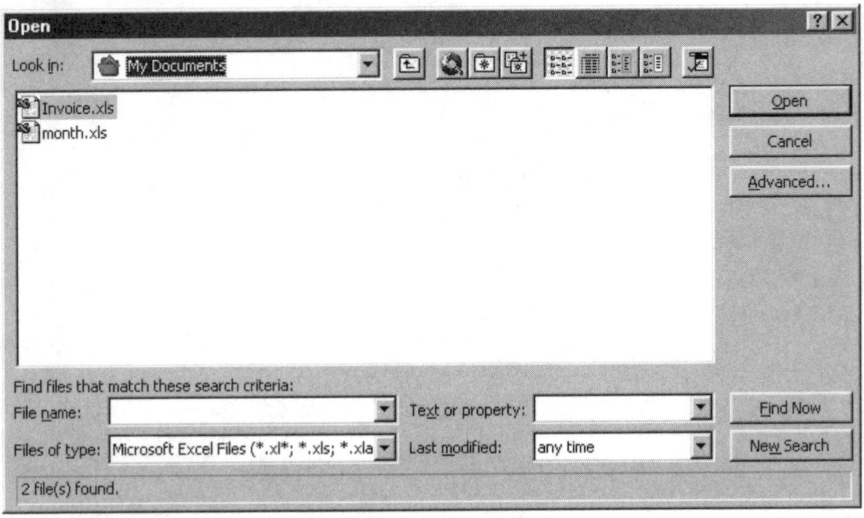

Fig. 3.19: The common *Open* dialog box (in Excel)

The *Look in* listbox

To open a document with the active application, open the *Look in* drop-down list box and select the drive on which the file to be opened is saved. Then move to the list below and, using double clicks, select the folder which contains the desired file. You can also move into subfolders by double-clicking on them. Documents of the *Office 97 Suite* are usually saved in the *C:\My Documents* folder.

Open button

Use the scroll bar to view files that are not displayed. When you see the document you want, select it with a mouse click and click the *Open* button. The document will be loaded.

Parent folder

Using the buttons in the *Open* dialog box, you can change the way the list of documents is displayed or move to parent folders. The *Up One Level* button ⬆ jumps from the folder in which you are currently, to the next folder level above. The current folder name is always displayed in the *Look in* list box.

Details button

The *Details* ▦ button will switch the display of the list box from the default *List* setting to *Details*. This will provide additional information on the documents listed such as file size and modification date. Using the *List* button ▦ you can switch back from the *Details* setting to *List*.

Tip!

The default file type of the active application is always shown in the *Files of type* list box in the *Open* dialog box. Which other file types can or cannot be opened with this application will be apparent when you open the *Files of type* drop-down list box by clicking on the drop-down button. The *All Files (*.*)* entry will display all files in the current folder in the list ox.

You can only open file types the application recognizes. For example, you can open text documents in a word processor program. Recently developed applications are often able to open dozens of different file types by using special conversion programs.

In the following table we have listed the standard file types of the components of the *Microsoft Office Suite*:

Office-Program	File type	Extension
Microsoft Word	Documents	*.DOC*
Microsoft Excel	Workbooks	*.XLS*
Microsoft PowerPoint	Presentations	*.PPT*
Microsoft Access	Databases	*.MDB*
Microsoft Binder	Binders	*.OBD*

Fig. 3.20: The file types of the Microsoft Office Suite

Using Applications to Save Documents

Windows 98 is a graphic operating system for many different kinds of programs. These applications can be used to execute specific tasks.

A word processor like *Word* can be useful if you want to write letters, for instance, while the *Windows 98* graphics program called *Paint* is a handy tool to have when you need to create a drawing. The documents created with the different programs are saved in the specific format of the application with which they were created.

File extension

Because of this you can only open specific file types within each application. For this reason programs attach a file extension, which is an abbreviation consisting of three letters. A *Word* document, for instance, has the *DOC* file extension which stands for *DOCument*, while a drawing in *Paint* will have an extension of *BMP* for *BitMaP*.

In order to save a document in an application in the program-specific format, first create the document.

***Save* command**

Select the *File* menu in the program and choose *Save*. If the application contains a toolbar, you can also click the *Save* button 🖫.

After you do this the *Save As* dialog box will appear, resembling the dialog boxes that are shown in Figure 3.21. Certain elements in the *Save As* dialog box are common to all *Windows 98* applications.

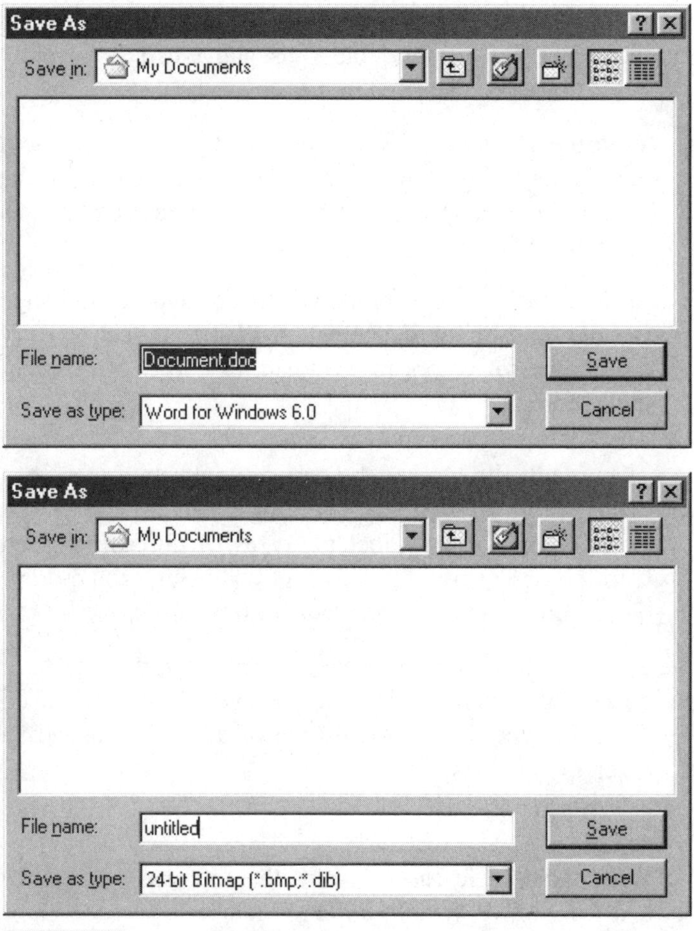

Fig. 3.21: The *Save as* dialog box (above in WordPad, below in Paint)

Target drive, target folder

To save a document in an active application, *Windows* needs four specifications: the target drive, the target folder, the file name and the file type. To select a target drive and folder, open the *Save in* drop-down list box and choose the drive in which the file is to be saved. In the list below, change to the target folder or subfolder in which you want to save the document.

The parent folder

Using the *Up One Level* button 🔼 you can move from the current folder to the folder just above it. The currently active folder is displayed in the *Save in* box.

Create
New folder

With the *Create New folder* button 📁 you can create a new folder and give it a name. Then enter a name for the document in the *Name* text box. File names can have as many as 255 characters.

In the *Save as type* drop-down list box, you can change the file type of the document. In *Paint* you can specify the number of colors in a bitmap, or choose a different image format.

The default file type of the current application is always displayed in the *Save as type* drop-down list box in the *Save As* dialog box. Other file types which can be saved with this application can be seen by clicking on the drop-down button of the *Save as type* list box.

Recently developed applications are often able to save dozens of different file types. However you will need these file types only if the files also have to be opened by other applications.

What is the difference between the commands *File/Save* and *Save As*? As long as a file has not been saved, both of these commands will call up the *Save As* dialog box. If the file has already been saved under some name, *File/Save* will update the existing version; *File/Save As* will always call up the *Save As* dialog box, allowing you to save the file under a different name.

Creating Empty Documents with Windows 98

Usually you will save a document in the program which you used to create it.

Windows 98 also offers the opposite possibility. You can create a new empty document, give it a name, and then open the application associated with the file type. Although that might sound terribly complicated now, it is actually very easy.

Explorer or My
Computer

Ideally, you would create the document in its final location. To do this, start *Explorer* or open *My Computer* and change to the folder or subfolder in which the document should be created. In *My Computer*, select the *New* command on the *File* menu of the target folder window. To do this in *Explorer*, the target folder has to be open. This can easily be done by selecting the folder in the tree view.

Context menu

Another way to do the same thing is to choose the *New* command from the context menu. In *My Computer,* this method does not require that an object be selected, while with *Explorer* the mouse cursor should be placed in the right window pane.

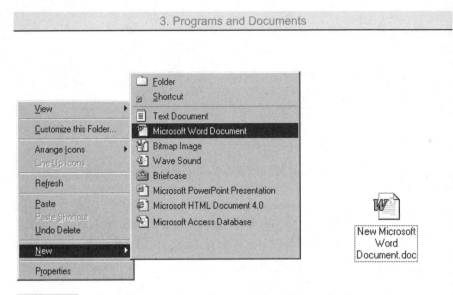

The file types are dependent on the installed applications.

New command

In the overlapping menu of the *New* item, all the file types which are available on your system for creating documents will be displayed in the lower command group. The number and type of documents which can be created thereby depends on which *Windows 98* applications have been installed on your PC.

Selected file type

Click on the selected file type of the document you wish to create. To create a document for the *Notepad* editor for example, choose the *Text Document* entry. For a *Paint* image select the *Bitmap Image*, and for text documents in *Word*, the entry *Microsoft Word Document*. In the same way you can create documents of all the various types that come with the *Office Suite*.

In the current folder, a new document icon will be displayed which is labelled *New [Type of file]...* (Figure 3.22, right). It will be selected for editing. Overwrite this by typing in the name of your choice. If the file extension is also highlighted, it is important to leave this suffix just as it is. Confirm with ↵, and open the empty document with a double click, along with the associated application.

File/Save

For new documents created using the *Microsoft Word Document* entry, this will start the *Microsoft Word* application. After making your changes choose *File/Save*. Entering a target location and file name and type is no longer neccessary when you use this method.

The *New Office Document* Command on the *Start* Menu

If you have the *Microsoft Office Suite* installed on your PC, then the *Start* menu offers another way of opening a new and empty *Office* document. This you can do by clicking on the *Start* button and choosing the *New Office Document* command above *Programs*.

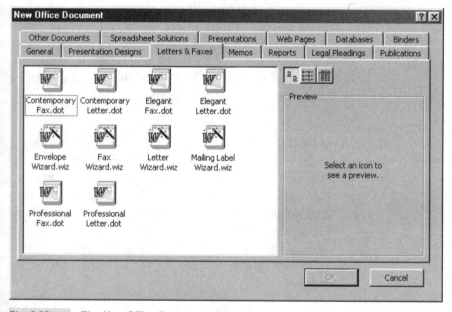

Fig. 3.23:   The *New Office Document* dialog box *t*

Microsoft Office options

The *New Office Document* dialog box displays all the types of *Microsoft Office* documents that can be created on several tab pages. Change to the tab page of the desired type and select the document template you want to use. When you've done that, confirm with *OK*.

Depending on the option selected the corresponding *Office* application will start with an empty document based on your choice. Go ahead and finish your document and save it using *File/Save*.

Creating New Office Documents Using the Microsoft Office Shortcut Bar

Templates

The *New Office Document* command is also available as a button 🔲 on the *Microsoft Office Shortcut Bar*. After clicking this button, the *New Office Document* dialog box will appear, in which all the templates of the *Microsoft Office* components are displayed on different tab pages. Change to the tab page with the template you are looking for and select it. Confirm with *OK* to open the corresponding *Microsoft Office* application along with a new document based on your choice.

Creating Shortcuts to Documents on the Desktop

Shortcuts give you quick and easy access to programs and documents which you use a lot. If you want to keep track of the hours you work in a document called *job hours*, you can create a shortcut to the *job hours* file on the desktop. You can then open the *job hours* document by simply double-clicking on the shortcut icon on the desktop.

Reference to the
file location

By using this method you avoid having to open the document with the source application each time. A shortcut will not change the file location of a document, since a shortcut only contains the reference to the actual file location and the file name. If you delete a shortcut, however, the original document will not be deleted.

Create a shortcut   You can create a shortcut for any object you want, such as programs, documents, folders, drives, or other computers and printers. Here is how to create a shortcut on the desktop. Click in a window of *My Computer* or *Explorer* on the object to which you want to create a shortcut, such as a program, a folder, printer, or computer. Choose the *Create Shortcut* command in the *File* menu or the context menu.

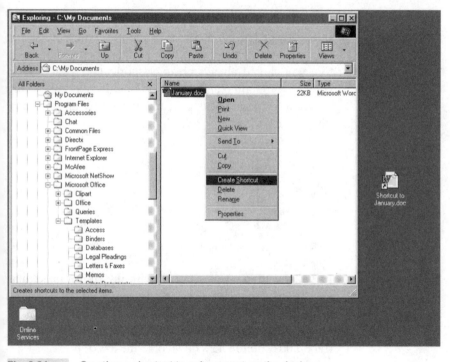

A copy of the object with the name *Shortcut to (filename)* is created. This shortcut icon can be dragged onto the desktop and positioned there. Once this is done, a double click on the shortcut is enough to open the document or object with a minimum loss of time.

 **Tip!** Only create shortcuts to really important documents or programs which you use very often, since otherwise the desktop will get cluttered up with too many shortcut icons.

Shortcut icons

Shortcut icons can always be recognized by this icon in the lower left-hand corner of the program icon. If you want to locate a program which is often used on the desktop, you should always create a shortcut. If you were to copy the program icon from its original location, the entire program file would be copied and would take up additional disk space.

Copy Here
Create Shortcut(s) Here
Cancel

Wordpad.exe

Fig. 3.25:   Creating a shortcut with the right mouse button

Right mouse button

It is faster to create a shortcut with the right mouse button. In order to create a shortcut to *WordPad* for example, open the folder *Program Files\Accessories* in *My Computer*. Then drag the icon of *WORDPAD.EXE* with the right mouse button held down onto the desktop.

Release the button and choose the *Create Shortcut(s) Here* command in the menu. You can cancel the operation by pressing Esc instead.

Tip! You can change all the shortcut properties (key combinations, icons, etc.) by clicking on the shortcut icon with the right mouse button and then choosing *Properties*. You can delete a shortcut by simply dragging it onto the *Recycle Bin*. The original object will remain in the location on the hard disk where it was saved.

Document Icons of Microsoft Office

The various *Windows* or *Office* applications will save your documents in a program-specific format, also called the file type.

File extension

This file type is entered into the *Windows 98* registry at the time the program is installed. *Windows*, with the help of the file extension, is able to recognize which application was used to create a document. The file type is indicated by an abbreviation consisting of three characters. A *Word* document normally has the file extension *DOC*, which is short for *DOCument*, while an *Excel* workbook has the extension *XLS*.

Windows also assigns a special document icon to registered file types. This icon allows you to immediately identify the source program of the document. In the table below, we have once again listed the most important document icons of the applications in the *Microsoft Office Suite*.

Office program	Document icon	File type
Microsoft Word		*.DOC*
Microsoft Excel		*.XLS*
Microsoft PowerPoint		*.PPT*
Microsoft Access		*.MDB*
Microsoft Binder		*.OBD*

Fig. 3.26: The document icons of the Microsoft Office Suite

Icons of Other Registered Applications

If you want to see a list of all the other registered file types on your computer, choose the *View/Folder Options* command in any folder window or, in *Explorer*, and select the *File Types* tab page.

The *Registered file types* list contains icons and descriptions of all registered applications. The description next to the icon is displayed in the *Detail* view in a folder window and in the *Type* column in *Explorer*.

File type details

Scroll down in the list box to get an overview of all the registered file types, both programs and documents. Click on a document icon to see details about it in the *File type details* box. The information displayed there will include the file extension which is associated with the icon and the program which will start after double-clicking on the icon in *Explorer*.

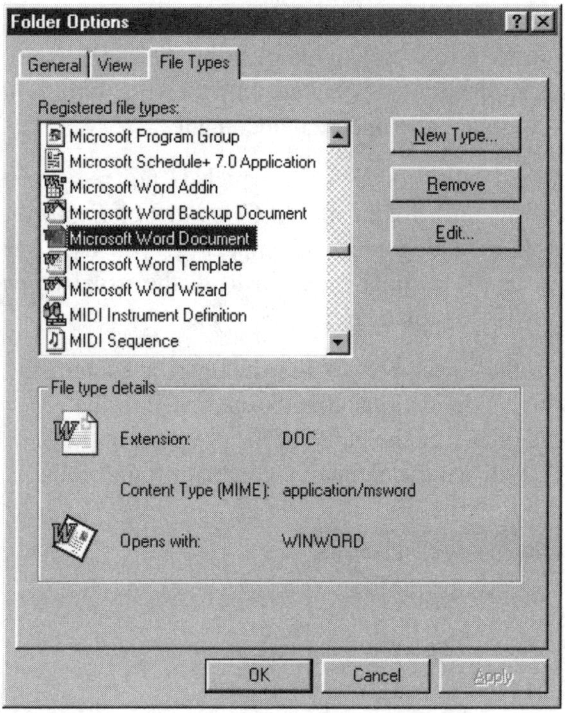

Fig. 3.27:   List of registered files using the *View/Folder Options* command

 **Tip!**   The icon of a selected file type can be changed using *Edit* and *Change Icon*. Click on *New* to register a program manually.

Opening a Document which has not been Registered

Every application will open only specific file types. Normally this file type will be the one which the program uses while saving, and which *Windows 98* recognizes by its file extension.

Open a document

To open a document in the *My Computer* folder or *Explorer*, all you have to do is double-click on the file name or icon. The application associated with the file type will start and automatically open the document.

Not registered

If you should try to open a file which is not registered with Windows in a folder of *My Computer* or *Explorer*, the *Open With* dialog box will appear. If you used the *File* menu or the context menu instead, the usual *Open* command will be replaced by *Open with*.

The list in the lower part of the dialog box contains all the Windows applications already entered into the registry. Instead of seeing the name of the program in the *Start* menu, you will see the name of the actual program file.

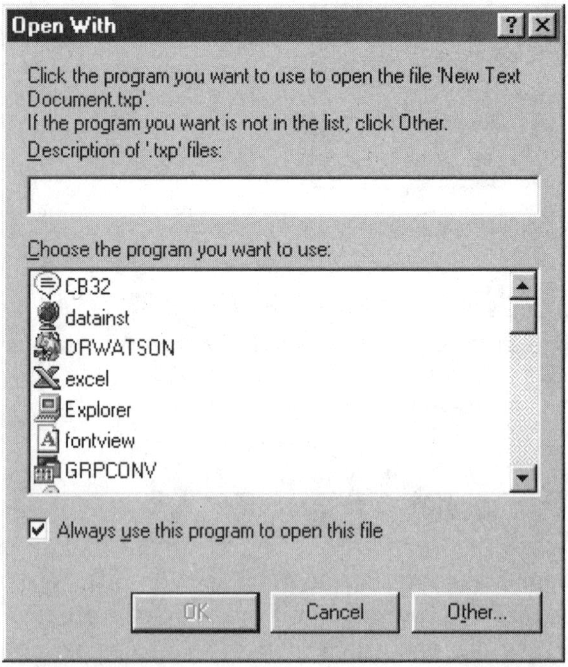

Fig. 3.28: List of registered programs in the *Open With* dialog box

Select the name of the required program in the list and click *OK* to open the file. You should be aware, however, that if the file type is not recognized by the selected program, you will just get an error message. The application and the file type should always be compatible, otherwise this method will not work.

Tip! If the selected program was able to open the file, check the *Always use this program to open this file* check box in the dialog. The *Other* button allows you select a different program which is not displayed in the list of registered programs.

Viewing Document Contents Without the Program

To view the contents of a document, you would normally open the file in the source program. A quicker method, as you already know, is to double-click on the document icon in *Explorer* or *My Computer*.

File viewer

Windows 98 offers yet another method. It comes along with a file viewer that can read the file types of the most important applications and display their contents quickly.

To make changes in the displayed file, the source program still needs to be opened. To get a preview of the document, change to the folder containing the document icon in *My Computer* or in *Explorer* and select the document you want to view. Then choose the *Quick View* command in the *File* menu or the context menu

Preview Document using the *Quick View* Program

There are two possible reasons why the *Quick View* command is not contained in the *File* menu. Either there is no file viewer available for this file type, or *Quick View* has not been installed on your system. At the end of this section, we will show you how to install *Quick View*.

If the *Quick View* command is listed, clicking on it will bring up a preview of the document in the program window of the file viewer. Try this with one of the bitmaps in the *Windows* folder, for example with the file *SETUP.BMP*.

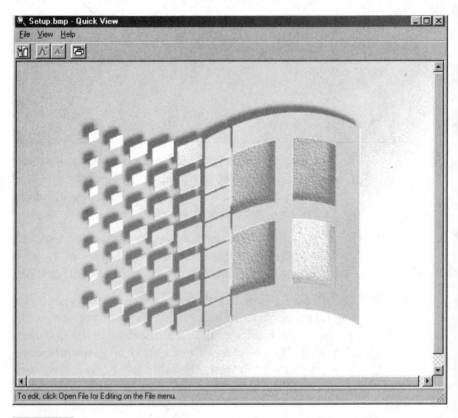

Fig. 3.29:   A bitmap image in Quick Viewt

You can change the way in which images are displayed in *Quick View* by selecting the *Landscape* command in the *View* menu. The document can be edited by selecting the *Open File for Editing* command in the *File* menu or by clicking on the *Open File for Editing* button.

Tip! You can display a different document in an open *Quick View* window by dragging the document icon into the *Quick View* window while holding down the mouse button.

Tip! *Windows 98* allows you to view the contents of compressed setup files (**.CAB*). To do this, select one of the *CAB* files in the *WIN98* folder on the Setup CD-ROM, and press the right mouse button. Select the *View* command in the context menu to view a folder with the contents of the archive. If you need a specific file select it and select the *Extract* command in the context menu. At this point, you have to select the target folder. You can now use the required file, for example, if the original has been damaged.

Installing the *Quick View* Windows Program

The *Quick View* program is a file viewer which allows you to view unknown file contents quickly and easily without having to start the source program. Unfortunately, *Quick View* is not automatically installed as part of the standard *Windows 98* installation. We will deal with this now, since the way to use *Quick View* has already been described above.

Quick View Command

Before following the steps described here, you should verify whether *Quick View* has already been loaded on your PC. To do this, open a folder containing a text file in

My Computer or Explorer, such as the C:\Windows folder. Select a text file and press the right mouse button. If the Quick View command is already available on the context menu, then you do not need to proceed with the steps outlined below.

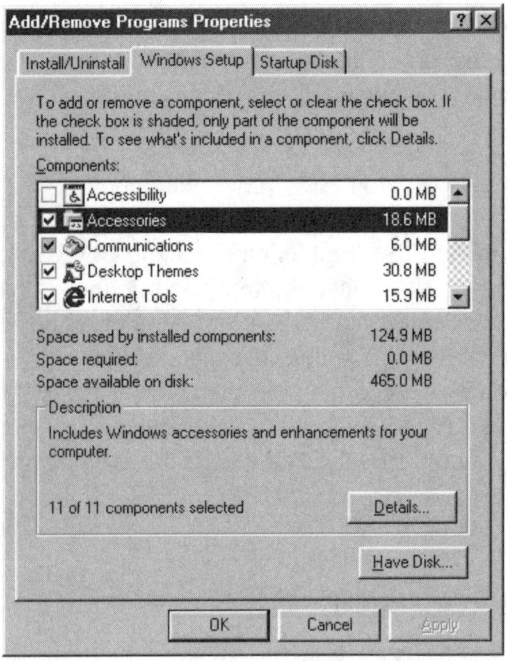

Add/Remove Programs Properties [?] [X]

| Install/Uninstall | Windows Setup | Startup Disk |

To add or remove a component, select or clear the check box. If the check box is shaded, only part of the component will be installed. To see what's included in a component, click Details.

Components:

	□ Accessibility	0.0 MB
	☑ Accessories	18.6 MB
	☑ Communications	6.0 MB
	☑ Desktop Themes	30.8 MB
	☑ Internet Tools	15.9 MB

Space used by installed components:	124.9 MB
Space required:	0.0 MB
Space available on disk:	465.0 MB

Description

Includes Windows accessories and enhancements for your computer.

11 of 11 components selected   [Details...]

[Have Disk...]

[OK]   [Cancel]   [Apply]

Fig. 3.30:   The Windows Setup

Control Panel

If the Quick View command is not available, continue as follows: Choose the Settings command in the Start menu and select Control Panel on the overlapping menu.

In the Control Panel folder, double-click on the Add/ Remove Programs icon. In the Add/Remove Programs Properties dialog box activate the Windows Setup tab page. Then wait until Windows 98 has searched for the installed components.

Accessories

Using the scroll bar in the *Components* list box, move through the list until the *Accessories* entry is visible, and select it. Then click on the *Details* button.

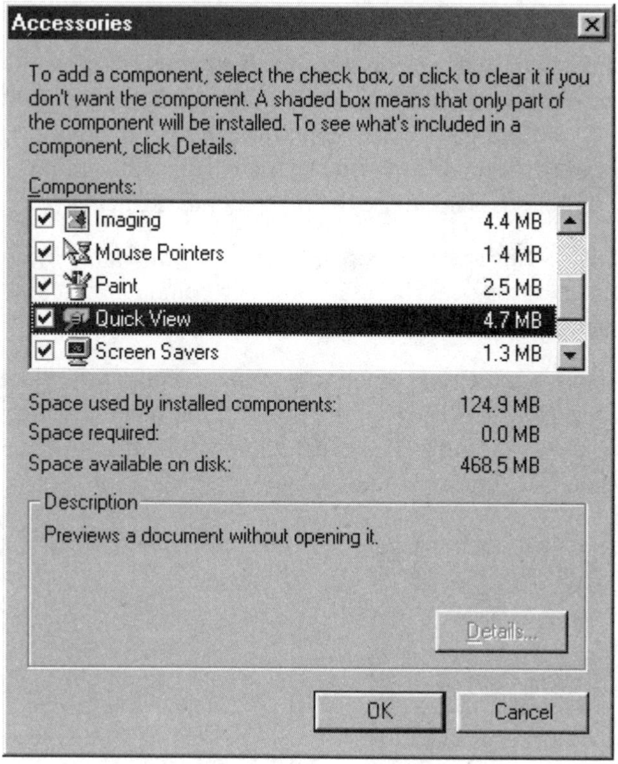

Accessories [×]

To add a component, select the check box, or click to clear it if you don't want the component. A shaded box means that only part of the component will be installed. To see what's included in a component, click Details.

Components:

☑ 📷 Imaging	4.4 MB	▲
☑ 🖱 Mouse Pointers	1.4 MB	
☑ 🎨 Paint	2.5 MB	
☑ 📄 Quick View	4.7 MB	
☑ 🖥 Screen Savers	1.3 MB	▼

Space used by installed components: 124.9 MB
Space required: 0.0 MB
Space available on disk: 468.5 MB

Description
Previews a document without opening it.

Details...

OK   Cancel

Fig. 3.31:   Installing Quick View

Windows 98 Setup

Use the scroll bar again to search the *Components* list. Select the check box in front of the *Quick View* item. Insert the *Windows 98* Setup CD-ROM in the CD drive and confirm twice with *OK*. The files will be copied. Close the *Control Panel*.

Using the Calculator for Calculations

Most people use their computers to write letters, create graphics, or play games.

Spreadsheets

If you use only these applications, then you will probably never need to do any calculations on the computer. But this is not the case when you work in applications that use spreadsheets or in those using a database, for in these you will often need to use the computer as a calculator.

Calculator

In this section we will explain how the *Calculator* Windows accessory can be used on your computer just like any normal calculator.

Program/
Accessories/
Calculator

To start *Calculator*, open the *Start* menu and select *Programs/Accessories*. In the overlapping menu click on the *Calculator* entry. The *Calculator* will be displayed in the standard display mode.

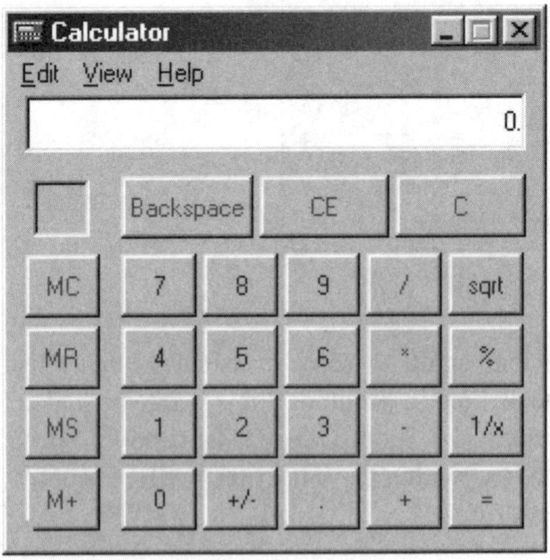

Fig. 3.32:   The standard Windows Calculator

View/Scientific

To change to the *Scientific Calculator* shown in Figure 3.33, select *View/Scientific*. Now, in addition to the basic arithmetic functions, you also have all the trigonometric functions at your disposal.

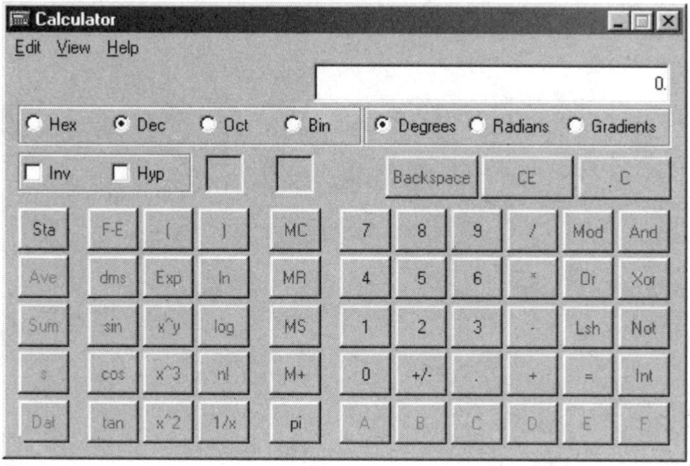

Fig. 3.33: The Scientific Calculator

Buttons

The calculator can be used with the mouse. Just click on the buttons for numbers or functions. You can also use the calculator with the keyboard, which is a faster way than using the mouse.

It is best to use the number pad on your keyboard, which first has to be activated with the [Num] key. Enter numbers and for the basic arithmetic functions, use the following keys: [*], [+], [-] and [/].

Tip!

The resulting totals can be copied to the clipboard using the *Edit/Copy* commands or the keyboard shortcut [Ctrl]+[C], and can be inserted into any Windows application at the inserting point using *Edit/Insert* or [Ctrl]+[V].

4. Desktop, Taskbar and *Start* Menu

In this chapter, we will discuss your electronic desk, the *Windows 98* desktop and its control elements. You will learn how to adapt the taskbar to suit your individual needs and how to switch between two open applications. In addition, you will learn all about how to configure the control center of *Windows 98* – the *Start* menu. You will be able to change the display and include new programs or program groups on the menu, and to delete shortcuts which you no longer need.

Changing the Display of the Taskbar

Apart from the *Start* menu, which can be called up with the *Start* button, the taskbar contains the control center of *Windows 98*. Viewed in this way, the taskbar can be seen as the most important element on the desktop.

Moving the Taskbar

Given this fact, it would be strange if you had to live and work with just the standard position at the bottom of the screen.

The position and the width

The position and even the width of the taskbar can be changed to accommodate your needs. If you would like to position the taskbar at the other side of the screen, click in a free area of the taskbar. Then move the taskbar to its new position while holding down the mouse button. If you approach the edge of the screen, a frame will be displayed indicating the new position.

To keep this position, release the mouse button. The *Start* menu and its submenus will also be moved along with the taskbar to the new location.

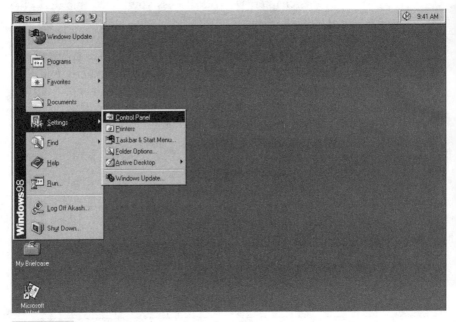

Fig. 4.1: The taskbar at the upper edge of the screen

Changing the Width of the Taskbar

When there are many open folders or running applications, the abbreviations on the buttons of the taskbar might be disturbing. If that's the case, you can display the taskbar in a larger size. To do this, point to the edge of the taskbar. The mouse pointer will change to a double-headed arrow. While holding down the mouse button, you can now set the width. The frame displayed indicates the future size. If you release the mouse button, the buttons will be spread out over several levels, and their labels will again be fully displayed.

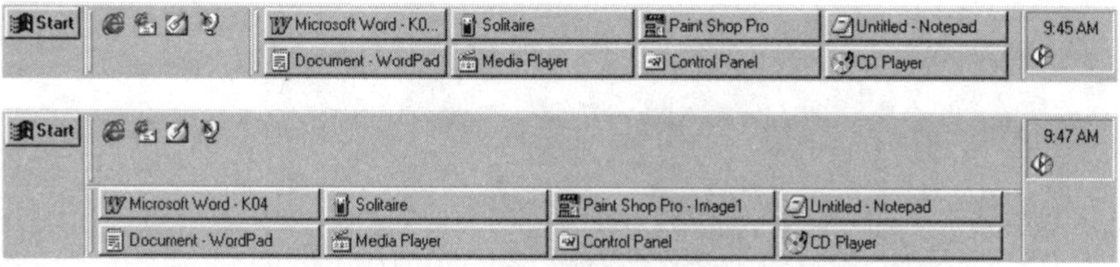

Fig. 4.2: Changing the width of the taskbar and the order of the buttons

Changing the width

The width as well as the position of the toolbars displayed on the taskbar can be changed. To change the width of the toolbar with the opened folders or applications, click the move handle of this toolbar which appears as a 3-D bar at the left edge and drag it to the right or to the left while holding down the mouse button (Figure 4.2, above).

Customize the arrangement

If you want to customize the arrangement of this toolbar and the channel bar, click the move handle of the toolbar and move the toolbar while holding down the mouse button (Figure 4.2, below).

Display or Hide the Taskbar

Since it is the most important control element of *Windows 98*, the taskbar can be customized to meet your personal needs. The default settings will always display the taskbar.

To configure the display of the taskbar, open the *Start* menu and point to the *Settings* entry. In the overlapping menu choose the *Taskbar & Start Menu* command. In the *Taskbar Properties* dialog box, the upper portion of the *Taskbar Options* tab page will display a preview of any changes you make.

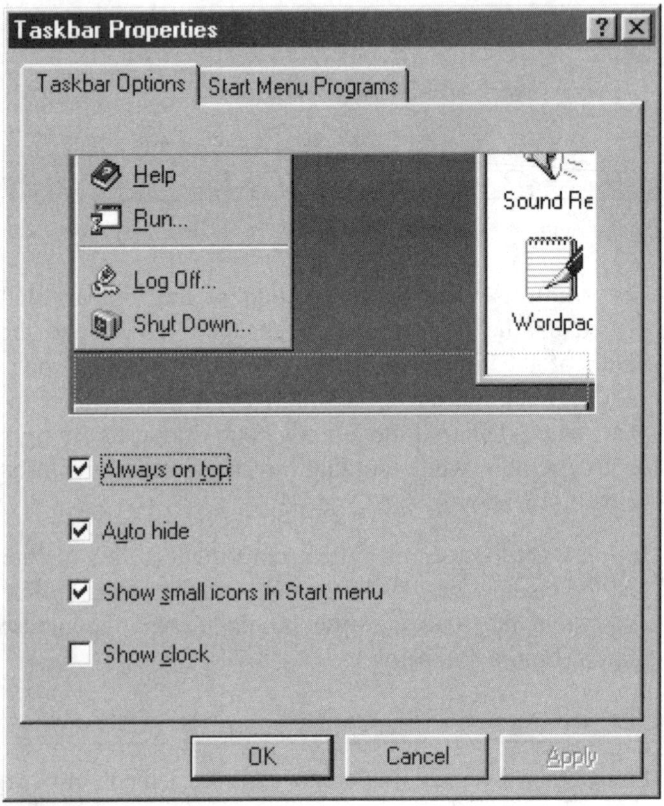

Fig. 4.3:   Configuring the taskbar

Always on top

Clear the *Always on top* check box if you want the task-bar to be in the background for maximized windows. In this way, the program window has more space for display; however, the size of the program window has to be reduced first if you want to switch between applications.

Auto hide

If you only want the taskbar displayed when you point to the lower edge of the screen, select the *Auto hide* check box. If you move the mouse pointer up, the taskbar will slide down and disappear.

Always on top

If you check both the *Always on top* and *Auto hide* check boxes, the taskbar will be hidden and displayed only with the movement of the mouse, even for maximized windows. Confirm with *OK* to make the changes to the taskbar.

Displaying the Time on the Taskbar

Normally *Windows 98* will display the system time in hours and minutes 12:45 on the right side of the taskbar. If this is not the case, it is possible that this option has been de-activated. In this section, we will explain how to display the time as well as how to receive additional information about it.

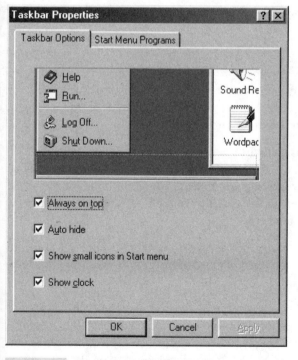

Fig. 4.4:   Displaying and hiding the time in the taskbar

Start/Settings

To configure the display of the taskbar, open the *Start* menu and point to the *Settings* entry. In the overlapping menu, choose the *Taskbar & Start Menu* command. The *Taskbar Properties* dialog box will be displayed.

Show clock

Check the *Show clock* option and confirm by clicking *OK*. Now the time 12:45 will be displayed (again).

Tip!
Place the mouse cursor over the time displayed on the taskbar. *Windows 98* will then display a *ScreenTip* with the current date.

Tip!
By double-clicking on the time displayed on the taskbar, the *Properties* window for the date and time, in which these settings can be changed, will be displayed.

Displaying the Resource Meter on the Taskbar

As a Windows user you might find it useful to have an easy-to-use application to keep track of the available system resources and display them.

System resources

This is exactly what we will deal with next. You will learn how to include the *Resource Meter* in the taskbar. This works as a kind of traffic light to monitor the actual demand on the system resources in a simple and easy to understand way

Accessories/
System Tools

Select *Programs/Accessories/System Tools* in the *Start* menu and then choose *Resource Meter* from the new menu.

Confirmation
message

When you begin the program it insists on showing you a confirmation message informing you that the *Resource Meter* program uses resources, too. Select the *Don't display this message again* check box if you do not want to see this message the next time you call up the *Resource Meter* program.

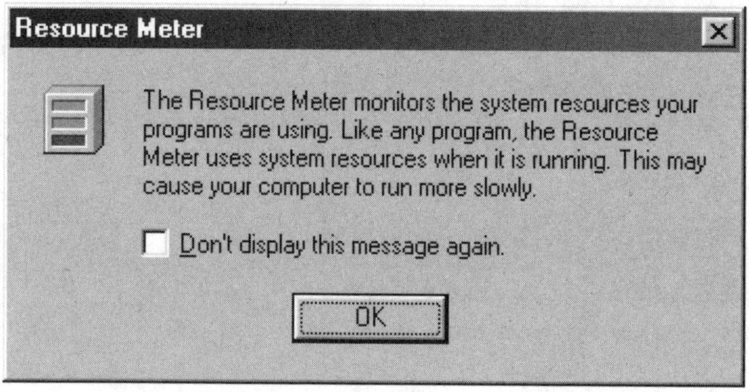

Fig. 4.5:   The *Resource Meter* confirmation message

Green bar

Click *OK* to include the *Resource Meter* ☰ in the taskbar tray next to the time display. As long as you see the green bar in the display, all is well. If you see an orange bar, this indicates that the system resources are almost completely used, and you should then close windows that you do not need. If the *Resource Meter* displays a red bar, save all your documents immediately, and after that, restart Windows again.

Tip!   The *Resource Meter* has to be called up again each time the system starts. You can copy the program icon of the *Resource Meter* into the *StartUp* program group to always display the meter in the taskbar tray.

To display the exact percentage of the *System, User,* and *GDI resources* available, double-click on the *Resource Meter* icon ☰ in the taskbar tray to display the dialog box shown below. This can be closed again by clicking on *OK.*

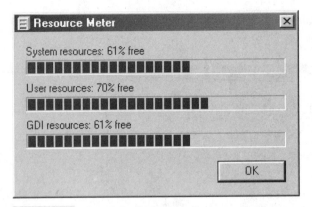

The dialog box of the Resource Meter

Tip!

In *Chapter 9*, we describe how the demand on the system can be monitored with the *System Monitor* system application. While this application is more powerful, it often requires the help of a professional to evaluate the results.

Switching Between Running Applications

The term *Windows* should be taken quite literally under *Windows 98*. Different windows can display any amount of information, as well as execute running programs. Thanks to multitasking this can all go on simultaneously. You can print a letter in a word processor, for example, while you are making a drawing.

Active window

Data can only be entried into the active window. There can only be one active window at a time. In case of several running applications you have therefore to be able to switch back and forth between the programs, for example, to exchange data. The simplest way to do this is to use the taskbar.

Switching Between Running Applications Using the Taskbar

Button of the
application

Every running program is represented by a button with its name and the description of the open document in the taskbar. The button of the active application will always be displayed as pushed down while the other buttons will be displayed in the normal manner.

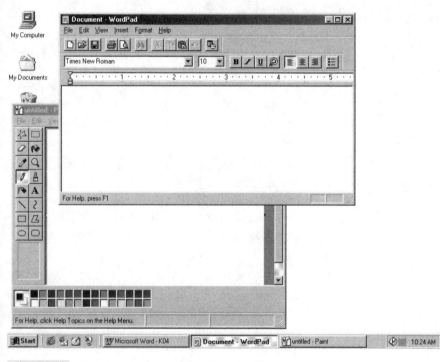

Fig. 4.7:   Switching between different applications

Taskbar button

To change between programs, click on the corresponding button on the taskbar. The program window will either be opened or appear in the foreground. You can now work in the window. If you want to change to another running application, click on the corresponding button in the taskbar.

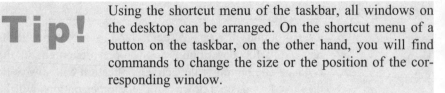

Tip! Using the shortcut menu of the taskbar, all windows on the desktop can be arranged. On the shortcut menu of a button on the taskbar, on the other hand, you will find commands to change the size or the position of the corresponding window.

Switching Between Running Applications Using the Keyboard

The big advantage of *Windows 98* is that several applications can be used at the same time. You can for example print a letter on your *WordPad* word processor while making a drawing in *Paint* or setting up tables in *Microsoft Excel*. *Windows 98* works with the so-called pre-emptive multitasking, which can actually run programs simultaneously.

More than one program
More than one program is in use when exchanging data between applications. In this case, you have to switch between applications in order to copy information from one program and insert it into the other program. For this switching, a keyboard combination can be used.

Press the ⌈Alt⌋ key and, while holding it down, press the *Tab* key ⌈↹⌋. A dialog box called the 'little task manager' will appear on your screen, containing the icons of all the running applications and open folders. The lower part displays the name of the selected application; the corresponding program icon above is marked with a blue box.

Next program
If you press the *Tab* key ⌈↹⌋ again, the task manager will switch to the next program or folder icon. Below it, you will again see the description. Keep pressing the *Tab* key ⌈↹⌋ until the task switcher displays the required application. At this point, release the ⌈Alt⌋ key and *Windows* will change to the selected application.

Tip!

If you are exchanging data between two programs, it is sufficient to press the [Alt]+[↹] keys to switch from one application to the other.

Changing the Display of the *Start* Menu

The *Start* menu is, as already mentioned, the control center of *Windows 98*. We will now show you how to add new items to the *Start* menu, how to delete existing entries, and how to include new program groups. To start with, you will learn how to customize the *Start* menu according to your needs.

Changing the Icon Size for the *Start* Menu

If you expect to find in the *Start* menu the same seemingly inexhaustible adaptability that *Windows 98* displays just about everywhere else on this menu, we unfortunately have to slightly dampen your hopes.

First level

You can only change the size of the icons in the first level of the *Start* menu. To do this, click on the *Start* menu button and point to the *Settings* entry. In the overlapping menu select the *Taskbar & Start Menu* command and change to the *Taskbar Options* tab page in the *Taskbar Properties* dialog box. Select the *Show small icons in Start menu* check box and confirm with *OK*. Verify the changes on the *Start* menu.

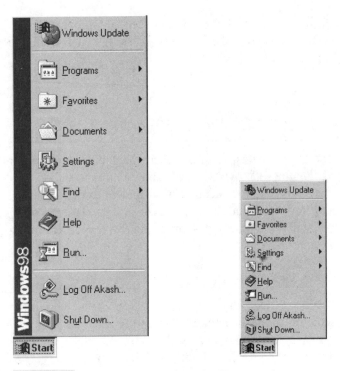

Fig. 4.8: Big and small icons on the *Start* menu*

Tip!

The 'small icons' are useful when you have a smaller monitor where *Windows* is displayed in the VGA resolution. Indirectly, the *Start* menu can be customized with the position of the taskbar and the display of *Windows* through the *Display* option in the *Control Panel*.

Customizing the *Start* Menu

The *Start* menu is the control center of *Windows 98*. Using it, you can call up all functions of the graphical operating system. After installing new programs, the shortcuts to the program files will automatically be included in the *Start* menu.

Adding New Entries on the *Start* Menu

This step can also be executed manually, for example in case of a problem or if you want to customize the *Start* menu according to your needs.

Start menu
programs

In this section, we will show you how to add entries to the *Start* menu using the properties window, which is one of the many ways this can be done. Click the *Start* button and point to *Settings*. After that click on *Taskbar & Start Menu* and change to the *Start Menu Programs* tab page.

Add

Now click on the *Add* button and, in the *Create Shortcut* dialog box, on the *Browse* button. At this point, you need to know the file location of the required program or the shortcut. We will use the *Windows 98* word processor *WordPad* as an example.

Program file

The program file of *WordPad* is called *WORDPAD.EXE* and it's located in the folder *C:\Program Files\Accessories*. Select the program file and click on the *Open* button. In the *Create Shortcut* dialog box, click *Next* and select the program group you would like to, put the shortcut in.

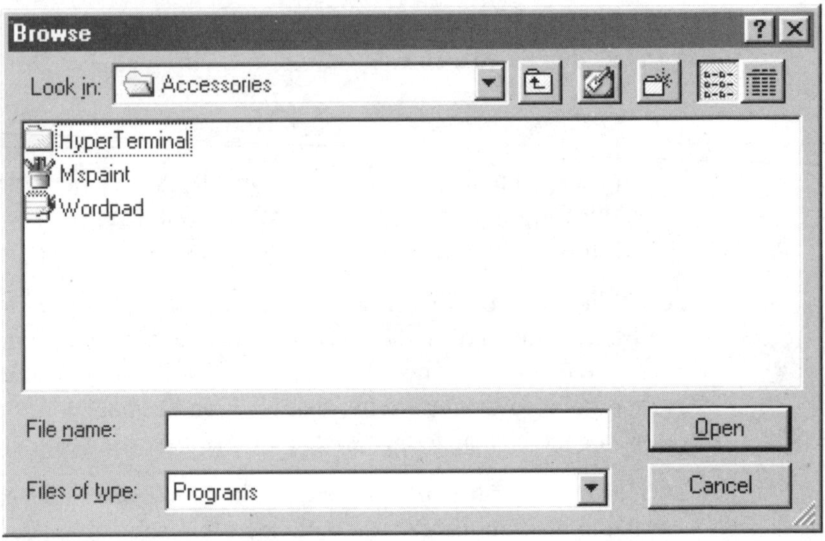

Fig. 4.9: Finding the file path of the programs file

Contents of the program group

Click *Next* and, in the text box, enter the name which should be shown in the program group, such as *Word Processing*. Now click the *Finish* button, close the properties window with *OK* and open the *Start* menu to access the new shortcut in the contents of the programs group.

With programs of the *Microsoft Office Suite*, you can straightaway use existing shortcuts which you will find in the folder *Program Files/Microsoft Office*, or in the *Programs* subfolder of the *Start* menu folder.

Customize the *Start* Menu Using Drag-and-Drop

Using the *Start* menu of *Windows 98*, all Windows components as well as additionally installed programs can be accessed. For programs which are often used, the *Programs* menu and its submenus can sometimes be time-consuming.

However, as you know, *Windows 98* is very flexible. The *Start* menu can, of course, be customized to suit your needs. You can go about adapting it in several ways.

The first level

To begin with, you will learn how to directly copy shortcuts of applications into the *Start* menu. The restrictions of the previous *Windows 95* version, when only the first level of the *Start* menu could be customized, no longer apply to *Windows 98*. Proceed as follows: First, highlight the shortcut or the program file of the application to be added to the *Start* menu. To do this, go to *My Computer* or *Windows Explorer*.

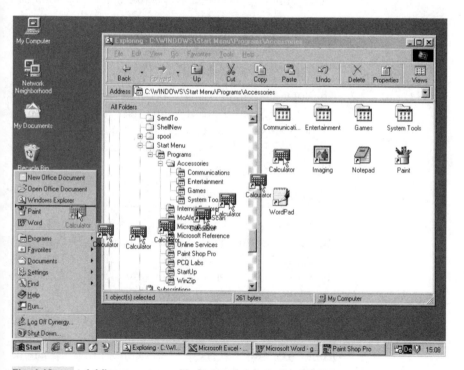

Fig. 4.10:   Adding programs with drag-and-drop to the *Start* menu

Pressing the
[Ctrl] key

Now drag the shortcut or the program icon of the selected application, while holding down the [Ctrl] key and the mouse button, onto the *Start* button on the taskbar. The menu will be opened. Point to the position where you want to insert it, which *Windows 98* will then display as a black bar.

Copy onto the
Start menu

If you release the mouse button, *Windows 98* will copy the program or shortcut icon onto the *Start* menu (Figure 4.10).

Copy into a
program group

If you want to copy the program into a specific program group, simply point to the respective entry. The submenu will be opened and here, too, a black bar will indicate the insertion position. If you release the mouse button now, *Windows 98* will copy the program or shortcut icon into the selected program group.

The copied program can now be started by clicking on its icon on the *Start* menu. If you do not use the [Ctrl] key, the program or shortcut icon will be moved, meaning that it will be deleted from the original program group and inserted on the *Start* menu.

Customizing the *Start* Menu Using Explorer

These days, a lot of companies offer information on CD-ROMs. Every computer discount shop offers programs or games on CD. Probably many of these CD-ROM applications will eventually find their way to your computer to be installed there.

Overloaded

Because of this, the *Programs* menu on the *Start* menu gets overloaded with program groups and application icons. After even a short while it may happen that the contents of the *Programs* menu do not fit on the screen anymore.

Sorting by topic

If you really need all these programs, you should now think about sorting and compiling your applications by topic in their own program groups on the *Start* menu.

The previous descriptions given for customizing the *Start* menu are not ideal for such a mammoth project, as already mentioned above. You will now learn how to comfortably organize the *Start* menu according to your needs using *Explorer*.

Shortcuts

Since the program groups in the *Start* menu only display shortcuts to programs and other program groups you are not working with the original files or folders. A shortcut only contains information about the file location and the name of the program file. Since shortcuts and the *Start* menu have equal rights under *Windows 98*, they can both be displayed in the *Explorer*.

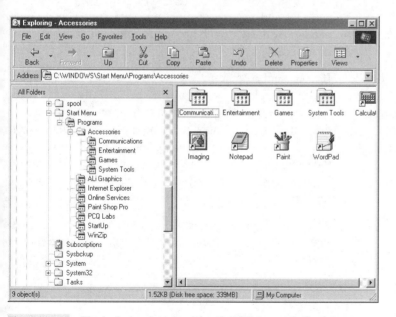

Fig. 4.11: Displaying and customizing the *Start* menu in Explorer

Folder structure of Explorer

To show the hierarchy of the *Start* menu in *Explorer*, expand the display by clicking on the plus sign ⊞ in front of the *My Computer* entry in the left window pane. Repeat this step for the drive icon of the hard disk (*C:*). After that, display the contents of the *Windows* folder and expand the display of the *Start Menu* program group. Click again on the plus sign ⊞ in front of the *Programs* entry. Now all program groups of the *Start* menu are displayed in the folder structure of *Explorer.*

Deleting program groups

When you select a program group in the left window pane, you will see its contents displayed in the right pane. New program groups can be created with the *File/New/Folder* command. Existing program groups can be renamed with the *File/Rename* command. Selected or empty program groups, or groups that are no longer needed, can be deleted with the ⌞Del⌟ key. This only deletes the shortcut and not the original program file. Those would need to be deleted in the program folder of the corresponding application.

Restructure the *Start* menu

If you want to restructure the *Start* menu, just copy and move the selected program groups. Ideally, you would first create new program groups that are compiled according to topic. Highlight the program groups that have to be moved. If you want to move several program groups at the same time, you have to make your selection in the right window pane. To select more than one program group, use the ⌞Ctrl⌟ and ⌞⇧⌟ keys.

Moving program groups

To move program groups using a key combination, press the ⌞Ctrl⌟+⌞X⌟ key combination after selecting the program group.

Now select the program group into which the other one is to be moved, and press the Ctrl+V key combination. If a program group contains shortcuts to start programs, these will be copied as well.

Copying program groups

You can copy a program group using the keyboard combination Ctrl+C. To move or copy program groups using the *Edit* menu, choose the *Cut* or *Copy* command on the *Edit* menu. Select the program group in which you want to insert the copy of the program group, and then select the *Paste* command on the *Edit* menu. In the same manner single shortcuts can be copied or moved from one program group to another.

Copy shortcuts

You can also copy shortcuts or program groups with commands on the shortcut menu. Point to the object and press the right mouse button. Choose the *Cut* or *Copy* command from the shortcut menu, and then select the program group into which the shortcut should be moved. Point to a free space and click the right mouse button. Choose the *Paste* command from the shortcut menu.

Drag-and-Drop method

If the shortcuts or program groups you want to move are in the right window pane and the target program groups are displayed in the left pane, or vice versa, you can also move the objects using the drag-and-drop method.

To do this, point to the shortcut or the program group and drag it onto the target program group. Then release the mouse button. If you want to copy it, hold down the Ctrl key at the same time.

Right mouse button

You can also copy shortcuts or program groups with the right mouse button and the drag-and-drop method. Click the shortcut or the program group and drag it with the right mouse button onto the target drive or the target program group. Release the mouse button, and choose the *Move Here* command from the context menu. To copy the item, hold down the $\boxed{\text{Ctrl}}$ key at the same time, and select the *Copy Here* command on the shortcut menu instead.

Deleting Entries from the *Start* Menu

With the plethora of information, programs or games offered on CD-ROM today, it's only a question of time until the *Start* menu becomes congested with all the new shortcuts or program groups.

Delete entries

If at this point you decide to separate the wheat from the chaff and delete programs or games which you no longer need, the shortcuts and program groups created by the application will not be deleted in most cases. The question then arises how to delete redundant entries from the *Start* menu.

Start/Settings

Select the *Settings* command on the *Start* menu and click on the *Taskbar & Start Menu* command in the overlapping menu. In the *Taskbar Properties* window, activate the *Start Menu Programs* tab page and click on the *Remove* button.

Remove Shortcuts/Folders

In the *Remove Shortcuts/Folders* dialog box, the *Start* menu is displayed in a structural view similar to that of the left pane in *Explorer*. Expand the structure by clicking on the plus signs ⊞ in front of the folders to select the entry to be deleted.

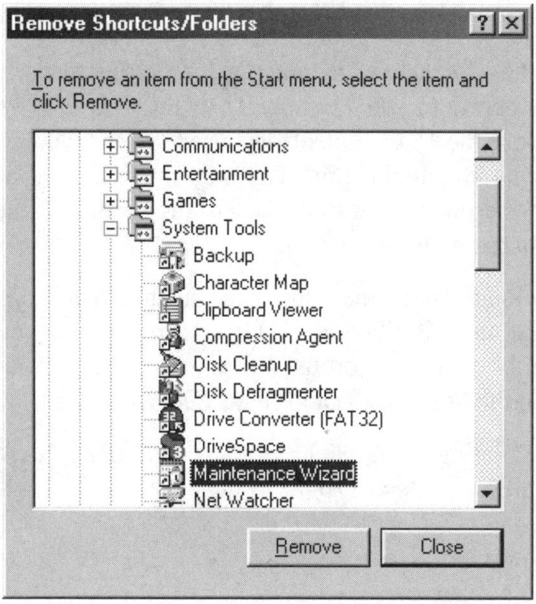

Remove Shortcuts/Folders   [?] [X]

To remove an item from the Start menu, select the item and click Remove.

- [+] Communications
- [+] Entertainment
- [+] Games
- [-] System Tools
    - Backup
    - Character Map
    - Clipboard Viewer
    - Compression Agent
    - Disk Cleanup
    - Disk Defragmenter
    - Drive Converter (FAT32)
    - DriveSpace
    - Maintenance Wizard
    - Net Watcher

[Remove]   [Close]

Fig. 4.12:   Remove obsolete shortcuts or folders

Remove

Select the program group to be deleted and click on the *Remove* button. The dialog box will remain open, and you can repeat the procedure for every program group or shortcut which is no longer needed.

Close the dialog by clicking on *Close* and confirm the changes by clicking on *OK*. In this way, only program groups or shortcuts are deleted. The connected folders and programs will have to be deleted separately.

Tip!

Obsolete entries in the *Start* menu can be deleted by an even faster and easier method: Open the *Start* menu and highlight the entry to be deleted. Now press the **right** mouse button and select the *Delete* command. Confirm the message with *Yes*.

Deleting the Contents of the *Documents* Menu

Through the *Documents* menu, you can open recently used documents. In the *Documents* menu, *Windows 98* keeps track of the 15 documents last used, independent of the corresponding application. The only qualification for this is that the file extension of the installed program has to be registered with *Windows 98*.

Start/Settings

If you no longer need the files listed in the *Documents* menu or the menu is filled up with too many entries, you can delete all the entries on the *Documents* menu. To do so, click on the *Start* button and select *Settings*.

Taskbar & Start
menu

In the overlapping menu click on *Taskbar & Start Menu* and go to the *Start Menu Programs* tab page.

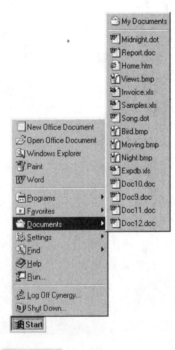

Fig. 4.13:   The display of the 15 most recently used documents

162

To irretrievably delete all entries, click on the *Clear* button in the *Documents menu* group box. After deleting them, this button will be disabled. Close the *Taskbar Properties* dialog box with *OK*. This function will, of course, delete only the menu entries, and not the actual documents on the hard disk.

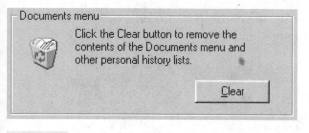

Fig. 4.14: Deleting all entries in the *Documents* menu

Changing the Appearance of the *Start* Menu

The *Start* menu can call up all Windows functions, start programs and open documents. Beginners will quickly learn how to use the *Start* menu because of its logical structure and the organized display of the Windows functions. When many programs are installed or a highly complex menu structure is used on the *Programs* menu, the *Start* menu sometimes turns into something of a treasure hunt.

Calling up
programs.

This will become obvious to you if you are repeatedly calling up programs. Should you want to check your hard disk for faults with *ScanDisk*, and after that optimize the fragmented files with *Disk Defragmenter*, you have to go twice to *Programs/Accessories/System Tools* from the *Start* menu.

Displaying the *Start* Menu as a Program Group Window

However, you can also display the *Start* menu in the form of a folder. To do this, point to the *Start* button and click the right mouse button. Select the *Open* command from the shortcut menu.

Program group window

The folder or the *Start Menu* program group window will appear. In the *Start Menu* folder, you will find, among other things, the *Programs* icon.

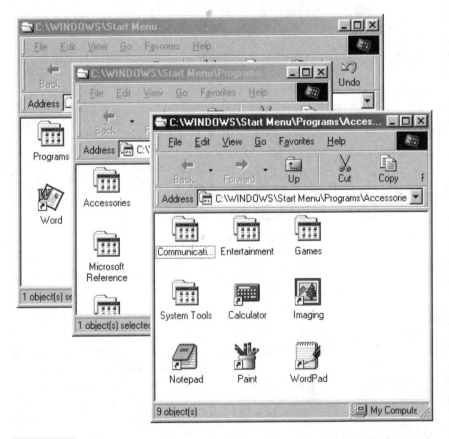

If you double-click on the *Programs* icon, or select it and choose the *Open* command from the shortcut menu or the *File* menu, another window will be displayed, the program group *Programs*. Here you will get all the menu entries of the *Programs* menu in the form of icons.

Tip! In order to avoid the contents of newly opened folders in *My Computer* being always displayed in the same window, select the *Folder Options* command on the *View* menu. On the *General* tab page select the option *Custom, based on settings you choose* and click on the *Settings* button. Select the *Open each folder in its own window* radio button in the *Browse folders as follows* option group box and confirm with *OK* and then *Close*. From now on every folder will be opened in its own window.

Program group icons

Program group icons ▦ indicate commands in the *Start* menu which open an overlapping menu. Inside the window you can open another window by double-clicking on a program icon ▦. Shortcuts inside a program group will start the application if you double-click on them.

Tip! The structure of the program group windows corresponds exactly to the structure of the *Start* menu. It is, however, limited to the *Programs* menu and its submenus. Users who have worked with the *Windows* version *3.x* will immediately feel at home with this display, since the *Windows 3.x Program Manager* displayed the program groups in the same manner.

The display of program groups is helpful especially if you often use different programs in submenus of the *Start* menu. In that case, open the often used program group and close the ones which are not in use.

Shortcut icons

The required shortcut icons are now displayed on the desktop, ready to be called up via a mouse click. Another advantage is that, when you shut down *Windows* with open program group windows, these will automatically be restored the next time *Windows* starts.

Tip!

If you want to avoid double-clicking to open a folder or program group, and prefer to open these with a single mouse click instead, select the *Folder Options* command on the *View* menu. On the *General* tab page select the *Custom, based on settings you choose* option and click on the *Settings* button.

Select the option *Single-click to open an item (point to select)* in the *Click items as follows* option group, and confirm by clicking *OK* and then *Close*. From now on any program group can be opened with a single mouse click. To select an item, you simply point at the item or folder. The user interface resembles that of a Web browser used on the WWW.

Microsoft Office Suite

Try out this procedure by placing all the program icons of the *Microsoft Office Suite* in a program group called *Microsoft Office 97* inside the *Programs* program group. This will provide you on the one hand with a 'slimmer' *Program* menu and on the other hand, you will have all the *Office* applications in a program group window on the desktop, ready to be called up at the click of an icon. If you are working with the *Microsoft Office Shortcut Bar*, there is no need to follow these steps.

5. My Computer and Explorer

In this chapter, you will become familiar with two *Windows 98* applications which are useful for the organization and administration of your data. You will browse folders on your hard disk with the *My Computer* system folder and the *Windows Explorer*, change the display style and order of the files, as well as learn how to copy, move and delete files. Of course we will also deal with creating and naming new folders, and the preparation of diskettes to receive data.

Working with My Computer

The *My Computer* folder is used for the organisation and administration of drives. Since it is strongly object-oriented, beginners especially like working with this folder. To open *My Computer*, double-click on the *My Computer* icon on the desktop.

Displaying the Contents of Drives in My Computer

System setup
The number of drives in this folder depends on your system configuration. Every drive is displayed with its own icon. Additionally, *My Computer* allows you quick access to the *Control Panel*, *Scheduled Tasks* and *Printer* folders. If you have installed the *Dial-Up Networking*, this folder will also be available in *My Computer*.

Browse
To browse a drive, select the desired drive icon and choose the *Open* command from the *Shortcut* menu or the *File* menu. Another faster way to browse a drive is to simply double-click its icon.

If you double-click *(C:)*, for example, *Windows 98* will automatically display, in a new window, all folders in the first level of this drive. The name of the drive will be displayed in the title bar of the respective window.

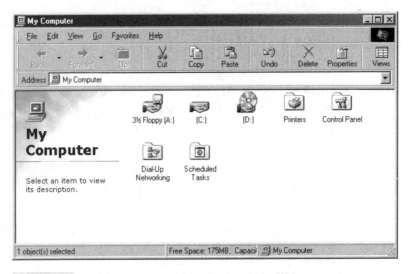

Fig. 5.1: The *My Computer* folder displayed as a Web page

Drive letter

Every kind of drive, (floppy disk, hard disk, CD-ROM, and network drive) has its own icon. Additionally, a description is displayed, which in the case of the hard disk, can even be changed. The drive letter used by MS-DOS is shown in brackets. The first floppy drive is called *(A:)*, and the first hard disk is called *(C:)*.

Tip!

If you have difficulty using the double-click to browse through folders in the beginning, just select the folder and press ⏎. You can also select the *Open* command from the shortcut menu or the *File* menu to open a folder. Yet another way to open a folder is the method described in the next tip.

Tip!

If you want to avoid using a double click to open folders in *My Computer* and want to use a single mouse click instead, select the *Folder Options* command on the *View* menu. On the *General* tab page select the *Custom, based on settings you choose* radio button and click on the *Settings* button.

Select the *Single-click to open an item (point to select)* option in the *Click items as follows* option group. Confirm by clicking *OK* and then *Close*. From now on, any program group can be opened with a single mouse click. To select an item, you simply point at the selected item or folder. Selected objects are displayed in a different color. The user interface resembles that of a Web browser like one used for the WWW on the Internet.

Browsing Folders with My Computer

When using *Windows 98* for the first time, most users prefer using *My Computer* to view the contents of drives and folders. It is not surprising, that due to the object oriented character of Windows, working with this folder is easy.

Open my computer

To open *My Computer*, double-click on the *My Computer* icon on the desktop. The number of drives in this folder depends on your system configuration. Every drive is displayed with its own icon.

Additionally, *My Computer* allows you quick access to the *Control Panel, Scheduled Tasks* and *Printer* folders. If you have installed the *Dial-Up Networking*, this folder will also be available in *My Computer*.

Browse a folder

To browse a folder, first open the required drive where the folder is located. To do this, double-click the desired drive icon, for example, *(C). Windows 98* will automatically display the contents of the first level in a new window. The name of the drive or folder will be displayed in the title bar of the respective window.

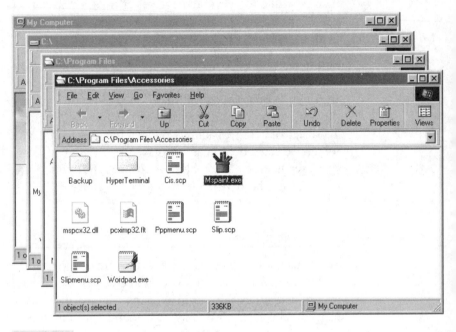

Fig. 5.2:   Browsing a folder with My Computer

Open a folder

To open a folder in the window, simply double-click on the folder name. If the folder contains a large number of files, use the scroll bar or change the display style of the objects in the folder, using the *View* menu (more on that below). If there are too many open windows on the desktop, change the display mode of the folder windows using *View/Folder Options* (see next section).

Changing the Display of My Computer

The strongly object oriented character of *Windows 98* is difficult for some people to use, especially for those who have switched over from the character and command-oriented operating system *MS-DOS* (*Microsoft Disk Operating System*) to the *Windows 98* graphic operating system.

Own window

This becomes obvious while working with *My Computer*. All folders viewed in *My Computer* are displayed in their own window. It is therefore only a matter of time until, as the saying goes, you cannot see the desktop for all the open windows.

Standard settings

This disadvantage of *My Computer* is very evident in the case of complicated folder structures. For such examples as this the *Windows Explorer* is often a better choice for the administration and organisation of your data. On the other hand, you do not have to work with the default settings of *My Computer*.

The display of the folders can be changed in such a way that all opened folders are shown in the same window. First of all, this gives you an overview of the desktop and secondly, it reflects the relation between the current and the parent folder in complicated folder structures more clearly.

Tip!

If you display the toolbar, using the *View/Toolbars/Standard Buttons* command, you can move up one level with the *Up* button 🖳 (in *Windows 95* the *Up One Level* 🖻 button) or, using the *Address Bar* | Address | 🖳 My Computer ▾ |, move directly to other folders.

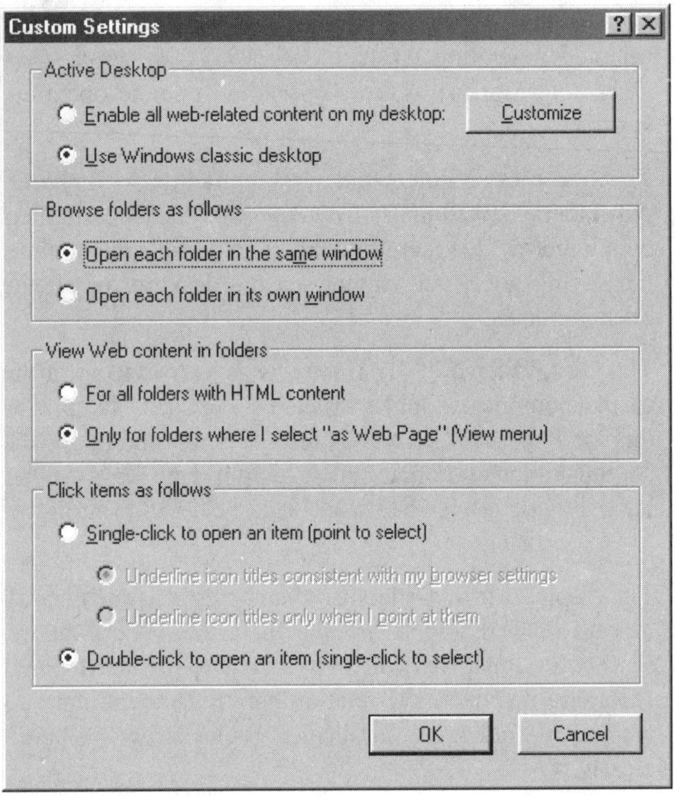

Custom Settings   ? X

Active Desktop

   ○ Enable all web-related content on my desktop: [Customize]

   ● Use Windows classic desktop

Browse folders as follows

   ● Open each folder in the same window

   ○ Open each folder in its own window

View Web content in folders

   ○ For all folders with HTML content

   ● Only for folders where I select "as Web Page" (View menu)

Click items as follows

   ○ Single-click to open an item (point to select)

     ● Underline icon titles consistent with my browser settings

     ○ Underline icon titles only when I point at them

   ● Double-click to open an item (single-click to select)

[OK]   [Cancel]

Fig. 5.3:   Selecting and changing display options for folders

View menu

To change the view, choose the *Folder Options* command from the *View* menu of any folder. On the *General* tab page select the *Custom, based on settings you choose* radio button and click on the *Settings* button.

Select the *Open each folder in the same window* radio button in the *Browse folders as follows* option group and confirm with *OK* and then *Close*. From now on you will work in only one window, the contents of which will be changed as you are moving between folders. This setting is applied to every newly opened window of *My Computer*.

Changing the View in My Computer and Folder Windows

With an object-oriented graphic operating system like *Windows 98*, all the elements of a computer, such as drives, folders, and the contents of folders in the form of files and documents, can be displayed as icons. This has the big advantage that every action under Windows can be performed using the mouse.

View/Large Icons

Large icons

To display objects in opened folders, *Windows* uses fairly large icons in the default setting, below which the name of the object is written. This display style is called *Large Icons*. On the *View* menu, the display can be customized in various ways.

View menu

To begin with, open the *View* menu and take note of the dot in front of the *Large Icons* item. The default setting is useful for the display of folder contents, and is helpful particularly for beginners on account of its clarity.

As Web Page

The display *View/Large Icons* (Figure. 5.4) can, however, only display a limited amount of icons in the window. For folders with large contents, scroll bars will automatically appear to enable you to view the parts that are not displayed. If the *View/as Web Page* option is selected, the window will be divided into two panes. In the left window pane, you will see the name of the current folder and a Help text, while the right pane will display the contents (see Figure 5.1).

```
C:\WINDOWS                                                    _ □ ×
 File   Edit   View   Go   Favorites   Help
  ⇦  ·    ⇨  ·   🔼      ✂       🗐      🗐      ↶      ✕      📝      🖽   ·
 Back   Forward    Up     Cut    Copy    Paste   Undo   Delete  Properties  Views
 Address  🗀 C:\WINDOWS                                              ▼
```

Windows

Warning

Modifying the contents of
this folder may cause
your programs to stop
working correctly.

Select an item to view its
description.

Downloaded Program Files, All Users, Application Data, Applog, Catroot, Command, Config, Cookies, Cursors, Desktop, Drwatson, Fonts, forms, Help, Inf, Java, Media, MsApps

```
:Show Files                    47.7MB                    💻 My Computer
```

Fig. 5.4:   View/Large Icons, (as Web Page) display style

The *Large Icons* display style can also be activated using
the toolbar of a document window. Select *View/Toolbars/
Standard Buttons* to display the toolbar. The size and
appearance of the icons depends on the settings of *View/
Toolbars/Text Labels*. The *Text Labels* display the corresponding text alongside the icon, as in the *Microsoft
Internet Explorer* Web browser.

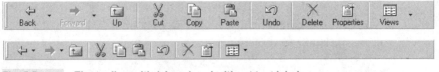

Fig. 5.5:   The toolbar with (above) and without text labels

Views button

To change the display to *Large Icons*, click the *Views*
button 🖽· and select the *Large Icons* command.

View/Small Icons

If you choose the *Small Icons* command from the *View* menu, the window contents will be displayed using smaller icons. The icons are arranged first by column and then by row. The *Small Icons* view can also be selected using a button on the toolbar. To do this, click the *Views* button ▦▾ and choose *Small Icons*.

View/List

The *List* item on the *View* menu shows a view which is not very different from the *Small Icons* view. Here *Windows 98* shows the contents of a folder in the form of a list, with the small icons displayed alongside the text.

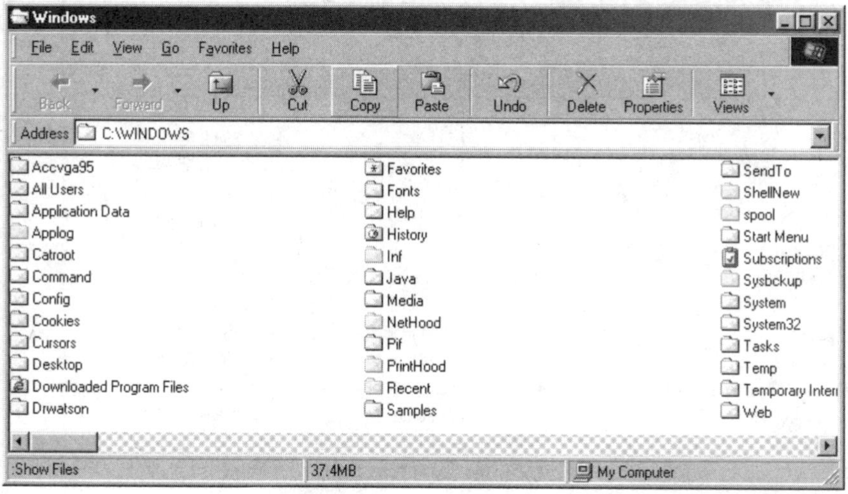

Fig. 5.6: The *List* view

If a window is too small to display all the objects in a row, a second or third row will automatically be created. The *List* view can also be selected using the *Views* button ▦▾ on the toolbar and choosing the *List* command.

Details View

If you change the view using the *View/Details* command, the contents of the folder will be displayed as a list in a single column. This list will not be displayed in more than one column even if there is not enough space in the window.

File size

In addition to the small icons, you will see information regarding size, file type, and the date of last modification (*Modified*), which is shown along with the time of the last modification.

Name	Size	Type	Modified
Accvga95		File Folder	10/9/98 3:24 PM
All Users		File Folder	10/7/98 6:52 PM
Application Data		File Folder	10/7/98 6:35 PM
Applog		File Folder	10/7/98 6:44 PM
Catroot		File Folder	10/7/98 6:33 PM
Command		File Folder	10/7/98 6:33 PM
Config		File Folder	10/7/98 6:37 PM
Cookies		File Folder	10/7/98 6:55 PM
Cursors		File Folder	10/7/98 6:34 PM
Desktop		File Folder	10/7/98 6:52 PM
Downloaded Program Files		ActiveX Cache Folder	10/7/98 6:54 PM
Drwatson		File Folder	10/7/98 6:37 PM
Favorites		Shell Favorite Folder	10/7/98 6:54 PM

Fig. 5.7:   A folder in the *Details* view

Using the scroll bar in the *Details* view, you can reach entries which are not displayed. The *Details* view can also be accessed by clicking on the *Views* button ▦▾ on the toolbar and choosing the *Details* entry.

Tip! The commands on the *View* menu have to be called up for each document window separately. This, too, can be modified. Customize the view of the present folder according to your preference, and then select the *Folder Options* command on the *View* menu. Click the *Like Current Folder* button in the *Folder views* group box on the *View* tab page. Confirm with *OK*, and all folders will be displayed in the same format as the current folder.

Tip! The *Large Icons* view is ideal for folders which contain only a few objects, while the *List* display is best used with folders that contain many objects. All *View* commands are also available in the the shortcut menu using the right mouse button. On the open shortcut menu click the *View* item and choose from the submenu.

Changing the Sorting Order in My Computer and Folders

Independent of the view settings, *Windows 98* automatically sorts the contents of open folders, normally in ascending alphabetical order. First, all the folders are listed from A to Z, followed by the files, which are again sorted by name. The way objects are displayed in a folder window depends on the selected setting.

In the *Large Icons* view, the objects in a folder are listed from left to right. Therefore, the icon of a folder will appear in the upper left-hand corner, along with the label of the folder starting with the letter closest to 'A' in the alphabet.

Right beside it, the second folder in the alphabetical order will be displayed, and so on. After the folders, all the file objects are shown, sorted in the same way.

The icons in the *Small Icons* view are presented in the same order. The *List* view, on the other hand, will sort the contents of a folder in a single column. As always, the folders come first, followed by the files.

Second column

For small windows with large contents, a second column will automatically be created, which will continue the list from the bottom of the first column.

Details view

Only in the *Details* view will an alphabetically sorted single column be shown, listing all the contents of a folder.

Tip!

If the *View/as Web Page* option is selected, the window will be divided into two panes. In the left pane, the name of the folder will be displayed, while the right pane will show the actual contents of the folder (Figure 5.1).

The sorting order can be customized for each individual folder in *Windows 98*. For this purpose, the *Arrange Icons* command is available in the *View* menu and the shortcut menu (no objects should be highlighted when this is called up).

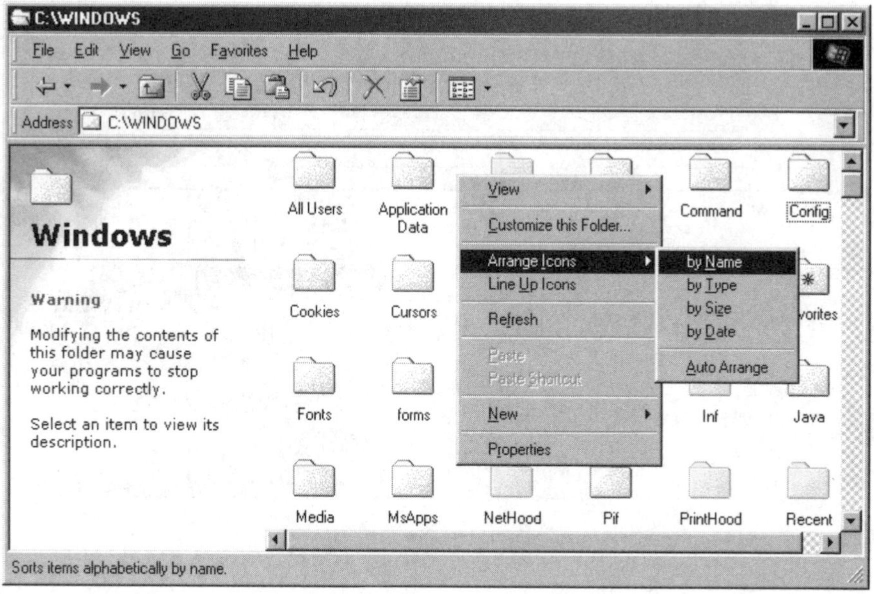

Fig. 5.8: The standard setting: Icons arraged by Name

Setting the sorting order
In the overlapping menu, the following five commands are available for sorting the contents of folders: *by name*, *by Type*, *by Size*, *by Date* and *Auto Arrange*. We will describe the *Auto Arrange* command at the end of the chapter.

By Name
The *View/Arrange Icons/by Name* command is the default setting in *Windows 98*. Here, the icons of the open folder are listed in ascending alphabetical order. The folders are shown first, followed by the files.

By Type
The *View/Arrange Icons/by Type* command will sort the contents of an open folder by file type. First shown are all the subfolders in ascending alphabetical order, then all the files, sorted according to file type. This command is useful if you are looking for specific file types such as *Bitmaps*, which are then shown in a column in the *List* or *Details* views.

179

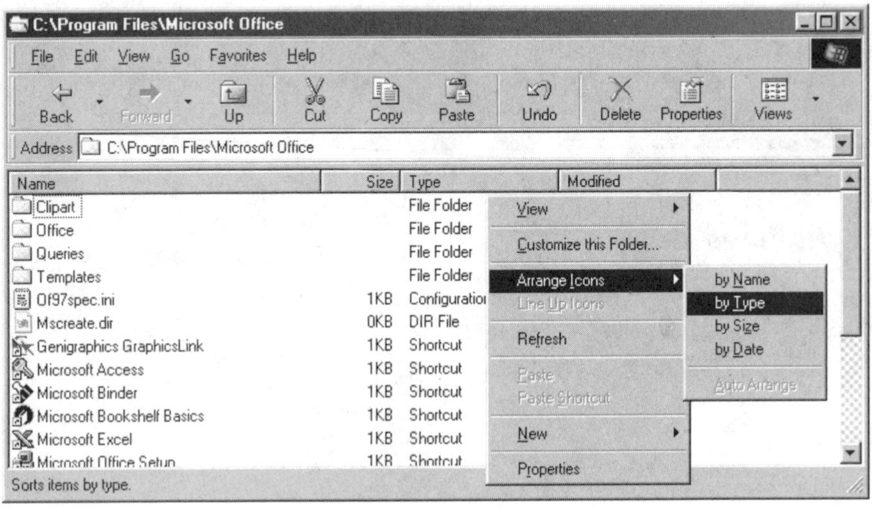

Fig. 5.9:   Contents of folders sorted *by Type*

The items are always sorted according to the label which you see in the *Details* view under *Type*.

By Size

The *View/Arrange Icons/by Size* command will sort the contents of an open folder according to file size. All folders will be displayed first, sorted according to file size, followed by the files, also sorted by size. The *by Size* command will list small files before big files, independent of the file name or the file type. For this reason, folders that are empty or folders containing only subfolders and no files are always found at the beginning of the list. The file size of a folder or a file can be 0 KB. This command should only be used if you know the exact size of the file you are looking for in a folder.

By Date

The *View/Arrange Icons/by Date* command will sort the contents of an open folder according to the date when they were last modified. First, all folders will be displayed, sorted according to date, followed by the file objects, also sorted by date. The *by Date* sorting option will list more recent files before older files, independent of the file name, the file type, or the size.

Tip!

Windows 98 recognizes three types of dates: the date an object was created, the date it was last modified and the date it was last accessed. The date of creation, *Created*, indicates the date when the object was saved for the first time. *Modified* indicates the date it was last modified as opposed to when it was created. *Accessed* shows the last time the file was opened without any changes having been saved.

Working with the Windows Explorer

By now you should be a little more familiar with the Windows desktop. The desktop dominates all Windows functions. The term 'desktop' can be taken quite literally. In a way, your Windows screen imitates your real desktop and, in this manner, allows you to perform all the tasks you have to do in a practical way.

Electronic desktop

To write a letter, you normally take a piece of paper and a pen, while on your computer you would start up your word processor. Correspondence which is completed, for example, is placed in the top drawer of your desk. If you want to be especially efficient, you will use a labeled folder.

Hierarchy

On the computer, you save the letter you've written with the word processor to your hard disk in a specific folder. We could go on and on with this analogy. The point we want to make is that behind everything there is a system and a hierarchy.

Displaying the Organizational Structure of Windows 98 in Explorer

Applied to *Windows 98*, this would correspond to the desktop. But how to do you go about it? The best way to view the Windows hierarchy is to use the *Windows Explorer*. This application displays all *Windows 98* objects in a hierarchy which resembles the structure of a tree. Some of you may already be familiar with this from having worked with MS-DOS.

Using the *Explorer*, the entire structure can be managed and organized in a better and clearer way than by using the windows of *My Computer*. The *Windows Explorer* view with its complicated folder structure is useful for Windows' experts.

To begin with, call up the *Windows Explorer* by opening *Start/Programs* and choosing the *Windows Explorer* item. A quicker way is to open the shortcut menu of the *Start* button and choose the *Explore* command. The application window of the *Windows Explorer* is divided into two panes. The left pane displays the folder structure and the right side, the contents of an open folder.

Take a look at the entries displayed in the left pane of *Explorer*.

The first entry is the *Desktop*. If this entry is not visible, use the scroll bar in the left pane to display it. Below it are the entries labelled *My Computer*, *My Documents*, *Internet Explorer* and *Recycle Bin*. If you are working on a network, you will also see the *Network Neighborhood* entry. If the briefcase is installed, you'll see *My Briefcase*, too.

Same level of the hierarchy

Click the plus sign ⊞ in front of the *My Computer* entry. As you can see, *Windows 98* looks at your volumes, which is to say your drives, as individual objects on the same level in the hierarchy. The number of icons displayed depends on your system configuration. In addition, you will see the icons for the *Control Panel*, *Scheduled Tasks* and *Printers*.

Drive icons

The type of drive can be identified from its description. The following icons are used for the different drive types:

▥ 🖫	*3½ Floppy (A:)*	3.5" Floppy Drive
▥ 🖫	*5¼ Floppy (B:)*	5.25" Floppy Drive
▥ 🖴	*[C:\] [Name]*	Hard Disk
▥ 💿	*[D:\] [Name]* or *[Number]*	CD-ROM Drive
▥ 🖥	*[Letter:\] [Name]*	Network Drive

Drive letter

In the case of floppy drives, the 3.5 inch floppy drive is generally used. If you have only installed one floppy drive, this will always be drive *(A:)*. The floppy description has been retained for reasons of compatability with the earlier *MS-DOS* operating system.

With the *5¼ Floppy* entry, *Windows 98* describes the good old floppy drives for 5.25 inch disks. The second disk drive has the drive letter *(B:)* in *MS-DOS*.

CD-ROM drives

The drive lettering which was used with the earlier *MS-DOS* operating system is used for hard disks, network drives and CD-ROM drives. However, you do not need to work with drive letters under *Windows 98*, all you have to do is click on the icon of the respective drive.

Do not be surprised at the sometimes strange sounding labels of the drives. In some cases only a number is assigned to a drive, in others it may be called *MS-DOS* or the name of a manufacturer such as *SEAGATE*, *MAXTOR* or *CONNER*, etc. We will show you how to change the drive label in Chapter 9.

First level

The first level of folders is the next step in the hierarchy, under the drive icons. If you want to display these folders click on the plus sign in front of a drive icon ⊞‥🖴. *Explorer* will expand the structural display to display all root folders in the drive, and the plus sign will be replaced by a minus sign ⊟‥🖴.

Hierarchy level

This sign indicates that the structure of a drive is visible. Under the drive, you will see more folders with plus signs ⊞‥📁, which in turn contain subfolders. Expanding and reducing folder structures will be discussed in the following sections.

System folders

Windows 98 displays three or four specific system folders on the same level as the drives.

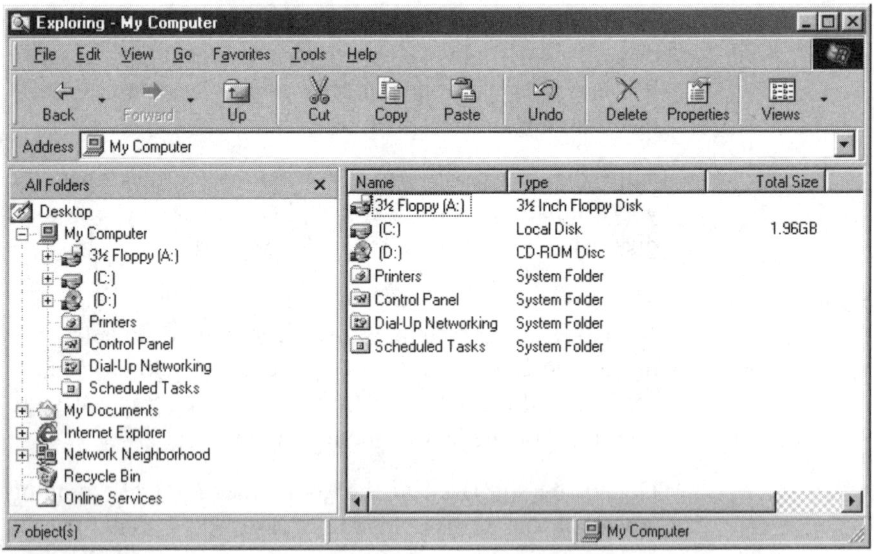

Fig. 5.10:   The desktop displays the first level of the object hierarchy

System folder

First comes the *Printers* folder, followed by the *Control Panel* which is used for the technical settings of the installed PC components and the software. With the *Scheduled Tasks* program, maintenance and fine tuning of drives can automatically be performed.

If you have *Dial-Up Networking* installed, this folder, too, will be displayed on the same level as the other drives.

Tip!

The hierarchical structure of the desktop and its objects is indicated with a dotted line in the left pane of *Explorer*.

This gives you an indication of how the system works in principle. All objects directly displayed on your desktop, which is to say saved on the desktop, are displayed in the hierarchy level below the desktop, on the same level as *My Computer*. This goes for any folders which you place on the desktop. (Of course these are only shortcuts, since the desktop is not a drive.) On the same level as *My Computer* you find a folder called *My Documents* for saving your personal files. The *Internet Explorer* (for Internet access) and the *Recycle Bin* icons are also listed at this level. If you are working with a network you will see the *Network Neighborhood* entry, too.

Difference of
My Computer

There are basic differences in the display of the hierarchy between *My Computer* and *Explorer*. Using *My Computer* you will get an overview of the drives installed on your computer. If you want to look further into the structure, the standard setting will display a different window for every level.

Displaying Drives and Folders in Explorer

The *Windows Explorer* is without a doubt the most powerful application of *Windows 98*. It is used primarily for file management. Only *Explorer* can provide you with a real overview of the organization of your files and the folder structure of your drives. In the *Windows Explorer*, the various Windows objects are displayed in a different way than in the strongly object-oriented *My Computer*, although both can actually execute the same functions. The most important difference in the *Explorer* is the view of the folder structure in the left pane.

Tree view

The display of the folder structure in the tree view allows you to work effectively with complicated folder structures. In this view, working with and organizing complex structures is easier than with the multi-window display of *My Computer*.

Working with *Explorer* is actually not that difficult. Call up *Explorer* using, for example, *Start/Programs* and then choose *Windows Explorer*. A faster way is to open the shortcut menu of the *Start* button on the taskbar, and then choose the *Explore* command.

Two panes

The application window of *Explorer* is divided into two panes. The left pane displays the folder structure and the right pane shows the contents of an open folder.

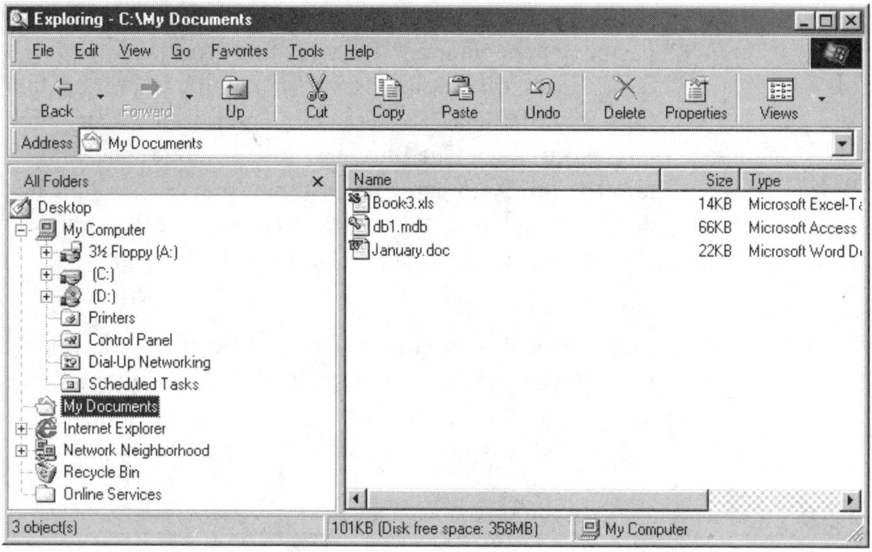

Fig. 5.11: The *Explorer* window: structure on the left, contents on the right

The default setting for the view in the right window is the *Large Icons* view. This setting can be changed using the *View* menu. The most helpful view is the *View/Details* setting which can be obtained by opening the drop-down menu on the *Views* button 🔲⁻ on the toolbar, and selecting the *Details* command.

Folder sturcture

In the left pane of the *Windows Explorer* the drive and folder structure are displayed. To expand or collapse the view, specific icons are used.

Folder structure

The most important control element is the little plus sign ⊞ in front of drive or folder icons. A drive icon ⊞⋯🖫 with a plus sign in front of it indicates that the drive contains folders. To display the folder structure in the left pane of *Explorer*, click on the plus sign. The plus sign will now be changed into a minus sign. ⊟⋯🖫.

Plus sign

This indicates that the structure of the drive is on display. In the list containing the structure, you will now see folder icons with a plus sign ⊞ ▢, which in turn contain further subfolders. To view subfolders in a folder, click on the plus sign. The plus sign will then be replaced by a minus sign. A folder with a minus sign ⊟ ▢ indicates that the structure of the folder has already been expanded. To collapse the structure, click on the minus sign.

Minus sign

Folder icons without a plus or minus sign ▢ represent folders that do not contain any subfolders. These folders may contain files. As long as you click only on the plus or minus signs in the structure window, the only thing that changes is the detail of the structure in the left pane.

Browsing Folders with Windows Explorer

While working with the *Windows Explorer* you should pay attention to the divided application window. The files contained in the folders can only be displayed in the right pane. Subfolders or drive contents can also be displayed in the right pane. The *Explorer* uses special icons in the left window which makes your work easy.

Folder icons with
a plus sign

To begin with, select a folder which you would like to open. To do this, use the following icons: Folder icons with a plus sign ⊞ ▢ contain additional subfolders which you can access by clicking on the plus sign. The plus sign will then be replaced with a minus sign ⊟ ▢.

Folder icons
without sign

If you see folder icons which do not have either a plus or a minus sign ▢ in the left window, it means that the folders do not contain subfolders. These folders can contain files, however. As long as you only click on the plus or minus signs in the folder structure pane, the only thing that changes is the detail of the strucure in the left pane.

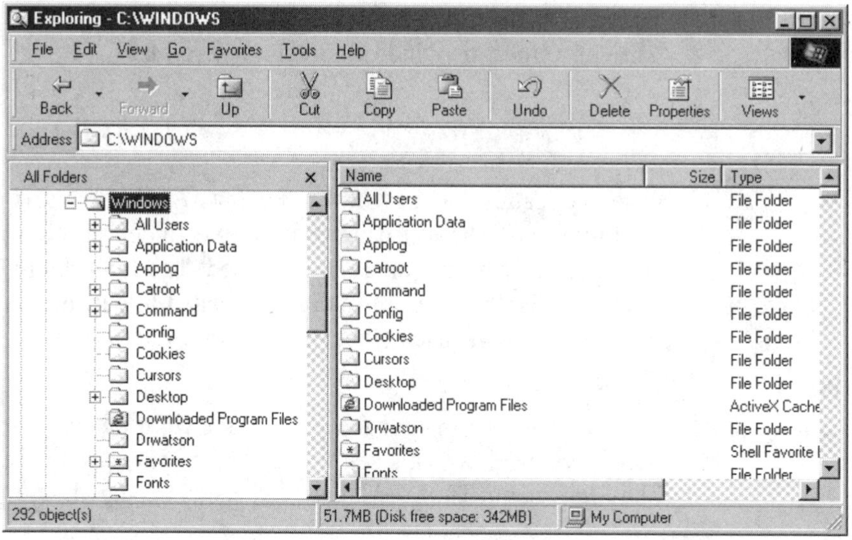

Fig. 5.12: The contents of the *Windows* folder is shown in the right pane

Folder name will
be highlighted

If you want to open a folder in order to display its contents in the right pane, click on the name of the desired folder to select it. An open folder can be recognized by its icon ⌐. The folder name will be highlighted, ⌐ **Windows** and displayed in the *Address Bar* as well ⌐ Address ⌐ C:\WINDOWS ▾. The *Address Bar* can be displayed or hidden using the *View* menu.

Tip!

If you show the toolbar using *View/Toolbars* and *Standard Buttons*, you can move up one level using the *Up* button ⌐ or move to other folders or drives with the *Address Bar* ⌐ Address ⌐ My Computer ▾.

Another way to
open folders

The view in the right *Explorer* pane depends on the settings in the *View* menu. Another way to browse through a folder displayed in the right pane is to double-click on it. In this case, only the icon of the opened folder changes, ⌐ and the label of the folder disappears. It is not necessary for the opened folder to be displayed in the structure since the window contains a scroll bar.

Changing the View in the Windows Explorer

The application window of the *Windows Explorer* is divided into two. The left pane displays the folder structure. This can only be expanded or collapsed. The right *Explorer* pane displays the objects in the opened folder. In this section, we will discuss the manner in which this takes place.

Standard setting

The standard setting for the view in the right pane is the *Large Icons* view. This setting appears as *Large Icons* in the *View* menu. The view, however, can be changed.

View/Large Icons

To begin with, open the *View* menu and verify whether the option *Large Icons* is marked with a dot. The standard display is not very useful for viewing the contents of folders in *Explorer*, and since *Explorer* is used for the organization of files, you will probably need more information than just the object name and the icon.

Scroll bars

The *Large Icons* view (Figure 5.13) can only show a limited number of icons in the *Explorer* window. For folders with large contents, a scroll bar will be displayed which can be used to reach parts of the window that are not displayed.

Display large icons

The *Large Icons* view can also be called up with the help of the *Explorer* toolbar, which will be illustrated when we describe the *View/Toolbars* and *Standard Buttons* commands. To change the display, click on the *Views* button ⊞ on the toolbar and select the *Large Icons* command.

Tip!

If the *View/as Web Page* option is selected, the window could be divided into three parts. The structure is displayed on the left. Beside it you will see the name of the opened folder and a Help text, while the contents of the folder are displayed on the right. The name of the folder may also be shown above the contents.

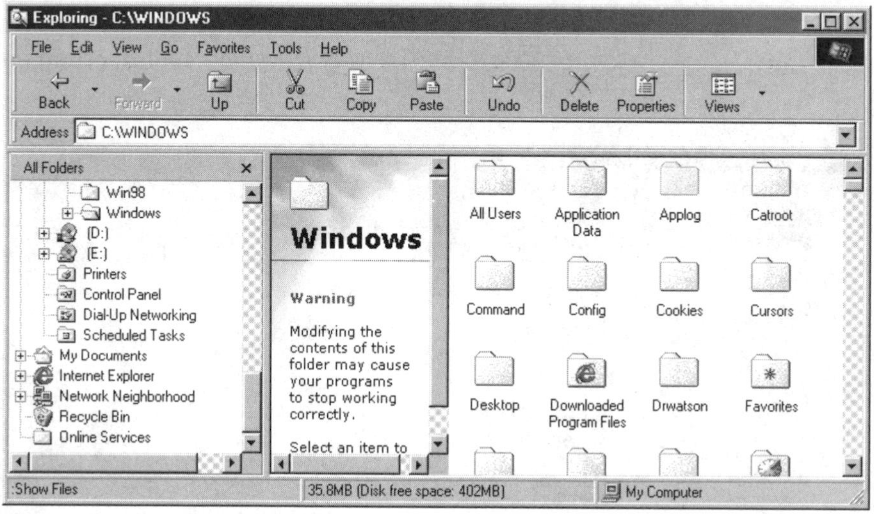

Fig. 5.13: The standard setting View/Large Icons (in this case as Web Page)

View/Small Icons

If you choose the *Small Icons* command from the *View* menu, the window contents will be displayed in a reduced size. The entries are shown side by side and then in lines, one beneath the other. The *Small Icons* option can also be selected with a button in the toolbar.

Views button

Click on the *Views* button on the toolbar and select the *Small Icons* command. Refer to the tip concerning *View/as Web Page* in the section on large icons.

View/List

The *List* command on the *View* menu shows a view which is not very different from the *Small Icons* view. Here *Windows 98* shows the contents of a folder in the form of a list in columns, with one entry below the other.

The *List* view can also be selected using the *Views* button ▦ · on the toolbar and choosing the *List* command. Refer to the tip concerning *View/as Web Page* in the section on large icons.

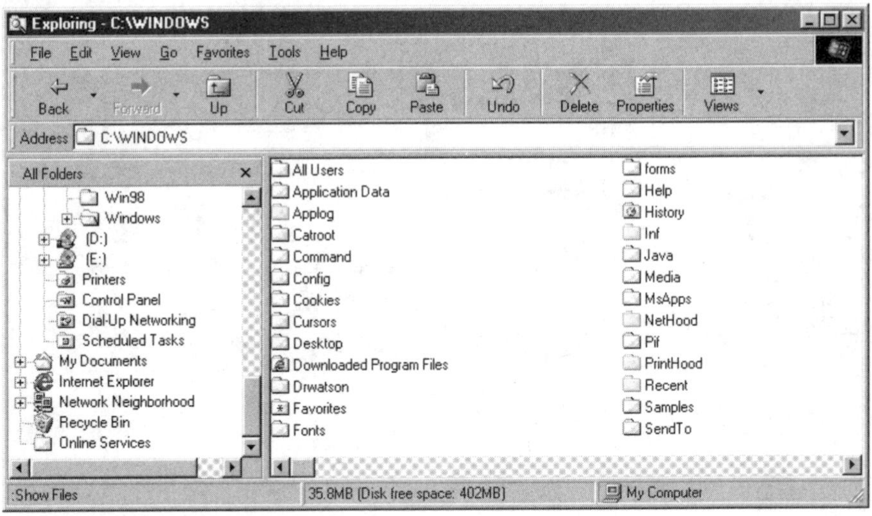

Fig. 5.14:   The *List* view in the right Explorer pane

View/Details

If you change the display using the *View/Details* command, the contents of the folder will be displayed as a list in a row. This list will not be displayed in more than one row, even it there is not enough space in the window.

In addition to the small icons, you find information regarding the size, file type, and date when it was last modified (*Modified*) which is displayed along with the time of the last modification.

Recomended
display

This is, in our opinion, the only worthwhile view in *Explorer*. Only with this additional information can files be properly managed and organized. Refer again to the tip concerning *View/as Web Page* above.

Permanent display

Once you select the *Details* view (or any other view option) the information will be permanently saved, and *Explorer* will always start with the selected view.

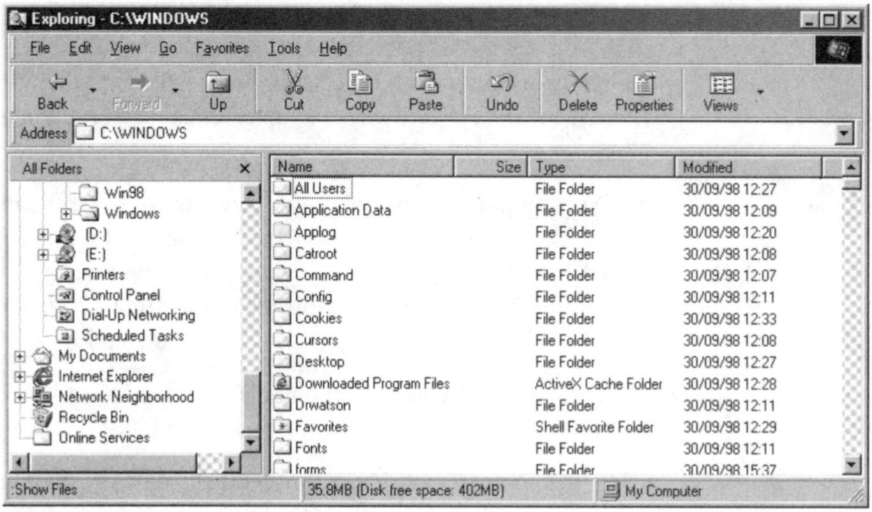

Fig. 5.15: The Explorer in the *Details* view

Scroll bar

Using the scroll bar in the *Details* view, you can reach entries which are not displayed. The *Details* view can also be selected by using the *Views* button 🔲▾, and choosing the *Details* command.

Tip!   The commands in the *View* menu have to be selected separately for each additional *Explorer* window which is running. All *View* commands are also available in the overlapping *View* menu on the shortcut menu, which is accessible using the right mouse button. If the option *View/as Web Page* is also checked, the *Explorer* window may be divided into three.

Changing the Sorting Order in Explorer

In this section, we will introduce the different methods by which you can change the sorting order in opened folders in the right window pane, the contents. The default setting which is used to sort objects in the right pane of the *Windows Explorer* is always by alphabetical and ascending order.

Selected setting   The sorting is independent of the view settings. To begin with, the available folders are listed from A to Z, followed by the files which are again sorted alphabetically by name. The order of the objects in the right *Explorer* window, however, depends on the setting selected.

Display large icons   In the *Large Icons* view, the objects in a folder are listed from left to right.

Thus the icon of a folder whose label begins with the letter closest to 'A' in the alphabet will appear in the upper left-hand corner. Right beside it, the folder coming second in the alphabetical order will be displayed, and so forth.

Following the folders, sorted alphabetically, come the files, which are also sorted in the same way.

Small Icons view

The icons in the *Small Icons* view are presented in the same order. The *List* view, on the other hand, will sort the contents of a folder in columns. As above, the folders come first, followed by the files.

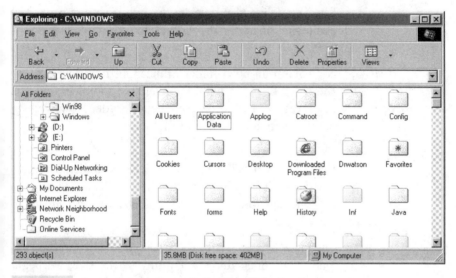

Fig. 5.16:   Icons sorted by name in Explorer (default setting)

Details view

If you are working with small windows that contain many items, a second column will automatically be created, which continues from the lower end of the first column Only the *Details* view will show an alphabetically sorted single column, listing the entire contents of a folder.

Arrange Icons
command

The sorting order can be customized individually for every copy of *Explorer* that is running. To do this, use the *Arrange Icons* command, which is available on the *View* menu or the shortcut menu (in which case no objects should be selected). In the overlapping menu, the following five commands are available to sort the contents of folders: *by Name*, *by Type*, *by Size*, *by Date* and *Auto*

Arrange. We will describe the *Auto Arrange* command at the end of the section.

By Name

The *View/Arrange Icons/by Name* command is the default setting in *Explorer*. Here the icons of the open folder are listed in alphabetical order in the right *Explorer* pane. The available folders are shown first, followed by the files.

By Type

The *View/Arrange Icons/by Type* command will sort the contents of an open folder in the right *Explorer* pane by file type. To begin with, the available subfolders will be displayed in ascending alphabetical order, followed by the files sorted according to file type.

This command is useful if you are looking for specific file types such as *Bitmaps* in the opened folder. The files are shown in a column in the *List* or *Details* view. The order always follows the description shown in *Type* in the *Details* view.

By Size

The *View/Arrange Icons/by Size* command will sort the contents of an open folder according to file size. To begin with, the available folders will be displayed and sorted according to file size, followed by the files, also sorted by size. The *by Size* command will list small files before big files, regardless of the file name or the file type. For this reason, folders that are empty or empty folders containing subfolders are always found at the beginning of the list. This command is only helpful if you know the exact size of the file you are looking for in a folder.

By Date

The command *View/Arrange Icons/by Date* will sort the contents of an open folder in the right *Explorer* pane according to the date it was last modified. To begin with, the available folders will be displayed and sorted by date, followed by the files, also sorted by date.

By Date

The sorting key *by Date* will list the more recent files first, regardless of the file name or file type. The *View/ Arrange Icons/by Date* command is useful if you are looking for a file in a folder with a specific date.

Tip!

Windows 98 keeps track of three types of dates. The date of creation, the date it was last modified and the date it was last accessed. The date of creation, *Created*, indicates the date on which the object was saved for the first time. The *Modified* entry indicates the date it was last modified as opposed to the date of creation. *Accessed* shows when the file was last opened without any changes having been saved. These dates can be seen by selecting a file, opening the shortcut menu, and selecting *Properties*.

Selecting Objects

The following section refers to the standard procedure of opening folders with a double click. Before issuing a command under *Windows 98* or executing an action involving an object, it has to be selected first. By this time, it should not be difficult for you to select objects. Simply click on the object (for example a file or a folder) in the respective window.

Selecting More Than One Object at the Same Time

Your daily work sometimes requires multiple selection: selecting more than one file or folder at the same time. To select more than one item, you cannot just click on several objects one after the other. Every click will remove the selection of the object previously selected!

Rules

If you want to select several files or folders at the same time, you have to observe certain rules:

- Multiple selection is only possible within the same window.

- In *Explorer*, multiple selections can only be made in the right window pane.

To select more than one file in *My Computer*, *Explorer*, or any document window of your choice, several different methods can be employed. You can choose between a combination of mouse and keyboard, just the mouse, or only the menu commands.

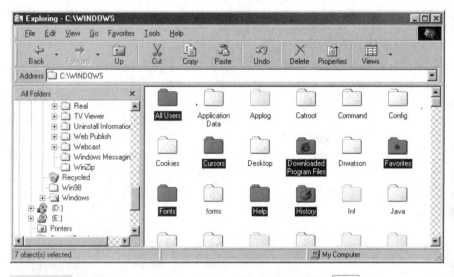

Fig. 5.17:   Independent multiple selection with the help of the `Ctrl` key

Mouse and keyboard

Let's start with the mouse and keyboard combination. Select the first file with a mouse click. Now press the `Ctrl` key and while holding it down, click the other objects to be selected one after the other.

Now release the ⟨Ctrl⟩ key. In this way several objects can be selected independently of each other.

Selecting in a vertical list

If you have selected the *List* or *Details* view, you can select objects shown in a vertical list or column by clicking on the first object in the list, and while holding down the ⟨◇⟩ key, clicking on the last entry in the list to be selected.

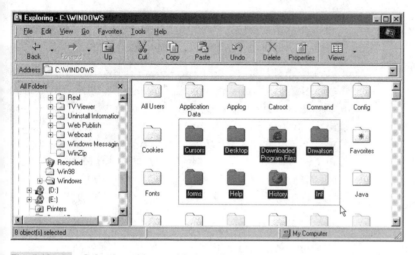

Fig. 5.18:   Selecting objects with the selection rectangle and the mouse

Holding down the ⟨◇⟩ key

Holding down the ⟨◇⟩ key will always select the objects contained in the area between the points where you clicked the mouse. This method can also be used in the *Large Icons* view, but the effect is not as clearly visible. The ⟨Ctrl⟩ and ⟨◇⟩ keys can also be used in combination.

Selection rectangle

Using the selection rectangle, objects which are side by side can be highlighted more quickly using the mouse. To do this, point at the first object to be highlighted, press the left mouse button and drag the *selection rectangle* in the required direction.

If the border of the selection rectangle touches an object or an object name, it will automatically be selected. Once you have selected all the required objects in this manner, release the mouse button.

Tip! If you open folders in *My Computer* with a single mouse click, (*View/Folder Options*, the option *Custom, based on settings you choose* on the *General* tab page and the *Settings* button, then the *Single click to open an item (point to select)* option selected in the *Click items as follows* option group), the highlighting works in a different manner.

To highlight, you simply point on the desired item or folder. Selected objects are displayed in a different color. The user interface resembles that of a Web browser for the World Wide Web (WWW) on the Internet. Another way is to use *View/Folder Options* to select the option to just underline selected objects, which helps to make things clearer. All the other methods for selection ($\boxed{\text{Ctrl}}$ and $\boxed{\diamond}$ etc.) will work in the manner explained above.

Selecting with menu commands

We will now deal with the selection of objects using menu commands. If all objects in a folder or in an *Explorer* window are to be selected, choose the *Select All* command from the *Edit* menu.

Tip! The *Invert Selection* command is also listed in the *Edit* menu. This can be used to select, for example, 49 out of 52 objects. To do this, select the three objects which are not required using the $\boxed{\text{Ctrl}}$ key. Then choose the *Edit/ Invert Selection* command which will simply reverse your previous selection.

Using the keyboard

Are you a keyboard maniac? Here is the method for selecting objects using the keyboard: Move to the first object to be highlighted with the ⬅, ➡, ⬆ or ⬇ keys. Then press the ⬦ key and move to adjacent objects which are to be selected with the ⬅, ➡, ⬆ or ⬇ keys.

Scroll bar

To select objects not displayed in the window, you can always use the scroll bar. Be sure to click **on** the scroll bar however, since, if you miss it, whatever you have previously selected will be lost.

Regardless of the selection method you choose, you should always keep an eye on the *Status* bar. This will give you information regarding the number of selected objects (left side) and their size.

Tip!

To highlight all objects in an opened folder, you can also use the Ctrl+A key combination, which corresponds to the *Edit/Select All* command.

Copying and Moving Files

The organization and management of files is one of the most common tasks a computer is asked to perform. While doing this, files are very often moved or copied, in order to rearrange the documents in a clear manner, for example. *Windows 98* offers you several methods of copying or moving files. To begin with, we will demonstrate how to copy or move files easily using the *Drag-and-Drop* technique.

Moving and Copying Files Using Drag-and-Drop

To copy or move files, you need *Windows* applications that display the actual file structure and folder contents of your hard disk. In the *Start* menu only the shortcuts and program groups are displayed, while the actual data is saved somewhere else. Therefore, you have to use *My Computer* or the *Windows Explorer* when you want to copy or move files.

Select the drive or the folder

Regardless of the method used to copy or move the files, you first have to select the drive or the folder which contains the files. Select this drive or folder. In *My Computer*, change to the required folder by double-clicking on the drive icon of the hard disk and then on the folder icons of the folders to be opened.

In *Explorer*, expand the structure in the left pane by clicking on the plus sign ⊞ in front of the *My Computer* entry, and repeat this step for the drive icon of the hard disk if necessary. By clicking on the plus signs ⊞ again, change to other folders and select the folder which contains the files to be copied or moved. If you want to copy more than one file at a time, you can use multiple selection in the right window pane.

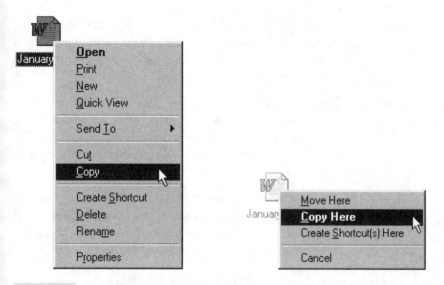

Fig. 5.19:   Copying objects using the shortcut menu

First select

The objects should be selected before they can be copied or moved. To do this, click on the object icon with the mouse. For multiple selection use the [Ctrl] or [⇧] keys.

To copy

To copy or move files with the mouse, the source folder should be displayed in one window, and the target folder or drive in another. In the *Explorer* this can be either the structure or contents view, or a second *Explorer* window.

Press [Ctrl]

To copy using the *Drag-and-Drop* method, point to the selected files. Be sure to hold down the [Ctrl] key during the entire operation! Drag the file(s) into the target drive or folder in the other window. First release the mouse button and then the [Ctrl] key.

To move

To move files using *Drag-and-Drop*, point to the selected files. Then simply drag the file(s) into the target folder in the other window and release the mouse button. If you move files between drives, press the [⇧] key at the same time.

Right mouse

Alternatively, files can also be copied or moved using the right mouse button and the *Drag-and-Drop* method (Figure 5.19, right). Let's look first at how to copy. Point to the selected files to be copied.

Copy with right mouse button

Hold down the Ctrl key and drag the objects using the right mouse button to the target drive or folder in the other window. First release the mouse button and then the Ctrl key. Choose the *Copy Here* command on the short-cut menu which appears.

Move with right mouse button

To move objects, point to the selected files. Drag the files with the right mouse button to the target folder in the other window. Release the mouse button and choose the *Move Here* command on the shortcut menu.

Copying and Moving Files with the Keyboard

Windows 98 offers many different methods to copy or move files. In this section we will show you how to move or copy files easily using keyboard combinations.

My Computer or Explorer

To copy or move files you should use *My Computer* or *Explorer*.

Regardless of the method used, first select the drive or the folder from which you want to copy or move files. Select the folder which contains the files to be copied or moved. Change to the required folder in *My Computer* by double-clicking on the drive icon of the hard disk and then on the folder icons of the folders to be opened.

Structure

In *Explorer*, expand the structure in the left pane by clicking on the plus sign ⊞ in front of the *My Computer* entry, and repeat this step, if necessary, for the drive icon of the hard disk. By clicking on the plus signs ⊞, change to other folders and select the folder which contains the files to be copied or moved. If you want to copy more than one file at a time, you can use multiple selection in the right window pane.

Multiple selection The objects should be selected before they can be copied or moved. To do this, click on a file icon with the mouse. For multiple selection use the ⌈Ctrl⌉ or ⌈⇧⌉ keys.

Key combination Press the ⌈Ctrl⌉+⌈C⌉ key combination to copy, or ⌈Ctrl⌉+⌈X⌉ to cut selected objects from the source folder. Then change to the target folder and paste the data from the clipboard with ⌈Ctrl⌉+⌈V⌉. For large files, a dialog box appears which shows the progress of the transfer.

Copying and Moving Files Using the *Edit* Menu

In this section, we will show you how to use the *Edit* menu to copy or move files.

My Computer Always use *My Computer* or *Explorer* to copy or move
or Explorer files. Regardless of the method used to copy or move, you have to start by selecting the drive or the folder from which you want to copy or move files.

Edit	
Undo Delete	
Cut	Ctrl+X
Copy	Ctrl+C
Paste	Ctrl+V
Paste Shortcut	
Select All	Ctrl+A
Invert Selection	

Fig. 5.20:   The *Edit* menu with the clipboard commands

First select the folder which contains the files to be copied or moved. Change to the required folder in *My Computer* by double-clicking on the drive icon of the hard disk and then on the folder icons of the folders to be opened.

Structure

In the *Explorer*, expand the structure in the left pane by clicking on the plus sign ⊞ in front of the *My Computer* entry, and repeat this step if required for the drive icon of the hard disk. By clicking on the plus signs ⊞ you can change to other folders and select the folder which contains the files to be copied or moved.

Multiple selection

If you want to copy more than one file at a time, you can use multiple selection in the right window pane. The files have to be selected before they can be copied or moved. To do this, click on a file icon with the mouse.

Second *Explorer* window

For multiple selection use the ⌈Ctrl⌉ or ⌈⇧⌉ keys. To copy or move files with the mouse, the source folder should be displayed in one window, and the target folder or drive in another. In *Explorer* this can be either the structure or contents display, or a second *Explorer* window.

Edit/Copy

To copy files using the *Edit* menu, select the *Copy* command on the *Edit* menu. To move files, select the *Cut* command. Then select the folder or drive to which the file should be moved, and choose the *Paste* command on the *Edit* menu.

Copy/Cut

You can also copy or move files with the shortcut menu, using the *Copy*, *Cut*, and *Paste* commands. Point to the selected file and press the right mouse button. Choose the *Copy* or *Cut* command in the shortcut menu.

Then select the folder or drive to which the file should be copied/moved. Point to a free space and click with the

Paste

right mouse button. Choose the *Paste* command from the shortcut menu.

Tip! Using the *Cut* command, the original file will be removed and a copy put on the clipboard. The *Paste* command will place the copy at the new location.

Tip! If you use a single click to open folders in *My Computer* instead of a double click, you only have to point at an object in order to select it.

Organizing Folders in My Computer and Explorer

What used to be called directories under *MS-DOS* are now called folders in *Windows 98*. This means that though the name has changed, it is still a container used for holding files. Folders are created while installing applications to contain program files. A folder can also contain more folders which are called subfolders.

File management

You should also create folders if you want to organize your files in a clear system according to topic. You could, for example, create folders for documents prepared with a word processor, which can be further subdivided into business and private correspondence. Do the same for folders containing drawings, diagrams or a database.

Creating and Naming New Folders

File structure

To create a new folder you need a Windows application which displays the file structure of your hard disk. The *Start* menu only displays shortcuts and program groups, while the actual files are saved in different locations.

Therefore use *My Computer* or the *Explorer* to create new folders.

Now change to the drive on which you want to create a new folder, or select the folder into which you want to place the new (sub)folder. For personal files, the *My Documents* folder used by the *Microsoft Office 97 Suite* can be used. It is located on the first level of the (*C:*) hard disk.

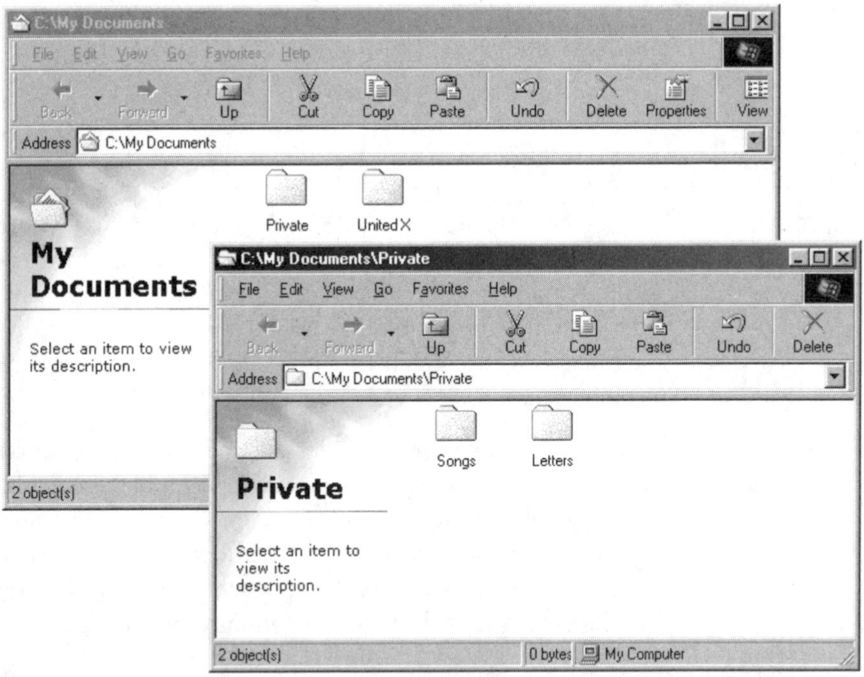

Fig. 5.21:   Creating folders with My Computer

My Computer

In *My Computer*, change to this folder by double-clicking on the drive icon of the hard disk, and double-click again on the *My Documents* folder.

Explorer

In *Explorer*, expand the structure by clicking on the plus sign ⊞ in front of the *My Computer* entry and, if necessary, repeat this step for the drive icon of the hard disk.

New command on the File menu

Now select the *My Documents* folder, and choose the *New* command on the *File* menu. Another way to call up the *New* command is by using the shortcut menu. In that case, no object should be selected in *My Computer* and in *Explorer*, the mouse cursor should be placed in the right pane.

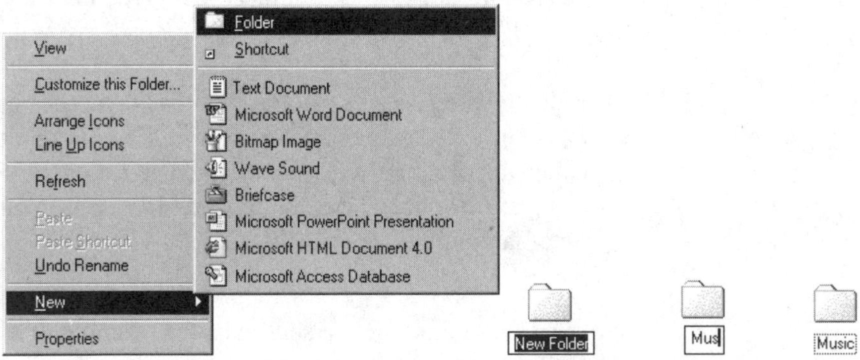

View	▨ Folder
	▱ Shortcut
Customize this Folder...	▤ Text Document
Arrange Icons	▨ Microsoft Word Document
Line Up Icons	▨ Bitmap Image
Refresh	◁ Wave Sound
	▨ Briefcase
Paste	▨ Microsoft PowerPoint Presentation
Paste Shortcut	▨ Microsoft HTML Document 4.0
Undo Rename	▨ Microsoft Access Database
New ▶	
Properties	

New Folder   Mus   Music

Fig. 5.22: Creating and naming a new folder

In the overlapping menu, select the *Folder* item. In the current folder a new folder icon labelled *New Folder* (Figure 5.22, right) will appear, with a highlighted name.

Replace with your name

Replace this with your own name, like *Text Documents* for example. If you confirm with ↵, the newly created folder will appear as a subfolder in the active folder. In the same way you can create more folders. Always select the parent folder when creating a subfolder.

Tip! You can file all the documents you create in your own folder. To do this, use the *Save As* command and select the drive and the target folder in your folder structure, using the list boxes. You can create specific folders for spreadsheets or presentations of *Microsoft Office*.

Renaming Folders and Files

It is easy to rename files and folders under *Windows 98*. The methods described in this section, however, should only be used for documents or folders which you have created yourself.

Tip! Never change the name of a folder that has been created by a program or the names of application files. If you do that, either the program will no longer be able to start or you will get error messages, or the program will crash because of faulty files.

An exception to this rule are shortcuts, for example those of the *Microsoft Office Suite*, which you find on the *Start* menu under *Programs*. These names can be changed, since the shortcuts only contain information regarding the file location and not the actual program or document file.

Only one object selected

To rename objects you have the choice of several options. To begin with, you should select the object to be renamed. Use *My Computer* or *Explorer* to do this. Only one object should be selected at a time. Select the *Rename* command from the *File* menu or the shortcut menu (Figure 5.23, right). The label of the object will be highlighted. Replace the old name and press ⏎. Pressing the Esc key will cancel the process.

Tip! If you open folders with a single mouse click as on the WWW, the renaming of objects will only work in the method described above!

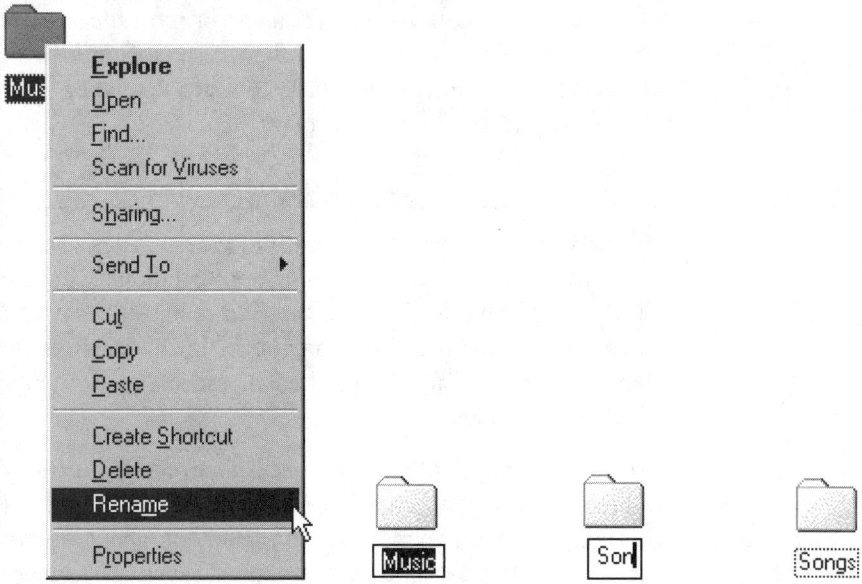

Explore
Open
Find...
Scan for Viruses

Sharing...

Send To   ▶

Cut
Copy
Paste

Create Shortcut
Delete
Rename

Properties

Music

Son

Songs

Fig. 5.23:   Renaming a folder

If you work with the standard double-clicking method, there is another way to rename an object. Click on an object, then wait a second and click on the object again. The object label will again be highlighted. Replace the name with a maximum of 255 characters and confirm with ⏎. If you repeat the click too fast, it will be considered as a double-click.

Tip! In case you have unchecked the *Hide file extension for known file types* check box in *View/Folder Options/View*, be sure to separate the original extension from the file name with a dot. Otherwise the file will become useless. In case of incorrect file names, an error message will be displayed which indicates invalid characters. Confirm the message in which invalid characters are displayed with *OK* and try renaming the file again.

Copying Folders

Folders can by copied in the same way as files. To do this, you can use the *Drag-and-Drop* technique with the left and right mouse buttons, the *Edit* menu, the shortcut menu, or the keyboard combinations. In this section we have summarized all the methods – especially for copying folders – once more.

Actual file
structure

To copy or move folders, you need *Windows* applications which display the actual folder structure of your hard disk. In the *Start* menu only the shortcuts and program groups are displayed, the actual data is saved somewhere else. Therefore, you have to use *My Computer* or the *Windows Explorer* to copy or move folders.

Select the drive

Independent of the method you use to copy or move a folder, you first have to select the drive or the folder from which you want to copy or move a folder, or select the folder to be copied or moved. In *My Computer*, change to the required folder by double-clicking on the drive icon of the hard disk and then on the folder icons of the folders to be opened.

Highlight

In *Explorer*, expand the structure in the left pane by clicking on the plus sign ⊞ in front of the *My Computer* entry, and repeat this step if required for the drive icon of the hard disk. After that, select the folder to be copied.

If you want to copy more than one folder at a time, you can use multiple selection in the right window pane. If you are using a single click to open folders, select the objects by simply pointing. Multiple selection will also work as described below.

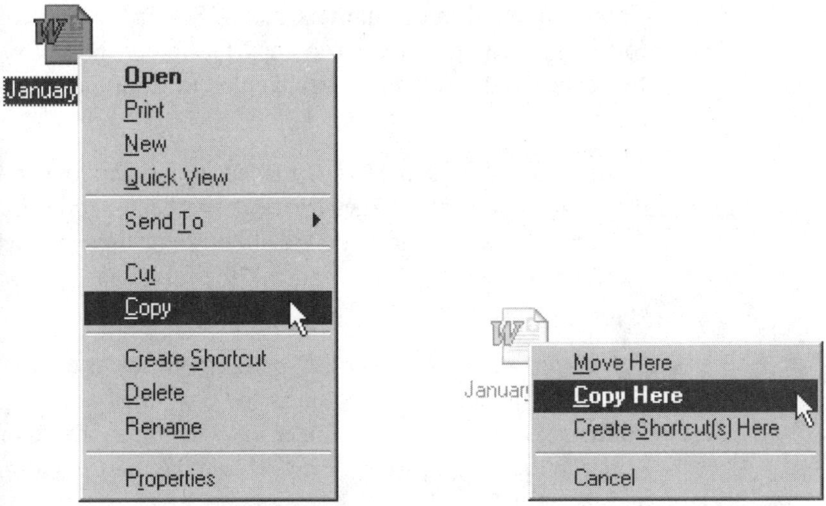

Fig. 5.24: Copying with the shortcut menu

Copy

Before copying, the folder should be selected. To do this, click on a folder icon with the mouse. For multiple selection, use the Ctrl or ⇧ keys. To copy a folder with a key combination, use the Ctrl+C keys.

Then point to the folder or drive into which the folder should be placed. Press the keyboard shortcut Ctrl+V at the insertion position.

Files will also be copied

If a folder contains files, these will also be copied. A dialog box will appear in which the copying process is shown. To copy folders using the *Edit* menu, choose the *Copy* command

213

from the *Edit* menu. Then select the folder or drive into which you want to copy the folder. Call up the *Edit* menu again and select the *Paste* command.

Shortcut menu commands

You can also copy folders using commands from the shortcut menu (Figure 5.24, left). Select the folder to be copied and press the right mouse button. Then choose the *Copy* command in the shortcut menu. Select the drive or folder into which you want to copy the folder, point to a free space and select the *Paste* command from the short-cut menu.

If the folder to be copied is displayed in one window and the target folder and target drive in another window (in *Explorer* this could either be the structure or the contents view, or another *Explorer* window), the folder can also be copied using *Drag-and-Drop*.

Drag-&-Drop

To copy using the *Drag-and-Drop* method, select the fol-der to be copied. Be sure to press the Ctrl key and keep holding it down. Drag the folder onto the target drive or folder in the other window. First release the mouse button and then the Ctrl key.

Right mouse button

Another way to copy folders is with the right mouse but-ton using *Drag-and-Drop* (Figure 5.24, right). To do this, select the folder to be copied. Then drag the folder onto the target drive or target folder while holding down the right mouse button. Release the mouse button and choose the *Copy Here* command from the shortcut menu which appears.

Moving Folders

With *Windows 98* you can move folders to another loca-tion in the same way as you do file objects. Be careful to move only folders you have created.

Tip!

If you move a folder created by a program, this appliction can no longer be started from the *Start* menu, since it will not be able to find its application files.

Drag-and-Drop

To move folders, you can use *Drag-and-Drop*, with both right and left mouse buttons, as well as the *Edit* menu, the shortcut menu or keyboard combinations.

Folder structure

To move a folder, you need a *Windows* application which displays the folder structure of your hard disk. The *Start* menu only displays shortcuts and program groups, while the actual files are saved in different locations.

My Computer or
Explorer

Therefore, use *My Computer* or *Explorer* to move folders. Regardless of the method used to move the object, change to the drive on which the folder to be moved is located, or select the folder which contains the folder or folders to be moved.

Select

Before moving a folder, it has to be selected. To do this, click on its icon with the mouse. If you are using the single click interface to open folders, select the object by pointing at it.

For multiple selection use the [Ctrl] or [⇧] keys. To copy a folder using the keyboard, press the [Ctrl]+[C] key combination. Then select the folder or drive into which the folder should be placed. Press the [Ctrl]+[V] keyboard shortcut at the insertion position. In case a folder contains files, these will also be copied. A dialog box will be displayed showing the progress of the transfer.

Cut command in
the *Edit* menu

To move folders using the *Edit* menu, choose the *Cut* command from the *Edit* menu. Then select the folder or drive into which you want to move the folder. Now choose the *Paste* command from the *Edit* menu.

Shortcut menu

You can also move folders using commands on the short-cut menu (Figure 5.24, left). Select the folder to be moved and press the right mouse button. Then choose the *Cut* command in the shortcut menu. Now select the drive or folder into which you want to move the copy of the folder. Place the mouse cursor over an empty space and click the right mouse button. Select the *Paste* command from the shortcut menu.

Explorer

In case the folder to be moved is displayed in one window and the target folder and target drive in another window (in *Explorer* this could be the either structure or the folder contents view, or another *Explorer* window), the folder can also be moved with *Drag-and-Drop*.

Right mouse
button

Another way to move folders is by using the right mouse button and *Drag-and-Drop* (Figure 5.24, right). To do this, select the folder to be moved. Then drag the folder with the right mouse button to the target drive or target folder in the other window.

Move here

Now release the mouse button. Choose the *Move Here* command in the shortcut menu that appears.

With *Cut* the original of the folder is removed and a copy is placed on the clipboard. The *Paste* command will place the copy in the new location.

Deleting files or folders will be discussed in Chapter 6.

Formatting Floppy Disks

A floppy disk has to be formatted before it can receive data. While formatting, the drive structure is established in the form of tracks and sectors. This is required by the operating system, in order to enable it to save data in such a way that it can be retrieved later on. Nowadays most floppy disks that are sold are preformatted; however it cannot do you any harm to know about the function.

1,44 MB

Today, 99.99 per cent of all floppy disks are in the 3.5" format, with a capacity of 1.44 MB. We will therefore not discuss the formats which were in use earlier.

Formatting a Disk

To format a disk, use *My Computer* or the *Windows Explorer*. The method of formatting is the same in both cases.

Select the drive icon in *Explorer* or *My Computer* which will receive the diskette to be formatted. Normally this would be the *3½ Floppy (A:)* entry. Then select the *Format* command from the *File* menu or the shortcut menu.

Capacity

Select the disk type in the *Capacity* list box. For 3.5" HD (*High-Density*) disks, this is always *1.44 MB*, while for the older 3.5" DD (*Double-Density*) disks the *720 Kb* entry should be selected. Select the *Full* radio button in the *Format type* option group for disks which are not yet formatted.

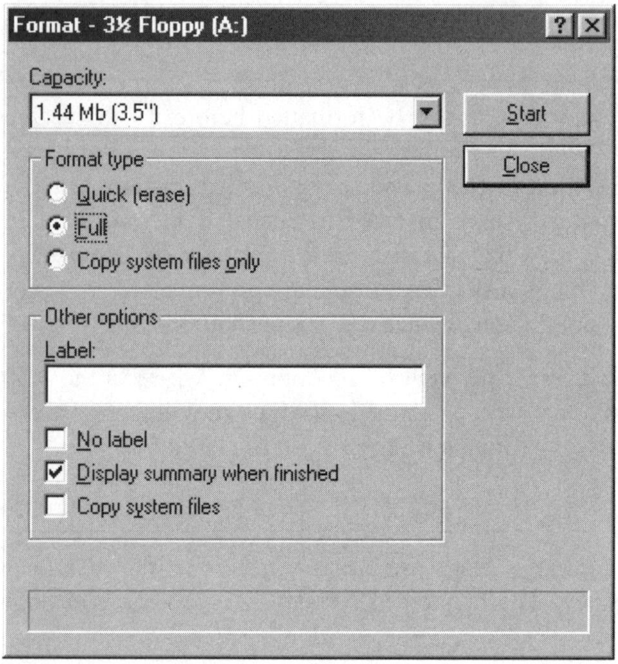

Format - 3½ Floppy (A:)

Capacity:

1.44 Mb (3.5")

Start

Close

Format type
- ○ Quick (erase)
- ⦿ Full
- ○ Copy system files only

Other options

Label:

- ☐ No label
- ☑ Display summary when finished
- ☐ Copy system files

Fig. 5.25: Formatting floppy disks

In case you want to name a disk, click in the *Label* text box and enter a name of a maximum of 11 characters without using any spaces.

Start the process of formatting

Start the process of formatting by clicking on *Start*. In the dialog box, the progress bar at the bottom shows the status of the formatting process. Once the formatting is complete, you will receive a status report. Click *Close* and likewise close the *Format* dialog box by clicking on *Close*.

Tip!

Do **not** use the *Format* command on hard disks. Formatting will irrevocably delete all data on a drive.

Copying Data to a Floppy Disk

To copy files onto a floppy disk, you can, of course, use all the methods of *My Computer* or *Explorer* that we have already discussed. But *Windows 98* has an additional command especially for floppy disk drives.

To begin with, you need to display the file structure of your hard disk and folders. To do this, use either *My Computer* or *Explorer.*

My Computer

Then change to the drive or folder from which you want to copy files to the floppy disk. In *My Computer*, change to the selected folder by double-clicking on the drive icon and the folder icons.

Explorer

In *Explorer*, expand the structure in the left pane by clicking on the plus sign ⊞ in front of the *My Computer* entry, and repeat this step if required for the drive icon of the hard disk. By clicking on the plus signs ⊞ in front of the folders, change to the subfolders and select the folder that contains the files to be copied.

Selection

If you want to copy more than one file at a time, you can use multiple selection in the right window pane of *Explorer*, or in the folder window. The files need to be selected before copying. To do this, click on a file icon with the mouse. For multiple selection use the Ctrl and ⇧ keys.

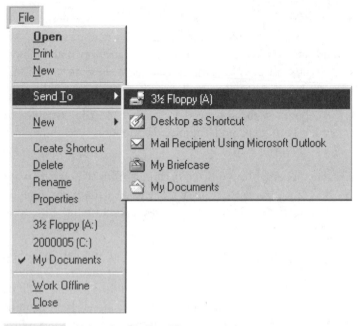

Fig. 5.26:   Using the *File/Send To* command

To copy files onto a floppy disk, choose the *Send To* command from the *File* menu or the shortcut menu. In the overlapping menu click on the entry for the required disk drive, for example, *3½ Floppy (A)*. For large files, a dialog box will be displayed in which the copy progress and the time remaining is indicated.

Automatically Arranging Icons

Using the entries in the overlapping menu of the *Arrange Icons* command on the *View* menu of any folder or window of *My Computer* or *Explorer*, the objects of open folders can be arranged according to various criteria such as *Name, Type, Size* and *Date*.

We have described these commands earlier in this chapter. In this section, we will show you how to automatically rearrange icons that have been moved in *Explorer* and on the desktop.

Icons are moved

While working with *Windows 98* it often happens that one or more icons are moved accidentally in a folder window or on the desktop, such as might happen when the double click is not yet perfectly mastered, for instance.

Confused display

Sometimes, the display of a window becomes confused and it is difficult to manually rearrange icons to their original positions. To rearrange displaced icons in any folder, choose the *Arrange Icons* command from the *View* menu.

Auto arrange

In the overlapping menu, click on the *Auto Arrange* command. The icons will immediately be arranged. This also works in *Explorer* and on the desktop.

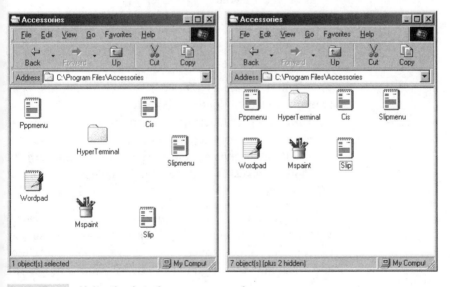

Fig. 5.27:   Using the *Auto Arrange* command

Automatically
arranged

If you now try to move an icon while holding down the mouse button, all the icons will again be automatically arranged as soon as you release the mouse button. Likewise, after changing the size of the window, the icons will be rearranged. This command has to be selected for each window that requires it!

Tip! The *Auto Arrange* command is only available in the *Arrange Icons* overlapping menu if you have selected either the *Large Icons* or *Small Icons* views.

Display All Files

Windows 98 tries to make your life as easy as possible while you are working with the computer. With this in mind, the graphic operating system has been designed to be as object-oriented as possible.

Almost every part of *Windows 98* can be displayed as an object, and because of this, almost every action can be performed using the mouse.

File extension

The default setting of *Windows 98* will display the contents of opened folders without the file extension used with *MS-DOS*. In addition, hidden system files, virtual device drivers, or program libraries are not displayed. This will help prevent people, especially beginners, from making mistakes like inadvertantly deleting important *Windows* files.

Automatic
registration

It is possible to do without the file extensions because Windows recognizes all files whose associated application has been automatically registered during installation, and it can thereby assign them to the respective program.

Experienced users may want to have a more in-depth look at their system. For this purpose, the display can be globally changed for all folders or for *Explorer*.

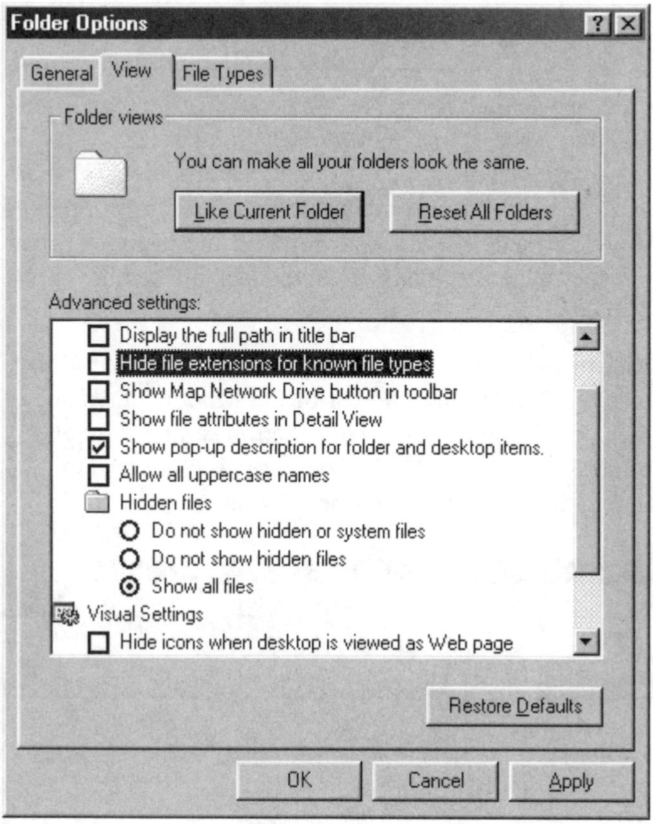

Folder Options   ? ✕

   General   **View**   File Types

Folder views

You can make all your folders look the same.

[Like Current Folder]   [Reset All Folders]

Advanced settings:

- ☐ Display the full path in title bar
- ☐ Hide file extensions for known file types
- ☐ Show Map Network Drive button in toolbar
- ☐ Show file attributes in Detail View
- ☑ Show pop-up description for folder and desktop items.
- ☐ Allow all uppercase names
- 📁 Hidden files
  - ○ Do not show hidden or system files
  - ○ Do not show hidden files
  - ⦿ Show all files
- 📑 Visual Settings
  - ☐ Hide icons when desktop is viewed as Web page

[Restore Defaults]

[OK]   [Cancel]   [Apply]

Fig. 5.28:   The *View* tab page is used to set the display of files

Folder options

Choose the *Folder Options* command in any folder of *My Computer* or from *Explorer*. Then change to the *View* tab page. Under *Hidden files* select the *Show all files* radio button to display even the hidden system files, virtual device drives, and program libraries.

Hide file extension

Clear the *Hide file extensions for known file types* check box if you want the file extension to be displayed after the file name. This file extension will indicate the source program of a file. Confirm your changes with *OK*.

Displaying the Complete MS-DOS Path in the Title Bar

Users switching from the previous character and command-oriented *MS-DOS (Microsoft Disk Operation System)* operating system to the graphic environment of *Windows 98* may be uncomfortable with the object-oriented way in which *Windows 98* works in the beginning, particularly when working with the default setting of *My Computer*.

Name of the

opened folder

All opened folders in *My Computer* are displayed in their own window. In the title bar of the window, the name of the opened folder is shown. When browsing through big folder structures with *My Computer*, sometimes the relation to the parent folders is not obvious.

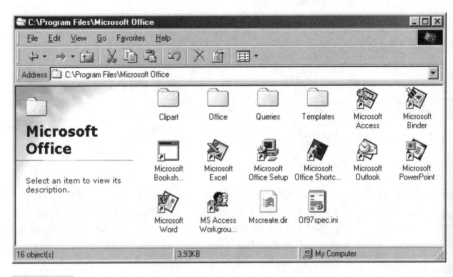

Fig. 5.29:   Folder window with the complete file path in the title bar

Complete file path

Do you remember that the *System Tools* folder is located in the *C:\Windows\Start Menu\Programs\Accessories* folder? With *Windows 98* you have the possibility to display the complete MS-DOS file path in the title bar of any folder opened in *My Computer.*

To change the display

To display the path, select the *Folder Options* command from the *View* menu of any folder window. Then change to the *View* tab page. Select the check box *Display the full path in title bar* and confirm by clicking the *OK* button.

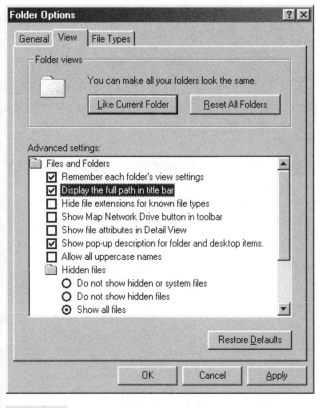

Fig. 5.30:   Here you can choose to display the file path

From now on, the complete file path of any folder is shown in the title bar using the standard MS-DOS conventions (Figure 5.29). This setting is also applied to *Explorer*.

Read-only Files

Windows 98 has several mechanisms to prevent the overwriting of an existing file by a new file with the same name.

Confirmation
message

In an application, if you try to save a file under an existing file name in the same folder, a confirmation message will appear, which informs you that this file already exists and asks you whether you want to replace the existing file.

If you click the *No* button, the *Save As* dialog box appears, and you can choose another file name. If you click on *Yes*, the existing file will be replaced.

The same applies when you create or rename a file or a folder and an identical file or folder already exists. Here, too, a confirmation message will appear to prevent you from replacing already existing objects.

Write-protect a file

Windows 98 allows you to set an additional protection, by write-protecting a file or a folder.

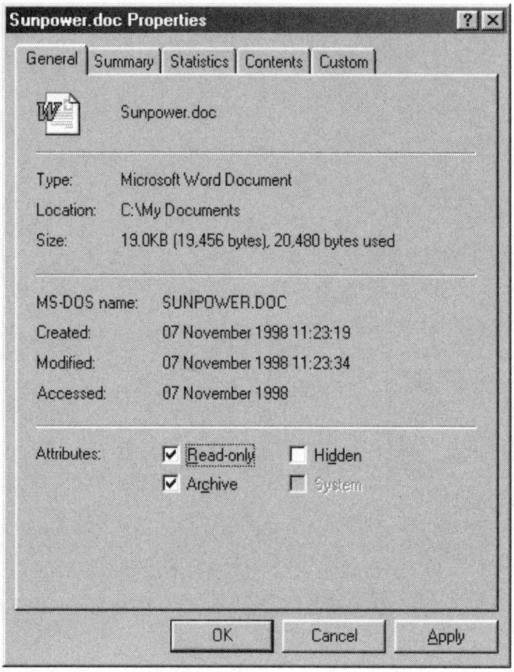

Fig. 5.31: Selecting the *Read-only* file attribute

Read only

To do this, select the file or folder in *My Computer* or the *Explorer*, and select the object. Then choose the *Properties* command from the *File* menu or the shortcut menu. In the *Properties* window, check the *Read-only* check box in the *Attributes* group and click *OK*. You will no longer be able to save changes in this file under its original name.

Tip!

If you try to save a read-only file, an error message will appear, which you should confirm with *OK*. After that the *Save As* dialog box is displayed, allowing you to save this file under another name. To remove the write-protection, clear the *Read-only* file attribute in the *Properties* dialog.

6. The Recycle Bin

This chapter deals exclusively with the deletion of files and folders, and the safety measures of the *Recycle Bin*. You will find out what happens to items once you've deleted them, how you can display the contents of the *Recycle Bin* as well as how to recover files you've deleted by mistake.

Deleting Files and Folders

Objects that are no longer needed can at any time be removed from *Windows 98*. At the beginning of this chapter, we will show you the keyboard and menu commands available for this purpose.

Attention

Be careful: While deleting files and folders, it is important to keep a few things in mind. Do not delete something just to try it out, even if you are already familiar with the *Recycle Bin*. In addition, you should only delete your own files and folders.

If you have deleted a folder of a program by mistake, the application can no longer be started with the *Start* menu, since it will not be able to find its files. If you have deleted only a specific program file, sometimes the program functions cannot be executed anymore, or error messages will constantly be displayed.

The actual file
structure

To delete files and folders you will need a *Windows* application which displays the actual file structure of your hard disk. The *Start* menu, for example, only displays shortcuts (instead of program files) and program groups (instead of file locations); the actual files can be saved somewhere else on the hard disk.

If you delete a shortcut (which can always be recognized by its icon 🡕), the original will still be saved on the drive.

Always use *My Computer* or the *Explorer* to delete files and folders. Regardless of the method used, change to the drive from which you want to delete a file or folder, or select the folder which contains the object(s) to be deleted.

Deleting Objects with the Del Key

Selection

Before deleting a file you have to select it first. You can make a multiple selection if you want to select several files and folders at the same time. The fastest way to delete a selection is using the Del key.

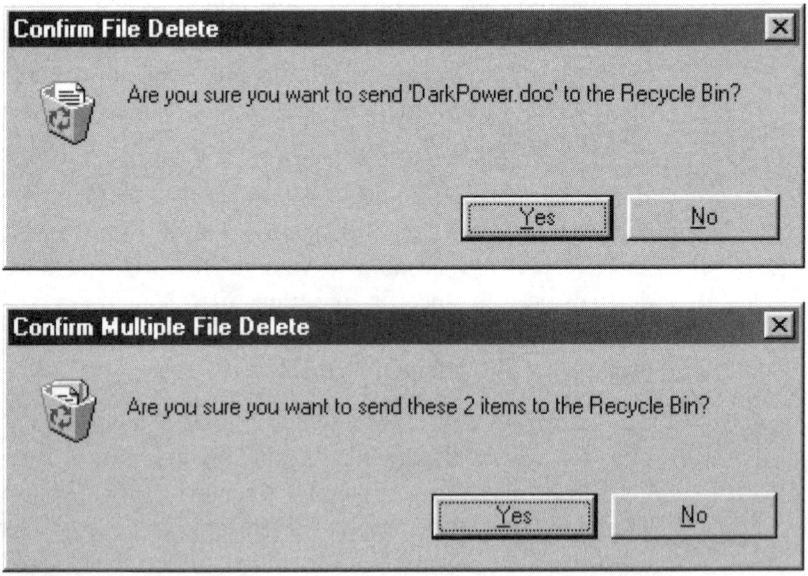

Confirm File Delete ✕

Are you sure you want to send 'DarkPower.doc' to the Recycle Bin?

Yes   No

Confirm Multiple File Delete ✕

Are you sure you want to send these 2 items to the Recycle Bin?

Yes   No

Fig. 6.1:   Confirming the deletion of a single file (top) and multiple files (bottom)

Recycle bin

Following this, a message box will appear asking you if you really want to move the file (name) to the *Recycle Bin*. If you choose *Yes*, the object will be deleted. A *No* will cancel the process. If you have selected multiple objects to be deleted, the confirmation box will be slightly different (see Figure 6.1, bottom). *Windows 98* will not give the name of the different objects to be deleted in this case.

Deleting Objects with the *File/Delete* Command

As an alternative to the ⌈Del⌉ key, selected objects can also be deleted with the *Delete* command on the *File* menu. The *Delete* command is also available on the shortcut menu of the selected objects.

Tip! The *Windows 98 Recycle Bin* is a special system folder in which deleted objects are placed. As long as you have not changed the settings of the *Recycle Bin* the objects are still available on the hard disk. They have just been removed from the folder in which they were originally stored.

Tip! The safety measure of the *Recycle Bin* only works with hard disks and not for floppy disks! If you delete an object on a floppy disk, then it is irretrievably deleted.

Deleting Objects with the Mouse Using Drag-and-Drop

Objects which are no longer required can also be deleted with the mouse. To delete files and folders in *Windows 98* using the mouse, first display the drive or folder contents in *My Computer* or *Explorer*.

Then select the object to be deleted and drag it, while holding down the mouse button, onto the icon of the *Recycle Bin*. As sson as you have reached the right place, the *Recycle Bin* will be highlighted. In this way, you can also delete several objects in one go. First select the objects with the selection rectangle, or with the `Ctrl` and `⇧` keys, and then drag them onto the 🗑 *Recycle Bin*.

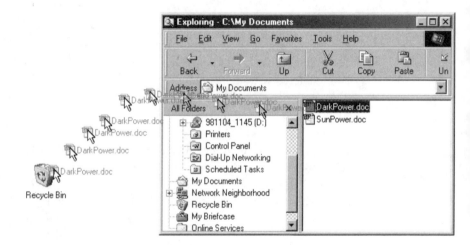

Fig. 6.2:   Dragging files to be deleted to the Recycle Bin

As long as you have not changed the settings of the *Recycle Bin*, the objects will still be available on the hard disk. They have just been removed from the folder where they were originally stored.

We have purposely mentioned the hard disk, since the safety measure of the *Recycle Bin* only works with the hard disk, and not for floppy disks. If you delete an object on a floppy disk, this will, after you confirm the message, be deleted once and for all!

Files deleted from the hard disk are not removed from the drive. *Windows 98* only moves these objects into a special folder, called the 🗑 *Recycle Bin*.

This does not just represent the fancy of a programmer, but a useful system. The 🗑 *Recycle Bin* prevents you from permanently losing data which may have been deleted by mistake.

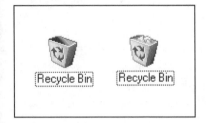

Fig. 6.3: Empty Recycle Bin (left) and full Recycle Bin

Tip! If you realize that you have deleted a file or a folder, but still need the data it contains, you should have a look at the *Recycle Bin*. It is easy to see whether the *Recycle Bin* is full by looking at its icon. If it contains files, a bunch of paper will be displayed inside it (Figure 6.3, right). Read more about this topic below.

If you wish to permanently delete objects instead of putting them in the *Recycle Bin*, drag the objects while holding down the ⬆ key onto the icon of the 🗑 *Recycle Bin* on the desktop. These objects will be deleted without any confirming message and cannot thereafter be recovered.

Delete button

Another way to move files to the *Recycle Bin* is with the *Delete* button ✖ (without *Text Labels*) or 🗑 (with *View/Toolbars/Text Labels*) on the toolbar of folders and

Explorer. Using this method, the process has to be confirmed by clicking *Yes*.

Viewing the Recycle Bin and the List of Deleted Objects

As long as you have not changed the settings of the *Recycle Bin*, the objects are still available on the hard disk. They have simply been removed from the folder in which they were originally stored.

Tip! We have purposely mentioned the hard disk, since the safety measure of the *Recycle Bin* only works with the hard disk, and not for floppy disks. If you delete an object on a floppy disk, it will, once you confirm the message, be irrevocably deleted!

Prevents loss of data

The *Recycle Bin* prevents loss of data when an object has been deleted by mistake. If you realize that you have deleted a file or a folder but still need the data contained in it, have a look in the *Recycle Bin*.

It is easy to see whether the *Recycle Bin* is full by looking at its icon. If it contains files, you will see a pile of paper displayed inside it.

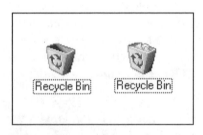

Fig. 6.4:   Icons for the empty Recycle Bin (left) and the full Recycle Bin

To view the contents of the *Recycle Bin* just double-click the *Recycle Bin* icon, or select the *Recycle Bin* icon and press [↵].

Recycle Bin folder

The *Recycle Bin* folder will be displayed. Using the selected view, all deleted objects will be shown either as *Large/ Small Icons*, as *List* or with all *Details* (see Figure 6.5).

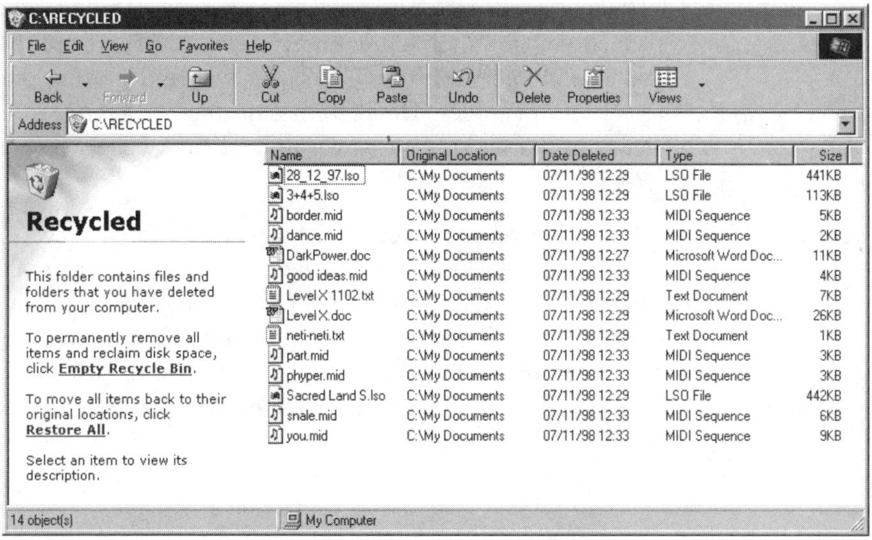
C:\RECYCLED
File Edit View Go Favorites Help
Back Forward Up Cut Copy Paste Undo Delete Properties Views
Address C:\RECYCLED
Recycled
This folder contains files and folders that you have deleted from your computer.
To permanently remove all items and reclaim disk space, click Empty Recycle Bin.
To move all items back to their original locations, click Restore All.
Select an item to view its description.
Name Original Location Date Deleted Type Size
28_12_97.lso C:\My Documents 07/11/98 12:29 LSO File 441KB
3+4+5.lso C:\My Documents 07/11/98 12:29 LSO File 113KB
border.mid C:\My Documents 07/11/98 12:33 MIDI Sequence 5KB
dance.mid C:\My Documents 07/11/98 12:33 MIDI Sequence 2KB
DarkPower.doc C:\My Documents 07/11/98 12:27 Microsoft Word Doc... 11KB
good ideas.mid C:\My Documents 07/11/98 12:33 MIDI Sequence 4KB
Level X 1102.txt C:\My Documents 07/11/98 12:29 Text Document 7KB
Level X.doc C:\My Documents 07/11/98 12:29 Microsoft Word Doc... 26KB
neti-neti.txt C:\My Documents 07/11/98 12:29 Text Document 1KB
part.mid C:\My Documents 07/11/98 12:33 MIDI Sequence 3KB
phyper.mid C:\My Documents 07/11/98 12:33 MIDI Sequence 3KB
Sacred Land S.lso C:\My Documents 07/11/98 12:29 LSO File 442KB
snale.mid C:\My Documents 07/11/98 12:33 MIDI Sequence 6KB
you.mid C:\My Documents 07/11/98 12:33 MIDI Sequence 9KB
14 object(s)
My Computer

Fig. 6.5: Contents of the Recycle Bin in the *Details* view (as Web page)

Choose *View/Details* to display under *Original Location* the original folder from which the file was deleted. The *Date Deleted* will also be shown in this view.

Tip!

If the *View/as Web Page* option is also selected, the window will be divided into two. The left window pane will display a Help text as well as options to empty the *Recycle Bin*, while the right pane will show the contents of the folder (view Figure 6.5).

Removing the Contents of the Recycle Bin

Windows 98 only moves objects that have been deleted to a specific folder, the *Recycle Bin*. In this way the *Recycle Bin* can help to prevent loss of data if a file has been deleted by mistake.

The question arises, of course, how do you get rid of data which you definitely do not need anymore? There are several possible methods. The safest way is by using the *Recycle Bin* folder. Double-click on the 🗑 *Recycle Bin* icon on the desktop to view the contents of the *Recycle Bin*.

File/Delete

Depending on the selected display, all 'deleted objects' will be displayed as *Large/Small Icons*, as *List*, or with all *Details*. Select those files in the *Recycle Bin* that you have deleted from the drive and which you now wish to delete permanently, and choose *File/Delete* or just press the ⌫Del key. If you confirm the message with *Yes*, all the objects will be deleted.

Fig. 6.6:   Deleting the full Recycle Bin, and the icon after this process

Empty Recycle Bin
To delete all the objects in the *Recycle Bin* in one go, choose the *Empty Recycle Bin* command from the *File* menu or the shortcut menu. If you confirm this message with *Yes*, all the objects will be permanently deleted.

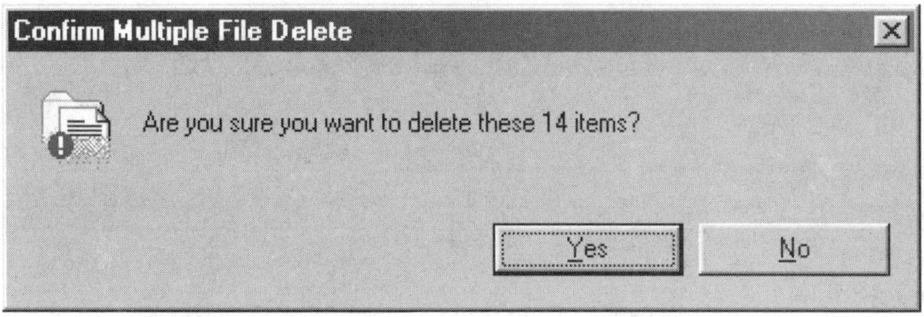

Confirm Multiple File Delete	✕
Are you sure you want to delete these 14 items?	
	Yes No

Fig. 6.7:   Confirmation message for deleting objects

Tip!
The *Empty Recycle Bin* command is also accessible via the shortcut menu of the *Recycle Bin* icon, without your having to open the folder. A faster way to delete objects is with *Drag-and-Drop*. Drag the objects to be deleted onto the *Recycle Bin*. By pressing the ⬆ key at the same time, they will be immediately and permanently deleted without further confirmation.

Recovering Deleted Objects with the Recycle Bin

The *Recycle Bin* prevents the loss of data when an object has been deleted by mistake. If you realize that you have deleted a file or a folder but still need its data, double-click on the *Recycle Bin* 🗑 icon on the desktop to view its contents.

Another method
Another method is to select the *Recycle Bin* 🗑 icon, and then press ↵. The *Recycle Bin* folder will be displayed.

Tip!   If you do not open folders in *My Computer* with a double click because the Web interface is enabled, open the *Recycle Bin* with a single mouse click. In this setting, objects can be selected just by pointing at them.

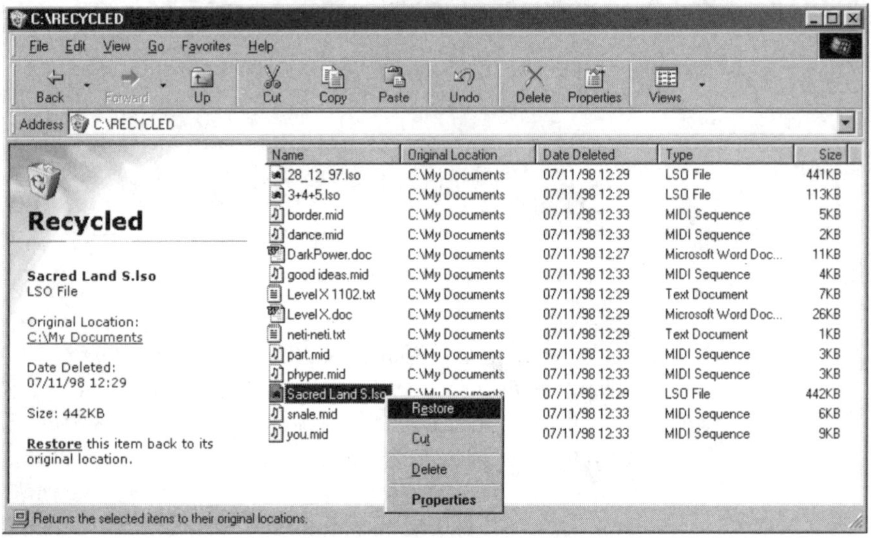

Fig. 6.8:   Restoring selected objects in the Recycle Bin

View/Details

Select the *Details* command from the *View* menu if the detailed contents of the *Recycle Bin* is not shown in the current view. In the *Original Location* column you can see from which folder the file was deleted. Additionally, the *Date Deleted*, the *Type*, and the *Size* of the file are shown.

File/Restore

Select the object which was deleted by mistake. To retrieve the object, select *File/Restore*. The *Restore* command is also available on the shortcut menu. The object will then be moved back into the source folder from which it had been deleted earlier.

Tip! Multiple selection in the *Recycle Bin* can be done with the [Ctrl] key. Point at the right edge of a column heading, for example, *Original Location*. By clicking and dragging the mouse cursor, the column width can be adjusted.

Changing the Properties of the Recycle Bin

Space on your hard disk

The deleted files in the *Recycle Bin* still take up space on your hard disk. If you want to use this space to store other data, or if you wish to remove objects that are no longer required without first putting them into the *Recycle Bin*, you can change the settings of the *Recycle Bin*.

Properties command

To do this, select the *Properties* command in the shortcut menu of the *Recycle Bin* icon on the desktop. The dialog box shown in Figure 6.9 will be displayed.

Hard disk space reserved

To increase or reduce the hard disk space reserved for the *Recycle Bin*, move the slider up or down from the 10% setting to a higher value (to reserve more hard disk space) or a lower value (to reserve less hard disk space).

Confirmation dialog box

If you have more than one hard disk installed, you can change this setting on different tab pages separately for each drive using the *Configure drives independently* option. To deactivate the confirmation message while deleting, clear the *Display delete confirmation dialog box* check box.

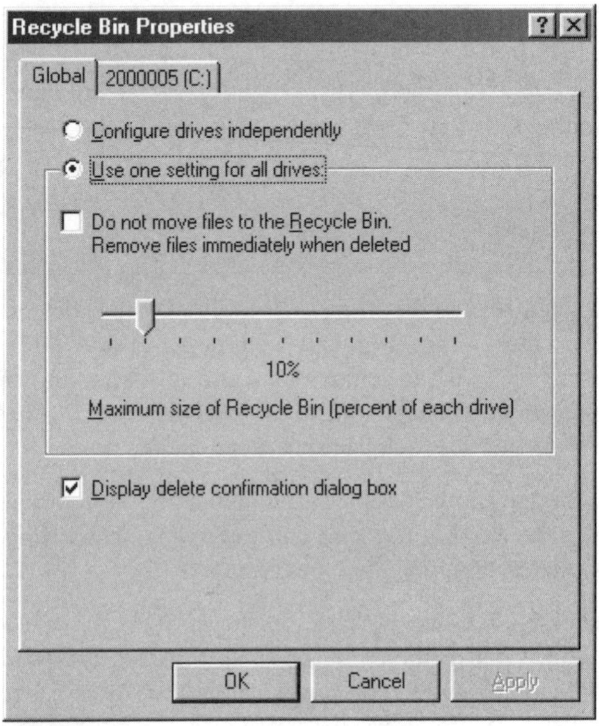

Recycle Bin Properties ▯?▯ ▯X▯

Global ▯ 2000005 (C:) ▯

  ○ Configure drives independently

  ⊙ Use one setting for all drives:

    ☐ Do not move files to the Recycle Bin.
      Remove files immediately when deleted

          10%

    Maximum size of Recycle Bin (percent of each drive)

  ☑ Display delete confirmation dialog box

    ▯ OK ▯   ▯ Cancel ▯   Apply

Fig. 6.9:   Setting properties of the Recycle Bin

Switch off the
Recycle Bin

If you want to switch off the *Recycle Bin* altogether, select the *Do not move files to the Recycle Bin. Remove files immediately when deleted* check box.

Be careful: In this setting, deleted objects will be destroyed immediately. Confirm your changes by clicking on the *OK* button.

7. Windows 98 Search

In your daily work with the computer, it happens quite often that a file which you require cannot be found in the place where you expected to find it. All over the world, customer support hot-lines are busy with emergency calls typically going like this: 'Just a moment ago I had a file and now it has disappeared. I do not believe this.' And yes, in most of these cases the file was not actually deleted but only misplaced.

Searching for files

Most people simply just do not pay attention to the destination folder they select when they save a file in the *Save as* dialog box. As a result, the file is saved in some random location and not where it was meant to go. So now, how can one retrieve lost files?

Finding Files and Folders

Windows 98 has a powerful search tool that can take care of such occurrences quite easily. In order to launch the finding tool, open the *Start* menu and click on *Find*. The overlapping menu then displays a number of options depending on the configuration of the computer:

- *Files and Folders* (finds files and folders on the the PC)

- *Computer* (finds computers on the network)

- *On the Internet* (launches Internet Explorer to search)

- *People* (finds addresses from the Outlook address book)

Find Files and Folders by Name

Find: All Files
dialog box

In order to find files and folders on your own PC, use the *Files and Folders* command. *Windows 98* will then bring up the *Find: All Files* dialog box.

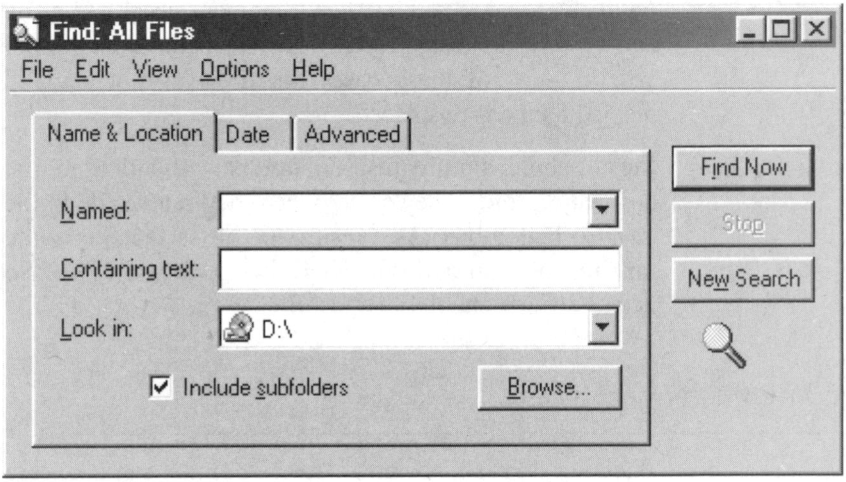

Fig. 7.1: *Find: All Files* dialog box

Named box

If you still remember the name of the file you are looking for, enter it in the *Named* text box. By default, the use of upper or lower case typing will not make any difference. However, if you do want it to exactly match your spelling, go to the *Options* menu and click on *Case Sensitive*.

Instead of using the file's full name, you can also limit it to a part of the name, in which case the result of the search might call up a greater number of files, since more of them might match the description.

Include subfolders

Verify whether the check box called *Include subfolders* is checked. If it is not checked, only the current level of the drive or folder selected in *Look in* will be searched.

Find Now button

In order to start the search, click on *Find Now. Windows 98* will then search all folders and subsequently expand the window to include the search results. If no files or folders were found, the results list will remain empty and the status bar will display the message *0 file(s) found*. If this is the case, you can repeat your search using a different search phrase.

Find Files and Folders by Location

Various volumes

The finding facility normally searches whatever drive is selected in the *Look in* box. If more than one drive is available you can open the list of this box in order to search a different drive. However, if you want to limit the search to a specific folder on one of the drives, click on *Browse*.

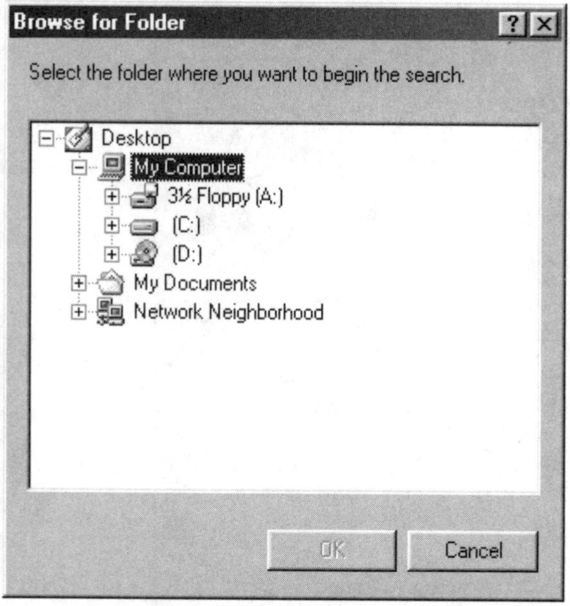

Browse for Folder [?] [X]

Select the folder where you want to begin the search.

```
⊟ 🧭 Desktop
   ⊟ 🖳 My Computer
      ⊞ 💾 3½ Floppy (A:)
      ⊞ 💿 (C:)
      ⊞ 💿 (D:)
   ⊞ 📂 My Documents
   ⊞ 🖧 Network Neighborhood
```

[OK] [Cancel]

Fig. 7.2: Search only specific drives or folders

Browse for Folder
dialog

In the *Browse for Folder* dialog box which will then open, you can select a drive and display its root directory by clicking on the plus sign ⊞ in front of the drive. In the same manner, go deeper into the levels of the folder hierachy until you reach the folder you are looking for. Select that folder and click the *OK* button.

Starting the search

In the *Look in* box, the new path will now be displayed. If you want existing subfolders to be included in the search, check the *Include subfolders* box. If you want to search the contents of only that particular folder, then uncheck this box. Verify if the search-phrase in the *Named* box is correct and start the search by clicking on *Find Now*.

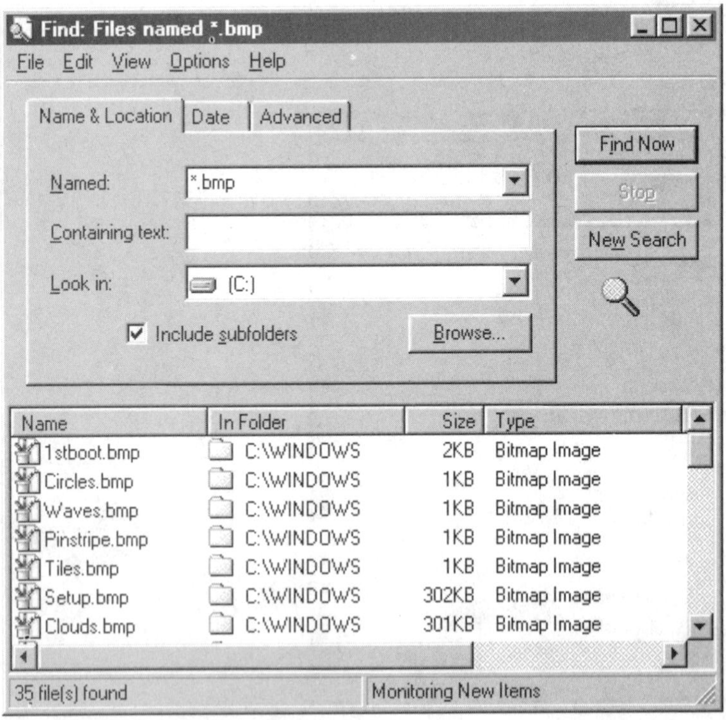

Fig. 7.3: The list of the search results is displayed at the bottom of the dialog box

Search results

Windows 98 will search the specified folders and expand the dialog window to display the list of results. If no files or folders are found, the result list remains empty and the status bar will display the message *0 file(s) found*. If this is the case, repeat your search using a different search phrase.

Stop button

Once the desired file appears in the list of results, you can stop the search at any given moment by clicking on *Stop*. By default, the list of results is displayed in the *Details* view mode. If that is not the case, you can use the *View* menu or, alternatively, the context menu to re-establish this view mode.

Further information

Next to the name of the file, the path of the file will be displayed listed under *In Folder*, and further information such as size and type of the file as well as its modification date is given. Documents from an installed application can be opened directly from this list of results.

Open a found file

In order to open a file, select the file and choose the *Open* command from the *File* menu or the context menu. A faster method, of course, is to double-click on the icon of the file. The associated application will then be launched and this document will be opened.

You can now save this document in the folder of your choice. The 'lost' copy of this file would remain in its former place in this case. However, with the commands on the *Edit* or context menu, the objects in the list of results can be copied or cut and then pasted into the target folder. For that, the target folder should be available as a window of *My Computer* or *Explorer*.

Tip!

Of course, it is also possible to move a file by dragging it straight from the list of results to the target folder in *My Computer* or *Explorer* and dropping it there.

Find Files by Type

You can also use other search criteria besides *Named* and *Look in*. Often objects of a very specific file type are being sought. Naturally, this would not apply if you were looking for just one of your letters and then found all of the text files on your hard disk. But it would make sense if you are planning to arrange all of the text files in a new order.

Find by file type

Even more useful is the search by file type on multimedia CD-ROMs or on the setup CDs of the *Office Suite* for *Windows 98*. These drives often contain hundreds of image, sound and video files and, on top of that, these might be located in hundreds of folders and subfolders. Here, it might be really handy to be able to list all of the existing image files, for example, in order to retrieve a specific picture from them.

Lost files

Sometimes, while saving a file, the user does not pay attention to the destination folder that he selects in the corresponding dialog box. Of course, the file is likely to be saved in some random location and not where it was meant to go. Here, too, it will be necessary to search for the lost file.

Advanced tab

In order to launch this find facility, open the *Start* menu and click on *Find*. In the submenu, click on the *Files and Folders* command. In the *Find: All Files* dialog box, select the *Advanced* tab.

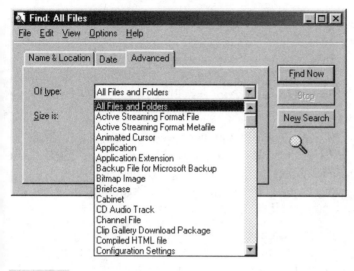

Fig. 7.4:   Limited search

Of type list

Open the *Of type* drop-down box and use the scroll bar to select the appropriate file type. The type descriptions in this list correspond to the information given in the *Type* column when you choose the *Details* view in an *Explorer* window. To select a type, click on an entry and it will appear in the *Of type* list box.

Starting the search

To execute the command, click on *Find Now*. *Windows 98* will then search all folders and subsequently expand the window by the search results. If no files of that type were found, the results list would remain empty and the status bar would be display the message *0 file(s) found*. If this is the case, repeat the search using a different drive or a different file type.

Name & Location tab

By default, *Windows 98* will scan all local hard disk drives. If you want to search for a file on a CD-ROM, switch back to the *Name & Location* tab after you have selected the file type. Now choose the target drive from the *Look in* list.

Verify whether the *Include subfolders* check box is checked. If it is not marked, only the root directory of the drive selected in *Look in* will be searched. To execute the search command click on *Find Now*.

Limited search

If you want to limit the search to a specific folder or drive, click on *Browse* and select the target folder. You can further limit the search to a file name by entering it to the *Named* box. *Windows 98* will regularly include each entry on all the tab pages.

New search

If you wish to define a new search, delete the items found so far by clicking on *New Search* and confirm with *OK*. Once the desired file appears in the list of results you can stop the search at any time by clicking on *Stop*.

Documents of a registered application can be opened directly from this list of results. In order to do so, select the file and choose the *Open* command from the *File* or context menu. Much faster, of course, is double-clicking on the icon of the file. The corresponding application will then be launched and the document will be opened.

Find Files and Folders by Date

Whenever you know the name and location or the file type of a file, you can use them as criteria for your search. If, however, you have forgotten the name of the file but you can recall the period of time in which it was created, you can use this information by limiting the search to that specific time period. In this way you could, for example, start your search for a letter which you might have as a print out in front of you.

**Find specific
versions**

Another version of this way of searching lies in the
option of using the version of a file as a criterion as long
as this is related to a specific date. In order to launch the
finding facility, open the *Start* menu and click on *Find*. In
the submenu, click on the *Files and Folders* command. In
the *Find: All Files* dialog box, select the *Date* tab page.

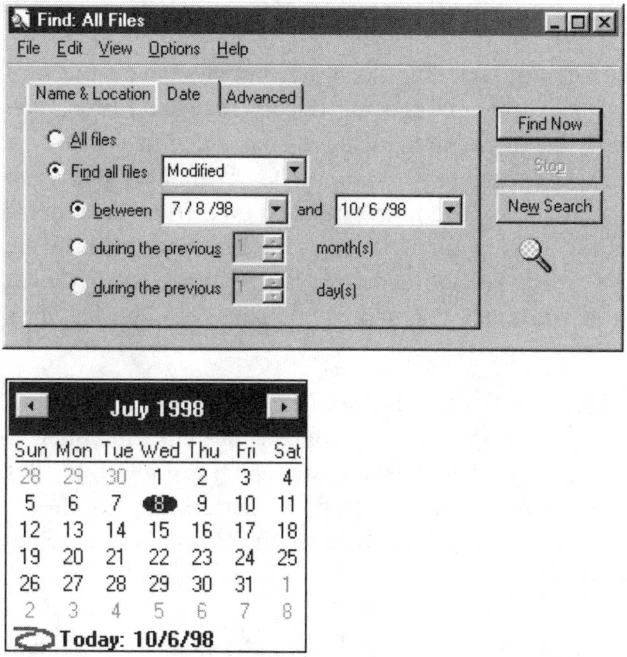

Fig. 7.5:   Limiting the search to a specific date

Define period

By default *Find: All Files* will search for files and folders
regardless of their date. If you want to limit the search to
a specific period of time, check the option *Find all files*
first. Now define the period. If you actually know the
exact date, like in the example of a letter given above,
click the *between* option and enter that date into the box
next to it using the format *DD/MM/YY*.

Now click on the text box behind and enter the terminating date there using the format *DD/MM/YY*. Alternatively, you could also click on the arrow button of the drop-down box. A mini calendar will pop up in which you can select the date (see Figure 7.5 above). Select a day by clicking on a number in the calendar. Month and year can be selected by using the  button to the left and the button to the right of the calendar.

During the previous ...

If you do not know the exact date but you have an idea of how many months ago the document was created, you can define the search using the *during the previous x month(s)* option. Enter the number of months you want the search to extend to into the text box. If the documents you are looking for have been modified or saved in the last few days, choose the *during the previous x day(s)* option and enter the number of days into the text box there.

Starting the search

To execute the search command, click on *Find Now*. *Windows 98* will search all folders and will subsequently expand the window to show the search results. If no files or folders are found in the given period, the results list will remain empty. In that case, repeat your search using a different set of dates.

> **Tip!** The results list might display a large number of system and program files which have to do with the loading of programs and which are therefore modified every time Windows and various other applications start. Thus these will also match your search criteria.

Searching a specific drive

By default, *Windows 98* will always search all document folders. If you want to search a specific drive, switch to the *Name & Location* tab page after entering the dates. Select the drive you want to search from the *Look in* list.

Verify whether the check box *Include subfolders* is selected. If it is not checked, only the root directory of the drive selected in *Look in* will be searched.

Starting the search

To start the search, click on the *Find Now* button. If you want to limit the search to a specific folder or drive, click on the *Browse* button and select the target folder. You can further limit the search to a specific file name by entering it to the *Named* box.

Entries on all
tab pages

The *Windows 98* search generally takes all the entries on tab pages into account. If you want to define a new search, clear the items in the present results list by clicking on *New Search* and confirm with *OK*. Once the desired file appears in the list of results, you can stop the search any time by clicking on *Stop*.

Searching Files and Folders by Size

Name, location and file type are not the only search criteria available when looking for a file. Sometimes you could be looking for objects of a particular size, and in this case you will want to narrow down the search results even further by including the size.

At least
At most

However, do not expect the described search technique to perform miracles since it merely allows you to define the file size using the boundaries *At least* and *At most* given in kilobytes (KB). Entering an exact file size, like 2345 KB, for example, is not possible.

File size

Naturally, in order to launch a search for files using minimum and maximum sizes, you should at least roughly know their actual size. Then, in order to launch the find facility open the *Start* menu and click on *Find*. In the submenu click on the *Files and Folders* command. In the *Find: All Files* dialog box select the *Advanced* tab page.

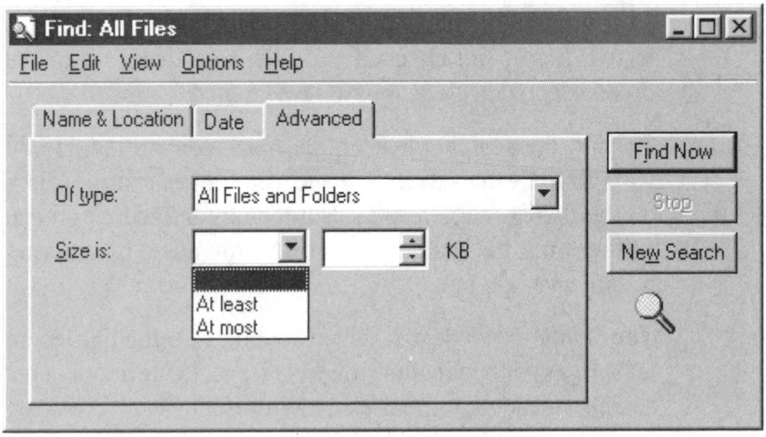

Fig. 7.6: Limiting searches to files of a specific size

Entering the file
size

Now open the *Size is* drop-down list and select one of the given search criteria which can be either *At least* or *At most*. Subsequently click in the spin box to the right of it and enter the file size in kilobytes. You can also make use of the spinners to alter the value.

Starting the search

To execute the search command, click on *Find Now*. *Windows 98* will then search all folders and, subsequently, expand the window to display the search results. If no files or folders of the given minimum and maximum size are found, the results list will remain empty. In this case repeat your search with a different set of sizes. The maximum value you can enter in the *At most* box is 99,999 KB, which is approximately equal to 98 MB.

By default, *Windows 98* will always search all the document folders. If you want to search a specific drive, switch to the *Name & Location* tab page after entering the sizes. Select the drive you want to search from the *Look in* list. Verify whether the check box *Include subfolders* is selected. If it is not checked, only the root directory of the drive selected in *Look in* will be searched. In order to start a search, click on the *Find now* button.

Limiting the search

If you want to limit the search to a specific folder or drive click on the *Browse* button and select the target folder. You can further limit the search to a file name by entering it in the *Named* box. *Windows 98* almost always uses information from the entries on all the tab pages. If you want to define a new search, delete the items from the current results list by clicking on *New Search* and confirm with *OK*.

Stop button

Once the desired file appears in the list of results you can stop the search at any time by clicking on *Stop*. You can also narrow down the search results for certain file types by using the file size as an additional search criterion.

Tip!

Documents of an installed application (such as all programs in the *Microsoft Office Suite*) can be opened directly from this list of results. In order to do so, select the file and choose the *Open* command from the *File* or context menu. A much faster method, of course, is to double-click the icon of the file. The corresponding application will then be launched and will open this document.

Searching for Files and Folders Using their Text Contents

Whenever the name and location of a file or the file type is known, you can use this information as the search criteria to start your search. If, however, you cannot even remember the name of an important document, but you are aware of the text of a passage which occurs within this document, you have the option of searching all documents using their textual content as a search criterion. Using this method, it would be possible, for example, to search for a letter when you clearly remember that it had the phrase 'contract negotiations' in it.

Name & Location tab

In order to launch the *Find* facility, open the *Start* menu and click on *Find*. In the the submenu, click on the *Files and Folders* command. In the *Find: All Files* dialog box select the *Name & Location* tab page.

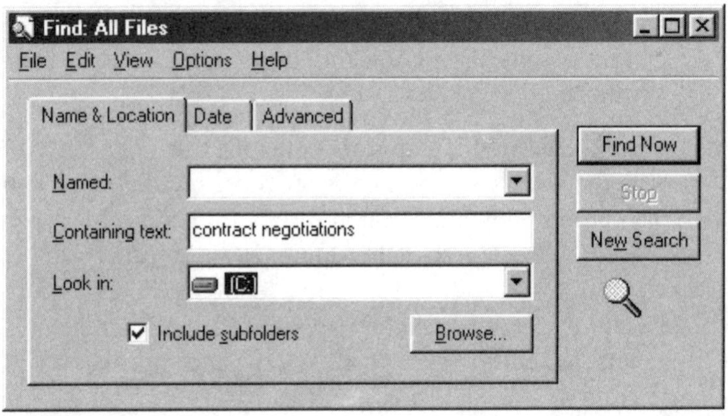

Fig. 7.7:   Search by containing text

Containing text box

Enter the passage of the text you want to use into the *Containing text* box. Naturally, only documents that actually contain text will be available when using this search option. A bitmap file which has text in the form of a headline in it will not be identified in this search since it is not classified as a text document.

Starting the search

To execute the search command click on *Find Now*. *Windows 98* will then search all files and folders and, subsequently, expand the window to show the search results. If no files or folders are found that contain the text passage you entered, the results list will remain empty. The status bar will display the message *0 file(s) found*. In this case, try searching again using a different text passage in the *Containing text* box.

Tip! The results list might well display many files belonging to the operating system and other applications which contain the specified text passage in addition to your files, since all existing files on this computer will have been scanned. This process might take quite some time, by the way. In such cases, limit your search to specific folders on the hard disk (*Name & Location* tab page, *Find Now* button).

Searching a
specific drive

If you want to search a different drive, switch to the *Name & Location* tab page and select the desired drive from the *Look in* list. Verify whether the *Include subfolders* check box is selected. If it is not checked, only the root directory of the drive selected in *Look in* will be searched. In order to start the search, click on the *Find now* button.

Tip! Generally, *Windows 98* always uses information from the entries on all the tab pages. If you want to define a new search, clear the items in the present results list by clicking on *New Search* and confirm with *OK*. Once the desired file appears in the list of results, you can stop the search at any time by clicking on *Stop*.

Documents belonging to an installed application (such as all programs in the *Microsoft Office Suite*) can be opened directly from the list of results. In order to do so, select the file and choose the *Open* command from the *File* menu or context menu.

A much faster method, of course, is to double-click on the icon of the file. The corresponding application will then be launched and will open this document.

Searching for Computers on the Network

If your computer is integrated into a local area network, you can also search for other computers connected to that network. To do so, click on the *Start* menu and move to the *Find* option. In the submenu that pops up, choose *Computer*. Now enter the name or part of the name of the computer in the *Find: Computer* dialog box and click on *Find Now*.

Fig.: 7.8:   Searching computers on the network

Windows 98 will then search the entire network and subsequently expand the window to include the search results. If no computer was found with the name given, the result list will remain empty. The status bar will then display the message *0 computer(s) found*. In this case, try searching using a different computer name as the search criterion.

8. Control Panel

In this chapter, we will deal with the various *Control Panel* elements of *Windows 98* and explain them in detail. With the help of this folder you will be able to adjust all the components of your computer to suit your requirements, as well as to add new hardware components and install new programs. You will learn how to adjust your mouse, the keyboard or your joystick and how to select new fonts as well as how to change the way in which Windows is displayed.

Furthermore, you will get to know how to install a driver for a new graphic card or printer, and how to make use of the energy-saving devices in your computer. To start with, you have to open the Windows *Control Panel* folder. You can do this by clicking on the *Start* menu and moving to *Settings*. In the overlapping menu select *Control Panel*. Otherwise, you can access the *Control Panel* folder through *My Computer* by double-clicking its icon there.

Double click

In the *Control Panel* folder, double-click the respective icon. If you have enabled the Web interface, then just move the mouse pointer over the object and click the mouse button once.

Adjusting the Properties of the Mouse

Without an appropriate pointing device to select objects, you ca not really use the *Windows 98* operating system. But even the smartest computer mouse still needs to be adjusted to your personal preferences.

Trackball

In this section, as well as in the following ones, we always refer to the use of a classic mouse. If you use a different pointing device such as a trackball, all the procedures described will also be applicable since these devices are similar.

Double click

Especially in the beginning, most users have a problem with the double-click speed of the mouse. The term *double-click* stands for quickly pressing the left mouse button twice. This action is used to open folders and launch programs.

Changing the Double-Click Speed of the Mouse

If, in the beginning, you really cannot manage to double-click successfully, it is usually due to the fact that you do not press the mouse button fast enough. The speed at which a double-click is performed is called the double-click speed, and it can be adjusted.

Fig. 8.1:   The Control Panel

Mouse properties

To do this, click on the *Start* menu and move to *Settings*. In the submenu select *Control Panel*. In the *Control Panel* folder, open the *Mouse* item (Figure 8.1, *Control Panel*). The *Mouse Properties* dialog box will appear.

Drag the slider in the *Double-click speed* group box in the desired direction with the left mouse button held down (for beginners, towards *Slow* is better).

Testing the settings

In order to try out the new settings, double-click into the *Test area* on the right side. If the double-click speed is good enough, a jack-in-the-box will jump out. If this does not happen, change the settings until the jack-in-the-box appears in the *Test area*. Close this dialog box.

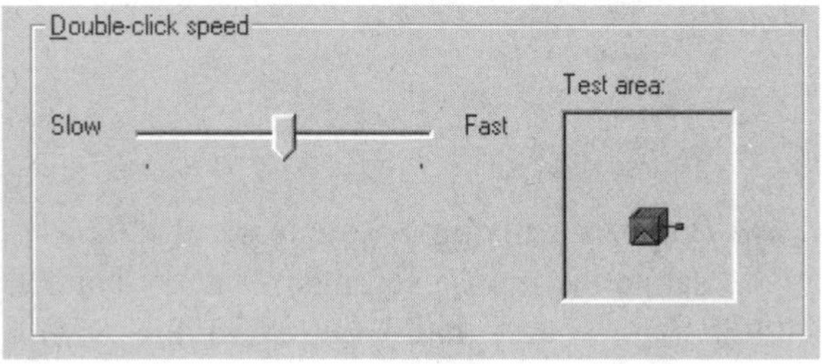

Fig. 8.2:   Using the Slider to change the double-click speed

Tip!

If you intend to change more settings for the mouse on other tab pages, do not click on *OK* but use the *Apply* button instead. The changes will then be saved and the dialog box will remain open.

Button Configuration

Since the mouse is the most important input device in *Windows 98*, you will want to make sure that you feel as comfortable as possible when you are using it. Experience has shown that left-handed people in particular encounter problems with the mouse. This is, of course, not their fault but is due to the fact that *Windows 98* is configured for right-handed people by default.

Left-hand
operation

But you've probably already guessed that this does not have to stay that way. It is possible to change it over to left-hand operation.

Start

Settings

To do so, click on the *Start* menu and move to *Settings*. In the submenu, select *Control Panel*. In the *Control Panel* folder, open the *Mouse* item.

Mouse

Fig. 8.3: Changing the properties of the mouse

Button
configuration

In the *Mouse Properties* dialog box, activate the *Buttons* tab page. To change the mouse settings for a left-handed user, click the *Left-handed* radio button in the *Button configuration* option group box.

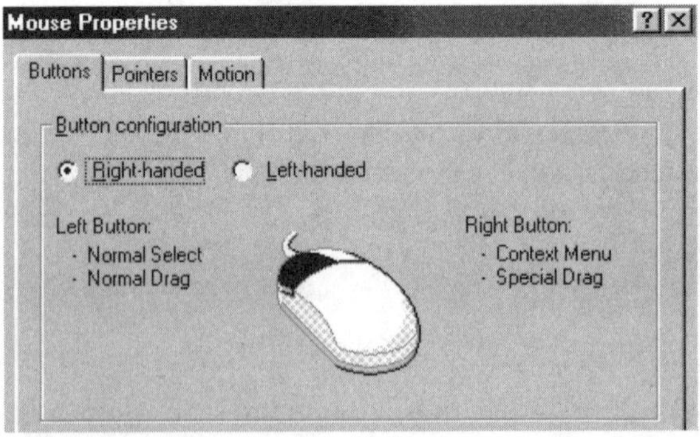

Mouse Properties	? X

Buttons | Pointers | Motion

Button configuration

⊙ Right-handed ⊙ Left-handed

Left Button:
· Normal Select
· Normal Drag

Right Button:
· Context Menu
· Special Drag

Fig. 8.4: Setting the button configuration to left-handed

Be careful with this, since the change will take effect immediately after you close the dialog box by clicking *OK* or as soon as you click the *Apply* button.

Multi-button mouse

A newer mouse might have three or more buttons and a wheel. They come shipped with appropriate software which will allows you to adjust the mouse or program the functions of those buttons. Some of these applications will install an item in the *Control Panel* folder.

Setting the Mouse Trail for Laptop Computers

On laptop computers with a passive matrix Liquid Crystal Display (LCD screen, Dual Scan, etc.) it is often difficult to see the mouse pointer and to trace it when it moves across the screen too quickly.

Laptop screens

This is not because you eyes are bad, but due to the inertia that is inherent in the passive LCD screens. However, *Windows 98* offers a solution for this problem. If you have problems tracing the mouse pointer on your screen, do the following: click on the *Start* menu and move to *Settings*. In the submenu select *Control Panel*. In the *Control Panel* folder open the *Mouse* item. Then, in the *Mouse Properties* dialog box activate the *Motion* tab page.

Pointer trails

In the area designated for *Pointer trail* settings, click the *Show pointer trails* check box and then start moving the mouse pointer. It will now be followed by a trail that looks a bit like a comet's tail and which will make it easily noticeable on the screen.

Show pointer trails

If the mouse trail appears too long or its inertia is too high, drag the slider under the *Show pointer trails* in the desired direction with the left mouse button held down. Move the mouse again to test the new setting. Then close the dialog box by clicking the *OK* button.

Fig. 8.5: The slider changes the length of the trail

Tip!

If you intend to change other settings for the mouse, do not click on *OK* but use the *Apply* button instead. The changes will then be saved but the dialog remains open.

Pointer speed

In the area set aside for the pointer speed, you can define the ratio between the mouse movement on the mouse pad and the movement of the mouse pointer on the screen. Setting it towards *Slow* will mean that you will have to move the mouse over a wider area in order to get the mouse pointer to move on the screen. Setting it to fast will mean that the pointer will respond with larger steps to even the smallest movements of the mouse. In this case, precise positioning of the cursor will also be more difficult.

Appearence of the Mouse Pointer

Windows 98 will translate each movement of the mouse into a change in the cursor position. Pointing to specific elements on the screen will automatically change the appearance of the mouse pointer. If you point to the edge of a window frame, for example, the pointer turns into a double-headed arrow which points in opposite directions. However, if you point to one of the corners of a window, it will turn into a diagonally positioned double-headed arrow.

Animated cursor

You can define whether the appearance of the mouse cursor should remain plain or acquire a fancy three-dimensional style, and even whether it should become an animated cursor when certain actions are being performed. To change the appearance of the mouse pointer, click on the *Start* menu and move to *Settings*. In the submenu select *Control Panel* and open the *Mouse* item in that folder. The *Mouse Properties* window will appear.

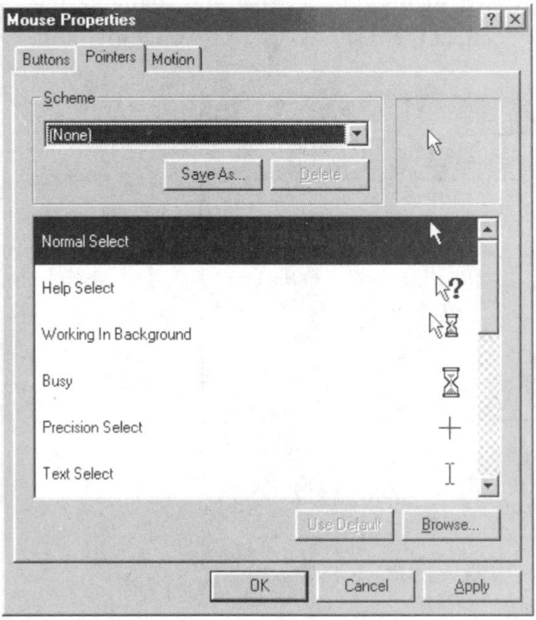

Fig. 8.6:   List of possible mouse pointer appearences

Pointers

Now activate the *Pointers* tab page. Open the *Scheme* drop-down list by clicking on the drop-down button and select an item from this list. In the large list box below it, all the available pointers will be displayed along with their respective context. Scan the whole list by using the scroll bar in order to view all possible options.

Pointer scheme

Once a pointer scheme has been selected it will affect the appearance of all mouse pointers in *Windows 98*. If this change is what you want, close the dialog box by clicking on the *OK* button. If you want to alter only a specific mouse pointer, first select the mouse scheme from the respective list.

Browse

Then select the mouse pointer you want to change from the list box below and click on *Browse*. The *Browse* dialog box will display all the cursors that are available under *Windows 98*. Select the desired cursor by clicking on it.

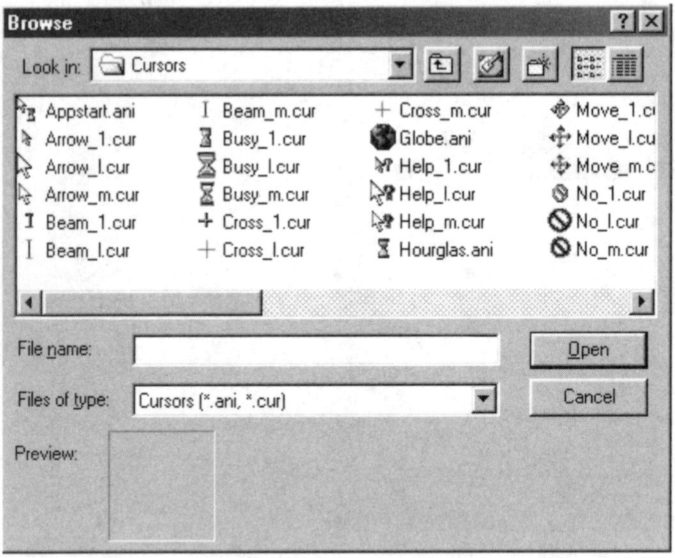

Fig. 8.7:   Each mouse pointer can be changed individually

Confirming your choice by clicking *Open* will add this cursor to the list in the *Mouse Pointers* window. Repeat this procedure for each cursor you want to change. When you are done, close the dialog box by clicking *OK*.

Tip!
Static Windows mouse pointers use the *CUR* file extension and are saved in the *C:\Windows\Cursors* folder. Animated mouse pointers are particularly interesting and can easily be identified by their *ANI* extension. If you select an animated cursor in the *Browse* dialog box you will be presented with an animated preview of it.

Tip!
Individual mouse pointer appearances will often occur only within *Windows 98*. Mouse pointers that you select will not necessarily be used by all programs. Applications of the Microsoft Office Suite, for example, will use their own specific mouse pointers.

Setting the Keyboard Properties

The keyboard is the most important input device for text entry. For this reason perfect adjustment to your personal requirements is most essential in this area. Unfortunately, most users hardly pay any attention to this option and spend their whole lives using the default settings of *Windows 98*.

Keyboard

To configure the keyboard settings you need to access the *Windows 98 Control Panel*. To do so, click on the *Start* menu and move to *Settings*. In the submenu select *Control Panel*, and in that folder open the *Keyboard* item. The *Keyboard Properties* window will appear.

Setting the Repeat Delay of the Keyboard

Speed tab

On the *Speed* tab page you can adjust the basic settings to meet your personal requirements. Dragging the slider, which is located below *Repeat delay* from *Long* to *Short*, will define the time span that elapses from the moment you hold down a key until the character starts to repeat itself.

Setting the Repeat Rate

Repeat rate

Dragging the slider positioned below *Repeat rate* from *Slow* to *Fast* will define the speed at which the character repeats itself whenever you keep held down a key.

Testing

To try out your new settings, click into the text field below and hold down any key. To close this window, confirm by clicking *OK*.

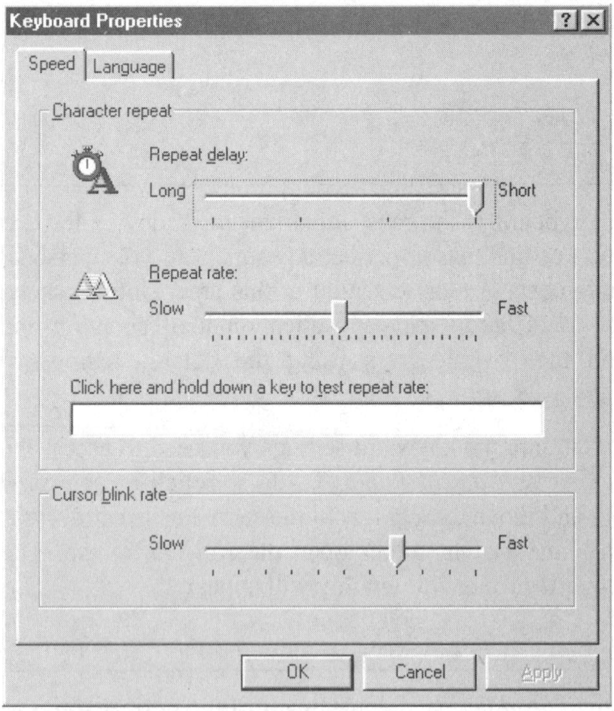

Fig. 8.8: Defining repeat delay and repeat rate

Setting the Cursor Blink Rate

To configure the keyboard settings, you need to access the *Windows 98 Control Panel*. To do so, click on the *Start* menu and move to *Settings*. In the submenu select *Control Panel* and once you are in that folder, double-click on the *Keyboard* item. The *Keyboard Properties* window will appear.

Speed tab

On the *Speed* tab page you can adjust the basic settings to your own requirements. Dragging the slider which is positioned below *Cursor blink rate* defines the speed at which the text cursor will blink. The current setting of this will be indicated by a blinking cursor which is positioned to the left of the slider.

Cursor within
a text

Changing the settings of the cursor blink rate will make it easier to detect the cursor within a text. Confirm your new settings by clicking *OK*.

Setting the Keyboard to a Different Language

The keyboard is the most important input device of the computer when it comes to entering text. But almost every country in the world has its own keyboard layout. This may be due in part to historical reasons but mainly it is due to the various characters which are used in those different languages.

The Danish language, for example, has some very specific characters which are not used anywhere else. Eastern European countries even have entirely different fonts and a Turkish keyboard has nothing in common with an English one except for the number of keys.

Keyboard
language

Windows 98 defines a keyboard layout as a *Language*. Configure the keyboard language you need to access the *Windows 98 Control Panel*. To do this, click on the *Start* button and move to *Settings*. In the submenu select *Control Panel*. In the *Control Panel* folder double-click the *Keyboard* item. The *Keyboard Properties* window will appear.

Language tab

The *Language* tab page allows you to adjust the language to your requirements whenever you happen to need a keyboard layout of a language other than English on your English keyboard. The language that is currently being used will be displayed in the *Language* list. If you are intending to install a new keyboard layout, click on *Add*. Then select the layout you need from *Language* list and close the *Add Language* dialog box by clicking *OK*.

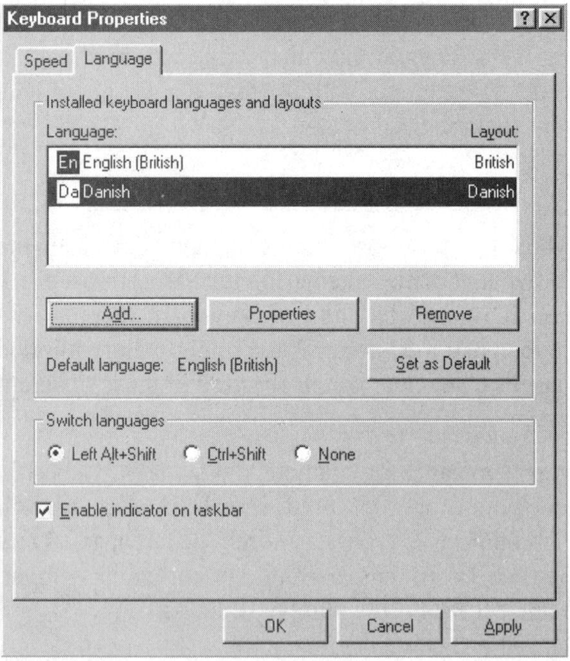

Fig. 8.9:   Setting the language of the keyboard

The new language will now appear in the *Language* list. Under *Switch languages*, you can select a keyboard shortcut which will allow you to switch between the different languages by using a key combination. Make sure the *Enable indicator on taskbar* option is checked. Then confirm by clicking *OK*.

Tip! Whenever you need the newly added keyboard layout press the key combination on the keyboard or click on the language indicator in the taskbar and select the language from the popup menu.

Managing System Fonts

Windows 98 uses two different types of system fonts. These are: 1. *Bitmap* fonts and 2. *TrueType* fonts. The latter offers a wider range of facilities.

Bitmap fonts

Bitmap fonts are basically raster fonts which come as separate files for each font size and contain detailed descriptions for each character in them. Like *pixel* images, Bitmap fonts assemble each character from a number of individual dots. They can never be used to describe a tilted or curved line perfectly, and thus, they will appear jagged when printed out. They are therefore only used for on-screen display.

TrueType fonts

TrueType fonts, however, are vector fonts which define the shape of each character through mathematical formulas that are contained in the font file. Therefore, Windows can freely scale them to any size you want using a single font file.

WYSIWYG
principle

The biggest advantage of *TrueType* fonts though is their ability to display the font on-screen in exactly the same way that it will appear when it is printed (WYSIWYG principle). Furthermore, the quality of *TrueType* fonts is far superior to that of *Bitmap* fonts - and this is true regardless of the font size.

Viewing the Installed *TrueType* Fonts

Fonts folder

In order to view all the fonts that are available on your computer open the *Control Panel* folder. Double-click the *Fonts* icon which contains all fonts that are installed on the system. The different fonts appear as icons. Freely scalable *TrueType* fonts are represented by the ⊺⊺ icon while *Bitmap* fonts are easily recognizable by the A icon.

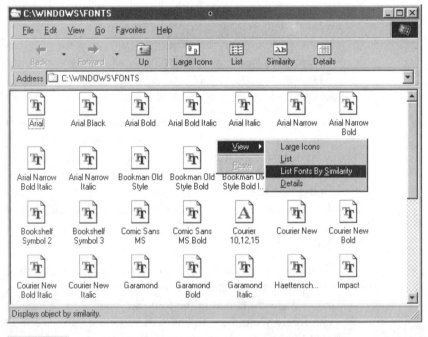

Fig. 8.10: Viewing the available Windows fonts

You can change the appearance of the *Fonts* folder by selecting a different option from the *View* menu. The same options are available through the shortcut menu by clicking the right mouse button anywhere in the *Fonts* folder window. In Figure 8.10 the *Fonts* folder is presented in the *Large Icons* view. By right-clicking one of the font icons you can obtain detailed information regarding its properties such as file size and date created.

List Fonts By
Similarity

The *List Fonts By Similarity* option will be described later on in this chapter. Very often, the *List View* option will be the most useful one.

All the listed fonts in the *Fonts* folder are available in the applications of the Microsoft Office Suite as well as in any other application that you are running.

List Installed Fonts by Similarity

To obtain a list of fonts that are installed on your computer you have to open the *Control Panel* folder and double-click the *Fonts* icon.

The *Fonts* folder contains all of the fonts that are installed on the system. The different fonts appear as specific icons. Freely scalable *TrueType* Fonts look like this ⊤ while *Bitmap* fonts are easily recognizable by this icon: A.

List Fonts By
Similarity

You can change the view of the *Fonts* folder to *List Fonts By Similarity* either through the commands on the *View* menu or through those of the shortcut menu. This can also be done by clicking on the *Similarity* button ⊞ on the *Standard Button* toolbar.

All of the fonts that are installed on the system will then be listed and compared to the font that is selected in the *List fonts by similarity to* drop-down list.

To change the font you want to be compared to all of the other fonts, click on the drop-down button of the *List fonts by similarity to* box and select a different font.

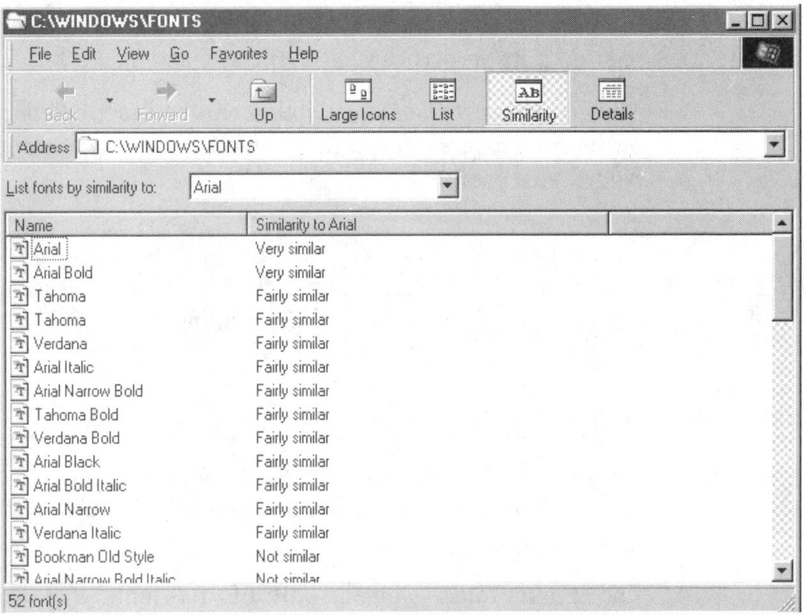

C:\WINDOWS\FONTS

File Edit View Go Favorites Help

Back Forward Up Large Icons List Similarity Details

Address C:\WINDOWS\FONTS

List fonts by similarity to: Arial

Name	Similarity to Arial
Arial	Very similar
Arial Bold	Very similar
Tahoma	Fairly similar
Tahoma	Fairly similar
Verdana	Fairly similar
Arial Italic	Fairly similar
Arial Narrow Bold	Fairly similar
Tahoma Bold	Fairly similar
Verdana Bold	Fairly similar
Arial Black	Fairly similar
Arial Bold Italic	Fairly similar
Arial Narrow	Fairly similar
Verdana Italic	Fairly similar
Bookman Old Style	Not similar
Arial Narrow Bold Italic	Not similar

52 font(s)

Fig. 8.11:   Listing fonts by similarity

Assessment

Apart from the font names in this list, an assessment will be given as to how similar the font is, such as *Very similar*, *Fairly similar* or *Not similar*.

Take the *Arial* font, for example, which has no serifs and compare it to the *Times New Roman* font which does have serifs. You will find the assessment given as *Not similar*. This option enables even users who have no typographical knowledge to gain at least a rough comparison between fonts, which is particularly useful when many fonts have been installed.

Tip!   All the listed fonts in the *Fonts* folder will be available in the applications of the *Microsoft Office Suite* as well as in any other application that you are running.

Printing the Type Faces of Installed Fonts

Many Windows applications come with a large number of *TrueType* fonts which are automatically installed during the setup process.

The CorelDRAW graphics suite, for example, ships with as many as 1,000 *TrueType* fonts. The *Microsoft Office Suite* also contains certain *TrueType* fonts which are installed automatically.

Hundreds of fonts

In this manner hundreds of fonts can accumulate on your computer after some time. Being able to remember what each of these fonts looks like would, even for professionals, be very difficult.

For this reason, recent graphics applications provide the user with a font menu which displays each font in its own type face.

No preview

Applications that are integrated in *Windows 98* do not provide such luxury and neither do the applications of the *Microsoft Office Suite* (the only exception to this is the *Style* list box in *Microsoft Word*). However, *Windows 98* does give you an option to view all the fonts that are installed on your computer and print them out if desired.

Fonts folder

To do so open the *Control Panel* folder through the *Start* menu or *My Computer*. Then double-click the *Fonts* icon. You are presented with a window of all the fonts installed on your system. If you want to, you can change the view of this window to *Large icons*, for example, using the *View* menu.

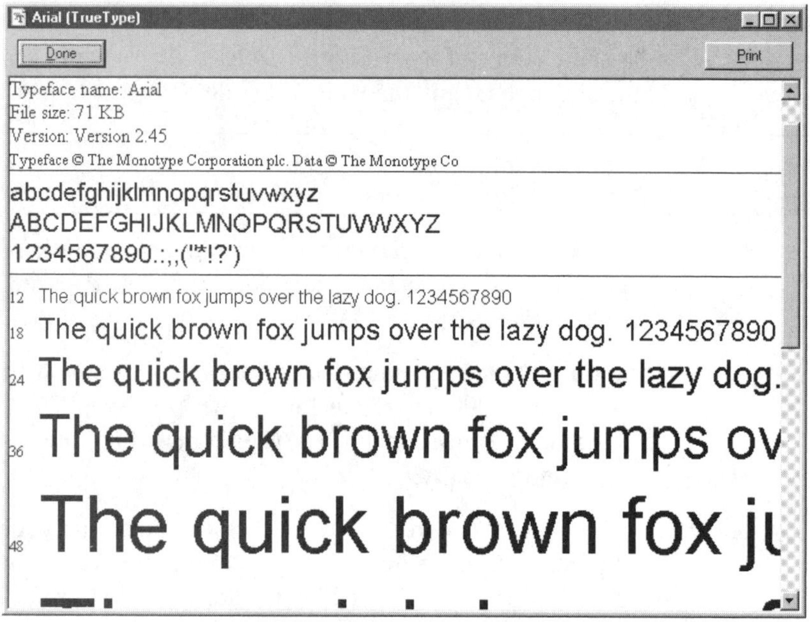

Fig. 8.12:   Displaying type faces on the screen or printing them out

Type face

The fastest and easiest way to display the type face of an unknown font is to double-click on the font icon or on the font name. Another way of doing the same thing would be to select the font and then choose the *Open* command from the *File* menu or else from the shortcut menu.

A window opens displaying a sample text for this type face: *'The quick brown fox jumps over the lazy dog'*. If you wish you can expand this window or make use of the scroll bar in order to view all of its contents.

Printing a sample text

While the [Done] button will close the window, the [Print] button gives you the option to print the sample text in the type face. Generally, the *Print* command is available in all windows through the *File* menu or alternatively through the shortcut menu.

Installing New TrueType Fonts

We have recommended the use of *TrueType* fonts earlier in this chapter. The reason for that is that *TrueType* fonts are freely scalable vector fonts which define the shape of each character through mathematical formulas stored in the font file. This saves storage space on the hard disk and allows you to use the fonts in any size without compromising the quality.

New TrueType fonts

Many applications these days are shipped with their own *TrueType* fonts which are automatically installed during the setup procedure.

The CorelDRAW graphics suite, for example, ships with as many as 1,000 *TrueType* fonts. Even the *Microsoft Office* CD ROM contains some *TrueType* fonts which are installed automatically.

If you intend to add more *TrueType* fonts to your system it is not enough to merely copy the font files onto your hard disk.

Installing new fonts

In order for *Windows 98* and all other applications to be able to use the installed fonts, you will have to open the *Control Panel* folder through the *Start* menu and *Settings* or through *My Computer*. Then open the *Fonts* folder by double-clicking its icon.

Add fonts

Now click on the *File* menu and select the *Install New Font* command. In the *Add Fonts* dialog box, use the *Folders* and *Drives* boxes to navigate to the target drive and folder that contains the font file which you want to install.

Windows 98 will then scan all font files in the target folder and add them to the *List of fonts*.

275

Add Fonts ☒

List of fonts:

Arial Alternative Regular (TrueType)	OK
Arial Alternative Symbol (TrueType)	Cancel
	Select All
	Help

Folders:
d:\...\reskit\desktop\minitel

Drives:

☐ d:\
  ☐ tools
  ☐ reskit
  ☐ desktop
  📂 minitel

d: Windows 98 ▼   Network...

☑ Copy fonts to Fonts folder

Fig. 8.13:   Adding new fonts to Windows 98

Select the font file(s) that you want to install from this list (for multiple selection, use the ⬚ or Ctrl key). In order to select all of the font files shown in the *List of fonts* simply click the *Select All* button. To proceed with the installation of the new fonts click *OK*. Then have a look at the *Fonts* folder to verify the result.

Tip!   Make sure that the *Copy fonts to Fonts folder* check box is selected to ensure that the new fonts are copied to *C:\Windows\Fonts*.

Removing TrueType Fonts You Do Not Want

Over time hundreds of fonts can accumulate on your computer. But each font file occupies space on your hard disk and has to be loaded into the memory every time *Windows 98* starts.

If you are in the habit of using only certain fonts for your work, you can always remove the fonts you do not need from your hard disk.

To remove superfluous fonts from your system, it is not advisable to simply delete the corresponding font files using the *Windows Explorer* or the *My Computer* system folder. There are two main reasons for this.

Firstly, it is almost impossible in some cases to conclude from a file name such as *TT1024M_.TTF* that the actual font name is *Futura MD BT*. Secondly, the link between the file and the *Fonts* folder also needs to be eliminated.

Fonts folder

To ensure that *Windows 98* and all other applications do not show the removed fonts anymore, you have to open the *Control Panel* folder through the *Settings* item on the *Start* menu or through *My Computer*. Then open the *Fonts* folder by double-clicking its icon.

List view

If a large number of fonts have been installed it would be advisable to change the view of the window to *List*. Select the font(s) you want to remove (for multiple selection use the ⟨ ⟩ or ⟨Ctrl⟩ key, or a selection frame holding the mouse button down while dragging).

Removing fonts

To remove the selected fonts choose the *Delete* command from either the *File* menu or the shortcut menu.

Confirming the warning message with *Yes* will cause all the selected fonts to be moved to the *Recycle Bin*.

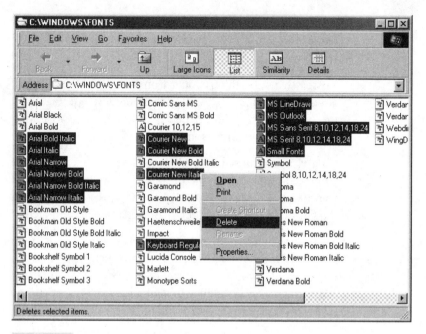

Removing TrueType fonts from the Fonts folder

Tip!

To actually delete all the fonts that have been removed from the *Fonts* folder and make the space on the hard disk available again, empty the *Recycle Bin*. For more information regarding this see Chapter 6.

Applications Displaying Only TrueType Fonts

As mentioned previously, *Windows 98* uses two different kinds of system fonts, which are: 1. *Bitmap* fonts and 2. *TrueType* fonts. The latter offers a wider range of facilities.

TrueType fonts are vector fonts which define the shape of each character through mathematical formulas that are

Freely scalable

contained in the font file. Therefore Windows can freely scale them to any size required using only one font file.

Superior quality

The biggest advantage of *TrueType* fonts, though, is their ability to display the font on the screen in exactly the same way that it will look when it's printed (WYSIWYG principle). Furthermore, the quality of *TrueType* fonts is far superior to that of *Bitmap* fonts, regardless of the font size.

Pixel images

Bitmap fonts, however, are basically raster fonts which come as separate files for each font size, containing detailed descriptions for each character in them. Like *pixel* images, *Bitmap* fonts assemble each character from a large number of individual dots which can never form a perfectly tilted or curved line. Thus, they appear as jagged lines when printed out. They are therefore only used for on-screen display.

Using only
TrueType fonts

We recommend that you use *TrueType* fonts, which are of superior quality and far greater adaptability. In order to avoid potential mistakes in future, it is advisable to limit the display of fonts in the *Font* drop-down list box in any of your applications, such as those of the *Microsoft Office Suite*, to *TrueType* fonts only. In order to do this you need to open the *Control Panel* folder.

TrueType
tab page

Open the *Control Panel* folder by navigating through the *Start* menu to *Settings*. Then open the *Fonts* folder window. The *Fonts* folder contains all of the fonts installed on the computer. Open the *View* menu and select the *Folder Options* command. Then activate the *TrueType* tab page.

Exclusivly
TrueType fonts

Check the *Show only TrueType fonts in the programs on my computer* check box and confirm with *OK*. From now on Windows will not list the bitmap fonts in any of the Windows applications. Instead, the list of fonts in the application will contain only *TrueType* fonts.

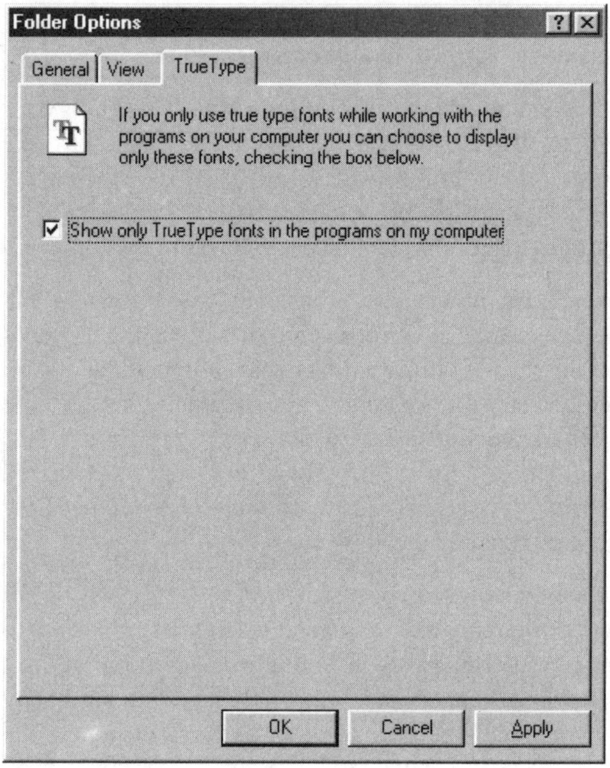

Folder Options [?] [X]

General | View | TrueType |

If you only use true type fonts while working with the programs on your computer you can choose to display only these fonts, checking the box below.

[✓] Show only TrueType fonts in the programs on my computer

[OK] [Cancel] [Apply]

Fig. 8.15: Show only TrueType fonts in the programs on my computer

Tip! The new settings take effect only after you have restarted the computer. Confirm the corresponding dialog box with *Yes*.

Configuring the Display Settings

You might have noticed that the windows on some computers are more colorful and fancy than on others.

Only some users take advantage of the options of the *Control Panel* settings to adjust the general appearance of the desktop and Windows to suit their personal taste.

Change Settings for Screen Elements

To change the general appearance of *Windows 98* you have to open the *Control Panel* folder, either through the *Start* menu or through *My Computer*. Then double-click the *Display* icon and activate the *Appearance* tab page.

Scheme list box

The easiest thing to do would be to change all the colors at the same time. To do this, open the *Scheme* drop-down list box and select one of the items.

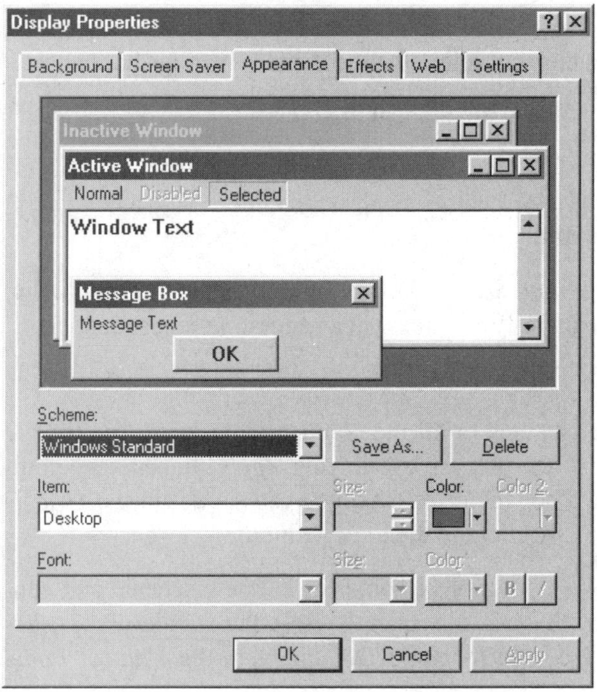

Fig. 8.16:   Changing the appearance of Windows 98

The changes you make will be displayed in the top half of the dialog box. If you want to see the effect it has on the entire screen, click on the *Apply* button.

Item list box

But nearly every single element on the screen can also be changed individually. You would be wise to first select an item from the *Scheme* drop-down list. Then in the top half of the dialog box, click on the particular screen element you want to change. The description of this element will then be given in the *Item* drop-down list. You can also use this list box to select the item you want to change directly, but it would require extensive background knowledge to know the exact meaning of each element described.

Possible settings

With the help of the remaining boxes, depending on the screen element selected, the following settings be changed:

- the *Size* of an element in pixels

- the *Color* and *Color 2* of the element from a set of predefined colors or, through *Other*, from a color pallette

- the *Font*, *Size*, and *Color* as well as the bold and italic attributes for all text occurrences in menus, dialog boxes, title bars, etc.

Saving a scheme

Make changes to all the elements you want to alter and confirm the process by clicking *Apply*. If you have composed a new color scheme you can save it in the *Scheme* list box by clicking the *Save As* button.

Choose a descriptive name for the new scheme and confirm with *OK*. Subsequently close the *Display Properties* dialog box by clicking *OK* and then the *Control Panel* folder.

Tip!

With the help of the *Display Properties* dialog box you can also indirectly change the appearance of the *Start* menu. By selecting the *Menu* item from the *Item* drop-down list you can change the font, font size and color, and in this way influence the appearance of the *Start* menu. However, this change will necessarily affect all the other menus in *Windows 98* as well.

Changing the Desktop Background

The term desktop background describes the surface of the Windows screen which is set to blue-green by default. You may have noticed, though, that other backgrounds are often used as well.

Background tab

To change the background open the *Control Panel* folder by navigating through the *Start* menu to *Settings*. Then open the *Display Properties* dialog box and activate the *Background* tab page. The monitor image on this tab page will display a preview of any changes you make. It will probably show the current blue-green area.

Background pattern

If you want to define a new background pattern, use the scroll bar to view the entire *Select an HTML Document or picture* list and select one of the items provided. Check the result through the preview in the monitor image. If all you see is a small area in the center, open the *Display* drop-down list and select *Tile*.

Pixel-images

Windows 98 will then generate copies of the bitmap picture and tile them alongside each other to fill the entire surface. The available bitmap images are designed in such a way that they seam together to provide a homogenous appearance. If you select one of the larger images (like *Setup*) you can also use the *Center* option. The background picture will then, however, have a border of a different color.

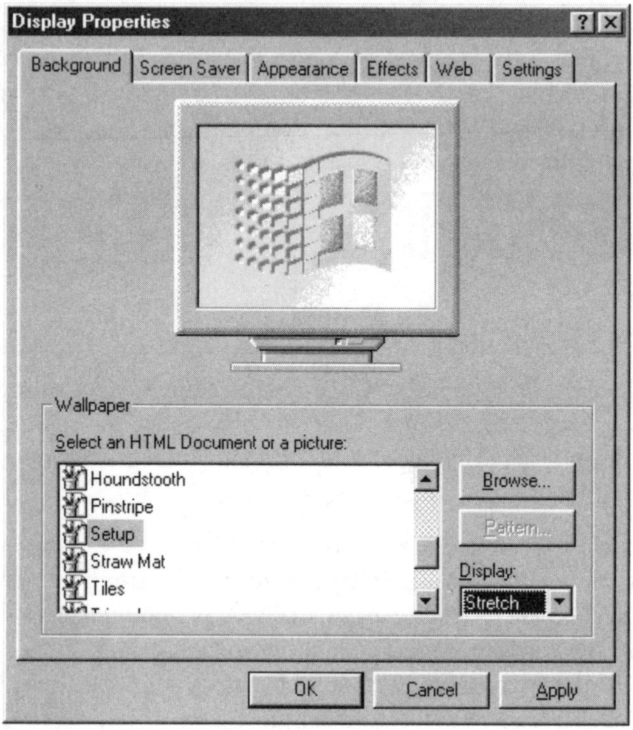

Fig. 8.17: Selecting a desktop background picture

Custom
background

Custom background pictures in the *Bitmap* format can also be selected by clicking on the *Browse* button. But large background pictures use a lot of memory. That is why *Windows 98* provides the *Stretch* option in the *Display* drop-down list.

Stretch

With this option, even smaller images will be stretched so that they fill the entire screen, even on high resolution monitors. However, with pictures that are too small (e.g., all those that are designed to be used with the *Tile* option), the quality will be reduced. Confirm the changes you have made by clicking the *OK* button and close the *Control Panel* folder.

Changing the Custom Font Size

The text appearance in all title bars, menus, dialog boxes or message boxes is defined not only by the settings in the *Appearance* tab page of the *Display Properties* dialog box, but also through the system fonts that are selected for the general display of text through the graphic card. These options, too, can be configured in the *Display Properties* dialog box, but they are located on a different tab page.

Font size list

To change these settings, open the *Control Panel* folder and double-click the *Display* icon. Bring the *Settings* tab page to the foreground and click the *Advanced* button. Make sure the *General* tab page is activated. From the *Font Size* drop-down list, you can choose the font size that Windows will generally use to display text. The *Other* item will depend on the graphic card which is installed on the computer. Not every graphic card supports this option.

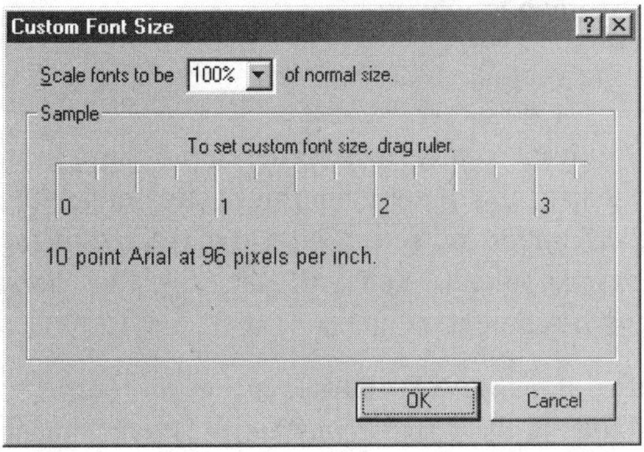

Fig. 8.18:   Setting the font size with the mouse

Small fonts and large fonts

At any rate, the *Font Size* drop-down list will give you the choice between *Small Fonts* and *Large Fonts*. Click on the *Other* option if you intend to make customized settings for the font size.

Preview

To change the original font size which is defined as 100% in the drop-down list box (Figure 8.18), point at the ruler and start dragging it with the mouse button held down to either side. The corresponding percentage values will be displayed in the drop-down list box above the ruler. A preview of the enlargement (values above 100%) or reduction (values below 100%) is provided by the ruler itself, which reflects the adjustments you are making. Confirm your setting by clicking the *OK* button.

Restarting
Windows

In the *Compatibility* group box, you can determine whether *Windows 98* should restart the computer after applying any changes. The *Restart the computer before applying the new color settings* option is required only for older graphic cards. If your graphic card supports changes in the display without restarting, choose the *Apply the new color settings without restarting* option. In this case you just have to confirm your setting by clicking the *OK* button in this dialog box and once again in a dialog box which will inform you of any possible problems.

Setting the Space Between Large Icons

Whenever you want to tidy up your desktop or any given file window, open the *View* menu and select either the *Line Up Icons* option or select *Auto Arrange* from the *Arrange Icons* submenu. You will also find the same commands in the context menu.

Invisible grid

In either case, *Windows 98* will use an invisible grid to line up the icons in the *Large Icons* view. The difference between the two options lies in the different horizontal and vertical spaces used between the icons.

Individual spacing

What is often very practical in one case might prove to be very annoying in another. Some users find the automatic spacing between the icons is simply too big, while others do not like it when long names in the text label under each icon are shortened using an ellipsis to represent the missing part.

Appearance tab

The setting that determines the spacing between the icons is actually quite well hidden. Open the *Control Panel* folder through the *Settings* item on the *Start* menu or through the *My Computer* folder. Double-click the *Display* icon and activate the *Appearance* tab page. The top half of the this dialog box provides you with the image of a miniature desktop which gives a preview of all relevant window elements. Part of this is the icon spacing.

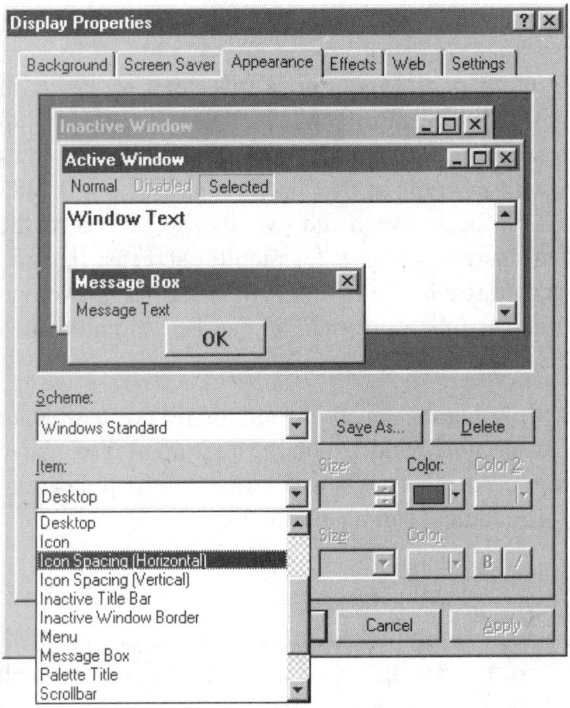

Fig. 8.19:   Changing the icon spacing

Change the icon
spacing

In order to change the icon spacing, open up the *Item* drop-down list box and scroll down to the *Icon Spacing (Horizontal* or *Vertical)* item. You will have to define the icon spacing twice: once for horizontal and once for vertical spacing.

Horizontal;
Vertical

Select *Icon Spacing (Horizontal)* or *Icon Spacing (Vertical)* with the mouse and enter the new spacing value in pixels into the *Size* box. Check your new settings by clicking on the *Apply* button. If necessary, make further alterations and confirm eventually by clicking OK. Then close the *Control Panel* folder.

Graphic Card and Monitor Settings

The resolution of the monitor is measured in *Pixels* in horizontal and vertical dimensions. Using a 640 by 480 screen resolution, for example, will display the Windows desktop with a width of 640 pixels and a height of 480 pixels. The ratio between the two figures relates to the ratio of measurements used for monitor screens. If, however, a screen resolution of 1024 by 768 is used, two and a half times as much information can be accommodated on the same screen.

Higher screen
resolution

Thus, with a higher screen resolution it is possible to arrange many more windows on the desktop next to, above and below each other. When working in an application, more of a document can be displayed.

Setting the Screen Resolution

Such a screen resolution, however, should not be used, regardless of the actual size of the monitor. On a 14-inch monitor, for example, you would hardly be able to read the text in any of the windows and menus since these monitors provide you with a diagonal width of only 34 cm. A 17-inch monitor, on the other hand, already measures 43 cm diagonally across the visible screen.

Recommendation

Therefore, when you want to define the resolution settings, follow the recommendations listed below:

- 14-inch Monitor (34 cm)   640 x 480 Pixel
- 15-inch Monitor (38 cm)   800 x 600 Pixel
- 17-inch Monitor (43 cm)   1024 x 768 Pixel
- 19-inch Monitor (48 cm)   1280 x 1024 Pixel

Changing screen resolution

To change the screen resolution, open the *Control Panel* folder and double-click the *Display* icon. Then bring the *Settings* tab page to the foreground.

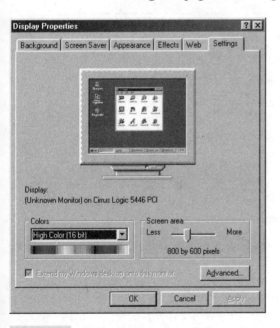

Fig. 8.20:   Setting the screen resolution

Resolution

Now start dragging the slider in the *Screen area* box with your mouse button held down to the left or to the right, until the desired resolution in pixels appears below it (for example, *1024 x 768 pixels*).

Then click on the *OK* button. If you do not make any changes to the color depth settings, then you will be prompted with the window shown in Figure 8.21, top. This message informs you of the process that's going to take place. Confirm it by clicking the *OK* button.

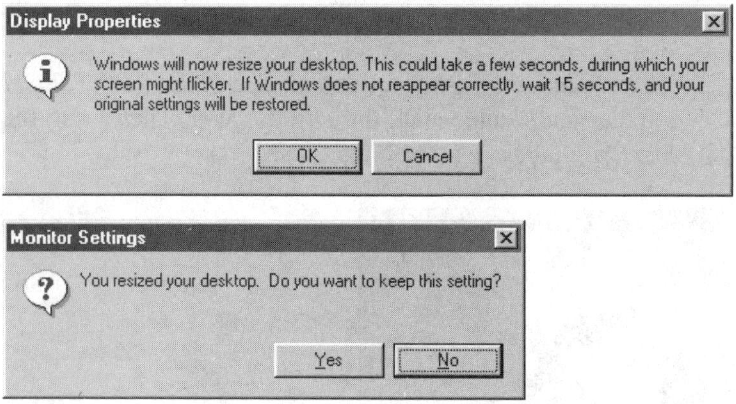

Display Properties

Windows will now resize your desktop. This could take a few seconds, during which your screen might flicker. If Windows does not reappear correctly, wait 15 seconds, and your original settings will be restored.

OK   Cancel

Monitor Settings

You resized your desktop. Do you want to keep this setting?

Yes   No

Fig. 8.21:   Messages before changing the resolution

If Windows cannot resize the desktop within 10 to 15 seconds it will restore the original settings. In this event, confirm the message you get by clicking *OK* and try a different resolution.

If the new resolution can be established, the color depth may be automatically changed as well. In this case you will be prompted with the message box shown in Figure 8.21, bottom. To accept the new settings, confirm the message within 10 seconds by clicking *OK*.

Tip! Changing the screen resolution can result in an automatic adjustment of the color depth (range of colors). The available resolutions depend on the chipset on your graphic card as well as on your monitor. The color depth will depend on the resolution and the amount of memory on the graphic card. **Warning**: incorrect settings can damage or even ruin the monitor.

Adjustment of the Color Depth

Within the context of the monitor design and the settings of the graphic card, the term *color depth* describes the range of colors that can be displayed on the monitor. This color depth will depend on the features of your graphic card and the amount of memory installed on it as well as on the screen resolution.

True Color
color depth

Using the regular VGA screen resolution, for instance, would theoretically allow you a *True Color* color depth of 16.8 million color shades, even with a so-called 1 MB graphic card. Using a screen resolution of 1024 x 768 pixels, though, that same 1 MB graphic card would only provide 256 colors, while a 2 MB graphic card would offer a *High Color* color depth of 65,000 shades. For a *True Color* display at this resolution you would require a 4 MB card.

To change the color depth, open the *Control Panel* folder and double-click the *Display* icon. Then bring the *Settings* tab page to the foreground and open the *Colors* drop-down list. Select the desired item from the list by clicking on it. Possible options in this list are: *16 Colors, 256 Colors, High Color (16 Bit)* = 65,536 colors, *True Color (24 Bit)* = 16.8 million colors and also possible *True Color (32 Bit)* = 4 billion colors.

The values available will depend on your graphic card, while which of these can be selected will depend on the resolution.

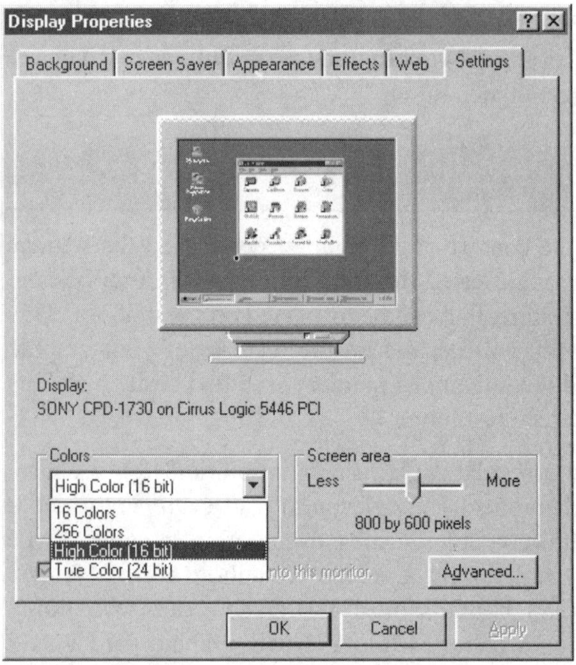

Fig. 8.22: Changing the color depth

Color depth

If your graphic card does not support the selected color depth at the current screen resolution, *Windows 98* will automatically reduce the resolution setting in the *Screen area* box. If you confirm by clicking *OK* you may be prompted to restart Windows, depending upon the settings you have made under *Advanced/General/Compatibility*, and, after restarting, the selected color depth will be used. Otherwise, just confirm the message which appears with *OK*.

Tip!

> More than 65,536 colors (*High Color/16 Bit*) are required only for professional purposes. But multimedia applications require a minimum of 256 colors.

Installing a New Graphic Card Driver

Besides processors, graphic cards are one of the computer components which tend to be replaced frequently, especially if you want to be up-to-date when it comes to speed in the area of graphic performance. Each graphic card requires its own driver in order for it to operate properly within the system. So, if you replace your graphic card you will have to install a new driver too.

Faulty driver

But there are a number of other occasions which may also require the installation of a new graphic card driver, for instance, if the current driver produces errors in certain applications or the screen display is just not optimal. Sometimes a new driver can even significantly improve the performance of the graphic card.

Display

To manually change the graphic card driver, open the *Control Panel* folder by navigating through the *Start* menu to *Settings* or through *My Computer*. Then double-click the *Display* icon.

Changing the driver

Bring the *Settings* tab to the foreground and click on the *Advanced* button. In the dialog box that follows, activate the *Adapter* tab page. This page displays the current graphic card driver, the software manufacturer and the version of the driver.

Selecting the driver

Now click on the *Change* button to launch the *Update Device Driver Wizard*. Click on the *Next* button and in the following dialog box select whether you want the wizard to search for a new driver or whether you want to do it yourself. To select an alternative driver manually, click on the *Display a list of all drivers in a specific location, so you can select the driver you want* radio button and then click *Next*. *Windows 98* will now load a database of graphic card driver information, provided that such a database already exists. The following dialog box will then display a list of all compatible drivers that have been installed on the computer so far. To change the driver, select an item from the list and click the *Next* button. Clicking on the *Show all hardware* radio button will display a complete list of all available drivers. For *Windows 98* drivers the Setup CD will be required.

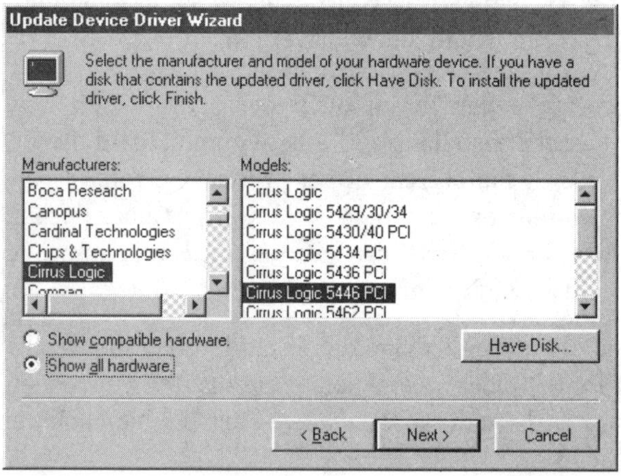

Fig. 8.23: Selecting a different graphic card driver

New graphic card

To continue, select a manufacturer and model from the respective lists. If you want to install a driver update from a manufacturer's diskette or CD, click the *Have Disk* button. Enter the path to the drive and folder that contain the data files which belong to the provided driver in the *Copy manufacturer's file from* list box and click *OK*.

Browse

Optionally, you can use the *Browse* button to navigate your way to the appropriate folder. Then select the *INF* file and click on the *OK* button to close the *Open* dialog box. Do the same for the *Install From Disk* dialog box. In the *Select Device* dialog box, select the correct model and confirm with *OK* again.

New graphic
card driver

The *Update Device Driver Wizard* dialog box now informs you of the graphic card driver you have chosen and its location. To finally complete the process of installation, confirm with *OK* and eventually with *Finish* in the last dialog box.

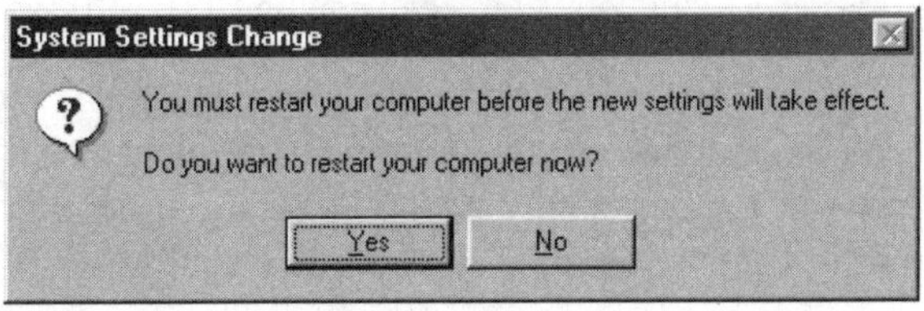

System Settings Change ⊠

(?) You must restart your computer before the new settings will take effect.

Do you want to restart your computer now?

[Yes] [No]

Fig. 8.24:   Changes will take effect after restarting

Restart

Finally, close all open dialog boxes until only the dialog box prompting you to restart the computer is left. If any documents are still open at this point, you will receive a message that allows you to save them. After restarting, check the quality of the screen display.

Tip!

If there are any problems with the new driver a message box will inform you of this. After confirming the message, the *Display Properties* dialog box will appear with the *Settings* tab activated. Repeat the steps described above to select a different driver. The wizard will inform you whether that driver is in fact newer than the one currently installed.

Choosing a Different Monitor

The model of your monitor is usually registered during the setup procedure of *Windows 98*. With the modern *Plug & Play* monitors, Windows can even recognize the manufacturer and model automatically and enter its technical specifications into the system registry.

Correct monitor

But then, what do you do if your monitor is not of the *Plug & Play* variety or if you have purchased a computer with *Windows 98* installed but want to use a different monitor? In this section you will learn why it is of essential importance to select the correct monitor type under *Windows 98* and how you can change the settings if necessary.

Incorrect technical
parameters

Even if you are not facing any imminent problems with your monitor at the moment, you should read this section very carefully because an incorrect monitor setting could have two major consequences. Firstly, running the screen with incorrect technical parameters could cause considerable damage or even totally ruin the monitor.

Refresh rate

And secondly, the refresh rate of the screen under *Windows 98* will depend entirely on the monitor type that has been selected. If that model has a lower performance than the screen you are actually using, however, you will probably end up working with an unergonomical refresh rate that results in a flickering display.

Verify monitor
setting

To verify that the settings of the monitor are correct, open the *Control Panel* folder by navigating through the *Start* menu to *Settings*. Then double-click the *Display* icon and bring the *Settings* tab to the foreground. Here, click on *Advanced*. In the dialog box that appears, select the *Monitor* tab. There you will find the monitor description and its energy-saving features. If the name of the brand

and the model matches that of your monitor, then everything is fine.

Changing the monitor

In this case click *Cancel* and subsequently *OK* to close the *Display Properties* dialog box. If, however, the selected type does not correspond to your monitor, click on the *Change* button to call up the *Update Device Driver Wizard*. Click on the *Next* button and determine whether you want the wizard to look for an updated driver or if you want to select one manually. If you choose the default option by clicking *Next*, all selected drives will be automatically scanned for driver databases. This option, however, is not very useful.

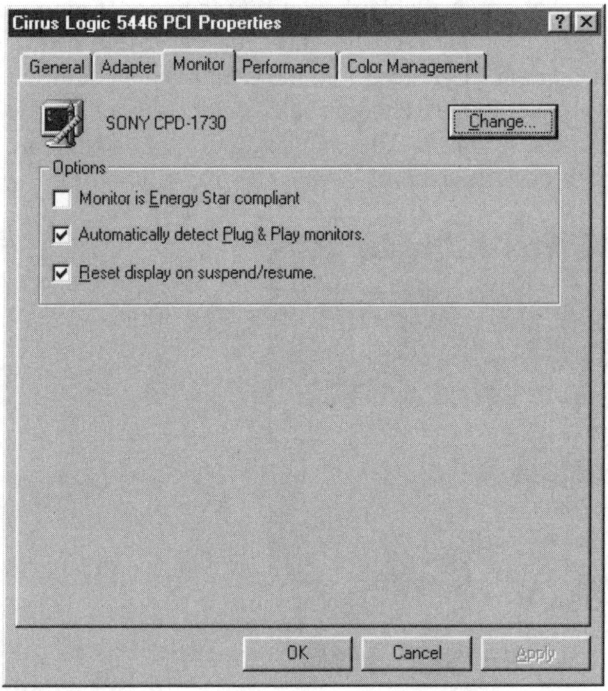

Fig. 8.25: Display of the current configuration

Configuration

If it happens that you are presented with a search result which differs from your monitor or from any of the *Standard...* or *Super VGA...* items, you should definitely take a very close look at this configuration.

Manual search

To perform a manual search, click the *Display a list of all drivers in a specific location, so you can select the driver you want* radio button and then click the *Next* button. The following dialog box will list all compatible drivers that already have been installed on your system.

Manufacturer
and model

Here, click on the *Show all hardware* radio button. Now select the manufacturer of your monitor from the list on the left side of this dialog box and go through the list of models that are available. If you find the correct item in both lists, continue reading when you get to the end of this paragraph. If you can find the right manufacturer but not the exact model, choose the monitor description that comes closest to it. If the manufacturer is not listed at all, select the *Standard monitor types* item from that list.

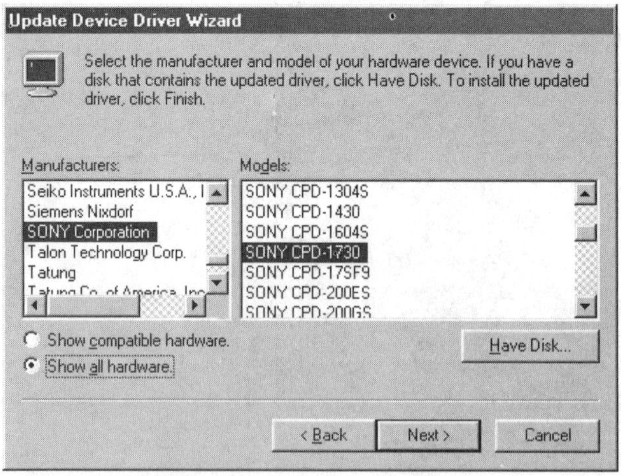

Fig. 8.26:   Selecting manufacturer and model

Maximum
resolution

From the *Models* list, select the item which provides the maximum screen resolution given in your monitor manual, for instance *Super VGA 1280 x 768*. Then confirm with *OK* and the screen will be switched over. If the monitor does not display properly, repeat this configuration with next item from the *Standard monitor types* list which has a lower resolution. Eventually, confirm with *Finish* in the *Update Device Driver Wizard* window and close the *Control Panel* folder.

Configuring the Screen Saver

Company and office computers very often remain turned on day and night, even though the time that someone is actually working with them may be only a fraction of that. Any bright areas on the screen, however, can damage the display, if they remain in the same screen area all the time.

That's the reason screen savers were created which allow you to deactivate the screen after a definable period of inactivity.

Screen saver

Windows 98 also provides screen savers which, by default, are not activated. To make use of them, you have to open the *Display Properties* dialog box and activate the *Screen saver* tab page.

Preview

Open the *Screen saver* drop-down list box and select one of the available items. The miniature monitor in the top half of the dialog box provides a preview of the selected screen saver.

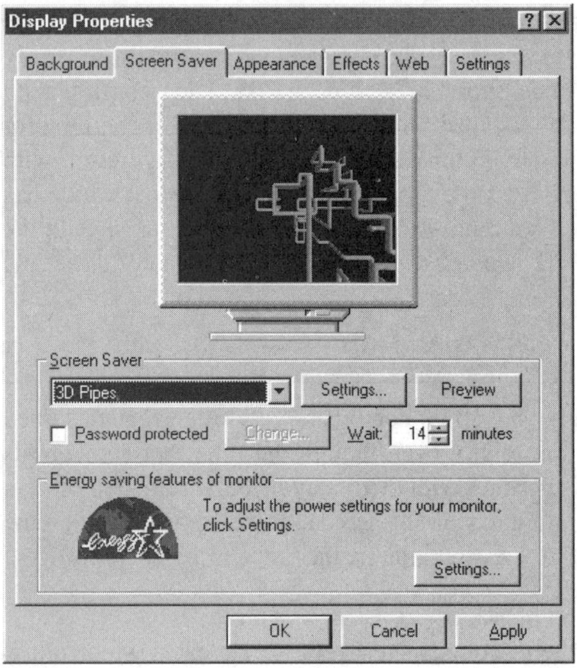

Fig. 8.27:   Setting the screen saver

Apply

If you want to see what the screen saver looks like when it fills the whole screen, click on *Preview*. As soon as you move the mouse you will return to the *Display Properties* dialog box.

Wait time

In the *Wait* text box you can define the period of inactivity in minutes which will have to elapse before the screen saver appears.

Settings

The *Settings* button in the *Screen Saver* option group allows you to further configure the screen saver to your individual requirements (*Blank Screen* as an exception). Once you have made all of the necessary changes close the dialog box with *OK* and then the *Control Panel* folder.

Installing and Setting a Printer

During the *Windows 98* setup process you were already asked to identify your printer. If you've just bought a new computer, however, that already had *Windows 98* installed on it, it's a different story. In this case your printer will not have been installed yet because the dealer could not possibly have known what kind of printer you would be using.

Installing a Printer

Printers control panel

New printers can always be added afterwards to do this. *Windows 98* will use the required driver software needed to transfer the data to the printer and control the printing process,. In order to install a new printer, open the *Printers* folder through *Start/Settings* or through *My Computer*. In the *Printers* folder window, double-click the *Add Printer* icon to launch the *Add Printer Wizard*. Confirm the first dialog box of the wizard with *OK*.

Add Printer Wizard

Click the manufacturer and model of your printer. If your printer came with an installation disk, click Have Disk. If your printer is not listed, consult your printer documentation for a compatible printer.

Manufacturers:

- Dataproducts
- Diconix
- Digital
- Epson
- Fujitsu
- GCC
- Generic

Printers:

- Epson SQ-2500
- Epson SQ-2550
- Epson Stylus 300 ESC/P 2
- Epson Stylus 800 ESC/P 2
- Epson Stylus 1000 ESC/P 2
- Epson Stylus COLOR ESC/P 2
- Epson Stylus Pro ESC/P 2

Have Disk...

< Back   Next >   Cancel

Fig. 8.28:   Add Printer Wizard

In the next dialog box you will be asked if the available printer is directly attached to your computer. If your computer is a stand-alone workstation click the *Local printer* radio button and continue with *Next*.The following dialog box then presents you with two list boxes from which to select the manufacturer and printer model.

Selecting the manufacturer

From the *Manufacturers* list box, select the appropriate name. To access the lower parts of the list use the scroll bar or directly type in the first letter of the manufacturer's name.

Selecting the printer model

The *Models* list box on the right side will display all the available drivers for that manufacturer. Select your printer model and confirm by clicking the *OK* button.

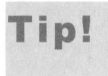

If the manufacturer and the model of the printer you are using is not listed, you will require the manufacturer's driver diskette and you will have to access it using the *Have Disk* button.

Selecting the printer port

In the next dialog box of the wizard, select the *LPT1: Printer Port* item in the *Available ports* list box and confirm by clicking on the *Next* button. You are then given the option of allocating a name of your choice to tis printer in the *Printer name* text box or of using the default name.

Default printer

If this is your only printer or if it is the printer you will mainly be using, select the *Yes* radio button in the lower half of the dialog box to make the printer the *Windows 98* default printer. Again, click on *Next*. In the following dialog box you are given the option of printing out a test page. If this is what you want to do click on *Yes* (this is recommended) and wait for the print to be completed.

Then answer the question asking whether the printout was acceptable or not in the message box which follows.

If you do not find it necessary to make a test printout, click on the *No* radio button and subsequently the *Finish* button. *Windows 98* will then copy the required driver from the Setup CD ROM and the new printer will appear as an icon in the *Printers* folder window.

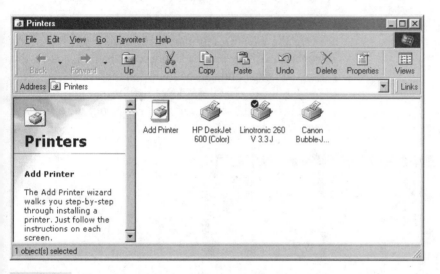

The printers folder with the installed printers in it (viewed as Web page)

Selected printers can be configured through the *Properties* item on the *File* menu. This procedure is described in the next section.

Setting the Properties of the Printer

After installing a new printer, *Windows 98* will use the default settings of the driver. In order for the printer to do a good job for you, you should adjust the printer properties to meet your own requirements. These settings can always be checked or changed through the *Printers* folder.

Properties

In order to do this, navigate through the *Start* menu to *Settings* or through *My Computer* and open the *Printers* folder. Select the icon of the printer you are using and open the *File* menu to select the *Properties* item from there. The possible settings which are available on a number of tab pages in the *[printer name] Properties* dialog box will depend on the type of printer. Activate the various tab pages to get an overview of the different options.

Print test page

In order to verify whether the printer is working properly activate the *General* tab page and click on the *Print Test Page* button. The printer connection is defined on the *Details* tab page and can be modified there. Use the *Print to the following port* drop-down list for that purpose. The current driver can be seen in the *Print using the following driver* drop-down list.

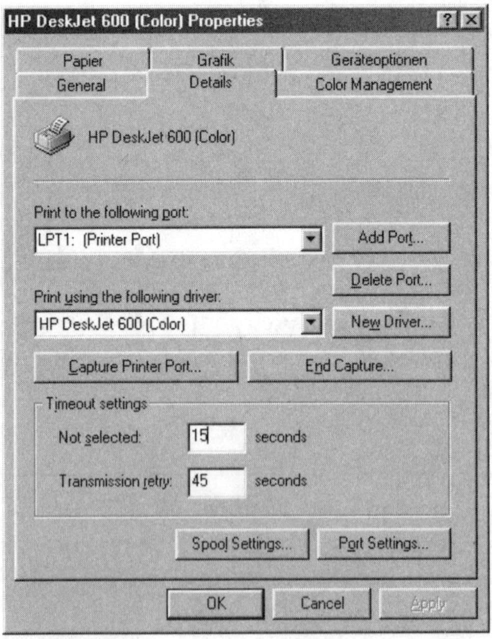

Fig. 8.30: Checking the settings of the printer connection

Tip! Help information on any of the elements on these tab pages can be obtained by clicking on the [?] button in the title bar and then on the element concerned.

Microsoft Office Suite

Changing the properties of a printer will affect the properties for every document that is printed with it. In order to change the settings for only one document, you will have to open the *File* menu of the respective application (such as the *Microsoft Office Suite*) and select either the *Page Setup* or the *Print* command from there. The settings you make in any of the dialog boxes related to these commands will affect only that particular document.

Selecting a New Printer Driver

The print quality is directly dependent on the performance of the driver that is installed. If you have found the manufacturer and model of your printer during the setup procedure, you should not run into any problems. If, however, only a similar model was available or the manufacturer provided a driver update on a diskette or via an online service, a different procedure has to be performed.

Change the printer driver

To change the printer driver you need to access the *Printers* folder, either by navigating through the *Start* menu to *Settings* or through *My Computer*. Open the folder and select the icon of the printer you are using. Then select the *Properties* command from the *File* menu and activate the *Details* tab page. Click on *New Driver* and confirm the following message with *Yes*.

Manufacturer list

Select the appropriate item from the *Manufacturers* list. To access the lower parts of the list use the scroll bar or directly type in the first letter of the manufacturer's name. The *Models* list box on the right side will display all the available drivers of that manufacturer. Select your printer model and confirm by clicking the *OK* button.

Tip!

If the manufacturer and the model of the printer you are using is not listed, you will require the manufacturer's driver diskette which you can access through the *Have Disk* button.

Internet

If the manufacturer provided a driver update on diskette or if you downloaded a new driver from an online service or the Internet to a folder on your hard disk, click on the *Have Disk* button. Enter the path to the file into the *Copy manufacturer's files from* text box or press the *Browse* button.

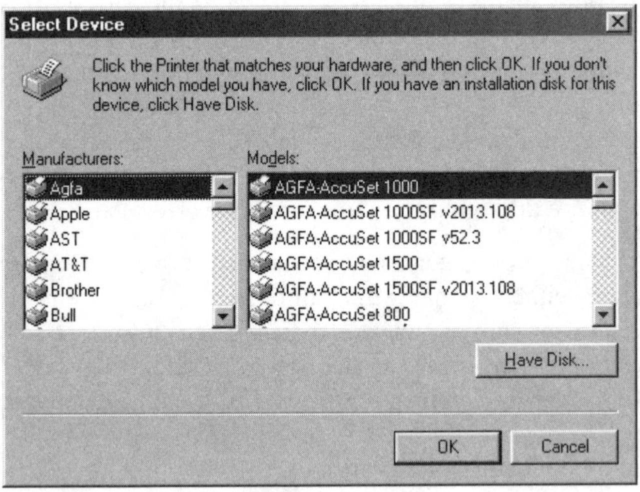

Select Device

Click the Printer that matches your hardware, and then click OK. If you don't know which model you have, click OK. If you have an installation disk for this device, click Have Disk.

Manufacturers:
- Agfa
- Apple
- AST
- AT&T
- Brother
- Bull

Models:
- AGFA-AccuSet 1000
- AGFA-AccuSet 1000SF v2013.108
- AGFA-AccuSet 1000SF v52.3
- AGFA-AccuSet 1500
- AGFA-AccuSet 1500SF v2013.108
- AGFA-AccuSet 800

[Have Disk...]

[OK] [Cancel]

Fig. 8.31:   Changing the printer driver

Target folder

Navigate to the appropriate drive and target folder using the respective list boxes to select the driver file and click the *OK* button. Subsequently confirm twice with *OK* and then select your printer model. After another confirmation, the files will be copied.

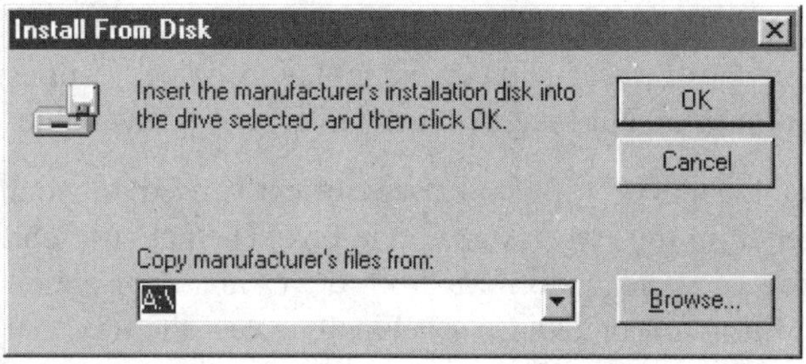

Fig. 8.32: Installing a new driver from diskette

Print test page

After this procedure, the new driver will appear in the *Print using the following driver* drop-down list on the *Details* tab page. Now activate the *General* tab page and click the *Print Test Page* button. If the quality of the print is satisfactory, confirm the *Properties* dialog box with *OK* and close the *Printers* folder.

Setting the Paper Size of the Printer

The properties of each printer installed under *Windows 98* can be adjusted in such a way that the settings will affect all applications that are running on this computer. In this section, we will explain how to define the paper size, paper format and paper tray for each available printer. For this purpose, you will have to open the *Printers* folder. This system folder is accessible in one of three ways:

- by opening the *Start* menu and choosing *Settings*

- through *My Computer*

- through the *Control Panel* folder in the *Windows Explorer*

Paper tab

After opening the *Printers* folder, select the icon of the printer you want to configure and choose the *Properties* command from the *File* menu or the shortcut menu. Then bring the *Paper* tab to the foreground. The number of options shown there will depend on the technical features of your printer, but several items will always be available.

Paper size

Select the paper format that is currently used in your printer from the *Paper size* option box. Then choose one of the two standard formats from the *Orientation* option group: *Portrait* or *Landscape*. Finally select the tray that supplies the paper size you have chosen in the upper part of the dialog box from the *Paper source* drop-down list and confirm with *OK*.

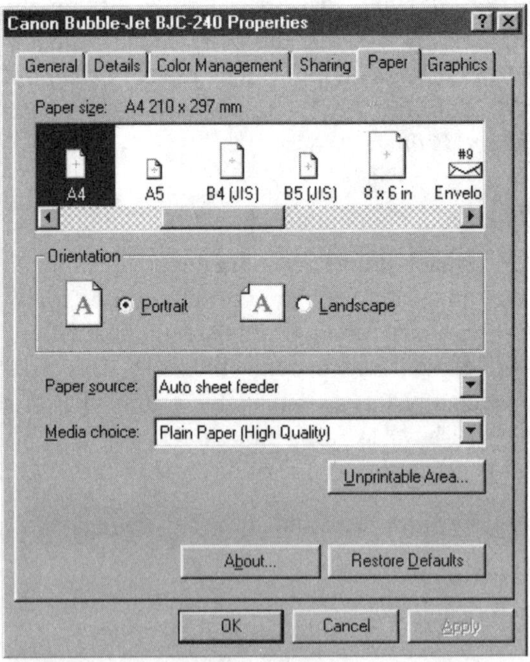

Fig. 8.33:   *Paper* tab page of the *Properties* dialog box of the printer

Information

With the *About* button, you can obtain detailed information regarding the driver version, while the *Unprintable Area* button provides information regarding the page borders (NB: not every driver provides this button).

Tip!

If a Windows application provides options and dialog boxes of its own that allow you to change the paper size and orientation, as is the case with *Microsoft Office Suite* programs, the settings you have made in the properties dialog box of the printer can be overridden. Ultimately, the effective settings are those of the application which is printing. But they are valid only for the documents currently being printed.

Setting the Graphics Properties of the Printer

The properties of each printer installed under *Windows 98* can be adjusted in such a way that the settings will be effective for all applications that are running on your computer. To define the dithering options you will have to open the *Printers* folder. This system folder is accessible in the following ways:

- through the *Settings* item on the *Start* menu

- through the *My Computer* folder window

- or through the *Control Panel* folder in the *Windows Explorer*

Graphics tab

After opening the *Printers* folder, select the icon of the printer you want to configure and select the *Properties* command from the *File* menu or the shortcut menu. Then activate the *Graphics* tab page.

The number of options that are provided on this tab page will depend on technical features of your printer model.

Dithering and Intensity	The *Dithering* and *Intensity* option group, however, will always be available for every *Windows 98* driver.

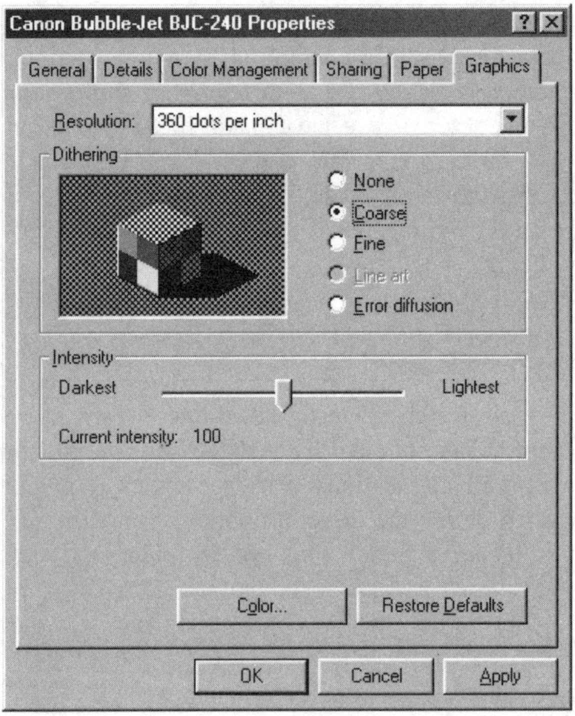

Fig. 8.34:   Setting the properties for the print of graphics

Error diffusion	Most *Windows 98* printer drivers allow you to choose from different types of dithering: *None, Coarse, Fine, Line art* and *Error diffusion*. The *Error diffusion* option provides a highly sophisticated printing result, even with a black and white laser printer. Ultimately, you can find out what works best for most cases by trial and error.

Intensity

The intensity slider allows you to regulate the brightness of the printout. Confirm the changes by clicking the *OK* button. Here, as in many other cases, the only way to find out the optimal setting is by printing out a number of variations and comparing the results.

Tip!

If the installed driver is not a *Windows 98* driver, this tab page could look entirely different or it might not be there at all. In such a case, follow the instructions given by the printer manufacturer.

Setting the Resolution of the Printer

The properties of each printer installed under *Windows 98* can be adjusted in such a way that the settings will take effect for all applications that are running on the computer. In this section we will explain how to set the resolution of your printer.

Printer resolution

Reducing the resolution of the printer could be a very sensible thing to do if, for instance, you need to print out a large number of drafts which do not need to be of a very high quality. To change the *dpi* value (dots per inch) you will need to open the *Printers* folder again.

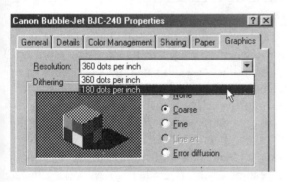

Fig. 8.35:   Changing the resolution of the printer

One way of accessing it is to navigate through the *Start* menu to *Settings* and select it from there. Then select the icon of the printer you want to configure and choose the *Properties* command from the *File* menu or shortcut menu. Then bring the *Graphics* tab page to the foreground.

Resolution list

The number of available options there will depend on the technical features of your printer model. The *Resolution* drop-down list, however, will always be there.

Dots per inch

Choose the *dpi* value that you want to apply when printing out all documents with the selected printer in future from the *Resolution* drop-down list. The lower the value of *dots per inch*, the faster the printing will be done. Finally, confirm by clicking on the *OK* button.

Tip!

If a Windows application provides options of its own that allow you to change the printer resolution, as is the case with *Microsoft Office Suite* programs, the settings you have made in the printer *Properties* dialog box can be overridden. Ultimately, the effective settings are those of the application which is printing.

Setting the Background Printing

Windows 98 allows you to run several applications at the same time and work with them simultaneously. This is very practical when you need to transfer data from one application to another and can generally save you a lot of time. You could be working with a spreadsheet application, for example, such as *Microsoft Excel* and be processing some data there while *Windows 98* looks after the printing of a number of *Word* documents which were created using sophisticated formatting. This is made possible by a feature of the operating system called background printing.

Automatic process   This whole process usually takes place without requiring any of your attention, i.e., it is fully automatic. The basic settings of the background printing can, however, be accessed and changed.

Individual settings   To do this, open the *Printers* folder by accessing it through *Start/Settings* or through *My Computer*. The settings for the background printing have to be configured for each printer individually.

Spool settings   Therefore, select the printer you want to configure and choose the *Properties* command from the *File* menu or shortcut menu. Then bring the *Details* tab to the foreground and click the *Spool Settings* button.

Spool print job   Using the default setting *Spool print jobs so program finishes printing faster* the print job will be temporarily saved to your hard disk as a file and you can then continue to work in the program while the printing is going on in the background.

Start printing after last page   The *Start printing after last page is spooled* option implies that the actual printing process will not start until all printer job data has been sent by the application.

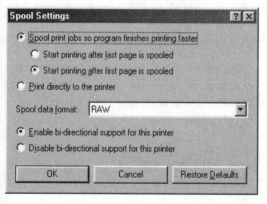

Fig. 8.36:   Changing the settings for background printing

Start printing after first page

In this way it is possible to continue working in the program, although this places demands on memory. The *Start printing after first page is spooled* option, however, will cause the printing procedure to start as soon as the first page is processed. This takes much less memory but it also means it will take longer before you can start working in the application again.

Bi-directional support

Checking the *Enable bi-directional support for this printer* option will enable data exchange between the computer and the printer. This kind of communication makes it possible for messages from the printer to appear. On the other, hand this also makes it a potential source of transmission errors.

Setting the Transmission Retry Value

Very complex printing jobs from applications such as *PowerPoint* or *Microsoft Excel* can create quite a strain on the processor as well as the printer.

In many cases you might have to wait for several minutes before the printing job is processed, and with laser printers the wait can be even longer before the printed data of an entire document is spooled to the printer memory and processed there. Ink jet printers, on the other hand, will process a print job line by line.

Problems

This is why very complex print jobs may occasionally cause some problems. In some cases error messages are displayed on the screen and disappear automatically after a moment. In other cases the print job gets aborted altogether.

In this chapter we will show you a trick which can take care of many of these problems.

Open the *Printers* folder by navigating through *Start/ Settings* and select the printer that is currently creating the problem.

Choose the *Properties* command from the *File* menu or the context menu and bring the *Details* tab to the foreground.

Increasing the transmission retry value

Transmission
retry

Now increase the value in the *Transmission retry* text box, which is in the *Timeout settings* option group, to a value between 60 and 120 seconds. This value defines how long Windows will wait for the printer to be ready before issuing an error message. Confirm this change by clicking on the *OK* button, close the *Printers* folder and try printing again.

Viewing the Print Jobs in the Print Queue

Multitasking

Windows 98 allows you to run and to work with several programs at the same time. This is called *multitasking* and can come in very handy when you have a lot to do. It will allow you to start a big printing job, for instance, from a word processor such as *Word* and then to go on working on a different document in the same program or even in an entirely different program such as *PowerPoint*.

Print status

Normally, you will not even notice the printing going on in the background, apart from the pages that the printer issues, of course. However, the current printing status can also be viewed.

If you want to check what's happening with the printing, point on the printer icon next to the clock in the taskbar. A *ScreenTip* pops up saying: *x document(s) pending for [user]* or : *x Documents are printing* and thus displays the current print status.

Printer icon in
the taskbar

Once the printing job is completed the printer icon will disappear from the taskbar. As long as it is visible you can also double-click on it in order to obtain more detailed information regarding the documents that are currently being printed out.

Print queue

The print queue of the active printer will appear along with a list of all the current printing jobs. This window provides you with information such as the status of the printing job and the owner of the document.

In addition to that you will get information about the progress of a printing job, such as *'page 4 of 8'*, for example, as well as the time the printing was started.

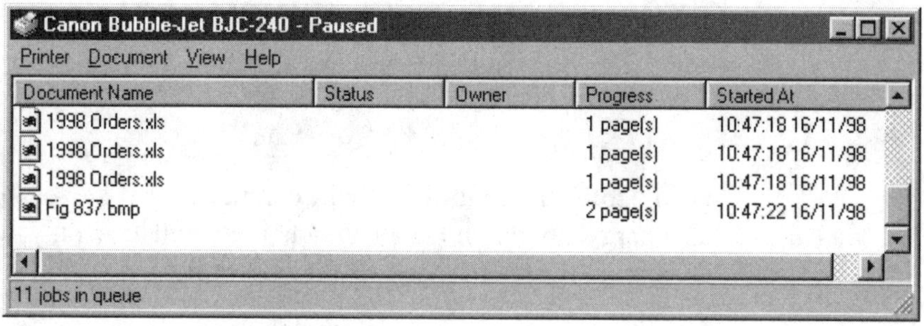

Canon Bubble-Jet BJC-240 - Paused					_ □ ×
Printer Document View Help					
Document Name	Status	Owner	Progress	Started At	▲
1998 Orders.xls			1 page(s)	10:47:18 16/11/98	
1998 Orders.xls			1 page(s)	10:47:18 16/11/98	
1998 Orders.xls			1 page(s)	10:47:18 16/11/98	
Fig 837.bmp			2 page(s)	10:47:22 16/11/98	

11 jobs in queue

Fig. 8.38:   Viewing the print queue

Tip!

If you want to cancel or abort any of the print jobs that you've already sent off, first select the respective document in the print queue window. Then open the *Document* menu and choose the *Cancel Printing* command.

If you encounter a problem with the printer such as a paper jam, for instance, open the *Printer* menu and select the *Pause Printing* command. Then solve the problem and select the same command again.

Close the print queue window with the *Close* command from the *Printer* menu or by clicking on the *Close* button in the title bar.

Setting the Energy-Saving Features

Company and office computers in very often remain turned on day and night. Statistically, only about 5 or 10 percent of the time they are on is someone actually using them. During the remaining time they are simply consuming precious energy, which can mean as much as 250 Watts per computer, plus the additional consumption of the monitor and other peripherals which may be switched on, such as printers or scanners. With modern computers this kind of energy waste can be avoided.

Configuring the Power Management of the Computer

Using software control, modern computers can be set to an energy-saving mode in which they will use only a fraction of the energy they require in normal mode.

To save power, the processor clock is reduced, for instance, and the hard disk(s) is deactivated. This section deals with the facilities of *Windows 98* that control these features.

Energy-saving
methods

Energy-saving is also important for notebook computers which require energy-saving methods to extend the period of time they can run on the power provided by the batteries, and thus be independent of the power grid.

In these cases the *Power Management* settings for monitors do not apply. They will be dealt with in the section *Setting the Power Management for the Monitor*.

The energy-saving features can only be utilised and configured on computers that actually support them. In addition to that, the *Power Management* option has to be activated in the BIOS.

Power management item

If those conditions are fulfilled, *Windows 98* will install the *Power Management* icon in the *Control Panel* folder. Open this item in order to configure the power management of your computer.

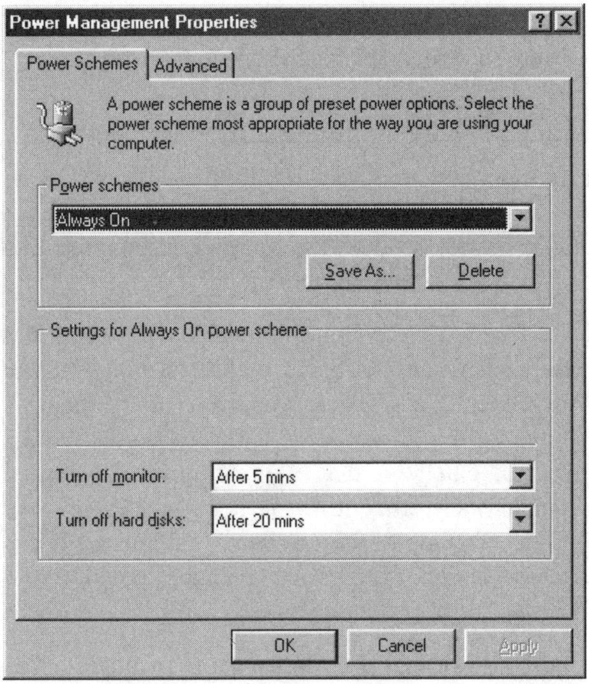

Power Management Properties

Power Schemes | Advanced |

A power scheme is a group of preset power options. Select the power scheme most appropriate for the way you are using your computer.

Power schemes

Always On

Save As...   Delete

Settings for Always On power scheme

Turn off monitor: After 5 mins

Turn off hard disks: After 20 mins

OK   Cancel   Apply

Fig. 8.39:   Configuring the power management

Desktop computer   In the *Power Management Properties* dialog box select the item from the *Power schemes* drop-down list which best matches your work situation. Choose *Home/Office Desk* if you are using a desktop computer, or *Portable/ Laptop* for a laptop computer, in order to make the best use of the existing features.

The *Always On* item will disable all energy-saving devices. Other possible options in this list will depend on your PC.

Laptop computer   If you are using a laptop computer, select the *Advanced* tab page and check the *Show power meter on taskbar* option in order to have an indication of the battery status displayed on the taskbar.

Otherwise, select the desired values from the *Turn off monitor* and *Turn off hard disks* drop-down lists.

Putting the Computer into Standby Mode

All modern computers have a facility that allows them to automatically switch to a stand-by mode using software control. This mode reduces the energy consumption to a fraction of what it uses in normal mode.

To find out whether the *Power Management* option has been activated in the BIOS, go to *Start/Settings/Contol Panel* and open the *System Properties* dialog box by double-clicking the *System* icon, and activate the *Device Manager* tab. Click on the + sign in front of *System devices* to check if the *Advanced Power Management support* item is on top of the sub-items that appear. If it is listed, power-saving features are available on the computer. Finally, close the dialog boxes.

Stand-by mode

The stand-by mode can also be triggered manually. This can be done by opening the *Start* menu and selecting the *Shut Down* command. Then select the *Stand by* radio button in the *Shut Down Windows* dialog box that appears and confirm with *OK*.

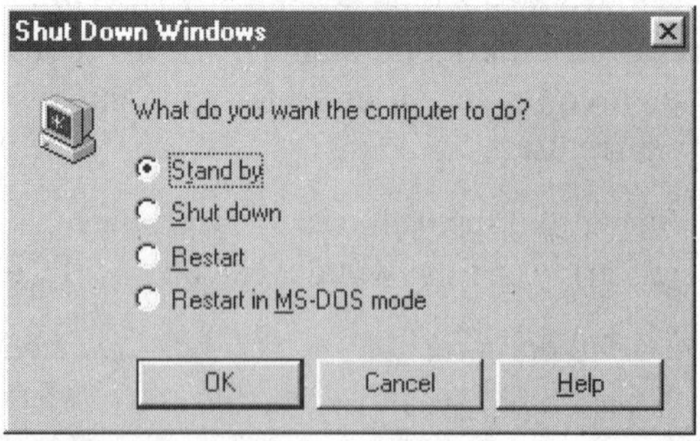

Fig. 8.40:   Putting the computer into stand by mode

Processor clock reduced

After that, depending on the configuration of the power management, the processor clock will be reduced step by step and the hard disk(s) will be turned off. This way, up to 95 percent of the power can be conserved.

On laptop computers these energy saving methods will significantly extend the length of time that a computer can run while not connected to the power grid. As soon as you move the mouse or press any key, the computer will return to normal mode and you can resume your work.

Tip!

The energy-saving devices of the monitor will be explained in *Setting the Power Management for the Monitor*. The *Power Management* option has to be activated in the BIOS of the computer in order to do this.

Setting the Power Management for the Monitor

By using screen savers under *Windows 98*, it is possible to protect the monitor's screen from becoming damaged. The steps required to activate this feature have already been explained earlier on in this chapter. In addition to that, it is possible to put the monitor into a stand-by mode and subsequently, even to turn it off after predefined periods of time. This not only protects the monitor but also helps to save a lot of energy and money.

To activate these energy-saving devices, your monitor would have to be compliant with the *Energy Star* standard. This implies that the monitor can be put into stand by mode and eventually, be shut down by software control. Besides this, your graphic card should also support this standard. With older models this is not necessarily so, in which case the respective options will not be available.

321

Screen Saver tab — Open the *Control Panel* folder by navigating through the *Start* menu to *Settings*. Then, open the *Display* icon. In the *Display Properties* dialog box activate the *Screen Saver* tab page.

Saving energy — In the *Energy saving features of monitor* option group click on the *Settings* button. In the *Power Management Properties* dialog box that appears, it is now possible to activate and configure the energy-saving devices that were explained above.

Monitor tab — The options available in this dialog box also depend on the settings that are made on the *Display Properties/Settings/Advanced/Monitor* tab page. Go there and make sure that the features supported by your monitor are activated in the settings. To configure the actual energy-saving devices, use the *Power Management Properties*.

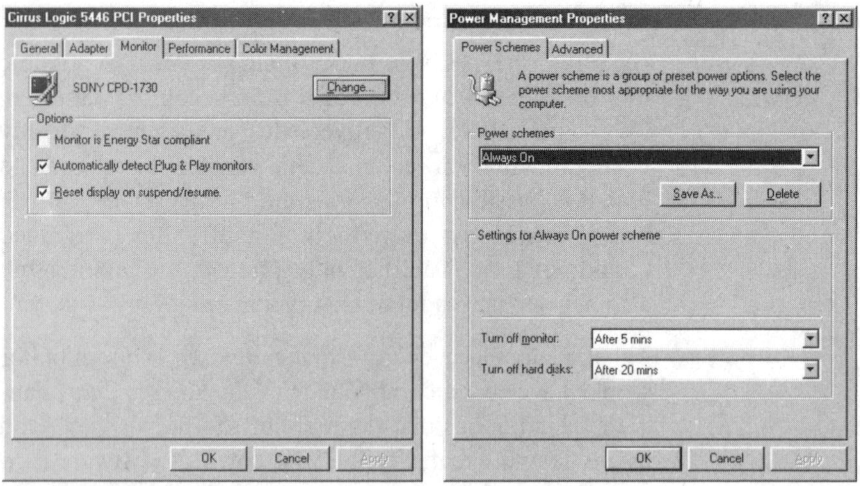

Fig. 8.41:   Checking the energy saving devices of the monitor (left) and activating them

Turn off monitor
after x mins

Click on *Settings* in the *Energy saving features of monitor* option group. Then select one of the *After X mins* items from the *Turn off monitor* drop-down list box and confirm your settings by clicking the *OK* button. Also, close the *Display Properties* dialog box and, subsequently the *Control Panel* folder.

Installing and Configuring new Hardware

Sooner or later, most users will upgrade their computer with new hardware components such as sound or video cards, an internal modem or an ISDN adapter card. These new hardware components need to be installed properly so that *Windows 98* can integrate their functionality into the entire system.

Plug & Play
hardware

Under *Windows 98*, it is irrelevant whether the new hardware is built-in before or after installing the Windows system software. If the new component falls into the category of *Plug & Play* hardware, it will ideally be configured automatically after rebooting the computer.

Installing Hardware Components

For the configuration of all other hardware, you will receive assistance from a wizard. To install new hardware, open the *Control Panel* folder through the *Start* menu and *Settings*. Then double-click the *Add New Hardware* icon to launch the *Add New Hardware Wizard*.

Add New Hardware Wizard

In the first dialog box of the *Add New Hardware Wizard*, you just need to click on the *Next* button. In the following dialog box also confirm with *Next* to start the recognition of hardware with *Plug and Play* support. Any new devices detected will be displayed in the next dialog box. There, select the device you want to install and click on *Next*.

Not Plug and Play compatible

If no new devices could be detected automatically, however, the *Add New Hardware Wizard* will carry on by informing you that there are two ways in which hardware that is not *Plug and Play* compatible can be installed.

Recognition

If you select the *Yes (Recommended)* option and click on *Next*, the automatic hardware detection of *Windows 98* will begin. This process will attempt to identify any hardware components that were added afterwards. This automatic process can take several minutes and is almost always recommended whenever any new hardware has been installed in the computer.

System-crash

In the event that your PC 'hangs' or 'crashes' during this automatic detection process, reboot the computer and start the wizard again, this time selecting the option for manual installation.

Manual selection

By clicking the *No, I want to select the hardware from a list* radio button and with a subsequent click on *Next*, you can select the category of hardware to which the component you want to install belongs.

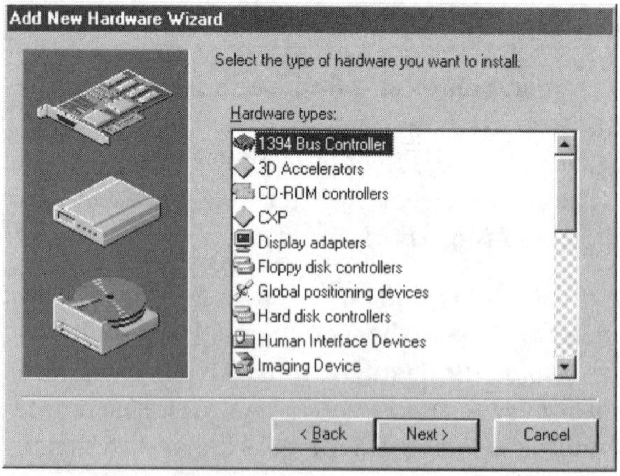

Fig. 8.42:   Selecting the type of the new hardware manually

Choose the appropriate item from the list and click on *Next* again. In the following dialog box you can then select the new hardware from the *Manufacturers* and *Models* list boxes.

Automatic detection

The *Hardware Types* list box will also appear if the automatic hardware detection process could not identify any new hardware.

Driver diskette

If the new hardware is not included in the list boxes, you will require the manufacturer's driver diskette. The driver files can then be located there after clicking on *Have Disk* and will be copied if you click on *Next*.

Depending on the type of hardware you are installing, you may now be presented with other dialog boxes which will allow you to configure the new component. Follow the directions on the screen in this case.

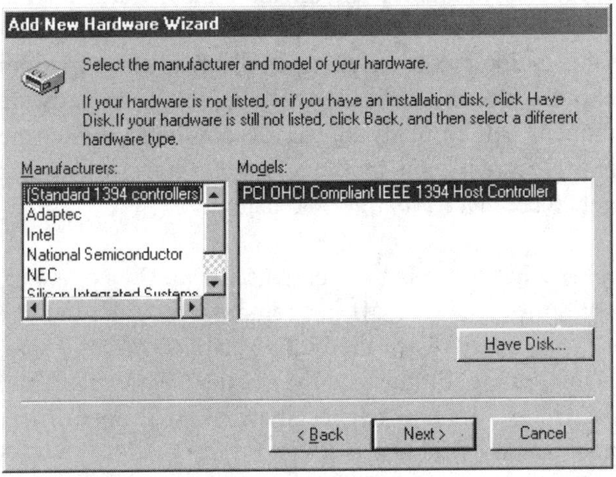

Add New Hardware Wizard

Select the manufacturer and model of your hardware.

If your hardware is not listed, or if you have an installation disk, click Have Disk. If your hardware is still not listed, click Back, and then select a different hardware type.

Manufacturers:
- [Standard 1394 controllers]
- Adaptec
- Intel
- National Semiconductor
- NEC
- Silicon Integrated Systems

Models:
- PCI OHCI Compliant IEEE 1394 Host Controller

Have Disk...

< Back   Next >   Cancel

Fig. 8.43: Selecting manufacturer and model of the hardware

Default settings

In the beginning, we suggest that you use the default settings of the new hardware. To do so, click on the *Next* button each time. Subsequently, the required drivers will be retrieved from the *Windows 98* setup CD ROM or from the manufacturer's diskette and copied onto the system.

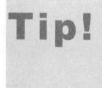 If a conflict is encountered with a hardware that is already installed, a message box will appear. If you click on *Next* the software for this hardware will be installed but the device itself will remain deactivated until the conflict is solved. Clicking on *Cancel* will abort the whole installation process.

Hardware conflict

If a hardware conflict arises after installing the component there will also be a corresponding message box. Normally it will also provide some suggestions as to how to solve the conflict.

When you have completed the whole process of new hardware installation, click on the *Finish* button. After that, you will be prompted to restart your computer. Confirm this dialog box by clicking on the *Yes* button in order to reboot. After the computer restarts, the new hardware component will be ready to use. To configure it later on, open the *System* icon in the *Control Panel* folder and activate the *Device Manager* tab page.

Tip! If the new hardware is not yet installed on the computer, exit Windows and turn off the computer in order to stick in the component. Turn the computer back on after that. But before doing this, be sure to read the following section which will explain how to check the resources upon which the new hardware depends.

Using the Device Manager to Check Hardware Components

Every computer is composed of various hardware components. The most basic elements are the motherboard and processor, memory, cache and drive controllers as well as storage components such as hard disk(s) and floppy drive(s). Depending on the hardware configuration, additional components will be added onto this, like a CD ROM drive, graphic card, sound card, video-, scanner- or *SCSI* card.

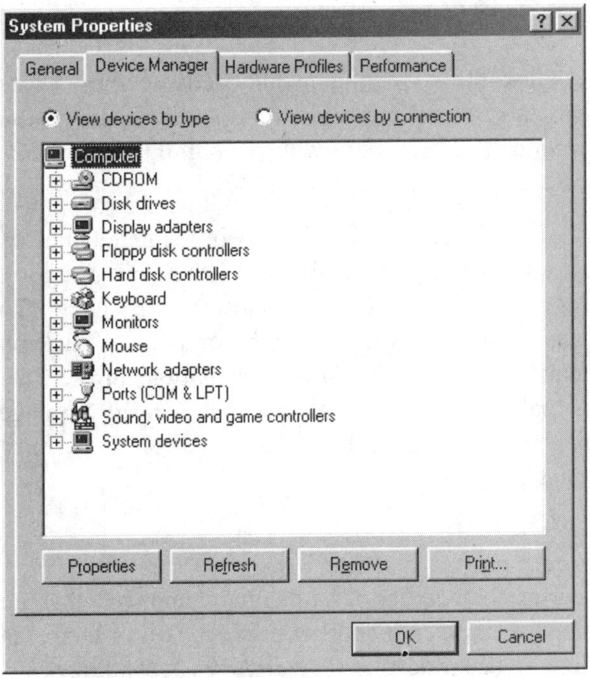

Fig. 8.44:   Installed hardware components listed in the device manager

Proper installation   All of these devices add to the functionality of the system. In order to make the best use of them, the hardware needs to be installed properly for the system to recognize them and all necessary drivers have to be installed and loaded. Usually *Windows 98* will do this automatically during the initial setup or after the installation of the new hardware and its drivers.

Plug & Play flaws

Unfortunately, *Plug and Play* technology does not always work as reliably in everyday use as the manufacturers claim it will. With the help of the *Control Panel* it is possible, though, to view the installed hardware components and, if need be, to change their properties. For this purpose, open the *Control Panel* folder through *Start/ Settings*.

Device manager

Double-click the *System* icon and activate the *Device Manager* tab page. Then select the *View devices by type* radio button. The list will now display all the major hardware categories.

Properties

Click on the plus sign in front of one of the items in order to view all the components that fall under that category. Clicking the minus sign will collapse the list again. To learn about the details of a certain component, click on that item and then on the *Properties* button. In the *Properties* dialog box for that object, the *General* tab page will display the status of this device, such as: *This device is working properly*.

Troubleshooting Hardware Conflicts with the Device Manager

Considering the number of hardware components that are built into a computer, a conflict between two of them can occasionally occur despite *Plug and Play* technology.

System conflicts of this kind will lead to the malfunctioning of the devices concerned or to the disabling of certain components. With the *Device Manager, Windows 98* provides you with a powerful tool to troubleshoot and eliminate hardware conflicts.

View devices by type

If this happens to you, open the *Control Panel* folder through the *Start* menu and *Settings*. Double-click the *System* icon and activate the *Device Manager* tab page. Then select the *View devices by type* radio button. The list will now display all the major hardware categories.

View all components

Click on the plus-sign in front of one of the items in order to view all the components that fall under that category. Clicking on the minus-sign will collapse the list again.

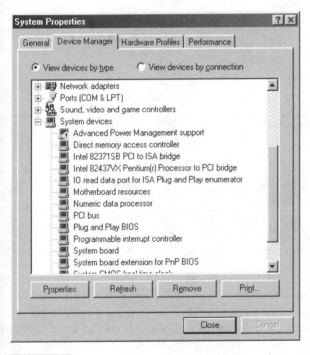

Fig. 8.45:   Troubleshooting hardware conflicts with the Device Manager

If the list of devices shows an exclamation mark in front of one of the item (see Figure 8.45), *Windows 98* is telling you that this is the component that is creating a problem or is in conflict with another device.

If you discover an 'X' on one of the icons (Figure 8.46) then this device has been disabled due to a hardware conflict.

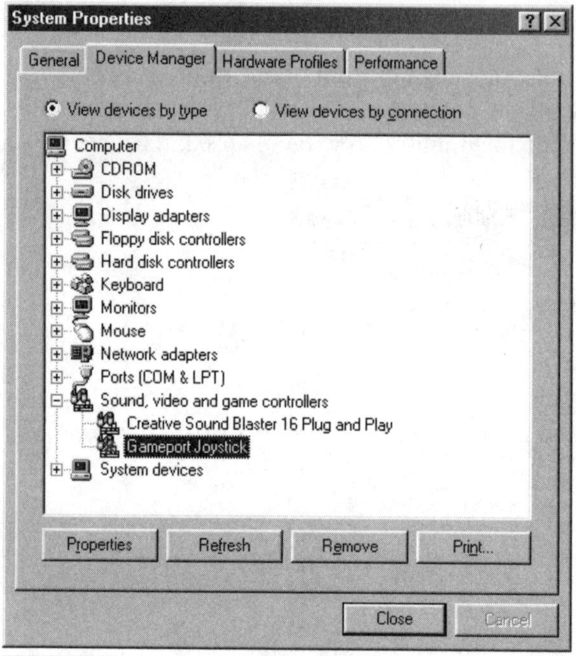

Fig. 8.46: Troubleshooting hardware conflicts with the Device Manager

Eliminating the conflict

To eliminate the conflict, select the item that has the exclamation mark or the red X and click on the *Properties* button. In the *Properties* dialog box of the same name, the *General* tab page displays the status of this device.

In the event of such problems the *Device status* box (Figure 8.47, left) will display a message such as: '*This device is either not present, not working properly, or does not have all drivers installed*'. Here is where the troubleshooting begins.

More tabs

Depending on the type of component, the *Properties* dialog box will contain more tabs. Through the *Driver* tab page you can obtain some data regarding the driver, and the *Driver File Details* button will provide you with even more information. Also, it is possible to re-install the manufacturer's driver from a diskette, for instance, by clicking on the *Update Driver* button.

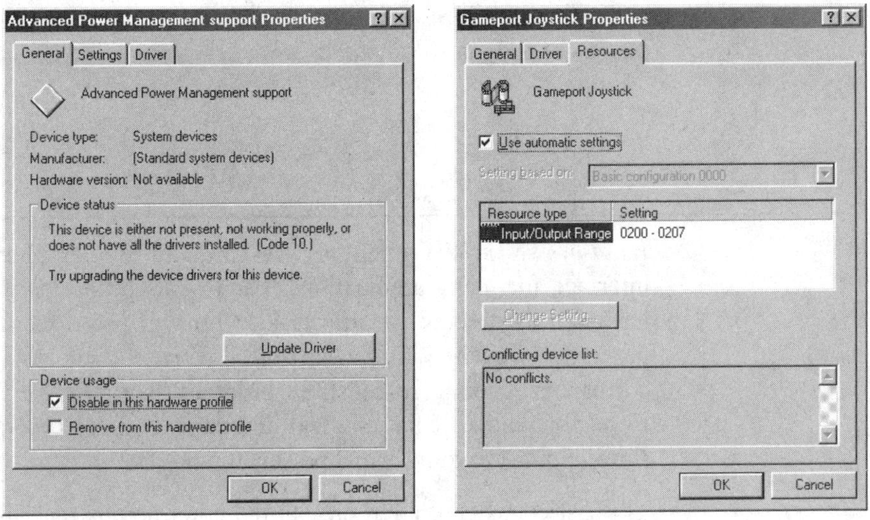

Fig. 8.47:   Identifying and eliminating problems

On the *Resources* tab page you can modify the system resources used by the hardware. These will depend on the hardware you have installed and could include *Direct memory access (DMA), Interrupt request (IRQ), Input Output I/O*, etc.. If you have not the slightest idea of what any of this means, you had better not touch it!

Use automatic settings

If you are familiar with these terms, however, you can clear the *Use automatic settings* check box. Then select the resource to be modified and click on *Change Setting*.

If no modifications are possible, a message will be displayed; otherwise, enter a different resource in the dialog box. Under *Conflict information* you will find more information. Confirm your settings, restart the computer and verify whether the modified component is working properly in the *Device Manager*.

Tip! Attention: If you deactivate the *Use automatic settings* check box, *Windows 98* may not be able to automatically configure *Plug and Play* hardware.

Installing Software and Windows Components

Windows 98 is the operating system and the graphic interface for many applications. Each of its programs is designed to execute specific tasks: you will use a word processor such as *Microsoft Word* for your correspondence; a spreadsheet program like *Microsoft Excel* for your calculations and diagrams; and *Microsoft PowerPoint* for your formal presentations.

This list could go on and on, but the point here is that all these programs for *Windows 98* have one thing in common: before you can use them on your computer, the program files have to be copied onto your hard disk. Of course you do not have to do all of this manually, because the setup and installation programs are meant for this purpose. Under *Windows 98*, calling up the setup program is child's play.

Installing Windows 98 Components

To install *Windows 98* programs on your computer, choose the *Settings* command from the *Start* menu and, in the overlapping, menu click on the *Control Panel* entry.

Double-click on the *Add/Remove Programs* icon and select the *Install/Uninstall* tab page in the dialog box.

Install button

Click the *Install* button. Insert the first program disk or the Setup CD-ROM into the respective drive and confirm with *Next*. *Windows 98* will search for the setup program, and will then display the found *SETUP* or *INSTALL* file in the command line.

Installation program

If you click the *Finish* button, the installation program of your new application will be started. From then on, follow the instructions of the setup program. After the installation, the entry of the new program will be displayed in the list box in the *Install/Uninstall* tab page.

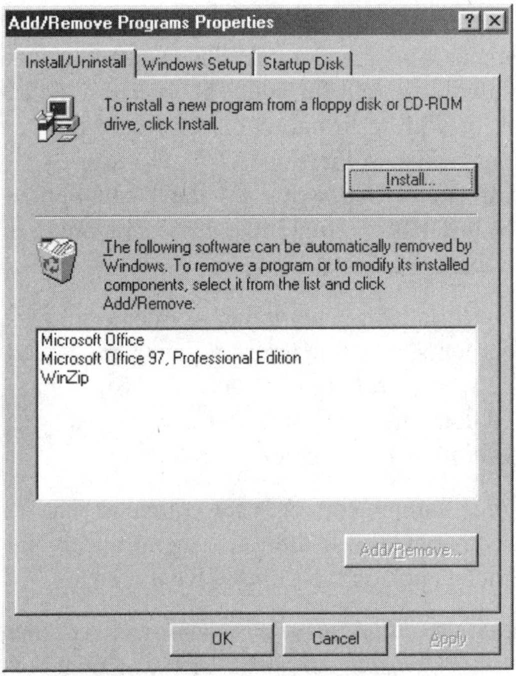

Fig. 8.48: Installing additional applications for Windows 98

Remove the
program

If you want to remove a program or add new components, select the respective entry in the list of the installed
programs and click the *Add/Remove* button.

Tip!

To subsequently add or remove *Microsoft Office Suite*
program components, use the procedure described above.
Select the *Microsoft Office 97 (Professional Edition)* entry
in the list box and click on the *Add/Remove* button. More
on this in the next section.

Installing Microsoft Office Components

Before using *Microsoft Office Suite* programs on your
computer, the program files have to be copied onto your
hard disk. Of course you need not do this manually, as the
setup program will do it all for you. The *Microsoft Office*
programs are, or will be, installed on your hard disk by
you or by your dealer in the same way. The size of the
installation can vary. Depending on the setup options
selected in the installation program, a different number of
files will be copied.

Standard
installation

In the *Standard* installation only the most often used files,
templates, help tools, and converter programs are copied.
If you realize, while working with an office application,
that a required component has not been copied onto your
system, you can do this installation anytime.

Office components

To install *Office* components on your computer, choose
the *Settings* command from the *Start* menu and in the
overlapping menu click on the *Control Panel* item.

Double-click on the *Add/Remove Programs* icon and then
select the *Install/Uninstall* tab page in the dialog box.
Select the *Microsoft Office 97 (Professional)* item in the
list and press the *Add/Remove* button. Insert the first pro-

gram disk or the Setup CD-ROM into the respective drive and confirm with *OK*.

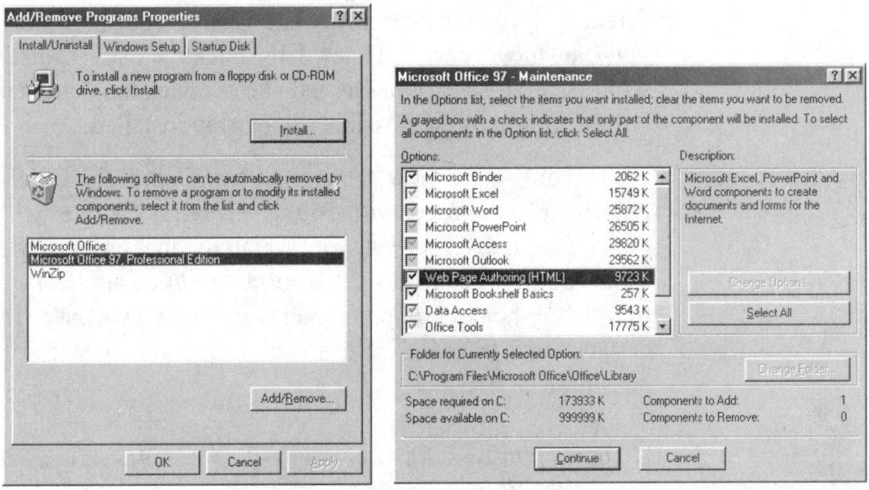

Fig. 8.49: Installation of additional Office components

Installed
components

The setup program will search for the installed components on your system. If the *Office Shortcut Bar* is displayed, you will be asked to close it. Follow the setup program instructions and click *Next* until the dialog box with the setup options is displayed on your screen. Click the *Add/Remove* button to select your components.

To begin with, select the program entry to which new components are to be added. If you have the *Microsoft Office Suite*, you first have to select the respective program. Then click the *Change Option* button. In the next dialog box you can further specify the selection. Select a topic and select the components installed in that category by clicking on the *Change Option* button.

Subtopics

If the *Change Option* button is not displayed, it means that no subtopics are available. Select the check box in front of the additional programs, help files, converters, or filters that you need. If you want to save your selection, you can move back one level by clicking *OK,*. *Cancel* will discard a selection. Greyed check boxes indicate that only a portion of the possible options are installed.

Installation can be started

Go on confirming your changes with *OK*, until the installation can be started with *Next*. The required files will then be copied. After that, confirm all the messages of the setup program, and start the respective *Office* application to verify whether the components are now available. In certain cases *Windows 98* has to be restarted before this is possible.

If you cannot find the *Microsoft Office 97* entry in the list box of the *Install/Uninstall* tab page, or you receive an error message after clicking on the *Add/Remove* button, start the setup program *SETUP.EXE* from the root level of the CD-ROM drive.

Installing Windows 98 Components

The number of installed Windows components depends on the type of installation. If the *Standard* or *Minimal* setup options are selected, then not all of the components are installed.

If you are missing one of the components described in this book, for example, a Windows accessories item, you have the possibility to install this component with the help of Windows setup.

Choose the *Settings* command from the *Start* menu and in the overlapping menu click on the *Control Panel* item. In the *Control Panel* folder double-click the *Add/Remove Programs* icon. Activate the *Windows Setup* tab page in the *Add/Remove Programs Properties* dialog box. Then wait for the automatic detection to be completed.

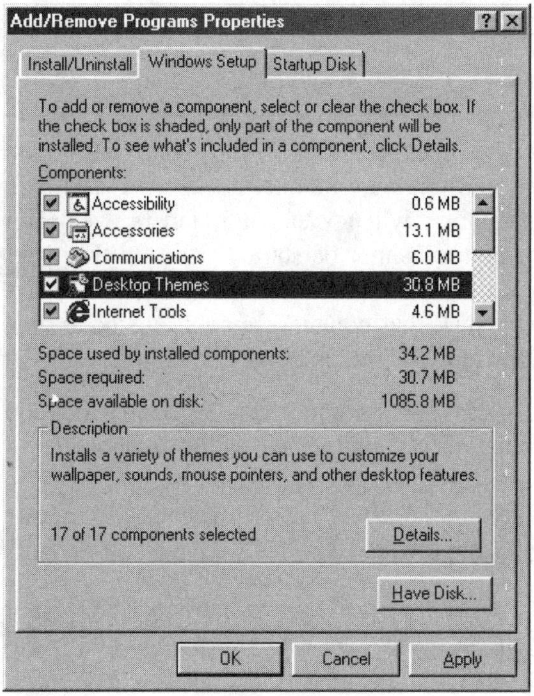

Add/Remove Programs Properties ? X

| Install/Uninstall | Windows Setup | Startup Disk |

To add or remove a component, select or clear the check box. If the check box is shaded, only part of the component will be installed. To see what's included in a component, click Details.

Components:

☑ 🔆 Accessibility	0.6 MB
☑ 🗂 Accessories	13.1 MB
☑ 🌐 Communications	6.0 MB
☑ 🎨 Desktop Themes	30.8 MB
☑ 🌐 Internet Tools	4.6 MB

Space used by installed components: 34.2 MB
Space required: 30.7 MB
Space available on disk: 1085.8 MB

Description
Installs a variety of themes you can use to customize your wallpaper, sounds, mouse pointers, and other desktop features.

17 of 17 components selected   Details...

Have Disk...

OK   Cancel   Apply

Fig. 8.50:   Installing additional Windows components

List *Components*   Use the scroll bar to go through the *Components* list. Once you find the component you are looking for, select it and click on the *Details* button if it is displayed. A list of all the programs contained in this category will appear. Use the scroll bar to go through the *Components* list box.

Select the
check box

Select or clear the check box of the required application and confirm with *OK*. Repeat these steps, if needed, for other entries. A partial selection is indicated with a grey check box on the *Windows Setup* tab page. Insert the *Windows 98* Setup CD-ROM into the CD drive and confirm with *OK*. The selected components will be copied. Finally, close the *Control Panel*.

Creating a Startup Disk

Sometimes the unexpected will happen, even under *Windows 98*, and this may be due to various reasons. In rare cases Windows will not start up, and in even rarer cases the computer cannot be started at all. In this case, you need a *Startup Disk*. A startup disk is a specially formatted floppy disk that contains, apart from the system files, the command line interpreter.

With these files your computer can be booted directly from the floppy disk. With the help of the diagnostic programs on the startup disk, experienced users can try to find the cause of the error that is preventing Windows from starting from the hard disk.

With the startup disk at least you will have access to your computer and can in this way copy any important documents onto other floppy disks if you need to send your computer for repair. If you want to be well prepared for an emergency such as this, you should always keep a startup disk on hand. You can easily create a startup disk with *Windows 98*.

Control panel

Call up the *Control Panel* with *Start/Setting* and double-click the *Add/Remove Programs* tab page. Change to the *Startup Disk* tab page and click on the *Create Disk* button.

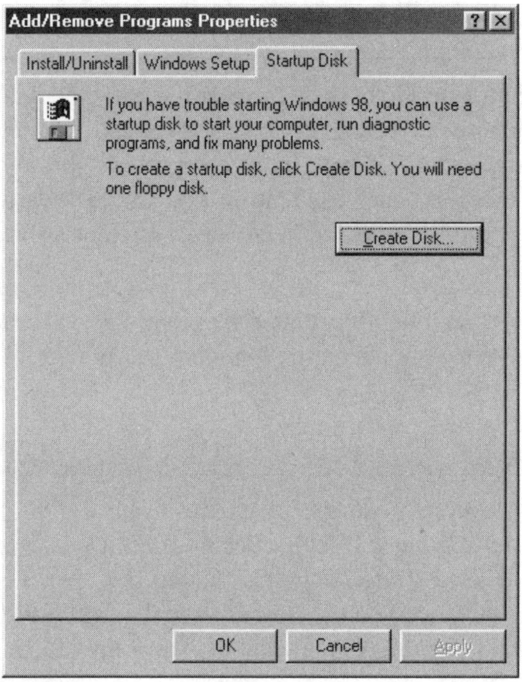

Add/Remove Programs Properties ? X

| Install/Uninstall | Windows Setup | Startup Disk |

If you have trouble starting Windows 98, you can use a startup disk to start your computer, run diagnostic programs, and fix many problems.

To create a startup disk, click Create Disk. You will need one floppy disk.

Create Disk...

OK | Cancel | Apply

Fig. 8.51: Creating a startup disk for emergencies

Windows 98
Setup CD

Insert the *Windows 98* Setup CD into the CD drive and a new floppy diskette into the floppy drive, and click on the *OK* button. *Windows 98* will copy all the required files and graphically display the progress of the copying. Close the *Add/Remove Programs Properties* dialog box with the *OK* button and subsequently close the *Control Panel*.

Clearly label your startup disk and keep it in a safe place. In case of problems, your computer can be started with the help of this disk.

Verifying and Setting the Date and the Time

Many program functions, such as inserting the date and the time, require an accurate system time and system date. Of course you also want your computer to display the correct time. A small element on your motherboard whose information is read by *Windows 98* is responsible for this task.

You can program this chip under *Windows 98*. This is what you have to do every time you change the date or the time.

Setting the Time and the Date

Programming
the chip

To change the system time, call up the *Control Panel* folder with *Start/Settings*. Double-click the *Date/Time* icon to display the *Date/Time Properties* dialog box. On the *Date & Time* tab page you can now change the date using the calendar and the time in the text box below the clock.

To set the month, open the respective drop-down list, and click on the name of the month. For the year, select the current year by using the spin buttons next to the year box.

Setting the day

The day can be selected by clicking on the day in the calendar. Finally click on the *Apply* button.

Correct the time

If you want to correct the time, click in the respective text box in hours, minutes, or seconds. Use the spin buttons to increase or decrease the values. You can also type the correct time directly into the text box. Confirm with *OK*, and close the *Control Panel*.

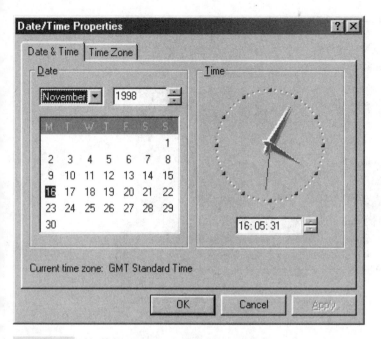

Fig. 8.52:   Verifying and correcting date and time

Fig. 8.52:   Verifying and correcting date and time

Tip!   A quicker way to call up the *Date/Time Properties* dialog box is by double-clicking on the time displayed in the taskbar. If you simply point at the time 🖥️ 19:30 in the taskbar, the date will be shown as a *ScreenTip*.

Automatic Adjustment of the System Clock to Daylight Savings Time

Automatically changes

You can set *Windows 98* in such a way that your computer automatically changes the system clock to daylight savings time. To do this, select *Start/Settings* and click on *Control Panel*.

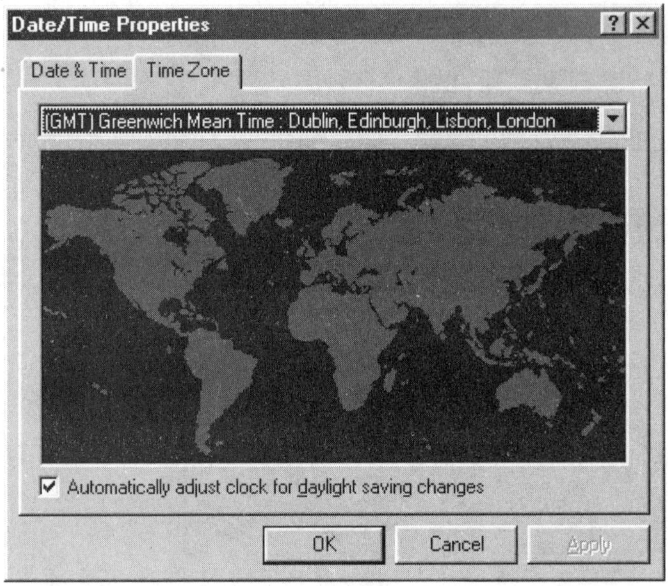

Date/Time Properties [?] [X]

| Date & Time | Time Zone |

(GMT) Greenwich Mean Time : Dublin, Edinburgh, Lisbon, London ▼

☑ Automatically adjust clock for daylight saving changes

[OK] [Cancel] [Apply]

Fig. 8.53:   Activate automatic time changes

In the *Control Panel* folder double-click the *Time/Date* icon. Activate the *Time Zone* tab page, and choose the option *Automatically adjust clock for daylight saving changes*. Then confirm with *OK*.

When you start your computer for the first time after the automatic switch-over, you will receive a message informing you of the changed time. If you confirm the message with ⏎, *Windows 98* will display the *Date/Time Properties* dialog box. Verify the system time and close the window with *OK*.

Configuring Regional Settings

Almost every country in the world uses a different format to write the date or time. Sometimes the 12-hour format is used, while in other cases the 24-hour format is used. The same applies to the date. The Americans put the month before the day and the year, while the Europeans, on the other hand, put the day before the month and the year.

Number and currency formats

This list can be continued for the various number and currency formats. Imagine what a job you'd have if you had to enter or change all those formats by hand! It's precisely for this reason that *Windows 98* has a choice of *Regional Settings*.

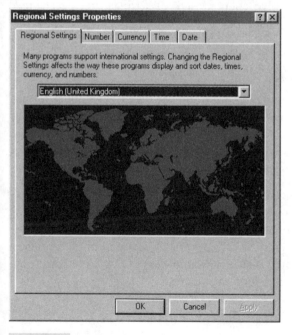

Fig. 8.54: Verifying and changing regional settings

You will find this function in the *Control Panel*, which you can access via *Start/Settings* or *My Computer*. If you double-click on the *Regional Settings* icon in the *Control Panel*, a dialog box with five tab pages will be displayed.

Regional settings

In the drop-down list on the *Regional Settings* tab page, choose the country whose number, currency, time, and date format you want to use. For the U.K. this would be the entry *English (United Kingdom)*. If you confirm with *OK*, these settings will be applied globally.

The *Regional Settings* tab page is useful if you are travelling with your notebook and want to create documents that are compatible with the time, number, date, etc. Format of the country where you are. It is enough to click on the respective country, and all settings will be changed automatically.

Changing the Number Format for Windows 98

Most countries in the world use their own number format. We are not talking here about the difference between Arabic and Chinese numbers, but the seemingly small differences like the digit grouping symbol, which in some cases is a space, in others a dot or a comma.

Specific fomat

To change all number formats of a country in one go, follow the steps detailed above concerning the changing of *Regional Settings*. In this section we deal with the specific number format. Sometimes you might require a particular format, for example when you have correspondence with a foreign country.

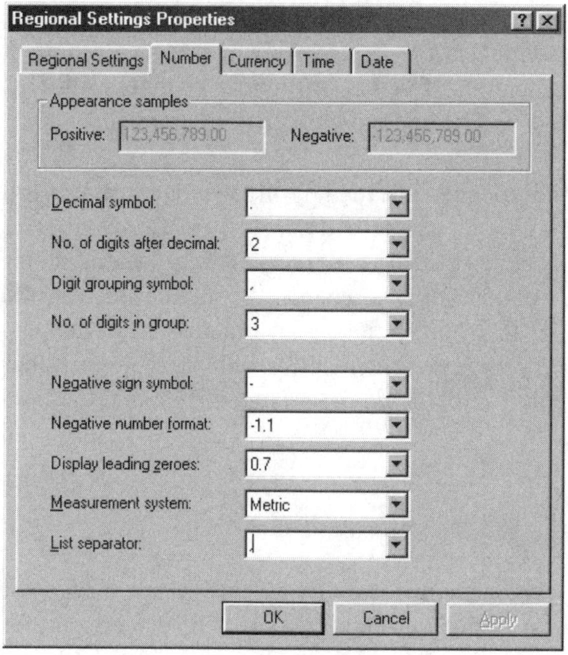

Fig. 8.55: The *Number* tab page

Flexible number format

Thanks to the flexibility of *Windows 98* you can modify the number format according to your requirements at any time. To do this call up the *Control Panel* with *Start/ Settings* or *My Computer*. Double-click the *Regional Settings* icon and change to the *Number* tab page. With the drop-down list boxes you can now individually select the settings for the *Decimal symbol, No. of digits after decimal, Digit grouping symbol*, etc.

Simply open the list next to the number format to be changed and select one of the available entries. The number of available entries depends on the country selected on the *Regional Settings* tab page. Using the *Measurement system* drop-down list, the metric system can be changed to the *US* format, (inches instead of centimeters, etc.). The entries in the *Negative sign symbol* and *Negative number format* drop-down lists are important for book keeping. If you confirm your changes with *OK*, the settings will be applied globally in *Windows 98*.

Tip! If an additionally installed Windows application (all *Microsoft Office Suite* programs, such as *Microsoft Excel* or *Word*, etc.) contains program-specific options, commands or dialog boxes to change the number format, the settings in that application are valid for only that program. The settings on the *Numbers* tab page, on the other hand, apply to all *Windows 98* components and applications.

Changing the Currency Format of Windows 98

Almost every country uses its own currency format for currency specification and symbols. The Americans for example write *US 250*, while the Germans write both *250 DM* and *DM 250*.

Settings for a country

If you want to globally change all the settings for a particular country, for instance, to write all your invoices in the dollar mark format, refer to the steps described above regarding changing the *Regional Settings*. Here we will discuss only the currency format.

Specific currency format

Sometimes a specific currency format is required, for example when you are corresponding with other countries or on account of specific business regulations. Fortunately, thanks to the flexibility of *Windows 98*, the standard currency setting (ex.: £ 123,456,789.00) can be customized to meet your needs.

To do this, call up the *Control Panel* with *Start/Settings* or *My Computer*. Double-click the *Regional Settings* icon

Decimal symbol | and change to the *Currency* tab page. With the drop-down lists you can now individually select the settings for the *Currency symbol, Position of currency symbol, Digit grouping symbol, Number of digits in group,* etc.

List currency format | Simply open the drop-down list box next to the currency format to be changed and select one of the available entries. The number of available entries depends on the country selected on the *Regional Settings* tab page. In the *Currency symbol* box you can also enter your own symbol, for example, *Pounds.* Simply enter your choice into the text box.

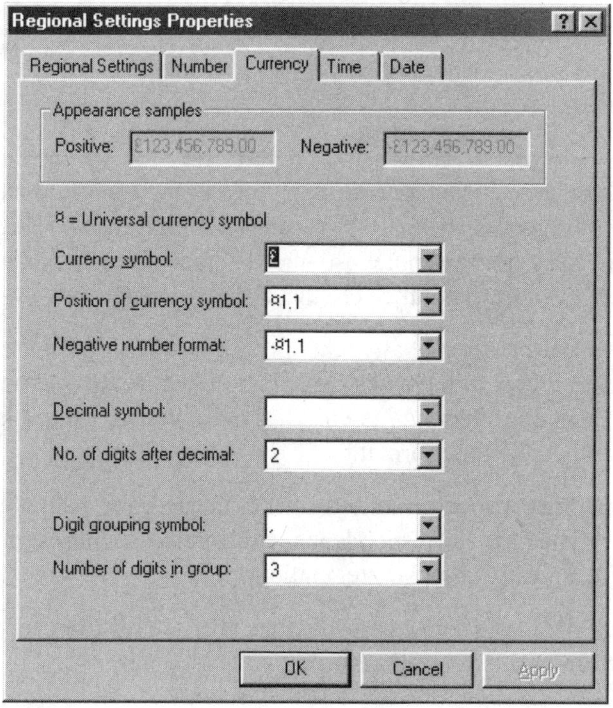

Regional Settings Properties | ? X

Regional Settings | Number | Currency | Time | Date

Appearance samples

Positive: £123,456,789.00   Negative: -£123,456,789.00

¤ = Universal currency symbol

Currency symbol: £

Position of currency symbol: ¤1.1

Negative number format: -¤1.1

Decimal symbol: .

No. of digits after decimal: 2

Digit grouping symbol: ,

Number of digits in group: 3

OK | Cancel | Apply

Fig. 8.56:   Changing the currency format under Windows 98

347

The settings in the *Position of currency symbol* and *Negative number format* drop-down lists are important for book keeping. If you confirm your changes with *OK*, the settings will be globally applied in *Windows 98*.

Tip!

If an additionally installed Windows application (any of the *Microsoft Office Suite* programs, such as *Microsoft Excel* or *Word* etc.) contains program-specific options, commands or dialog boxes for changing the currency format, the settings of the application are valid only for documents within that application.

The settings on the *Currency* tab page, however, will apply to all *Windows 98* components and applications.

Changing the Time Format in Windows 98

Almost every country uses its own date and time format. The differences in hour formatting are well known. The Americans for example use the 12-hour format, while many European countries use the 24-hour format.

Global settings

If you want to globally change all the settings for a country, refer to the steps described above in the section on changing *Regional Settings*. For now we will talk about just the time format.

Time format

Sometimes a specific time format is needed, for example when you have correspondence with foreign countries, or due to specific company regulations.

Since *Windows 98* is very flexible, the default time format can be customized according to your needs.

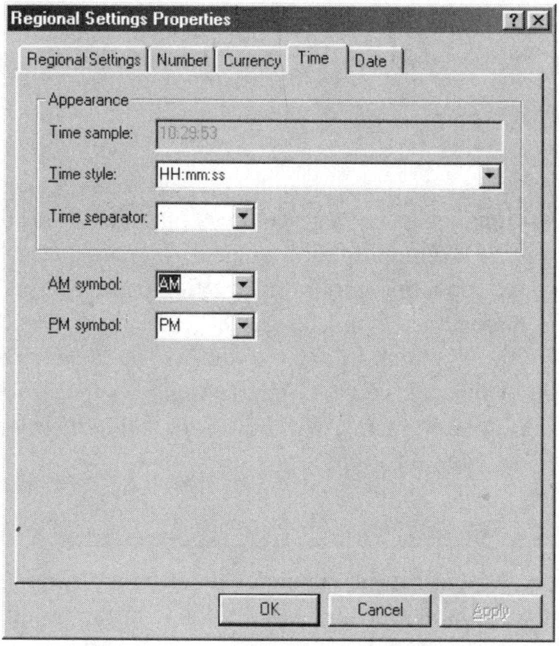

Regional Settings Properties

Regional Settings | Number | Currency | Time | Date

Appearance

Time sample: 10:29:53

Time style: HH:mm:ss

Time separator: :

AM symbol: AM

PM symbol: PM

OK   Cancel   Apply

Fig. 8.57: Changing the time display under Windows 98

Time tab page

To do this, call up the *Control Panel* with *Start/Settings* or *My Computer*. Double-click the *Regional Settings* icon and activate the *Time* tab page. With the *Time style* drop-down list, you can now change the settings for the display format for hours, minutes and seconds.

Syntax

The following characters, using the capital and lower case letters indicated, are used to compose the time format:

- 24-hour time format:
  H or HH (with leading zero)

- 12-hour time format:
  h or hh (with leading zero)

- Minutes:
  m or mm (with leading zero)

- Seconds:
  s or ss (with leading zero)

- AM/PM:
  xx (two letters)

Tip!

If an additionally installed Windows application (all *Microsoft Office Suite* programs, such as *Microsoft Excel* or *Word* etc.) contains program-specific options, commands or dialog boxes to change the time format, the settings of the application are only valid for the documents within that application. The settings on the *Time* tab page, on the other hand, will hold for all *Windows 98* components and applications.

Changing the Date Format in Windows 98

Almost every country uses its own date and time format. The most well known differences are those in the month format. The Americans, for example, put the month before the day, while in most European countries the day comes before the month. Different date formats occur even within the same country, for instance, *Saturday, 14 February 1999,* or *14/02/99.*

Global date
settings

If you want to globally change the date settings for a country, refer to the steps described above in the section which deals with changing the *Regional Settings*. Here, only the date format will be discussed.

Sometimes you may need a specific date format, for example when you are in touch with a foreign country or bound by specific company regulations.

Since *Windows 98* is very adaptable, the standard date format can be customized to suit your requirements. To do this call up the *Control Panel* with *Start/Settings* or

Date tab page

through *My Computer*. Double-click the *Regional Settings* icon and change to the *Date* tab page.

Syntax

With the *Short date* and *Long date* group boxes you can select settings for two different date formats. Use the characters given below, including capital and lower case letters, to compose the date format:

- Years:
  y or yy (with leading zero)

- Days:
  d or dd (with leading zero)

- Month:
  M or MM (with leading zero)

- Abbreviation with three characters:
  ddd and MMM

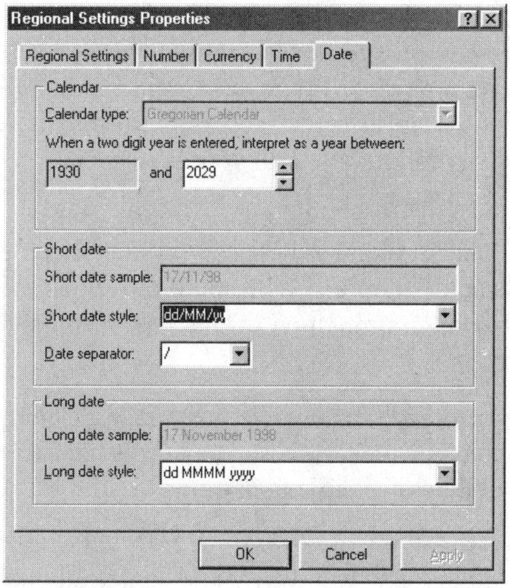

Fig. 8.58:   Configuring the date format under Windows 98

351

Date separator

Using the *Date separator* you can choose other separators for the days, months and years. If you confirm your changes with *OK*, the settings will be globally applied in *Windows 98*.

Tip!

If an additionally installed Windows application (all *Microsoft Office Suite* programs, such as *Microsoft Excel* or *Word*, etc.) contains program-specific options, commands or dialog boxes to change the date format, the settings of the application are only valid for documents in that program. The settings on the *Date* tab page will apply to all *Windows 98* components and applications.

Setting the Windows Password

The access to computers with *Windows 98* can be restricted using a password. If a password is assigned, Windows will ask for the *User name* and the *Password* after the startup. Assigning a password is as easy as pie, although the configuration of an effective access protection is a task for the systems administrator of your network.

Personal settings

In this section we will show you how to protect your personal settings using a password. These settings include the contents of the desktop and its display as well as the customized personal configuration of the *Start* menu and the program groups.

Other users can protect their own settings on your computer. Such protection makes sense, especially in cases where a PC is used by the whole family.

Passwords icon

To set a password call up the *Control Panel* with *Start/Settings*. Double-click the *Passwords* icon and select the *User profiles* tab page. Select the *Users can customize their preferences and desktop settings...* radio button and choose one or both check boxes if required.

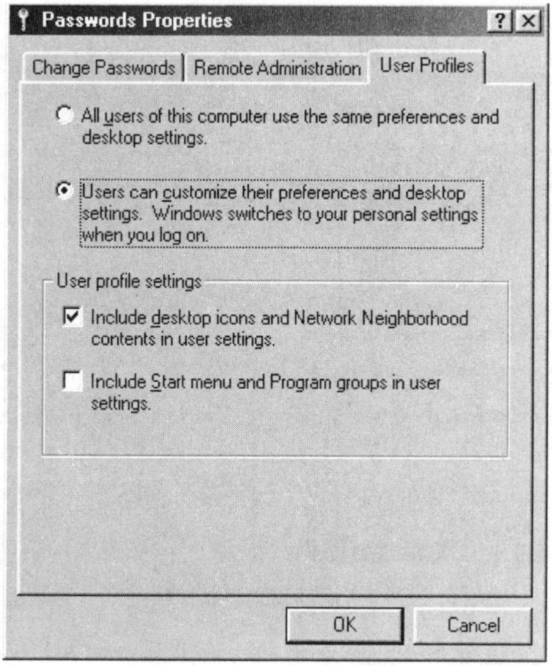

Fig. 8.59: Changing the *Change passwords* tab page

With the *Include desktop icons...* check box you can specify whether the icons on the desktop are saved for each user separately.

Individual settings

The *Include Start menu and Program groups...* option will save individual settings for the *Start* menu and program groups.

Make your selection and change to the *Change Passwords* tab page. Click the *Change Windows Password* button.

Asterisks

Enter your password in the *New Password* text box. Your entry will be displayed as asterisks, and will have to be confirmed in the *New Password* text box. After that click on *OK*. If the two entries are not identical you will receive an error message, in which case you should type in the entry again.

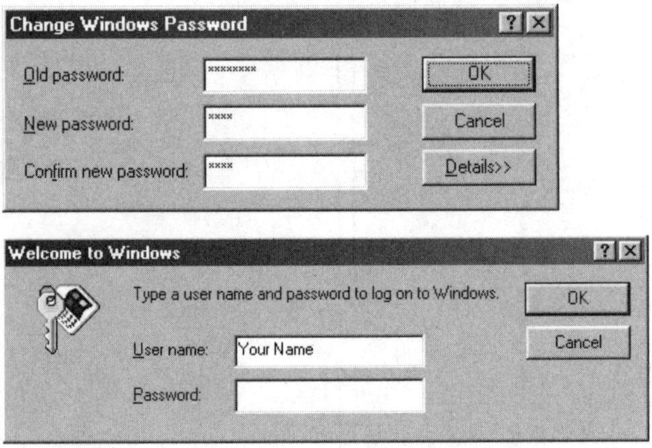

Fig. 8.60: Entering a password (above), and the prompt at Windows startup

Restart

Windows 98

Confirm the final message with *OK*, and close the *Password Properties* dialog box. You will now be requested to restart *Windows 98*. Click *Yes* to automatically restart the system.

Password prompt

After restarting you will be prompted to enter your password and your user name. Enter this information and click *OK*.

From now on, if this option is selected, changes in the *Start* menu will be saved in the subfolders of the *C:\Windows\Profiles* folder. The subfolder will have your user name and contain the entire program structure of the *Start* menu.

Tip! Using this method, the password does not provide real protection. By closing the password prompt, you can access the *Windows 98* desktop without any difficulty. You can also change the user name in the prompt and log on under another name to enter the system without a password. In the next section you will learn how to protect *Microsoft Office* applications from unauthorized access.

Saving Documents in Office Applications with a Password

All programs of the *Microsoft Office Suite* offer three mechanisms for protecting your documents from unauthorized access. These methods are especially useful where confidential documents such as client lists, tax declarations, or private material are concerned. Of course you only have to protect your files from unauthorized access if you share your computer with other users or if they have access to it.

This is the case more often than it might appear at first glance. Good examples include company PCs and network computers as well as Internet or Online access. In all these cases, unauthorized persons could have access to the computer you are using.

Office application

For this reason, the *Microsoft Word* and *Microsoft Excel Office* applications offer protection for documents. These options are not available with *Microsoft PowerPoint*. *Microsoft Access* offers even more complex protection mechanisms which can, however, only be used if the security administration account mode is activated.

Password to modify

The maximum protection for files is offered by the *password to open* option. Without the password, a file cannot be opened again. Not even by you. If you have forgotten the password, it cannot be recovered again. If you want to save a document with very important private or secret contents using a password, go to *File/Save As*.

In the *Save As* dialog box, change to the folder where the document is to be saved and enter the file name. Then click the *Options* button.

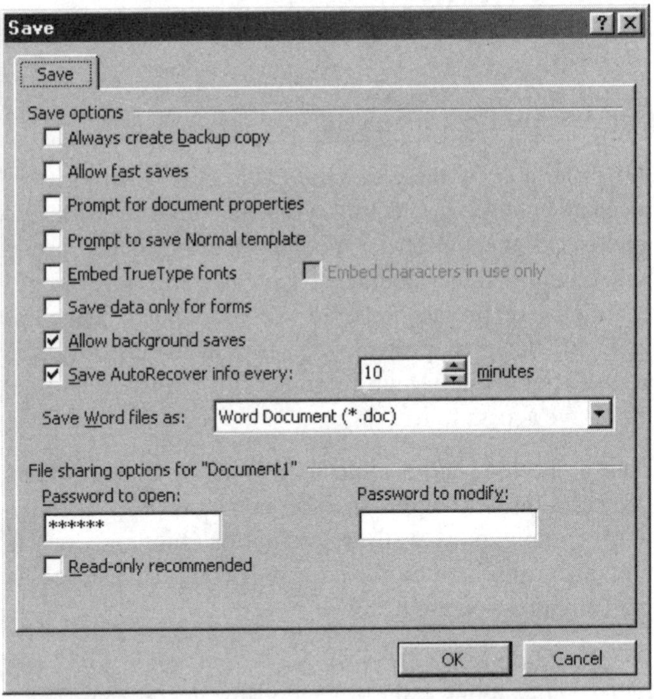

Fig. 8.61:   Activate the password to open (here, Word 97)

Enter a password   Enter a password in the *Password to open* text box if what you want is to allow only authorized users to open the document, to accept or reject modifications, add or delete comments, as well as to modify protected tables or formulas, or even to cancel the protection of the document.

A good password

Your password is displayed only as asterisks * so that nobody else who is present when you enter your password can read it. A good password contains no less than four characters and should not be identical with the first name of either you or your wife/husband.

No birthday dates

Number combinations of birthday dates are also not advisable. This type of password can easily be guessed. Pay attention to upper and lower case letters and confirm with *OK*.

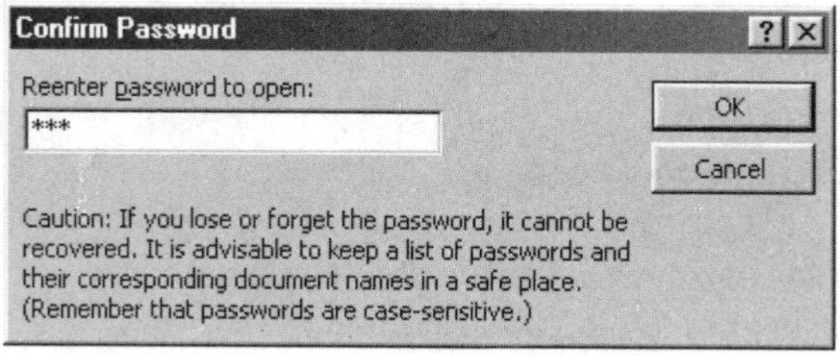

Fig. 8.62:   Confirming the password

Confirming the password

For reasons of security, *Word* and *Excel* will display a new dialog box in which the identical password has to be entered again. Confirm with *OK*.

If the two passwords are not identical, an error message will be displayed and the confirmation will have to be repeated. Click on *Save* in the *Save As* dialog box to complete the protection of the file.

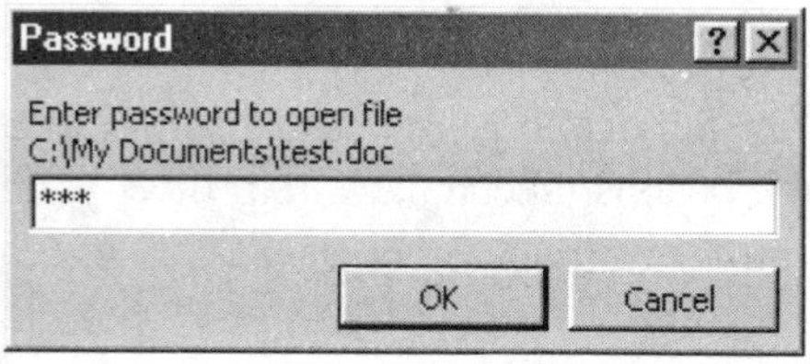

Fig. 8.63:   Password prompt when opening the file

Password
dialog box

Close the file and try to open the document using the *File* menu. The *Password* dialog box appears, asking you to enter the password. Correctly enter the password and confirm with *OK*.

The Word or Excel Office applications will then open the document. If you enter the wrong password, you will receive an error message, so try it again with *File/Open*.

Microsoft Access

With *Microsoft Access* select *Tools/Security/Set Database Password*. Enter the password in the *Password* text box and retype it in the *Verify* box, then click *OK*.

Tip!

In order to assign a password to a database with *Microsoft Access,* the database has to be opened in the *Exclusive* mode. After organizing the *Security Administrator Account*, further mechanisms will be available if more than one user needs access to a database. Get more information on this from the *Office-Assistant* of *Microsoft Access*.

Changing the Password in Office Applications

Changing the password with *Microsoft Word* and *Microsoft Excel* is only possible with files that have been opened with that password. Use the *Save As* dialog box and click *Options*. Delete or change the password which is displayed and confirm with *OK*.

Saving Documents with Passwords in Office Applications

The *Microsoft Office* applications *Microsoft Word* and *Microsoft Excel* offer various mechanisms to protect your documents from unauthorized access or accidental overwriting.

These methods are useful especially in the case of confidential documents with sensitive contents such as client lists, tax declarations, or product and item lists.

Prevent overwriting

Here you will learn how protected documents can be saved under another name, to prevent overwriting the information in the original. *Word* and *Excel* offer a three fold protection for documents.

Read only

Step 1 is the *Read only recommended* option, which allows you to open the file in the read-only mode. With step 2, the *Password to open*, only people who know the password can open the document and save it under its original name.

Password to modify

Step 3 is the *Password to modify*, without which a file can only be read but not saved. To protect a document in this manner, choose *File/Save As*. In the dialog box go to the target folder and enter the file name. Then click on *Options* to display the *Save* dialog box.

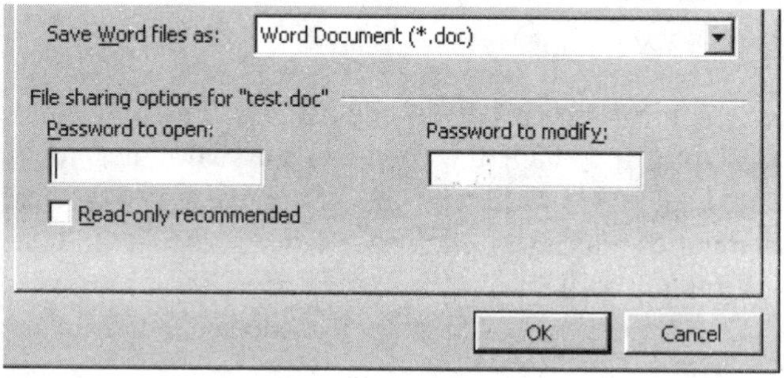

Save Word files as:	Word Document (*.doc) ▾

File sharing options for "test.doc"

Password to open:	Password to modify:

☐ Read-only recommended

OK   Cancel

Fig. 8.64:   *Read-only recommended* and *Password to open* boxes

Enter a password

Enter a password in the *Password to open* text box to allow only authorized users to open the document.

Without the password the file cannot be opened at all, so be sure to remember the correct password.

Tip!

Your password will be displayed in the form of asterisks * to prevent anyone present from reading it. A good password contains no less than four characters, which can be letters as well as numbers. It also should not be identical with the first name of you or your wife/husband.

Passwords which use combinations of birth dates or similarly important dates can prove equally unsecure. These passwords can be guessed all too easily. It is important to pay attention to lower and uppercase letters. Confirm the password entry by clicking on *OK*.

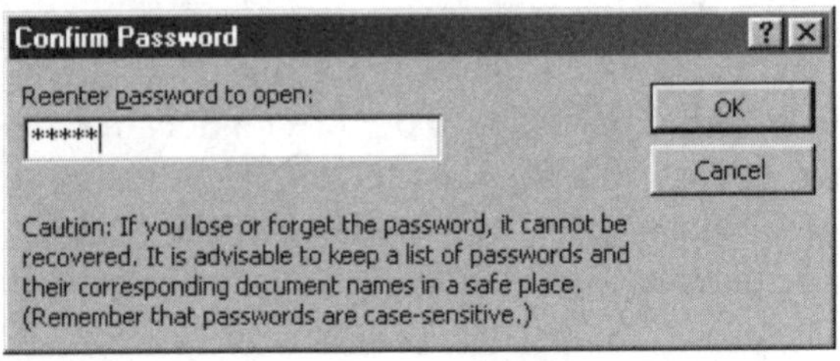

Confirm Password	? X
Reenter password to open: *****|	OK Cancel
Caution: If you lose or forget the password, it cannot be recovered. It is advisable to keep a list of passwords and their corresponding document names in a safe place. (Remember that passwords are case-sensitive.)	

Fig. 8.65:   Confirming the password

Password confirmation

For reasons of security, *Word* and *Excel* will display a new dialog box in which the identical password has to be entered again. Confirm with *OK*. If the two passwords are not identical, an error message will be appear and the confirmation will have to be repeated. Click on *Save* in the *Save As* dialog box to complete the protection of the file.

Open the document

Then close the file and try to reopen the document, for example using the *File* menu. The *Password* dialog box appears asking you to enter the password. Correctly enter the password and confirm with *OK*. The document will then be opened without restrictions.

To open a document that is protected with *password to modify* as read-only, click the *Read Only* button. If you open a document as read-only, and then modify the document, it can only be saved under another name.

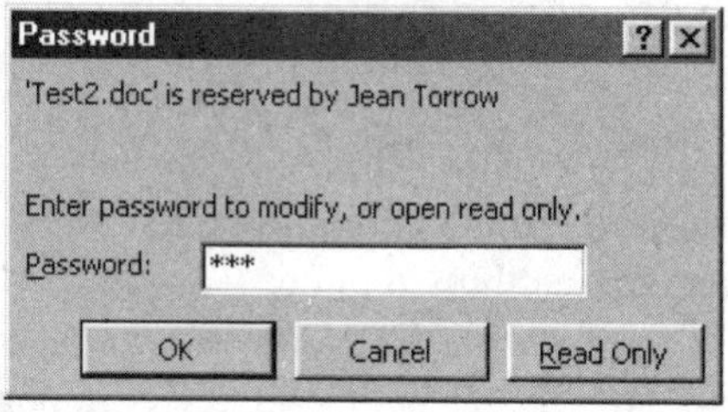

Password	? X
'Test2.doc' is reserved by Jean Torrow	
Enter password to modify, or open read only.	
Password: ***	
OK Cancel Read Only	

Fig. 8.66: Password prompt when opening the file

Saving Documents in Office applications with *Read only recommended*

To save a document with *Read only recommended*, choose *File/Save As*. In the dialog box, change to the folder and enter a file name. Click on the *Options* button and select the *Read only recommended* check box. Confirm with *OK* and *Save*.

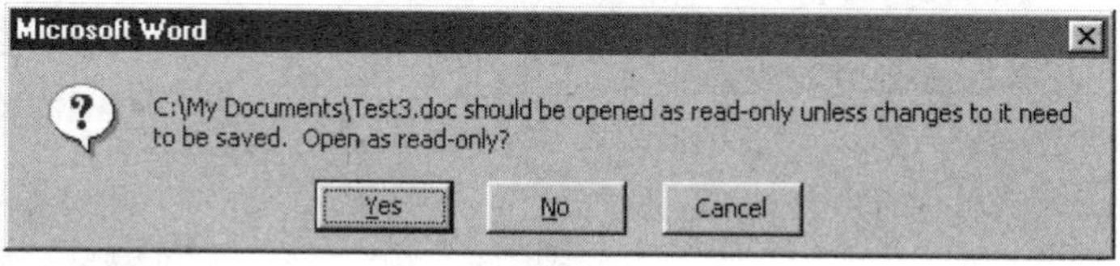

Microsoft Word	X
C:\My Documents\Test3.doc should be opened as read-only unless changes to it need to be saved. Open as read-only?	
Yes No Cancel	

Fig. 8.67: Read only recommended (with Word)

Prevent overwriting

When opening the document you will get a read-only recommendation message which should be answered with *Yes*.

This is only for your protection, to prevent any accidental overwriting of the original. Clicking *No* will open the document with full access.

Installing and Configuring Game Controllers

People who like computer games cannot avoid coming into contact with the *Joystick*. Only by means of this device can flight simulators, race cars or space ships be properly controlled. Those who have tried to do this using the keyboard or the mouse will understand why.

Like every device connected to the computer, even a joystick can be configured and calibrated under *Windows 98*. This is possible due to the fact that *Windows 98* claims to be able to run most *MS-DOS* games directly under *Windows 98*. If you have connected a joystick to your computer, or if the computer has a port for the joystick (this could be on the sound card), *Windows 98* will display an icon labelled *Game Controllers* in the shape of a joystick in the *Control Panel*. Check it out right now.

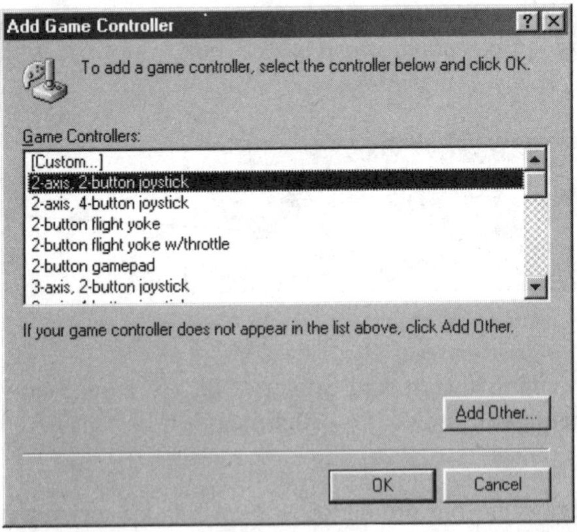

Fig. 8.68:   Adding and configuring the game controllers

Properties window

Choose *Start/Settings* and click on the *Control Panel*. In the *Control Panel*, double-click the *Game Controllers* icon. The properties window of the *Game Controllers* will be displayed, indicating the status at the top.

Windows 98 offers you the possibility to use 16 different joysticks which can be configured independently of each other. Select the highlighted entry in the list box of the *Game Controllers* dialog box and click the *Properties* button to configure the model you are using.

Installing a new
gamecontroller

To install a new game controller, on the other hand, click the *Add* button. Choose the manufacturer and the model. If you cannot find the manufacturer in the list, take one of the standard entries such as *2 axis, 2 button joystick* or *2 button flight yoke*, etc. If you click on *Add Other*, the *Add New Hardware Assistant*, which has been described earlier in this chapter, will be started. After copying the required files and restarting the computer, the new game controller will be ready for use.

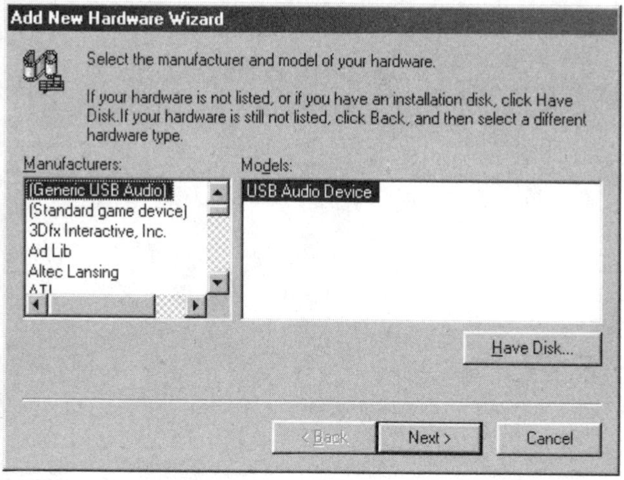

Fig. 8.69: Adding a game controller

Properties window   Choose *Start/Settings* and click on the *Control Panel*. In the *Control Panel*, double-click the *Game Controllers* icon. The properties window of the *Game Controllers* will be displayed, indicating the status at the top.

Properties window   Choose *Start/Settings* and click on the *Control Panel*. In the *Control Panel*, double-click the *Game Controllers* icon. The properties window of the *Game Controllers* will be displayed, indicating the status at the top.

9. System Tools

This chapter deals with everything that has anything to do with drives. To begin with, you will learn how to see the amount of free space available on your hard disk(s), and how to change the name of your drives. Then we will introduce the *System Monitor*, an application which allows you to monitor the usage of the system down to the last detail.

ScanDisk

After that we will show you how to check your hard disk for errors with the *ScanDisk* program, how to optimize the file structure with the *Disk Defragmenter* application, how to set both programs to run automatically with the *Maintenance Wizard* or to set a timetable for execution with *Scheduled Tasks*.

Compress drives, protect files

At the end of this chapter we will discuss in detail how to compress drives with *DriveSpace* and how to protect data with *Microsoft Backup*. You will learn how to compare and restore files, what kind of backup is available and how to customize the programs according to your needs.

Free Space and the Drive Label

Windows 98 applications, as a rule, require a lot of disk space. The fully installed *Microsoft Office Suite* for example will use anything upto 350 MB. Even the *Windows 98* operating system with all its components and accessories can take up 120 MB. Because of this, the standard capacity of modern hard disks, which seemed so huge to begin with, looks very small by comparison.

Only half of the original 4.3 Gigabytes will be available after all the programs have been installed.

Free hard disk
space

Because of this, it is often useful to have a tool under *Windows 98* to regularly monitor the free hard disk space. This type of tool is available, more than one of them in fact. Let's start with the easiest method.

Monitoring Free Hard Disk Space

To monitor the free or used disk space on a drive, select the respective drive icon. This can be done in *Explorer* or *My Computer*. Then select the *Properties* command from the *File* menu. Another way to call up the *Properties* command is using the shortcut menu of the drive icon.

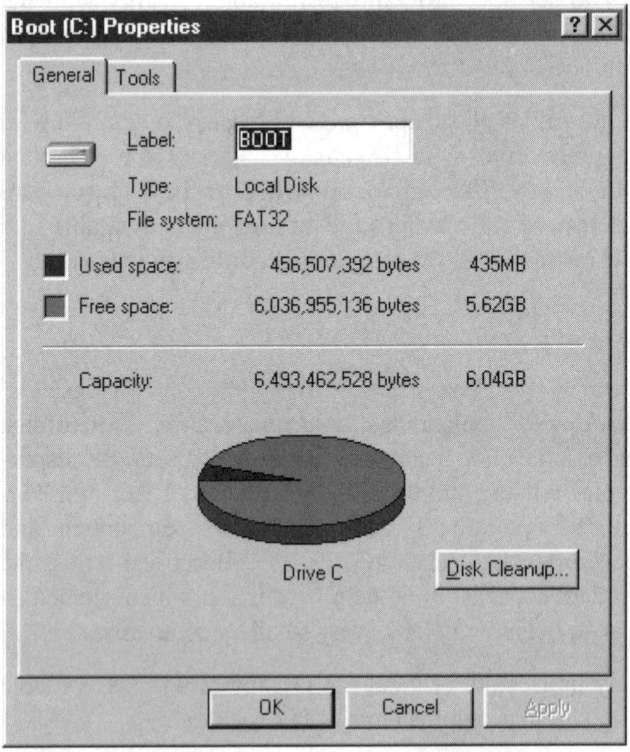

Fig. 9.1:   Viewing disk space with a pie chart

Used/free space

In the *Properties* dialog box of the selected drive all the required information will be displayed. In the upper part of the dialog box under *Used space/Free space*, the details are given in *bytes* and *megabytes (MB) / gigabytes (GB)*.

Below that you will see the total capacity of your hard disk. To top it all off, the relation between the used and the free space is displayed as a 'pie chart'.

Tip! Do not be surprised if the capacity in the *Properties* dialog box turns out to be less than that listed on the computer invoice. Dealers like to advertise the unformatted hard disk size, which is given in bytes. The *Properties* dialog box can also be shown for floppy drives.

For information about the free disk space on drives, you do not necessarily have to open the *Properties* dialog box. The *Windows Explorer* and *My Computer* also display this information in the status bar at the lower edge of the window.

My Computer

If the drive icon is selected, you will see the free space as well as the capacity (only with *My Computer*) of the drive in the status bar. If it is not visible, you can display the status bar through the *View/Status Bar* command.

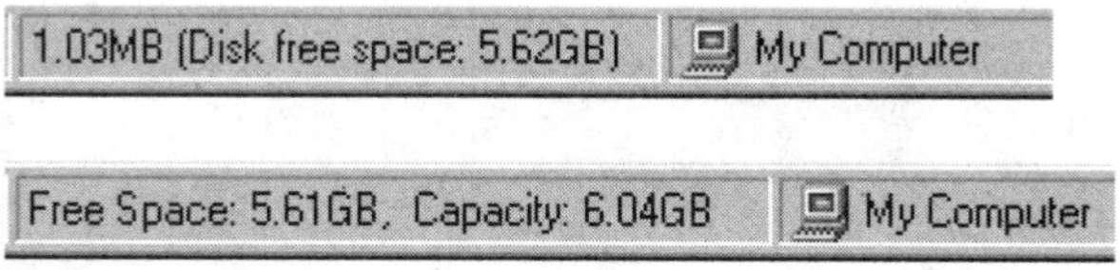

| 1.03MB (Disk free space: 5.62GB) | 🖳 My Computer |

| Free Space: 5.61GB, Capacity: 6.04GB | 🖳 My Computer |

Fig. 9.2:   Usage information in the status bar of *Explorer* (above) and *My Computer*

Explorer

In *Explorer*, the free space is displayed as soon as any folder in a drive in the left window pane is selected. This is especially useful when working with floppy disks, since you can always see how many bytes can still fit on the drive.

Units

The unit (bytes, KB, MB and GB) used in the status bar depends on the size of the drive.

Changing Your Drive Label

You might have been surprised at the strange label of the drive icon for your hard disk. Sometimes one encounters labels like *Ms_dos6* or *1353_436cky*, or what appears to be an advertisement for something. This variety of names might make you conclude that the label names can be changed freely.

Properties

This just happens to be true. Not, however, with the command used for normal objects, since *File/Rename* is not available for hard disk icons. To rename a hard disk or a floppy disk, select the respective drive icon. This can be done in *Explorer* or *My Computer*. After that, choose the *Properties* command from the *File* menu.

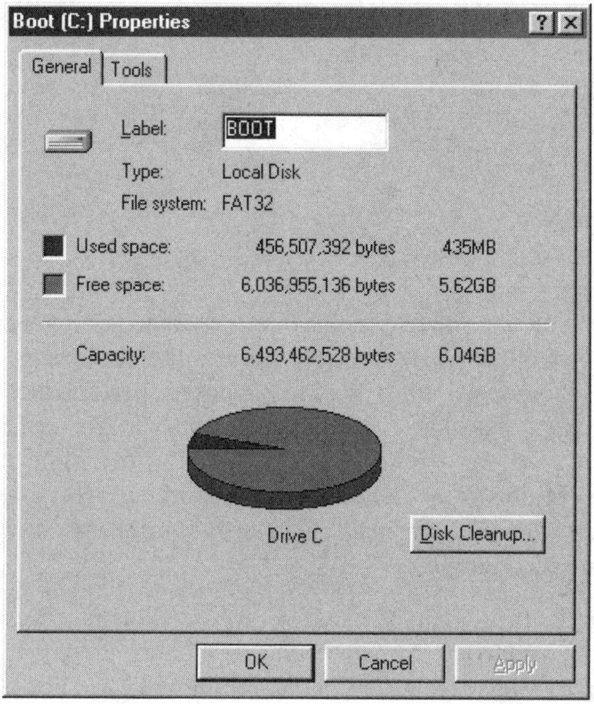

Fig. 9.3:   A maximum of 11 characters for hard disk names

Label text box

The *Properties* command can also be selected from the shortcut menu of drive icons. In the *Properties* dialog box of the selected drive, the *Label* text box is displayed in addition to information regarding free and used space.

The displayed label can be changed by entering a name of your choice at any time. This should contain no more than eleven characters, without spaces or the special characters * ? % & / : \ /. Moreover, there is no distinction between upper and lower case letters. If you confirm your settings with *OK*, Windows will change the drive label.

Tip! You can call your hard disk *Hard disk*. If there is more than one hard disk by this name, *My Computer* will distinguish between them by *Hard disk (C:)*, *Hard disk (D:)*,etc. CD-ROM drives cannot be labeled.

Monitoring System Resources with the System Monitor

Monitor programs

Maybe you have already noticed after working with your computer all day, the system somehow seems to slow down. Sometimes this kind of reduced performance happens all of a sudden. *Windows 98* contains a powerful system program that graphically displays the system usage. In this way, while you are working you can monitor the preformance of defective programs and respond accordingly.

System monitor

This system program is called *System monitor* and was originally intended for networking, to monitor the server resources. But it can also be called up and used for a stand-alone computer.

System tools

To do this, point in the *Start* menu to the *Programs/ Accessories* entry and then to *System Tools*. In the overlapping menu click on the *System Monitor* command. Before the *System Monitor* can graphically display the usage of your resources, you should indicate which resources you would like to monitor.

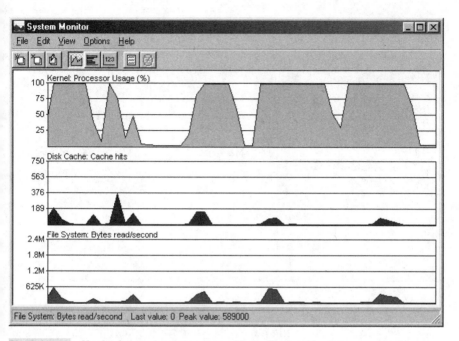

Fig. 9.4: Monitoring system resources with the System Monitor

Add item

Select the *Add Item* command from the *Edit* menu. In the dialog box of the same name, select the required *Category*. The most interesting and representative ones are the *File system, Kernel* and *Disk Cache* categories.

Add Item [?] [X]

Choose an item to add to the chart. For more information on a particular item, select that item and then click 'Explain'.

Category:
```
Dial-Up Adapter
Disk Cache
File System
Kernel
Memory Manager
```

Item:
```
Processor Usage (%)
Threads
Virtual Machines
```

[OK]

[Cancel]

[Explain...]

Fig. 9.5:   Selecting an item to be monitored

Display diagrams

In the right part of the window, the *Item* list box shows all the processes which can be monitored and displayed graphically. Select the desired entry and click *OK*. If you want to monitor more processes, select those with *Edit/Add Item* and confirm with *OK*. You have to wait a bit for the current values to be displayed in the chart. Charts that are no longer required can be removed with the *Edit/Remove Item*.

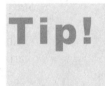

Using *Options/Chart* you can set the update interval of the values in the chart. Drag the slider to the required position in seconds and confirm with *OK*. But remember that even just monitoring uses additional system resources.

Check the process

To check the processes or applications, start the application or execute the command while the system monitor is open.

Update interval

Taking the update interval into consideration, you can come to certain conclusions about the usage of the system resources displayed in the *System Monitor*.

Monitoring Drives and Correcting Errors

While working with files that are stored on magnetic drives such as hard disks, errors can always occur. These may be due either to physical damage to the magnetic surface, or simply incorrectly saved files or fragmented files.

Switch off your
computer

The latter can be the case if you switch off your computer without properly closing *Windows 98* or after program crashes.

Checking the Hard Disk with ScanDisk for Errors

In any case lost file fragments, cross-linked files, invalid date and time or other disk errors can lead to errors in your daily work.

ScanDisk
command

Windows 98 has a system program which can track down and automatically remove the most frequent drive errors. If you want to check your hard disk(s), choose *Start/ Programs/Accessories/System Tools* and select the *Scan-Disk* command in the overlapping menu. This program is part of the *Maintenance Wizard* which additionally starts the *Disk Defragmenter* and frees space on the hard disk.

Drive(s) you want to check

In the *Select the drive(s) you want to check for errors* list box, select the drive(s). For multiple selection press the `Ctrl` key and click the required drive entries one by one.

Standard option

Select the *Standard* radio button in the *Type of test* option group box to check only files and folders for errors. Check the *Automatically fix errors* check box to let *ScanDisk* remove any eventual disk errors automatically.

Start the test

Then click the *Start* button to start the test. The progress is indicated with a progress bar. At the end of the checking the *ScanDisk Results* dialog box will appear, giving details regarding the errors found and fixed.

ScanDisk result

The *ScanDisk Results* dialog box contains all the relevant information about the checked drive as regards the number of available bytes, number of folders, number of hidden files, total disk space, number of bytes in each allocation unit, etc.

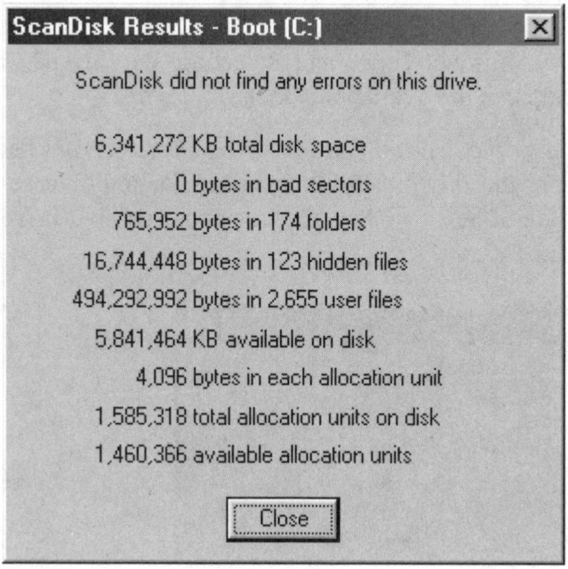

ScanDisk Results - Boot (C:)   ☒

ScanDisk did not find any errors on this drive.

6,341,272 KB total disk space

0 bytes in bad sectors

765,952 bytes in 174 folders

16,744,448 bytes in 123 hidden files

494,292,992 bytes in 2,655 user files

5,841,464 KB available on disk

4,096 bytes in each allocation unit

1,585,318 total allocation units on disk

1,460,366 available allocation units

[Close]

Fig. 9.7:   *ScanDisk* results

Use ScanDisk
regularly

Click on the *Close* button to close the results window and close *ScanDisk* with the *Close* button. Use *ScanDisk* regularly, at least once a month.

You can use *ScanDisk* together with other system programs by using the *Maintenance Wizard* or *Scheduled Tasks (*for time scheduling).

Configuring the ScanDisk System Utility

The *ScanDisk* system utility regularly tracks down the most common drive errors and corrects them automatically.

Customize
ScanDisk

You can customize the way *ScanDisk* works. To do this, first call up the program by choosing *Start/Programs/ Accessories/System Tools* and selecting the *ScanDisk* command from the overlapping menu.

Select the drive(s)

In the *Select the drive(s) you want to check for errors* list box, select the drive(s) to be checked. For multiple selection, press the Ctrl key and click the required drive entries one by one.

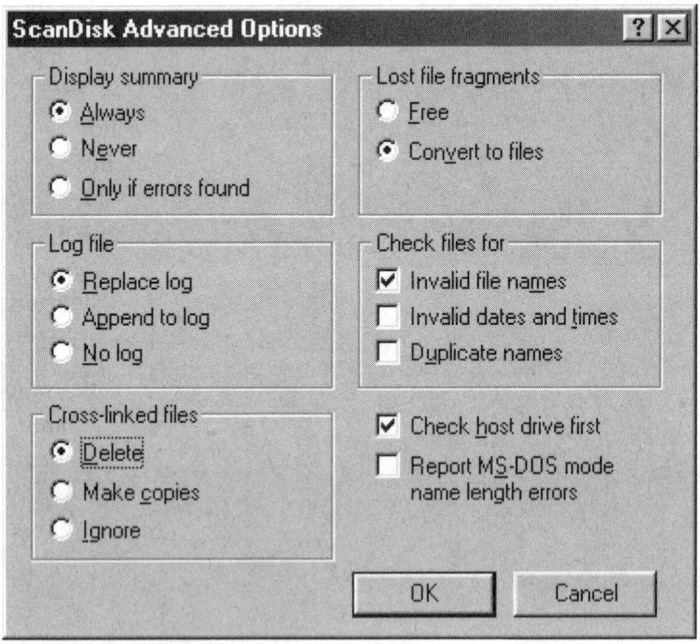

Fig. 9.8:   Configuring ScanDisk

Advanced button

To configure *ScanDisk,* click on the *Advanced* button. In the *Display summary* option group, select whether the *ScanDisk Results* dialog box should be displayed, after checking for errors, from among the *Always, Never*, or recommended *Only if errors found* entries.

Determine the log file

With the *Log File* option group you can determine whether *ScanDisk* should display a log, or save the results in the *SCANDISK.LOG* file on the root of the *(C:)* drive. With *Append to Log*, the results are always added to the end of the file.

Cross linked files

Now, for the most important configuration options: in the *Cross-linked files* option group, you can determine how *ScanDisk* should deal with files that simultaneously use the same cluster on the drive. Since nothing can be done with these files anyway, it is best to select the *Delete* option.

Lost file fragments

Under *Lost file fragments* you can determine how *Scan Disk* should deal with file fragments. These file fragments may contain useable data, but normally they only take up space. If you select the *Free* radio button, the file fragments will be deleted. Choose *Convert to files* to create files in the root folder with the *CHK* extension, which can then be read with suitable text editors.

Check files for

In the *Check files for* group box, you can tell *ScanDisk* to check files that cannot be opened for *Invalid file names* or check files for *Invalid dates and times*. The *Duplicate Names* option can lead to the incorrect sorting of files, or errors with archive programs such as *Microsoft Backup.* Choose the required options and confirm with *OK*.

Configure the test method

In the *ScanDisk* window you can configure the test method under *Type of test*. The *Standard* option will only check files and folders. The *Thorough* option will execute the standard test and, after that, check the surface of the hard disk for any physical damage.

Don't fix errors

This process may take some time. Clear the *Automatically fix errors* check box if you want to get messages from *ScanDisk* when disk errors are found, asking for futher instructions.

Start the test

Then click the *Start* button to start the test. The progress is indicated with a progress bar. At the end you will get the *ScanDisk Results* dialog box showing the details regarding the errors found and whether or not those errors could be fixed.

Optimizing Your Hard Disk

As long as you install all the necessary programs one after the other, and save the documents created with the applications, all the data on your hard disk will be stored sequentially. But in your daily work you may sometimes delete documents or programs which are no longer needed.

'Holes' in the data structure

This will soon create 'holes' in the data structure. If you save new documents or install new programs, it can happen that one chunk of this data is saved in one of these 'holes', and the other chunk somewhere else.

Fragmentation of files

You should not have to worry about this since as a user you are not aware of this process. But the fragmentation of files slows down the access to the hard disk. This is because the drive head has to move around to different locations in order to read the information of a document or a program file.

Restructuring Fragmented Data with Disk Defragmenter

Windows 98 comes complete with a system utility which can, to put it in the simplest terms, plug these holes. The *Disk Defragmenter* application analyzes your hard disk(s) and rewrites all the data contained therein. The result is that all data is defragmented and the hard disk works faster. This program is part of the *Maintenance Wizard* which additionally starts *ScanDisk* and deletes files that are no longer needed.

Disk defragmenter

To start the hard disk tuning program, select *Start/ Programs/Accessories/System Tools* and click on the *Disk Defragmenter* command in the overlapping menu.

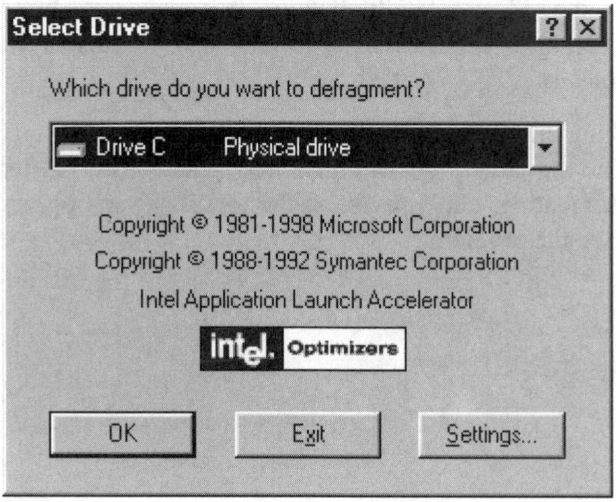

Select Drive ? X

Which drive do you want to defragment?

Drive C   Physical drive ▼

Copyright © 1981-1998 Microsoft Corporation
Copyright © 1988-1992 Symantec Corporation
Intel Application Launch Accelerator

intel. Optimizers

OK   Exit   Settings...

Fig. 9.9:   Drive selection

Select the drive

In the dialog box which appears, select the drive to be defragmented. With the *All Hard Drives* entry, all available drives will be checked one after the other. *Windows 98* will no longer recommend optimization like in earlier versions, but will instead start optimizing after you select the drive and click *OK*.

Status display during defragmenting

Show details

With the *Show Details* button, the read and write operations in the different sectors will be displayed graphically.

Clicking the *Legend* button will display a dialog box which explains the multicolored characters. After defragmenting, click on *Yes* in the message that appears to leave the program.

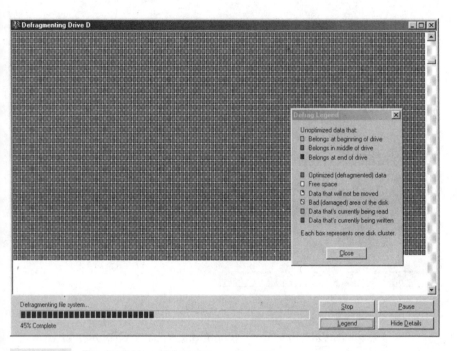

Fig. 9.11: The detail view while defragmenting

Tip! You should not work with your PC during defragmentation, although theoretically it would be possible. Defragmenting large or compressed drives can take several hours.

Configuring the Disk Defragmenter System Utility

The *Disk Defragmenter* application analyzes your hard disk(s) and rewrites all saved data. After all the data is defragmented, the hard disk will work noticeably faster. *Disk Defragmenter* can be customized according to your personal needs.

To start the defragmentation program select *Start/ Programs/Accessories/System Tools* and click on the *Disk Defragmenter* command in the overlapping menu. In the dialog box, select the drive to be defragmented.

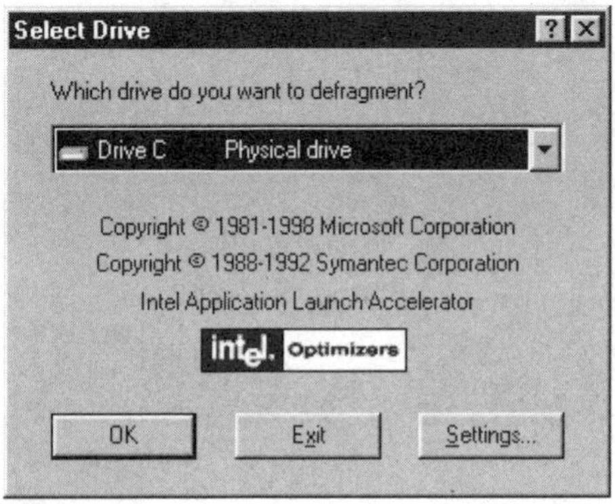

Fig. 9.12: Drive selection and the Settings button

Customizing disk   With the *Settings* button, *Disk Defragmenter* can be
defragmenter   customized to suit your individual requirements.

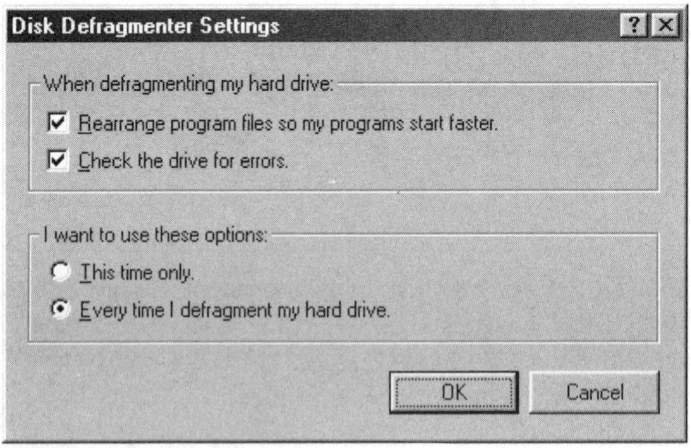

Fig. 9.13: Configuring the Disk Defragmenter system utility

Defragmenting options	In the *When defragmenting my hard drive* option group you can set the type of defragmentation that should take place. The quickest defragmentating method occurs when no check boxes have been selected. In this case the sorting of program files and the error checking with *ScanDisk* will be omitted.
Rearrange program files...	By selecting *Rearrange program files so my programs start faster*, all the program files will be placed at the beginning of the drive, and additionally all files will be stored in connected chunks. This will considerably accelerate the starting time of *Windows 98* applications.
Check the drive for errors...	If you select the *Check the drive for errors* check box, the *ScanDisk* system utility will automatically start before *Disk Defragmenter*. Whenever errors are found, the *Disk Defragmenter* will, in any case, be interrupted.
Standard settings	With the remaining radio buttons, you can determine whether your settings should apply only for the current defragmentation process *(This time only)*, or if they should become the standard settings (*Every time I defragment my hard drive*). Make your choices and confirm with *OK*.
Start defragmentation	Start defragmenting by clicking the *Start* button. The progress of the defragmentation will be displayed in a progress bar.
Quit the program	After the defragmentation, click on *Yes* in the message box which appears in order to quit the program.

Tip! You should not work with your PC while you are defragmenting, although theoretically it would be possible. Defragmenting large or compressed drives can take several hours. Click on *Details* to produce a graphic display of the defragmentation process.

You can set the *Maintenance Wizard* or *Scheduled Tasks* to automatically perform the defragmentation process. Both applications can be found in the *System Tools* program group. You can set up a schedule to start *ScanDisk* and *Disk Defragmenter* automatically at a fixed time. For this the computer has to remain switched on.

Compressing and Decompressing Drives

With modern hard disks having a standard capacity of 3 to 4 GB, disk space is not a problem in most cases. This is not the case, however, if you are working with older models whose capacity is less than 1 GB. With many programs installed, space can become a problem. You have two possibilities to eradicate this problem.

One way would be to go out and buy a new hard disk and install it in parallel. Another way might be just to use the *DriveSpace* system utility.

Tip! *DriveSpace* can only compress *FAT* drives (not *FAT 32*) with a maximum of 850 MB capacity. Larger disks have to be divided into several drives of 850 MB each for the compressed drive to be able to work.

Compressing Drives with DriveSpace

Using *DriveSpace* the capacity of a hard disk can roughly be trebled. The good thing about that is that it's absolutely free. Of course a few things should be considered before using *DriveSpace*. These have to do with the safety of your data. To begin with we will describe how *DriveSpace* works.

Cluster size

The additional space has of course nothing to do with magic. All data saved on your hard disk requires a specific amount of clusters. The bigger the hard disk, the larger the clusters. If a file has 1,025 bytes, then three clusters are needed for hard disks with a cluster size of 512 bytes (such as 2 Gigabyte hard disks): 2 clusters containing 512 bytes each, and one cluster containing one byte but which , even so, uses up 512 bytes of disk space. From this you can imagine how much space is wasted by using this method.

Compression programs

Compression programs like *DriveSpace* use the clusters in a more economical way. Basically, only as much space as is really needed is used. In addition, *DriveSpace* analyzes the contents of each file.

Compression factor

For pixel graphics files, contiguous areas of the same color are no longer saved pixel by pixel. Similarly, recurring character patterns that are contained in text files are saved as abbreviations. In this way, depending on the file type, up to 98 per cent of a file can be compressed. On an average *DriveSpace* achieves a compression ratio of 2:1 or 3:1.

Decompressed

DriveSpace can compress not only files, but even entire disks. For a compressed disk, *DriveSpace* will insure that every new file is automatically compressed. If you want to read such a file, it has to be decompressed first.

System files

You will not be aware of this process. The compressed disks behave exactly like uncompressed disks. All compressed files are saved by *ScanDisk* in a very big file, which acts like a normal drive in *Windows 98*. A small part of the hard drive reserved for important system files will not be compressed.

Host drive

This part is called the host drive This drive does not actually physically exist on your computer.

DriveSpace
command

Enough theory for now. To start the *DriveSpace* program select *Start/Programs/Accessories/System Tools* and click on the *DriveSpace* command in the overlapping menu. In the program window, select the drive to be compressed. Before compressing your hard disk, you should first practice the process on a floppy disk.

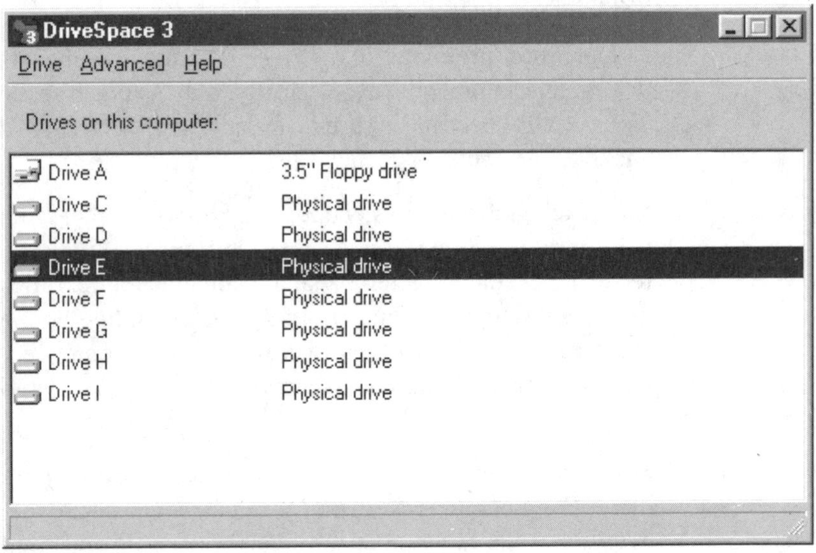

Fig. 9.14: The program window of DriveSpace

Select the *Compress* command from the *Drive* menu. In the dialog box, you will get information about the amount of free space on the disk before and after compression (see Figure 9.15). The next section deals with the compression options available. Clicking on the *Backup Files* button will start *Microsoft Backup* to enable you to protect the data (more aboaut this at the end of the chapter). Click on the *Start* button.

```
┌─────────────────────────────────────────────────────────┐
│ Compress a Drive                                 [?][X]  │
├─────────────────────────────────────────────────────────┤
│ Compressing drive E will make it appear larger and contain more free │
│ space.                                                   │
│ ┌─Drive E (now)──────────┐  ┌─Drive E (after compression)─┐ │
│ │                        │  │                            │ │
│ │                        │  │                            │ │
│ │                        │  │                            │ │
│ │   ■ Free space         │  │   ■ Free space             │ │
│ │   ■ Used space         │  │   ■ Used space             │ │
│ │                        │  │                            │ │
│ │ Drive E currently contains │ After compression, Drive E will │ │
│ │ 846.92 MB of free space.   │ contain approximately 1.65 GB │ │
│ │                        │  │ of free space.             │ │
│ └────────────────────────┘  └────────────────────────────┘ │
│          [    Start    ]   [ Options... ]   [  Close  ]  │
└─────────────────────────────────────────────────────────┘
```

Fig. 9.15:   Overview of the compressed drive

Errors

Before compression, the drive will be checked for errors by the *ScanDisk* system utility. If errors are found those will automatically be corrected. Be prepared for the compression process that follows to take up to several hours!

Restart

For hard disks you will get a message asking you to restart the computer after the successful completion. For floppy disks, the result of the compression will immediately be displayed, hence restarting is unnecessary. Once you've done this you will have a drive which is outwardly unchanged, but which has two or three times its original capacity.

Configuring the DriveSpace System Utility

If you are familar with the basics of compressing drives or if you have already done the first tests with *DriveSpace*, you may want to select the options for the compression of drives.

DriveSpace options

If you want to select the *DriveSpace* options before compression, start the *DriveSpace* program by selecting *Start/Programs/Accessories/System Tools* and clicking on the *DriveSpace* command in the overlapping menu.

Select the drive to be compressed in the program window. Then choose the *Compress* command from the *Drive* menu. A dialog box will appear containing information about the free disk space before and after compressing.

Options button

If you click the *Options* button, the *Compression Options* dialog box will appear. You can then change the *Drive letter of host drive* by opening the drop-down list and selecting another letter.

```
┌─────────────────────────────────────────────────┐
│ Compression Options                      [?][X]  │
├─────────────────────────────────────────────────┤
│ When Windows compresses drive E, it creates an   │
│ uncompressed host drive. The host drive contains │
│ the volume file for drive E and other files      │
│ that are uncompressed.                           │
│                                                  │
│ Windows will create the new uncompressed drive   │
│ using the following settings:                    │
│                                                  │
│ Drive letter of host drive:  [K        ] [▼]     │
│                                                  │
│ Free space on host drive:    [2.00  ]  MB        │
│                                                  │
│ ☑ Hide host drive                                │
│                                                  │
│              [    OK    ]  [  Cancel  ]          │
└─────────────────────────────────────────────────┘
```

Fig. 9.16:   Selecting options for compressing

This is especially useful in the case of networks, because you can ensure that the *Drive letter of host drive* will be fixed, for example 'M'. For this the *AUTOEXEC.BAT* file must contain the command *LASTDRIVE=[X]*, where *[X]* is the last letter which you want *Windows 98* to use for your drives.

Hide host drives

Select the *Hide host drive* check box in the *Compression Options* dialog box, if you do not want to display the uncompressed host drive in *Explorer* or *My Computer*.

Uncompressed drive space

With the *Free space on host drive* text box, you can set the size of the uncompressed drive space on the host drive. Bigger entries are necessary when working with programs or files which cannot be compressed.

Compress drive

Confirm your changes with *OK* and click on the *Start* button. Following this, the computer has to be restarted, and you will get a status report with information on the additional disk space.

All settings can be changed after the compression of a drive using the commands in the *Advanced* menu of *DriveSpace*.

Compressing and Mounting Floppy Disks with DriveSpace

There is no basic difference between compressing a floppy disk and compressing a hard drive. Refer to the section on 'Compressing a Hard Drive with *DriveSpace*' in this chapter. But while using compressed disks in your daily work is no different than using uncompressed disks, floppy disks are another matter altogether.

Automatically mounted

Compressed hard disks will automatically be mounted during the window start. The host drive will in most cases be hidden, which means basically that the user will not notice the compressed drives except for the increased disk space. With a compressed floppy disk the situation can be slightly different: Depending on the settings of *DriveSpace*, it is sometimes not very easy to access the contents of a compressed floppy disk. This is because under *Windows 98*, compressed floppy disks can be read only by the *DriveSpace* compression program.

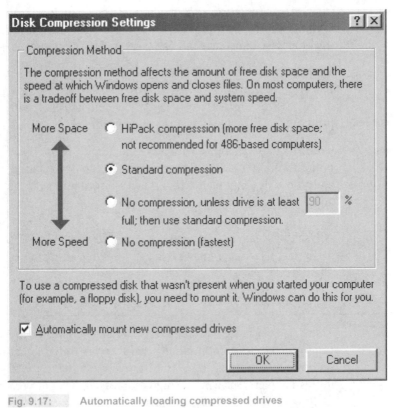

Fig. 9.17:   Automatically loading compressed drives

Without *DriveSpace*, the *Windows Explorer* or *My Computer* will show the contents of a floppy disk as two files, the compressed file *DRVSPACE(.000)* and one information file called *Readthis(.TXT)*.

Text file

The first file contains all the compressed data of the floppy disk, while a manual on how to use the compressed data is provided in the text file. Before you open the information file, go on reading this section. Use the *Start* menu to call up the *DriveSpace* program by clicking on *Programs/Accessories/System Tools*. We need to 'mount' the floppy disk with *DriveSpace*.

Mount command

Select the floppy disk drive in the list box. Then choose the *Mount* command from the *Advanced* menu. The message *Drive A:/B: has been mounted* appears. If a floppy disk is not compressed, you will get a message informing you of this fact.

Compression
properties

After confirming this message with *OK*, the drive letter of the floppy disk drive will be replaced by the entry *Compressed floppy disk*. A double click on this entry will display the compression properties. Click on *OK* to hide this information. After mounting the disk, you can access the compressed data as usual. *Explorer* or *My Computer* will now show the data contained in the floppy disk, instead of the compression and information files.

Automatically
mount

Mounting compressed floppy disks can also be done automatically. To do this, choose the *Settings* command in the *Advanced* menu of *DriveSpace* (see Figure 9.17). Select the *Automatically mount new compressed drives* check box, and confirm with *OK*. From now on, new compressed floppy disks will automatically be mounted after Windows starts.

Decompressing Compressed DriveSpace Drives

Compressed drives are a useful thing. Unnoticed by the user, the *DriveSpace* program works in the background and can multiply the disk space of older drives by three times. However, how do you go about changing a compressed drive back to its original condition? Well, the answer is simple – it is called decompression. Unfortunately there is one small snag.

At this point the circumspect reader will be inclined to think that working with *DriveSpace* is not really safe. Be assured, therefore, that the snag has nothing to do with safety of your data, even though it is better to save all your data with *Microsoft Backup* prior to decompressing. The snag is rather the need for additional space, which is usually the reason for using *DriveSpace* in the first place.

Running out of space

Normally the program is used when you are running out of disk space on smaller drives. After compression, you will suddenly have lots more disk space available, so that more applications can be installed or new data (compressed) can be saved. Unfortunately, the space available is often not enough for the data which is not compressed.

Security mechanism

It is for this very reason that *DriveSpace* has a built-in safety mechanism. To decompress a drive, use the *Programs/Accessories/System Tools* command in the *Start* menu and click on the *DriveSpace* command in the overlapping menu. Select the drive you want to decompress in the program window.

Uncompress command

Choose the *Uncompress* command from the *Drive* menu. *DriveSpace* will now verify the disk space on the drive. If there is not enough space available for decompression, you will recieve a message to this effect. If this happens, all you can do is to confirm with *OK* and delete data which is no longer required.

Before and after

If there is enough disk space available, the *Uncompress a drive* dialog box will appear with information regarding *now* and *after uncompression*. To start uncompressing, click the *Start* button.

ScanDisk

Before uncompressing, the drive will be checked for errors by the *ScanDisk* system utility, and if any are found, they will automatically be corrected.

Yes button

To start uncompressing hard drives, click on the *Yes* button in the message box that appears. The following process of uncompression can take several hours!

Tip!

During this time you cannot work on your computer. For hard disks, you will receive a message after successful uncompression, asking you to restart your computer. For floppy disks, the results of the uncompression will immediately be displayed, and restarting is not necessary.

After this the uncompressed hard disk will be at your disposal, outwardly unchanged, but with only one-third of the compressed disk space.

Liberating Disk Space with Disk Cleanup

In the course of time, any hard disk will collect many unnecessary files, called temporary files. These originate from software installations or program crashes and unnecessarily take up space on your hard disk. *Windows 98* has a system utility to delete these unneeded files, called *Disk Cleanup*.

Disk cleanup

To start it, select *Start/Programs/Accessories/System Tools*, and choose the *Disk Cleanup* command. Select the drive to be cleaned and confirm with *OK*.

You now have to wait for the calculation of the disk space that will be reclaimed. The number of available items to delete depends on your system configuration. In

Temporary Internet files
the *Disk Cleanup* dialog box, select the *Temporary Internet files* and *Downloaded Program files* check boxes if you have Internet access. Read the information displayed under *Description*.

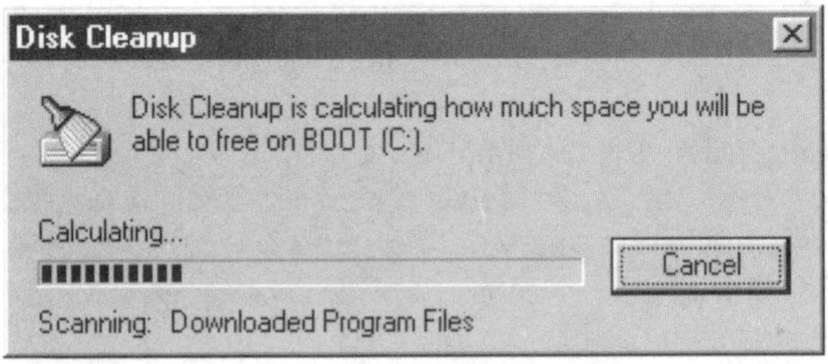

Disk Cleanup ☒

Disk Cleanup is calculating how much space you will be able to free on BOOT (C:).

Calculating...

▐▌▌▌▌▌▌▌▌▌▌▌ [Cancel]

Scanning: Downloaded Program Files

Fig. 9.18: Verifying the disk space to be gained

Without Internet access, clear the *Temporary Internet files* and *Downloaded Program files* check boxes. Select the *Recycle Bin* check box if you are sure that these files are no longer required.

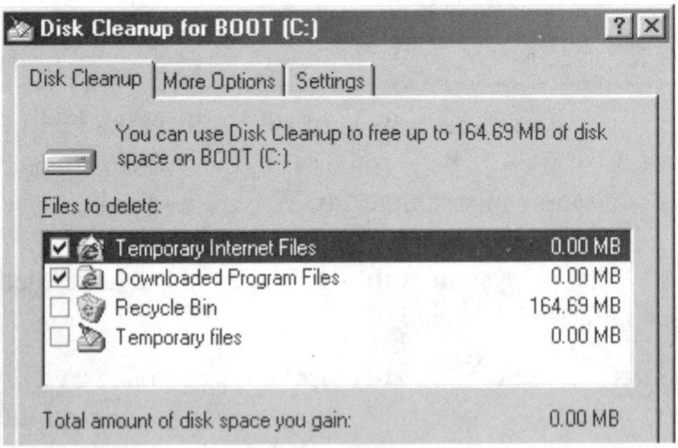

Disk Cleanup for BOOT (C:) ? ☒

| Disk Cleanup | More Options | Settings |

You can use Disk Cleanup to free up to 164.69 MB of disk space on BOOT (C:).

Files to delete:

☑ 🗔 Temporary Internet Files	0.00 MB
☑ 📄 Downloaded Program Files	0.00 MB
☐ 🗑 Recycle Bin	164.69 MB
☐ 🗂 Temporary files	0.00 MB

Total amount of disk space you gain: 0.00 MB

Fig. 9.19: Which files should be deleted?

Always select the *Temporary files* check box, to remove all the unneeded files. With the *Temporary Windows Setup files* check box, backup copies of a *Windows 98* update can be removed (about 50 Mbytes). The *View Files* button will show you a list of files to be deleted.

Start the process
of deleting

Start the process of deleting by clicking *OK*. If you also reply to the following confirmation message with *OK*, *Windows 98* will start the *Disk Cleanup*.

Tip!

The *Disk Cleanup* will only delete the selected temporary files, not documents or program files. These temporary files are definitely not required any longer. Deleting the temporary Windows setup files makes it impossible to uninstall *Windows 98* after an update.

If you delete the temporay Internet files and the downloaded program files (ActiveX controls and Java applets from Web sites), accessing these sites through the WWW can take a little longer, since these files have to be transferred again because they cannot be read from the hard disk.

Backup with Windows 98

With the *Windows 98* system utility called *Microsoft Backup,* you can save your data from the hard disk onto tapes. *Backup* will also make copies onto floppy disks. In addition, you can also use *Microsoft Backup* to transfer large files from one computer to another.

Data safety

Regularly backing up files with *Microsoft Backup* will increase the safety of the data on your computer. This will become clear to you when you lose data for the first time, for example after a sudden power cut, or on account of a defective hard disk. To protect your data you need suitable tools!

Data Safety with Microsoft Backup

Start *Microsoft Backup* to begin copying your files. To do this, point to the *Programs/Accessories/System Tools* entry in the *Start* menu and select the *Backup* command.

Backup device

If you have a backup device (Tape streamer, etc.) which has not yet been installed, click on the *Yes* button in the first *Backup* dialog box, asking you whether the *Add New Hardware* Wizard should be run. This happens the first time you start *Backup*. Follow the instructions to install a streamer device, or a *ZIP*- or *JAZZ* drive. If the drive has a driver disk, or CD-ROM, install the driver from those drives by clicking on the *Have Disk* button in the *Add New Hardware* Wizard.

No backup device

If you do not have a backup device and want to use *Backup* with floppy disks, answer this message with *No*. Now you can either work with the *Backup Wizard*, or use *Backup* with the conventional method.

With or without Backup Wizard

To call up the *Backup Wizard* select the option *Create a new backup job* in the first *Microsoft Backup* dialog box and confirm with *OK*. To proceed without the Wizard, just click on *Close*. The procedure is almost identical.

Backup tab page

Without the *Backup Wizard*, you can go straight to the *Microsoft Backup* window. Change to the *Backup* tab page where you can determine the kind of backup to be done, the *backup job* in the option group with this name.

With the backup wizard

To work with the *Backup Wizard*, choose the option *Back up selected files, folders and drives..*, in the first step of the *Backup Wizard* dialog box, in order to determine yourself which files to save. After that click on *Next*.

The program window of Backup

Regardless of whether or not you are working with the Wizard, you have to select the data to be backed up. To do this, use the boxes under *What to back up*.

Select the data to backup

In the left window pane the drives and folders which contain the data to be backed up can be selected by clicking on the check boxes next to their icons. If you do not want to backup the whole drive, you should select the objects to be backed up one by one.

Back up the hard
disk

For this purpose several options are offered. All objects in a hard disk can be selected by selecting the check box ☑▭ C: - [Boot] in front of the entry for the hard disk.

Backup single
folders

Single folders or subfolders can be selected by checking the ☑ check box in front of the respective folder name in the left window pane. Single files can be selected by checking the ☑ check box in front of the respective file name in the right window pane. It might be necessary to open the folders to do this. The display in the left window can be expanded with the plus sign ⊞ just like in the *Explorer*. The contents of the folder will be displayed in the right window pane after clicking on the name of the folder.

After having made your selection, click on the *Next* button in the *Backup Wizard*. In the following window determine *What to back up*. Without the Wizard, the process is identical, just use the *What to back up* option group in the *Microsoft Backup* program window. The *All selected files* radio button is the standard setting, and this will backup all selected data. You have to use this option the first time you do the backup. Then choose the *Next* button in the Wizard.

Backup
destination

Now choose the destination for the backup. In the *Backup Wizard,* open the *Where to back up* [IOMEGA TapeStreamer ▼] drop-down list and choose the backup device. In the program window of *Backup* you will find the list on the lower left side. If you have no backup device, choose the *File* [File ▼] entry. To backup onto a floppy disk, click on the ▣ button. The dialog box shown in Figure 9.21 (below) will appear.

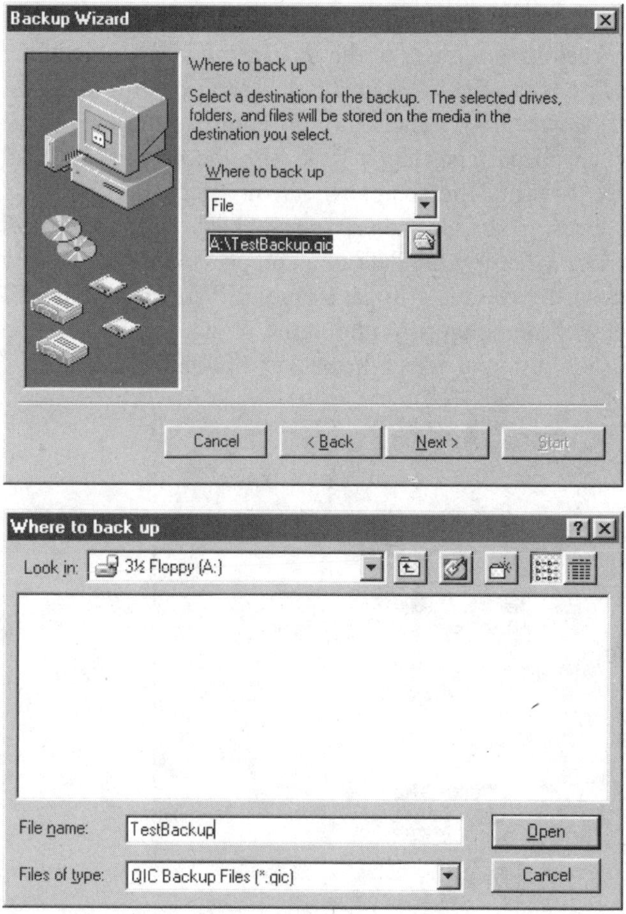

Fig. 9.21:   Selecting the destination for the backup

File name

Use the *Look in* list to go to the backup drive, in this case the floppy disk drive *A:*. Give it a clear file name by entering this in the *File name* text box, so that later on you will be able to distinguish it from other backup jobs. The file type will automatically be *QIC Backup files (*.qic)*. Confirm the dialog box with *Open*.

Backup options

Click again on the *Next* button in the Wizard. Now select the backup options. In the *Backup Wizard*, select the check boxes of your choice. Select the *Compare original and backup files...* check box to compare the data to be backed up on tape/floppy disk with the original data, in order to verify the accuracy. If you select the *Compress the backup data to save space* check box, *Microsoft Backup* will copy the data in a compressed form onto the backup drive. This will save tape or disk space, but will take a little longer. Without the Wizard, click on the *Options* button to select the backup options.

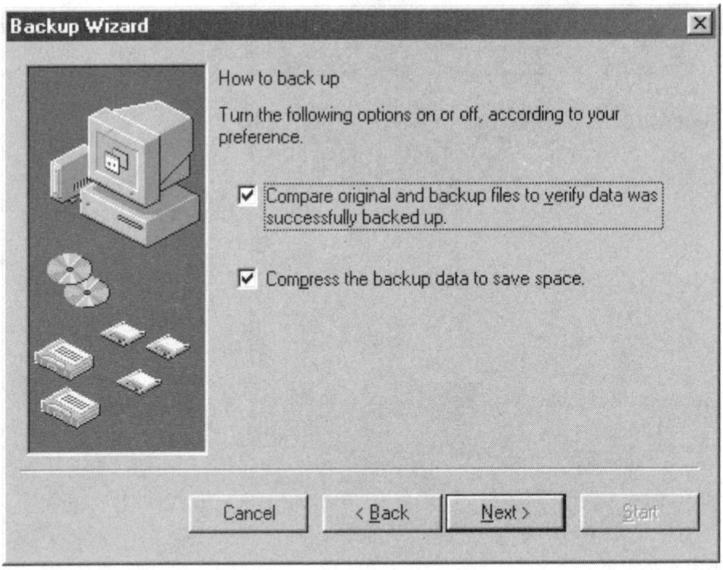

Fig. 9.22:   Setting backup options (Wizard)

Backup job

Click again on *Next* in the *Backup Wizard*. Enter a name for the backup job in the *Type a name ...* [Untitled ▼] text box to save all backup options. Without the Wizard, use the list *Backup Job* [Untitled ▼] box in the *Microsoft Backup* window.

start the backup
job

If you click the *Start* button after this, *Backup* will start the backup job. The progress is graphically displayed in the *Backup Progress* dialog box. In the case of floppy disks, follow the instructions regarding the changing of disks.

Backup
successfully
completed

If the data has been successfully copied onto the disk, the message *Operation completed* appears. Confirm it with *OK*. Close the *Backup Progress* dialog box with *OK*, to get back to the *Microsoft Backup* program window.

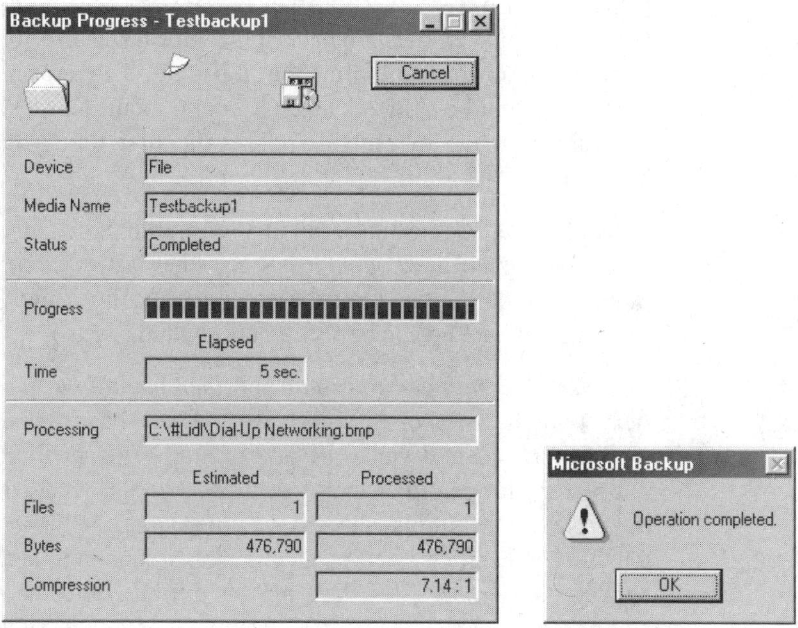

Fig. 9.23: The backup progress and completion message (right)

Selecting the Backup Type in Microsoft Backup

After you've done the first backup with *Microsoft Backup* you can change the type of backup, for example to copy only new or modified files. In addition, the backup options can be defined in greater detail. To set this configuration, do not work with the *Backup Wizard*, but instead, work directly in the *Microsoft Backup* program window.

Configuration

To configure the type of backup, first start *Microsoft Backup*. Point to the *Programs/Accessories/System Tools* command in the *Start* menu and click on *Backup*. Then click on *Options*.

Type of backup

If you want to select the type of backup, activate the *Type* tab page (Figure 9.24). With the *All selected files* radio button, all selected files are backed up. This takes up a lot of tape or disk space and time, but it has to be done once before you will be able to backup new and modified files. You always have to use this option the first time you back up.

Files that have changed

After that you have the possibility of backing up only those files that have changed since the last backup. *Backup* uses the archive attribute to identify those files. This type of backup can be further configured.

Incremental backup type

The *New and changed files only* and *Incremental backup type* options will only copy files which have been modified or created since the last backup. This method will verify, for each file that is to be backed up, whether the archive attribute is selected, in other words, whether the file has been changed or newly created since the last backup. Only those files showing this attribute will then be backed up. This means that files which have not been modified will not be on your backup disks. After the backup, the archive attribute will be cleared to ensure that the next backup will only save the files that have been modified since the last *Incremental backup*.

In practice this means that you first have to do a complete backup with the *All selected files* option and then, for

Quick backup

example, once a week, an *Incremental backup*. The advantage of this is that the backup is faster, since it only updates the original backup. The disadvantage is that restoring data is slower, since the full backup set has to be read.

Differential backup type

The *New and changed files only* and *Differential backup type* options also copies files which have changed since the last complete backup. The disadvantage of this method is that the modified files are not transferred into the last complete backup, but into a new smaller backup file each time.

In any case, with the passage of time a mountain of floppy disks or tapes will be created. You can document your changes from one backup job to the next. The actual backup is slower, but the restoring is faster.

You only have to deal with the other types of backup if you want to have an all-round security. If you want to backup only specific files such as a document in a word processor, then you will in any case always backup using *All selected files*.

Regardless of which backup type you use, one thing is important: regular practice. You should backup your data at least once a month, and once a week would be even better. Keep your floppy disks in a safe place and label your disks in a clear way. Take special care to annotate the date and name of the backup and the backup type.

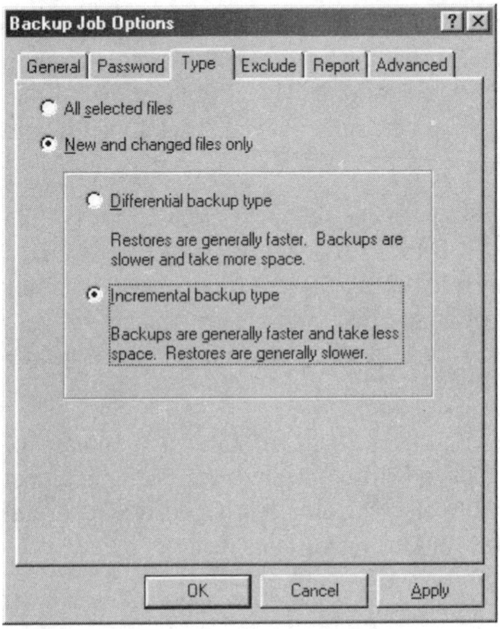

Fig. 9.24: Selecting the backup type in Microsoft backup

New and changed files option

Select the *New and changed files only* radio button if only the data that has changed since the last complete backup should be backed up on a tape or a disk. Confirm your settings with *OK*, then select the data to be backed up and the destination of the backup job and begin the backup by clicking on *Start*.

Customizing the Backup Options in Microsoft Backup

The standard setting of *Microsoft Backup* assumes a backup of *All selected files*, whereby all selected files will be backed up. These data will be saved in a compressed format on the backup tapes or floppy disks.

Customize backup

You can customize *Backup* anytime according to your personal needs. To configure the *Backup* function, start *Microsoft Backup*. In the *Start* menu choose *Programs/*

Accessories/System Tools and click on the *Backup* command in the overlapping menu.

Without the wizard In the first dialog box, click the *Close* button to work without the Wizard. In *Microsoft Backup* select the *Options* command from the *Job* menu. Alternatively, change to the *Backup* tab page and click on the *Options* button.

Options Normally *Microsoft Backup* copies the data to the backup drive in a compressed format. This saves tape or floppy disk space, but requires more time.

Compress data Select the *Compress data to save time* radio button to speed up the process of compression, but then it does not perform very effectively.

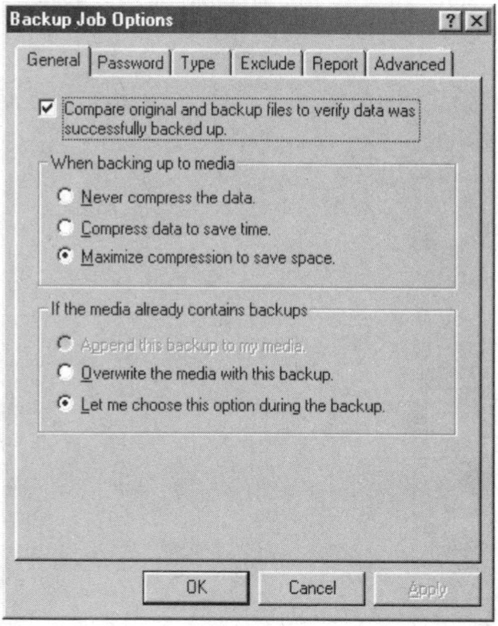

Backup Job Options ? X

| General | Password | Type | Exclude | Report | Advanced |

☑ Compare original and backup files to verify data was successfully backed up.

When backing up to media
  ○ Never compress the data.
  ○ Compress data to save time.
  ◉ Maximize compression to save space.

If the media already contains backups
  ○ Append this backup to my media.
  ○ Overwrite the media with this backup.
  ◉ Let me choose this option during the backup.

[OK]   [Cancel]   [Apply]

Fig. 9.25: Customizing options to backup data

Save time

You can also save time by clearing the *Compare original and backup file...* check box which automatically compares the backed-up data with the original data while backing up. This increases the data safety but takes longer.

Overwrite the media

Select the *Overwrite the media with this backup* radio button if the backup is done using floppy disks or tapes whose contents are no longer required. For reasons of security, we do not advise using this option.

Password

With the *Password* tab page you can give an added protection to your backup with a password. To do this, select the *Protect this backup with a password* check box. Enter the identical password (with a maximum of eight characters) into the *Password* and *Confirm password* text boxes and click on *Apply*. Only those who know this password will have access to the data on the backup media.

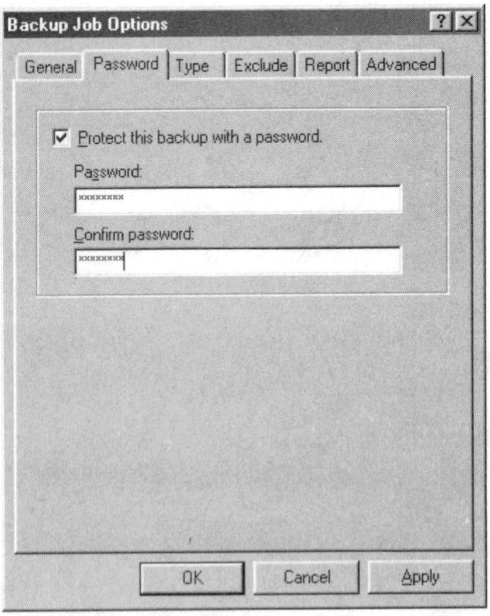

Backup Job Options

General | Password | Type | Exclude | Report | Advanced

☑ Protect this backup with a password.

Password:
[xxxxxxxx]

Confirm password:
[xxxxxxxx]

OK | Cancel | Apply

Fig. 9.26:   Setting a password protection for a backup

Report

With the *Report* tab page you can select how *Backup* reacts to errors during a backup, and if the backup can be left unsupervised, meaning it does not require further user input. It is best to leave the default settings here.

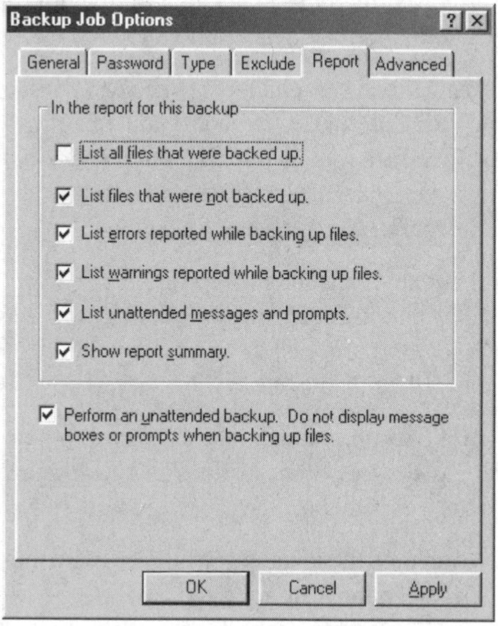

Fig. 9.27: Selecting options for the report of the backup

Start the backup

Confirm your settings with *OK*. Select the data to be backed up, the destination drive, etc. and start the backup.

Restoring Files with Microsoft Backup

With the *Restore* function of *Microsoft Backup* you can restore the data from tapes and floppy disks back to the hard disk.

Transfering large files

You can also use *Microsoft Backup* for transferring large files from one computer to another. To use the *Restore* function start *Microsoft Backup*.

To do so, select *Programs/Accessories/System Tools* from the *Start* menu and choose *Backup*.

Open backup job

In the first dialog box of *Backup*, select the *Open an existing backup job* radio button and click *OK*. Choose an available backup job in the *Open Backup Job* dialog box and confirm by clicking on the *Open* button.

If *Backup* is already running, change to the *Restore* tab page. A message appears asking if you want to refresh the current view. Confirm this by clicking on *Yes*. *Backup* will then read the available backup jobs and displays the contents in the *Select Backup Sets* dialog box.

Select backup sets

Choose the name of an available backup set, in the *Select Backup Sets* dialog box and confirm by clicking the *OK* button. After the logging process, the program window of *Microsoft Backup* will be displayed.

As in the case of a backup, you can use a Wizard to help to restore data. To do this, choose the *Restore Wizard* command from the *Tools* menu.

Restore

Now select the source of the backup job. If you are using the *Restore Wizard,* open the *Restore from* `IOMEGA TapeStreamer ▼` drop-down list and select your backup device. In the program window of *Backup* the list is in the upper right-hand corner. If you do not have a backup device choose the entry *File* `File ▼`. To restore from a floppy disk, click on the ⊞ button and select the drive and the backup file. Click *Next*.

Refresh the current view

A message appears, asking whether you want to refresh the current view. Confirm this by clicking on *Yes*. *Backup* will then read the available backup jobs and display the contents in the *Select Backup Sets* dialog box. Choose the name of an available backup set in the *Select Backup Sets* dialog box and confirm by clicking the *OK*. After the logging process, you have to select what to restore.

What to restore

This step also occurs in the program window of *Microsoft Backup* if you are not using the Wizard. Select the *Restore* tab page. Graphically, the selection of *What to restore* is the same as that of backing up. To begin with, select the folder(s) in the left window pane that contains the required data.

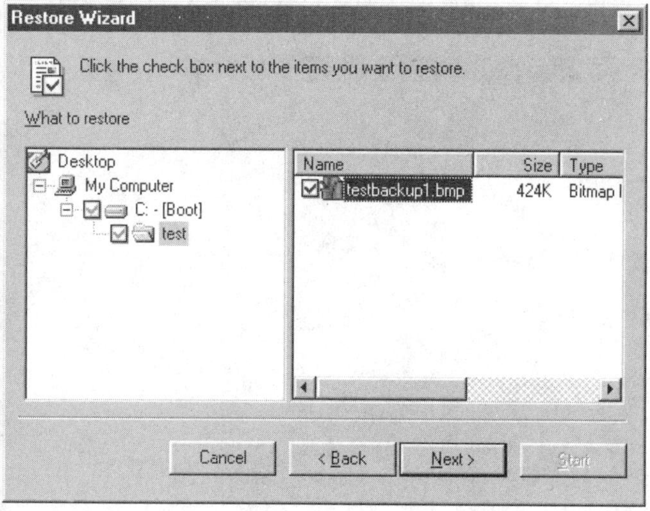

Fig. 9.28: Selecting what to restore (using the Wizard)

View of the structure

To expand the view of the structure, click on the plus sign ⊞ in front of a folder name. *Microsoft Backup* will list the file path from which the backup of the file was done. Click on the name of the folder to display its contents.

Restore backup job

You can select all objects of a backup job by checking the ☑ C: - [Boot] check box in front of the entry with the name of the drive.

Restore single folders

Single folders or subfolders can be selected by clicking the ☑ check box in front of the respective folder name in the left window pane. Single files can also be selected by clicking the ☑ check box in front of the name of the file in the right window pane. To do this, the corresponding folder has to be open. The display of the left window pane can be expanded using the ➕ plus signs like in *Explorer*. The contents of the folder will be displayed in the right window pane after clicking on the name of the folder. Once you have made a selection, click on *Next*.

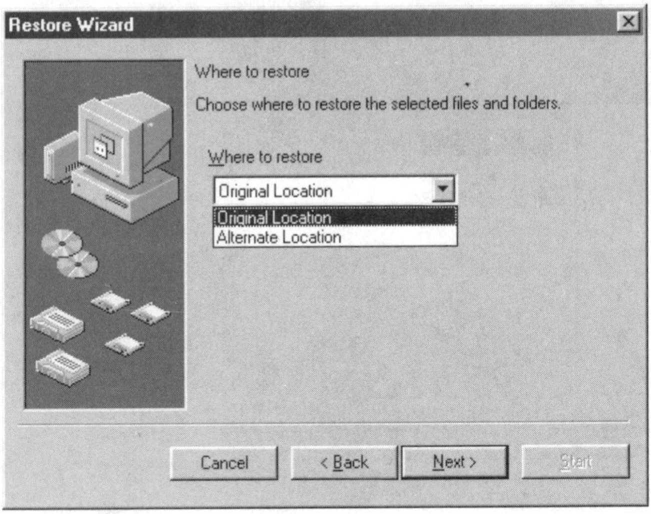

Fig. 9.29: Selecting the destination for the restored files (using the Wizard)

If you are using the *Restore Wizard* you can now select the destination for the restored files. To do this, use the *Where to restore* drop-down list. If you keep the standard setting *Original Location, Microsoft Backup* will restore the backed up files into the original folder(s) specified in the backup job.

Alternate Location

Select the *Alternate Location* entry if you want to restore the backup job into a folder other than the original folder.

410

To select the new target folder use the 🖳 button. After selecting the restore location, click *OK*.

Do not replace the file

Click on *Next* in the Wizard and choose how to restore the files. Select the *Do not replace the file on my computer* radio button to avoid overwriting a recent file of the same name with an older backup version. In the program window of *Backup* you can do this on the *General* tab page after clicking the *Options* button.

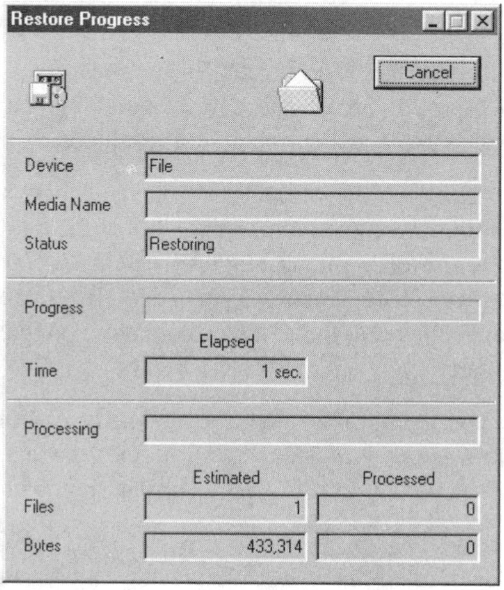

Fig. 9.30:   Restoring the backed-up files and the operation completed message

Restoring the backup job

Start restoring now by clicking on the *Start* button. *Microsoft Backup* will restore the backed up files. (Figure 9.30, left). For floppy disks follow the instructions when asked for a change of disk.

Operation completed

If the data has been successfully restored to the disk, the message *Operation completed* will be displayed. Confirm it with *OK*. Close the *Restore Status* dialog box with *OK* to get back to the *Microsoft Backup* program window

Customizing the Restore Options of Microsoft Backup

If you start restoring without using the *Restore Wizard*, the standard settings of *Microsoft Backup* will always restore a backup job to the original location on the hard drive. If, for example, you have backed up files from the *My Documents* folder, *Microsoft Backup* will restore the backup into this folder.

Original folder deleted

If the original folder has been deleted in the mean time, *Microsoft Backup* will create the folder including any subfolders again and place the backed up files there.

Customize restore options

You can customize the *Restore* options in such a way that the backed-up files are copied to other folders of the hard disk. To set the *Restore* options, start *Microsoft Backup*. Point to *Programs/Accessories/System Tools* from the *Start* menu and click on the *Backup* command in the overlapping menu.

Click on the *Close* button in the first dialog box, and change to the *Restore* tab page. Confirm the message asking whether you want to refresh the current view with *Yes*.

Backup will then read the available backup jobs and display the contents in the *Select Backup Sets* dialog box. Choose the name of an available backup set in the *Select Backup Sets* dialog box and confirm by clicking the *OK* button. After the logging process, the program window of *Microsoft Backup* will be displayed again.

Where to restore

Open the *Where to restore* listbox if you do not want to restore the backup at the original location. Choose the entry *Alternate Location*. Now you can determine the target folder by clicking the ⬛ button.

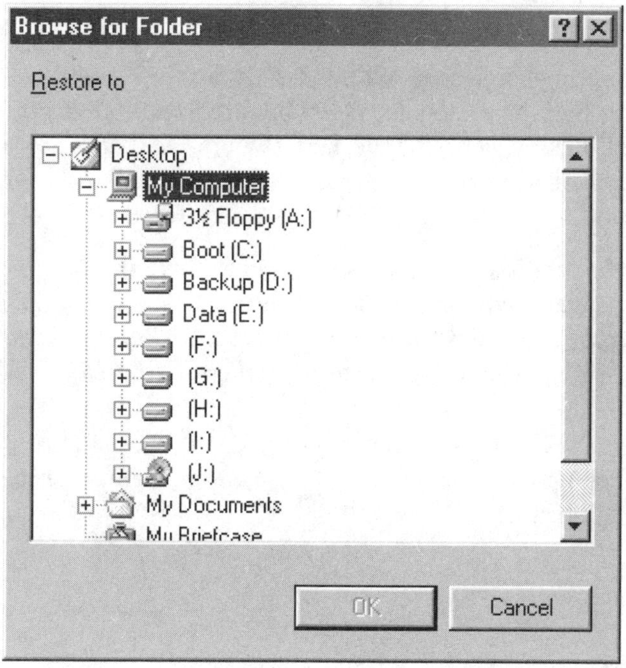

Browse for Folder   ? X

Restore to

```
☐ ✎ Desktop
   └ ☐ 🖳 My Computer
        ├ ⊞ 💾 3½ Floppy (A:)
        ├ ⊞ 🖴 Boot (C:)
        ├ ⊞ 🖴 Backup (D:)
        ├ ⊞ 🖴 Data (E:)
        ├ ⊞ 🖴 (F:)
        ├ ⊞ 🖴 (G:)
        ├ ⊞ 🖴 (H:)
        ├ ⊞ 🖴 (I:)
        └ ⊞ 🖴 (J:)
   ⊞ 📁 My Documents
      🖳 My Briefcase
```

OK   Cancel

Fig. 9.31:   Choosing other target folders

Select target drive or folder

Display the structure of the desired target drive or folder by clicking on the plus sign and select the target folder by clicking on its name. Confirm your changes with *OK*.

More options

For further options, click the *Options* button and change to the *General* tab page. Select the *Replace the file on my computer only if the file is older* radio button if *Microsoft Backup* should overwrite older files with more recent versions from the backup. The *Always replace the file on my computer* radio button will replace all (even more recent) files with the backed up version!

Report

On the *Report* tab page, you can select how the *Backup* will react to errors during a backup, and whether the backup can be left unsupervised, meaning without further user input. It is best to leave the standard settings here.

Restore

Confirm your settings with *OK* and start the *Restore* process by clicking on the *Start* button. *Microsoft Backup* will then restore the backup (Figure 9.30, left). For floppy disks, follow the directions when asked to change disks.

Operation completed

If the data has been successfully copied onto the disk, the message *Operation completed* (Figure 9.30, right) will be displayed. Confirm it with *OK*. Close the *Restore Status* dialog box with *OK* to get back to *Microsoft Backup*.

Tip!

The *Backup Wizard* and the *Restore Wizard* can also be called up from the main *Microsoft Backup* window using the *Tools* menu.

10. Multimedia Applications

DVD, digital TV, audio and games

In this chapter, we will introduce you to the most important multimedia applications integrated in *Windows 98*. *Windows 98* supports digital video, DVD, digital audio, the latest generation of *DirectX* games, digital TV reception via the Internet, and the connection of digital camcorders via *IEEE 1394* (Firewire).

You will learn about how to play audio files, how to apply effects or make recordings. You will also find out how to play midi files for digital *MIDI* instruments, video clips and music CDs.

Naturally, we will also have a look at the configuration of the necessary drivers and show you how you can tell *Windows 98* to play certain sounds whenever a particular system events occurs. The indispensable condition for all of the functions mentioned above is that your system has an integrated sound card with connected speakers and a CD-ROM drive.

How to Apply Sounds to System Events

Do you want *Windows 98* to start with drums and trumpets, or error messages to appear with a little jingle, and to celebrate the opening of a window with a soft 'plop'?

Individual sounds

This is no problem. You can apply individual sounds to each system event in *Windows 98*. The sound will be played as soon as the event takes place. Naturally, you will need to have a sound card and speakers connected to it.

To apply sound files to system events open the *Control Panel* via *Start/Settings/Control Panel* or via *My Computer*. Double-click the *Sounds* icon. In the *Events* list of the *Sounds Properties* dialog box, select the *Windows 98* action which you want to make audible. Open the *Name* drop-down list and select one of the displayed sounds using the mouse. In both lists you can use the scroll bar if necessary to view the entries not displayed in the list.

In the *Events* list, all events that are already linked to a sound file are marked with the speaker icon ◁. You can play the sound applied to the selected event with a click on the *Play* button ▶. Repeat this procedure for any events to which you want to apply sounds.

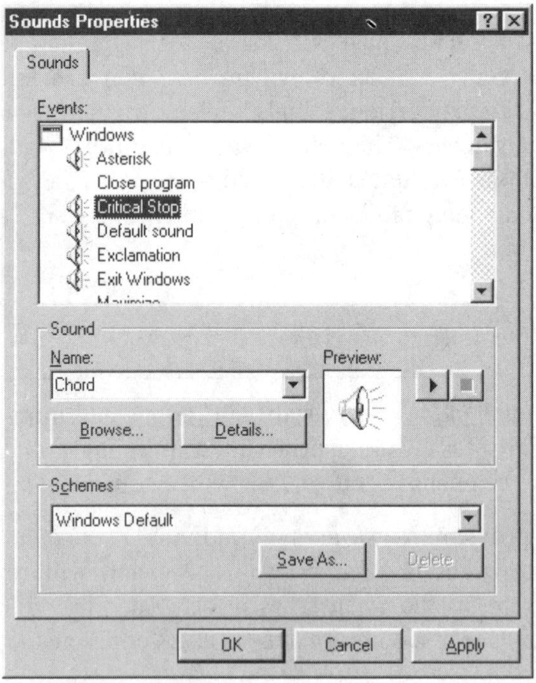

Fig. 10.1: Assigning individual sounds to system events

Tip!

To regulate the volume of the sounds for system events double-click the speaker icon on the taskbar and pull the slider to the desired position. The files displayed in the *Name* list are saved in *C:\Windows\Media.* Your own sounds can be loaded using the *Browse* button.

Installing and Setting Windows 98 Sound Schemes

You can apply an individual sound to every system event in *Windows 98.* This sound will be audible whenever the event occurs. In this section we will explain how to apply sounds from a *Windows 98* sound scheme to a selection of system events at the same time.

Sound schemes

A sound scheme contains various sounds that will be automatically applied to certain events. In addition, the schemes and their sounds are connected to a theme or a section. You have the choice between a wide range of sounds ranging from musical instruments to jungle sounds to the clatter of a robot.

Sounds

To use a sound scheme, open the *Control Panel* dialog box via *Start/Settings/Control Panel* or via *My Computer.* Double-click the *Sounds* icon, open the *Schemes* drop-down list and select one of the offered sound collections using the mouse.

Events list

In the *Events* list box, all events to which the scheme applies a sound are marked with the speaker icon. You can listen to the sound applied to a selected event with a click on the *Play* button.

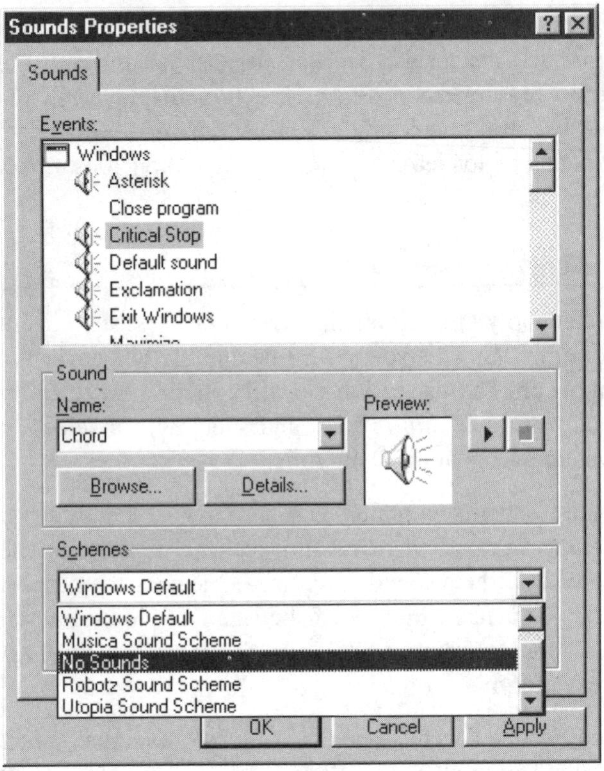

Fig. 10.2:   Changing the system sounds with sound schemes

Installing schemes   If the *Schemes* list contains no schemes or only the *Windows Default* scheme, open the *Control Panel* dialog box via *Start/Settings/Control Panel*. Then double-click the *Add/Remove Programs* icon.

In the *Add/Remove Programs Properties* dialog box, activate the *Windows Setup* tab. Scroll through the *Components* list with the scroll bar until you see the *Multimedia* entry. Select the *Multimedia* check box, then click the *Details* button.

Check the *Multimedia Sound Schemes* check box, insert your *Windows 98* setup CD into the CD-ROM drive and confirm twice with *OK*. The data will be copied. You can now apply the new schemes via *Control Panel/Sounds*.

Tip!

To regulate the volume of the system event sounds, double-click the speaker icon 🔊 on the taskbar and pull the slider to the desired position. If you do not hear any sound at all, check to see whether the speakers are turned on.

Setting the Volume for Sound Playback

With the corresponding audio hardware, *Windows 98* can play and record almost any kind of digital sound file. The playing and recording of audio files is handled by special multimedia applications in the *Accessories* program group. These applications will be explained separately. Here our topic is setting the volume for sound playback and the setting of the recording level. All sound applications use the *Windows 98* mixer to set the volume.

Volume Control with the Windows 98 Mixer

But you will not find the mixer anywhere if you look for it under this name. You will find the application in *Start/ Programs/Accessories/Entertainment* and *Volume Control*. The *Volume Control* window will pop up (the name displayed in the title bar will vary from sound card to sound card), looking similar to the one displayed in Figure 10.3.

Volume control

In the next tip you will read how to call up the volume control much more quickly than by the method described above.

By selecting *Options/Properties* you can individually configure the display of your mixer with the various check boxes in *Show the following volume controls* list box. In the *Properties* dialog box you can also determine with the radio buttons whether the controls for *Playback* or *Recording* or *Other* should be displayed or not.

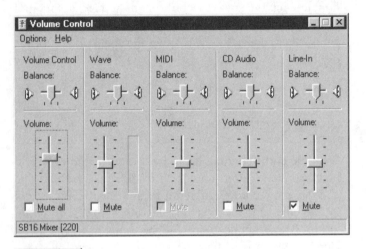

Fig. 10.3:   Volume control for playback. Above: the extended view

Total control

To regulate the total volume use the left slider called *Volume Control*. The volume for different sound sources (for example *Wave*, *CD* or *MIDI*) can be regulated independently using the respective controls. The changes are immediately effective.

Tip!

To open the volume control in future with a single click, go to the *Control Panel* and double-click the *Multimedia* icon. On the *Audio* tab page select the *Show volume control on the taskbar* check box to display the speaker icon ⏸ 12:09 on the taskbar (Figure 10.3, below). You can then access the *Volume Control* dialog box with a double click on ◁.

Setting the Properties of Multimedia Devices

Every recent and decent computer comes with a sound card. With a sound card, you can play system sounds and audio CDs, and if you connect a microphone to it, you can even make your own recordings.

Plug and Play
technology

The installation and configuration of the sound card has probably been done for you. However, you may want to upgrade your sound card and therefore you have to do the job yourself. Luckily, most sound cards work with the *Plug and Play* technology. Ideally you just have to insert the card into the slot in the computer and install the software that comes with the card. The fascinating world of multimedia then opens its gates for you.

Multimedia
option

The audio hardware can also be manually configured. In this section we will describe how to adjust the basic settings for playback and recording, how to choose the right options for the recording quality and lastly, how to make the handy volume control icon visible on the taskbar. To configure multimedia devices, click the *Start* button, open the *Control Panel* from *Settings* and double-click the *Multimedia* icon. Click the *Audio* tab page if it is not already activated.

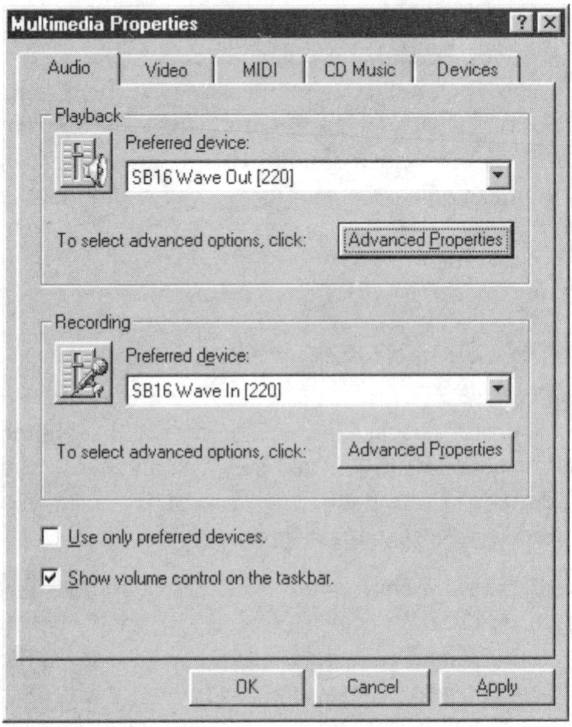

Fig. 10.4: Selecting preferred devices for playback and recording

Playback and recording device

With the drop-down list in the *Playback* option group you can select the *Preferred device* for the playback of system sounds. This list normally shows the name of the active sound card. If your sound card supports several sound standards, choose from the various options after opening the drop-down list.

Use only preferred devices

If you use programs that require certain hardware, select this hardware in the *Preferred device* drop-down list. Additionally, you can select the *Use only preferred devices* check box for these programs.

The basic volume and recording level can be controlled in the *Volume Control* dialog box after clicking the *Playback* button 🔳 or the *Recording* button 🔳 (as described previously).

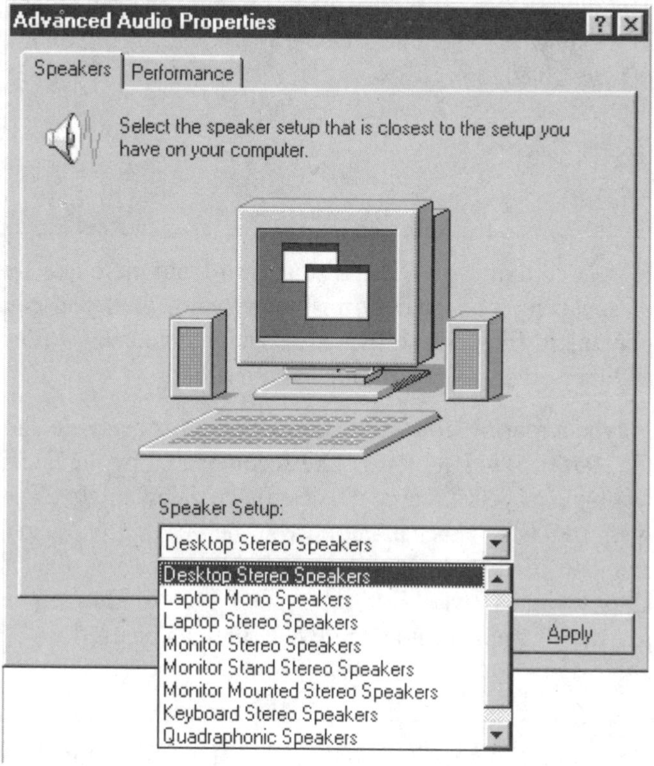

Advanced Audio Properties

Speakers | Performance

Select the speaker setup that is closest to the setup you have on your computer.

Speaker Setup:

Desktop Stereo Speakers

Desktop Stereo Speakers
Laptop Mono Speakers
Laptop Stereo Speakers
Monitor Stereo Speakers
Monitor Stand Stereo Speakers
Monitor Mounted Stereo Speakers
Keyboard Stereo Speakers
Quadraphonic Speakers

Apply

Fig. 10.5:   Setting the properties of the speakers

Setting properties   With the *Advanced Properties* button, you can adjust some more basic settings for playback and recording. For example, in the *Advanced Audio Properties* dialog box, you can set the type of speaker you are using with your PC (Figure 10.5). On the *Performance* tab page you can set the quality of the sample conversion. All changes have to be confirmed with *OK*. Click on *Restore Defaults* to restore the default settings.

Tip!

The playback and recording level can only be controlled via the *Control Panel* if the audio hardware supports this. This is the case with most of the sound cards available. To be able to do so, click the *Show volume control on the taskbar* check box ◄ 12:09 .

Playing Audio Files

If your computer provides a sound card and there is a set of speakers connected to this sound card, then you can play audio files. These files are usually called *Wave* files and they are also used for the system sounds.

Wave files

Maybe a roaring lion will announce an error message and the start of *Windows 98* will be accompanied by the latest hit single of your favorite musician. A window might close with a squeak. This can get on your nerves pretty quickly and one of the nicest features of *Windows 98* is that it allows you to switch off the system sounds. But this is just one example of how the *Wave* files can be used.

Playing Audio Files with Sound Recorder

You can use *Sound Recorder* to play audio files stored on your hard disk. To start *Sound Recorder*, choose *Start/ Programs/Accessories/Entertainment* and click on *Sound Recorder* in the overlapping menu.

Integrated sound files

Select the *Open* command from the *File* menu. By default, *Sound Recorder* opens in *My Documents*, where you probably do not have any sound files if you have not downloaded any from the Internet. To choose a file, go to *C:\Windows\Media* where the sound files integrated in

Windows 98 are stored. Select a sound from the list box or change to a different source folder. Click the *Open* button to load the file.

Open

Look in: ☐ Media

My Hit	Jungle Default	Jungle Minimize
Chord	Jungle Error	Jungle Open
Ding	Jungle Exclamation	Jungle Question
Jungle Asterisk	Jungle Maximize	Jungle Recycle
Jungle Close	Jungle Menu Command	Jungle Restore Down
Jungle Critical Stop	Jungle Menu Popup	Jungle Restore Up

File name: My Hit   [Open]

Files of type: Sounds (*.wav)   [Cancel]

Fig. 10.6: The *Media* folder for Windows 98 sounds

Buttons

The *Play* button ▶ starts the playback of the sound file. Click the *Stop* button ■ to stop the playback. The *Seek to Start* button ◀◀ takes you to the start of the file and *Seek to End* ▶▶ to the end. You can move the slider ⊣├ with the mouse to move to a particular position in the file.

Fig. 10.7: Playback of *Wave* files

On the left side of the *Sound Recorder* window the current position of the playback is displayed in increments of hundredths (1/100) of a second.

The right side of the window displays the total length of the sound file. The level is graphically displayed in the black box in the middle of the *Sound Recorder* window.

If you do not hear much of the sound file or even none at all, double-click the speaker icon ◀⁞ on the taskbar and adjust the volume with the *Wave* volume control or the main *Volume Control*, or both, and start the playback again.

Tip! To control the volume of the system sounds, simply click the speaker icon ◀⁞ on the taskbar and use the corresponding slider in the dialog box which appears to adjust it.

Tip! With *Sound Recorder* and a microphone you can also make your own recordings. Use the *Record* button ● More about recording is given further ahead in the chapter.

Playing Sound Files with Media Player

The *Media Player* in *Windows 98* is used to play all kinds of multimedia files. You can choose to play video clips (*AVI files*), sound files (*WAV* files), *MIDI* sequences (*MID* and *RMI* files) and audio CDs.

To start *Media Player*, go to *Start/Programs/Accessories/* and *Entertainment*, then select the *Media Player* item in the overlapping menu.

Choosing the device

First choose the type of media to be played back in the *Device* menu. For now we just want to hear sounds, so choose *Sound*. The *Open* dialog box appears, and the

Files of type drop-down list shows the default *Sound (*.wav)* entry. Change to the source folder of your choice.

Select the file you want to listen to and click the *Open* button. The title bar of *Media Player* will display the name of the file and the current status.

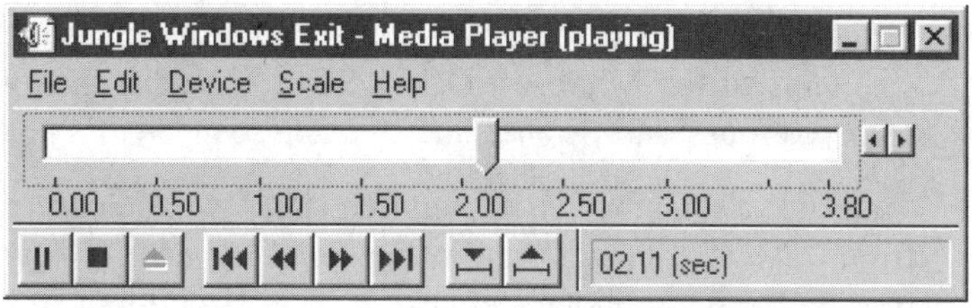

Fig. 10.8:   Playback of a sound file with Media Player

The actual playback is controlled with the buttons in *Media Player*. Start the playback with the *Play* button ▶ and stop the playback with the *Stop* button ■.

Click the *Next Mark* button ▶▶ to jump to the next mark created with one of the *Start Selection* ⬐ or *End Selection* ⬏ markers.

You can *Fast Forward* with the ▶▶ button and *Rewind* with the ◀◀ button. You will find sample sounds in the *C:\Windows\Media* folder.

Tip!

Use the *Edit* menu to create a selection and copy it to the clipboard. In another application, you can choose the *Paste* command to paste the part of the object at the cursor position. With *Edit/Options* you can determine properties such as the *Auto Rewind* after playback or the *Auto Repeat* function for continuous replay. Furthermore, you can set the *OLE* Options for the data exchange with other *Windows 98* applications.

Recording Sound Files

If your computer provides a sound card and you connect a suitable microphone to it, you can make your own recording anytime you want and save it as a digital *Wave* file. These *Wave* files can be inserted or embedded into virtually all modern *Windows 98* applications, such as the programs of the Microsoft Office Suite. In addition, any recorded sound can also become a system sound.

To record a sound with a microphone start *Sound Recorder* from *Start/Programs/Accessories/Entertainment*. Now pick up the microphone and click the *Record* button ⬛. With the mouse of course, not with the microphone.

Stop recording

Speak or sing into the microphone. The recording time is displayed on the left side below *Position* in seconds. Click the *Stop* button ⬛ to finish the recording. With the *Play* button ▶ you can start the playback of your recording. The *Seek to Start* button ◀◀ brings you to the start of the file and *Seek to End* ▶▶ to the end of it. You can move the slider ─┤─ with the mouse to move to a particular position in the file.

Microphone level

If your recording is not audible, it may be that the volume level just was not high enough during recording. Double-click the speaker icon 🔊 on the taskbar and increase the *Microphone* level with the respective slider. Depending on the sound card and where you plugged in your input, you might have to increase the *Line in* level too. If you do not see the microphone level, it means it is still hidden, in which case you can go to *Options* and select *Properties*. In the *Show the following volume controls* list box, scroll down till you see the *Microphone* item. Select the check box to display the volume control. Increase the level and try recording again.

Fig. 10.9: With a sound card and microphone you can record your own sound files

Saving sound files

In order to save the recordings as a sound file on the hard disk, choose *File/Save As*. By default, sound files are saved in *My Documents*. If you want to use your recording as a system sound, change to the *C:\Windows\Media* folder. The advantage is that you can assign your recording to a system event simply by choosing it from the *Name* list in the *Sound* option group in the *Sounds Properties* dialog box. You find this dialog box in *Start/Settings/Control Panel/Sounds*. Whatever folder you choose to save the file in, click the *Save* button to save it.

Tip!

The *Sound Recorder* always records in the format (by default *PCM*) displayed in the *Save As* dialog box next to *Format*. The settings can be changed by clicking the *Change* button.

Effects for Sound Files

Not only can you record sound files with the *Sound Recorder*, but you can also create special effects on *Wave* files. The results are definitely simplistic, but they may be good enough for the initial steps concerning sound editing with the computer. To experiment with the effects,

429

either record your own sound file or choose a sound file from the *Media* folder in *Windows 98*.

Setting Effects for Sound Recorder

Start *Sound Recorder* with *Start/Programs/Accessories/ Entertainment* and choose from the overlapping menu *Sound Recorder*. Record your own file as described above. You can also choose a sound from the *Windows 98* sound files in *C:\Windows\Media*.

Buttons

The *Play* button ▶ starts the playback of the sound file. Click the *Stop* button ■ to stop the playback. The *Seek to Start* button ◀◀ brings you to the start of the file and *Seek to End* ▶▶ to the end. You can move the slider ─╟─ with the mouse to move to a particular position in the file.

Playback position

On the left side of the *Sound Recorder* window the current position in the playback is displayed in increments of 1/100 of a second. The right side of the dialog box shows the total length of the sound file. The level is graphically displayed in the black box in the middle of the *Sound Recorder* window.

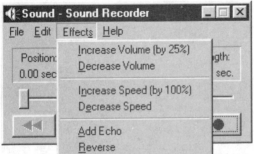

Fig. 10.10:   The *Effects* menu in Sound Recorder

The *Effects* deals with the manipulation of the opened sound file. All available effects will affect the whole file:

- *Increase Volume (by 25%)*
  Increases the volume by 25 percent. The command can be repeated several times, but there will soon be distortion.

- *Decrease Volume*
  decreases the volume. This command can also be executed several times in a row.

- *Increase Speed (by 100%)*
  doubles the playback speed of the sound file. Obviously, the pitch of the recording will go up. The command can be repeated several times.

- *Decrease Speed*
  cuts the playback speed of the sound file by half. Of course the pitch of the recording will go down. The command can be repeated several times.

- *Add Echo*
  adds a digital echo to the sound file. The procedure can be repeated for stronger effects.

- *Reverse*
  plays the sound file backwards.

Tip!

The quality of the sound file decreases with the number of effects you apply. If you use effects with opposite results several times in a row, the sound file will become very distorted. The *Revert* menu item on the *File* menu will restore the file to the last saved condition. Confirm the dialog box with *Yes*.

Playing Audio CDs

Playing audio CDs is not reserved anymore to the exclusive domain of stereo systems. If you have a CD-ROM drive in your computer, you can use your PC to play audio CDs.

Sound card and
speakers

Unless you have a sound card and speakers, you will need to use a set of headphones connected to the headphone output of the drive in order to do this. Most sound cards available on the market can connect to the CD player from inside the computer and play the sound through the speakers.

Using CD Player to Play CDs

AutoPlay

To play an audio CD on the computer just open the CD drive and put the CD onto the tray. Close the drive and wait a few seconds. By default *Windows 98* automatically starts the playback of the first song.

CD Player

If this is not the case or if you want to change the order of the titles use the *CD Player* application.

Click the *Start* button and go to *Programs/Accessories/* and *Entertainment*. In the overlapping menu choose *CD Player*.

Titles and
position

The top left corner of the application window displays the current title number and the current position in seconds. To the right of this window are the control buttons for the CD drive. The design of the interface resembles a stereo system.

Audio CDs can be played with CD Player

Control buttons

To interrupt the playback temporarily, click the *Pause* button ⚏; to stop the playback click the *Stop* button ■, and to resume the playback use the *Play* button ▶. A click on the *Next Track* button ▶▶ jumps to the next title. The *Previous Track* button ◀◀ will jump to the previous track or the beginning of the current track.

Opening the tray

The *Skip Forwards* button ▶▶ will move forward by one second, while the *Skip Backwards* button ◀◀ will move backward by one second. The *Eject* button will open and close the tray. If you want to jump to a particular title, use the *Track* drop-down list.

Continuous play

The *Options* menu offers you the *Random Play* and *Continuous Play* items, as well as a short preview of every track called *Intro Play*. The status bar shows the total length of the CD on the left side and the length of the current title on the right side.

Enabling and Disabling Continuous Play

Normally you just have to open the tray, insert a CD, close the tray, and then wait for a few seconds in order to listen to the first title.

AutoPlay-
function

This is called the *AutoPlay* function and for many users it is a practical feature, because they do not have to do anything. The same function ensures that an application on a CD-ROM is launched as soon as you insert the CD.

However, sometimes this automatic start is not what is wanted. People who want to decide by themselves what the PC does and does not do can disable the *AutoPlay* feature on the computer.

Device Manager
tab page

To do so, go to the *Control Panel* with *Start/Settings* and double-click the *System* icon. In the *System Properties* dialog box, view the *Device Manager* tab page.

Select the *View devices by type* radio button and double-click the *CD-ROM* entry in the list.

Auto insert
notification

The entry of your CD-ROM drive will appear. Double-click this entry as well. You will then see the *Properties* dialog box of your CD-ROM drive. Change to the *Settings* tab page and clear the *Auto insert notification* check box. Confirm both dialog boxes with *OK* and close the *Control Panel*.

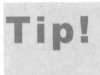

To manually control the playback of a CD, use the *CD Player*. Click to the *Start* button and open *Programs/Accessories/Entertainment*. In the overlapping menu choose *CD Player*. How to work with this program is described above.

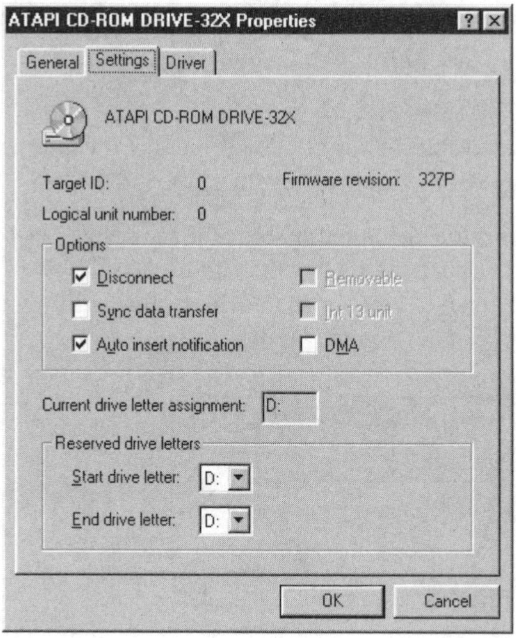

ATAPI CD-ROM DRIVE-32X Properties ? X

General | Settings | Driver |

ATAPI CD-ROM DRIVE-32X

Target ID: 0   Firmware revision: 327P

Logical unit number: 0

Options
- ☑ Disconnect   ☐ Removable
- ☐ Sync data transfer   ☐ Int 13 unit
- ☑ Auto insert notification   ☐ DMA

Current drive letter assignment: D:

Reserved drive letters
Start drive letter: D: ▼
End drive letter: D: ▼

OK   Cancel

Fig. 10.12:   Here you can switch off the AutoPlay feature

Playing Video Clips

The *Media Player* can be used to play all kinds of multimedia files. These files include video clips (*AVI* files), sound files (*WAV* files), *MIDI* sequences (*MID* and *RMI* files) and audio CDs. To start the application, choose *Start/Programs/Accessories/Entertainment* and then click on *Media Player*.

Playing Video Clips with Media Player

Video for Windows   First of all, you have to choose the type of multimedia object to be played using the *Device* menu. For *AVI* video clips choose *Video for Windows*. The *Open* dialog box pops up and you will only see all the available *AVI* files, because the *Video for Windows (*.avi)* entry is selected.

Change to the source folder of your choice. If it contains *AVI* files, they will be immediately displayed in the list.

Select the file you are looking for and click the *Open* button. You can read the title of the clip in the title bar of *Media Player*. At the same time you will get the first frame of the video clip in a separate window. (Figure 10.14).

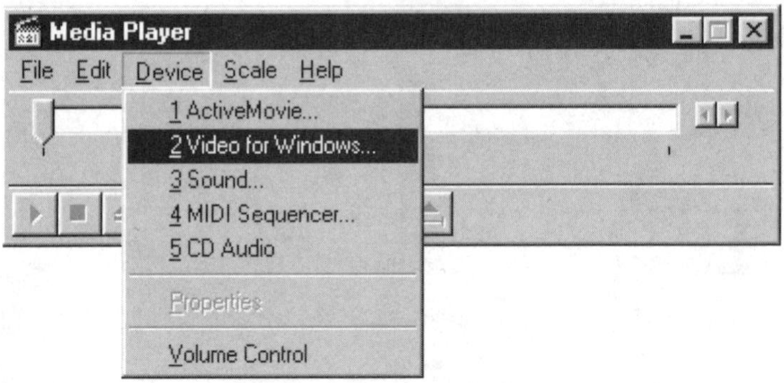

Fig. 10.13:   Choosing the multimedia type

Controls

Here is a short description of the controls in Media Player: you can start the playback with the *Play* button ▶ and stop the playback with the *Stop* button ■.

Selection

Click the *Next Mark* button ▸▸ to jump to the next mark created with one of the *Start Selection* ⊻ or *End Selection* ⊼ buttons.

Fast Forward with the ▸▸ button and *Rewind* with the ◂◂ button.

Time slider

In the *Scale* menu you can switch the way the time slider is displayed from the default *Time* to *Frames*.

Current position

During playback, the slider shows the current position and a box on the right at the bottom of the Media Player application window displays the current position in tenths of a second.

You can drag the slider with the mouse and move it by sight, to search for a particular position in the video.

Fig. 10.14:   Playback of a clip with Media Player

If you want to copy a section of the video into the clipboard, choose *Edit/Selection* and determine in the *Set Selection* dialog box the size and position of the section to be copied. Copied selections can be pasted into other applications at the cursor position. With *Edit/Options* you can determine properties such as the *Auto Rewind* after playback or the *Auto Repeat* function for continuous replay. Furthermore you can set the *OLE* options for the data exchange with other *Windows 98* applications.

Tip! *ActiveMovie* video clips from the Internet can be played back with *ActiveMovie Control*. Choose *Start/Programs/ Accessories/Entertainment* and click the *ActiveMovie Control* entry. You can also play *MPEG* files with this application, however, it is not possible to edit them.

Tip! Sample videos can be found on the Setup CD-ROM of *Windows 98* in the *\cdsample\videos* folder, for example. Video files have the *.AVI* extension, and *MPEG* clips the *.MPG* extension. Both formats can be played in full-screen mode without any difficulty. To do so, click the *Maximize* button ▣. Start the playback with *Run* ▶, and stop the playback with the *Stop* button ■.

Setting the Properties for Video Playback

An essential part of the PC's multimedia capability is the playback of video clips. As long as you only play existing video clips you will not need any special hardware. The playback of *AVI, MPEG* or *ActiveMovie* videos is software-controlled and displayed by the graphic card.

Setting the
window size

Therefore, the playback of video clips can be controlled individually on every Windows computer. To do so, choose *Start/Settings/Control Panel*.

Multimedia icon

Double-click the *Multimedia* icon and change to the *Video* tab page (Figure 10.15). On the top of the dialog box you see an iconized monitor which provides a preview of your video settings.

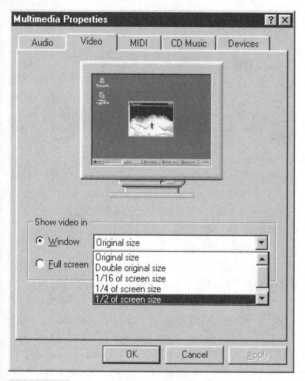

Fig. 10.15:   Setting the window size

Multimedia
properties

In the *Show video in* option group you can determine the window size for the playback of *AVI* files. With the *Full screen* radio button, you can choose to play the video in full-screen mode. You will need a graphic card of superior quality which supports hardware based video acceleration in order to get good results with this.

Jerky video

With old graphic cards the result will be jerky, particularly in full-screen mode. It will help to play the clip in a smaller window. The computer and the card have less work and more time to improve the quality of the playback. From the drop-down list choose a window size that provides a reasonable quality and is large enough to enjoy the video clip.

Tip!

The above-determined settings will affect only the playback of video clips that have been started with a double click on *AVI, MPEG* or *ActiveMovie* files in *Explorer* or *My Computer*. In these cases, the *ActiveMovie Control* will be launched automatically.

Sample videos can be found on the Setup CD-ROM of *Windows 98,* for example in the *\cdsample\videos* folder. Video clips have the *AVI* extension, and *MPEG* clips the *.MPG* extension. Both formats can be played in full-screen mode without problems.

Playing music with MIDI Instruments

Start *Media Player*

The Media Player is used to play all kinds of multimedia files. These files include video clips (*AVI* files), sound files (*WAV* files), *MIDI* sequences (*MID* and *RMI* files) as well as audio CDs. To start the application, choose *Start/ Programs/Accessories/Entertainment* and *Media Player*.

MIDI-Sequencer
command

First you have to choose the type of multimedia files to be played from the *Device* menu. For .*MID* midi sequences choose *MIDI Sequencer*. The *Open* dialog box pops up and you will only see the available *MID* files, since the *MIDI Sequencer (*.mid *.rmi)* entry is set.

Source folder

Change to a folder that contains MIDI files. *C:\Windows\ Media* would be an excellent place to look. Select the

desired file and click *Open*. The name of the MIDI
sequence is displayed in the title bar of Media Player.
The status bar shows the current position in the piece in
minutes and seconds.

Playing a midi file with Media Player

Controls

Here is a short description of the controls of *Media
Player*. You can start the playback with the *Play* button ▶
and stop the playback with the *Stop* button ■.

Selection

Click the *Next Mark* button ▶▶| to jump to the next mark
created with one of the *Start Selection* ⌐ or *End Selection* ⌐ buttons.

Fast Forward with the ▶▶ button and *Rewind* with the ◀◀
button.

Tip!

Use the *Edit* menu to determine a selection and copy it to
the clipboard. In another application you can choose the
Paste command to paste the selected part of the object at
the cursor position. With *Edit/Options* you can determine
properties such as the *Auto Rewind* after playback or the
Auto Repeat function for continuous replay. In addition,
you can set the *OLE* options for the data exchange with
other *Windows 98* applications.

Checking and Changing Multimedia Drivers

Nowadays, one often hears the term multimedia in connection with computers. This means the integration of various media like text, graphics, tables and diagrams, as well as animation, sound and videos.

For this wide spectrum of possibilities you need additional hardware like a sound card or a video card. These devices have to be recognized by the operating system on your computer.

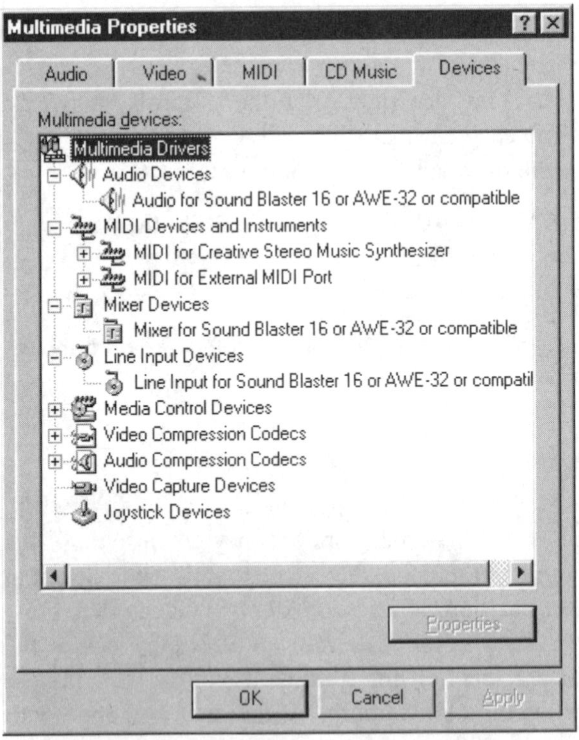

Fig. 10.17: Displaying installed multimedia devices

The necessary internal programs to control this hardware are called drivers and have to be installed in *Windows 98*. Normally *Windows 98* does this automatically.

Plug and Play-technology

Unfortunately, the *Plug and Play* technology does not always work as well as the manufacturers claim it will. You can help matters yourself using the *Control Panel*. The *Control Panel* lists all available multimedia devices and their respective drivers and properties. Often you can adjust properties and change drivers.

Fig. 10.18: Checking the properties of multimedia drivers

Multimedia properties

Click the *Start* button and choose *Settings/Control Panel*. Double-click the *Multimedia* icon and change to the *Devices* tab page. The *Multimedia Drivers* list shows all the recognized main components on your PC. Click the plus sign in front of the main category to list the individual devices within the group. Double-clicking on the category name will do the same.

Status of the device

If you have a device which does not work or which gives you some other kind of trouble, select it in the list and click the *Properties* button. The *Properties* dialog box displays the status of the respective device. If you see the message *Driver is enabled and active* everything should be fine with your configuration. If you have a deactivated driver or a driver which is not being used, you can usually configure the device by clicking the *Settings* button. The *Remove* button removes the drivers of the device from the configuration. If the device is conflicting with other devices on your system, you can also switch off a device which you do not need at the moment by selecting the *Do not [...] this device* radio button.

11. Online Features

Internet-Look

This chapter deals exclusively with *Windows 98*'s most important Online features. The *Windows 98* interface is consequently oriented around the Internet so that there is no difference for the user, at least visually, whether he is looking at data from his own hard drive or data from the Intranet of the company's network or even at data from the Internet itself.

Internet Explorer

You are already familiar with the surface of the desktop and its capability to display Web contents like animations or pictures. You might also have noticed the similarity of folder icons and similar elements to the *Microsoft Internet Explorer 4.0* interface. However, before you can connect your *Windows 98* PC with the big webbed world outside, some configuration work needs to be done.

A modem is essential for working with online features. First, you will learn how to install and configure this necessary piece of hardware on your system. Then we will take a look at the *Dial-Up Networking*, an application used by the *Microsoft Internet Explorer* integrated Web browser to establish a connection with the Internet.

Subsequently, we will introduce you to *Internet Explorer* and its various features. You can use *Internet Explorer* to display information from the World Wide Web (WWW).

Phone Dialer

In the next section we will introduce the *Phone Dialer*, an application that lets you use your computer to dial certain phone numbers.

But before all that, we have to take care of the technical requirements. Unless you have a correctly installed modem or ISDN adapter, you cannot access the Internet.

Installing a Modem in Windows 98

In order to access the Internet and use online services such as *America Online* or *CompuServe*, you need additional hardware in the form of a modem. This device converts digital data into analog pulses and vice versa, since the computer deals exclusively with digital data while the telephone lines transfer analog pulses.

Modem connection

So the receiving modem converts the analog pulses back into digital data which can be understood by your PC. Before you can work effectively with the modem, your computer has to know where it is. Therefore, you have to install it. In this chapter we assume that you have a correctly installed modem.

Modem installation

Switch on your modem. To install it click the *Start* button and choose *Settings* and then *Control Panel*. Double-click the *Modems* icon 🖥. This should launch the *Install New Modem* wizard.

Add button

If the *Modems Properties* dialog box pops up instead, click the *Add* button to start the *Install New Modem* wizard from here. Check the *Don't detect my modem; I will select it from a list* check box. In this way you can provide a manual configuration. Click the *Next* button.

Fig. 11.1:   Selecting the manual configuration

Manufacturers and
models

In the next step of the wizard, select your modem from the *Manufacturers* list and the *Models* list. If your modem is not listed, select *(Standard Modem Types)* in the *Manufacturers* list.

Install New Modem

Click the manufacturer and model of your modem. If your modem is not listed, or if you have an installation disk, click Have Disk.

Manufacturers:

[Standard Modem Types]
[VoiceView Modem Types]
3Com
3X
Accton Technology Corpor
Aceev

Models

Standard 9600 bps Modem
Standard 14400 bps Modem
Standard 19200 bps Modem
Standard 28800 bps Modem
Standard 33600 bps Modem
Standard 56000 bps K56Flex Modem
Standard 56000 bps X2 Modem

Have Disk...

< Back   Next >   Cancel

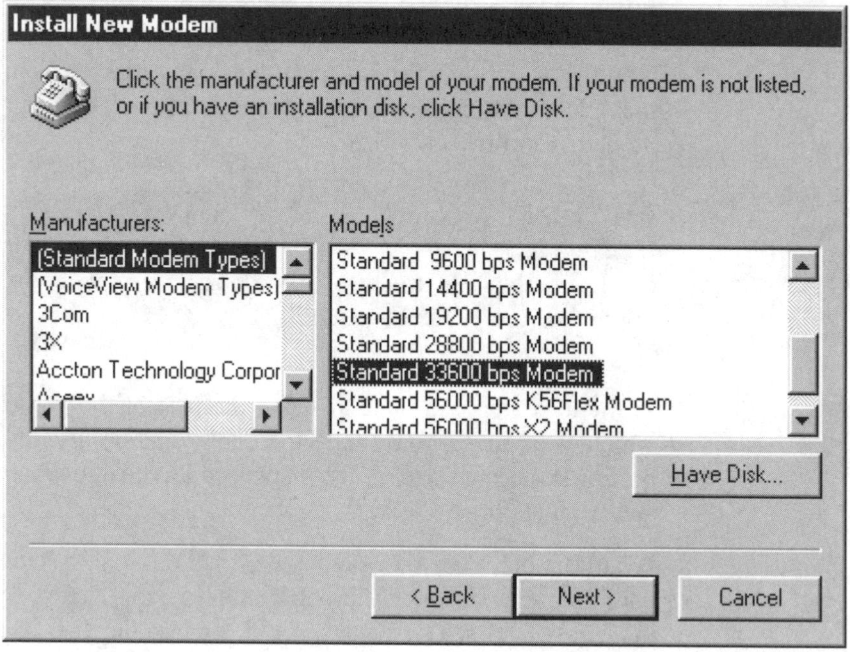

Fig. 11.2:   Selecting the modem manufacturer and model

Select in the *Models* list box the speed your modem supports, for example, *Standard 28,800 bps Modem* for a V.34 modem and *Standard 33,600 bps Modem* for a V.34bis modem.

For an older *V.32* modem, choose the entry *Standard 14,400 bps*; for a new high-speed-modem at 56,000 bits per second, choose the entry *Standard 56,000 bps X2* or *K56Flex*.

V.90 modem

For a modern *V.90* modem, either choose the manufacturer and the model, or click the *Have Disk* button and read the driver information from the floppy disk or from the CD-ROM provided by the manufacturer of your modem. Confirm with *Next*.

Be careful with the standard modem types in *Windows 98*, you might run into certain limitations later on. It is advisable to install the correct type with the original driver, if you have it.

COM- port

In the next step you have to select the port of the PC to which your modem is connected. This will be a serial port or serial interface. A list displays all available serial and parallel ports.

What this list looks like exactly depends on your system configuration. Check which port you have connected your modem to and select the respective one in the list, for example, *Communications Port (COM2)*.

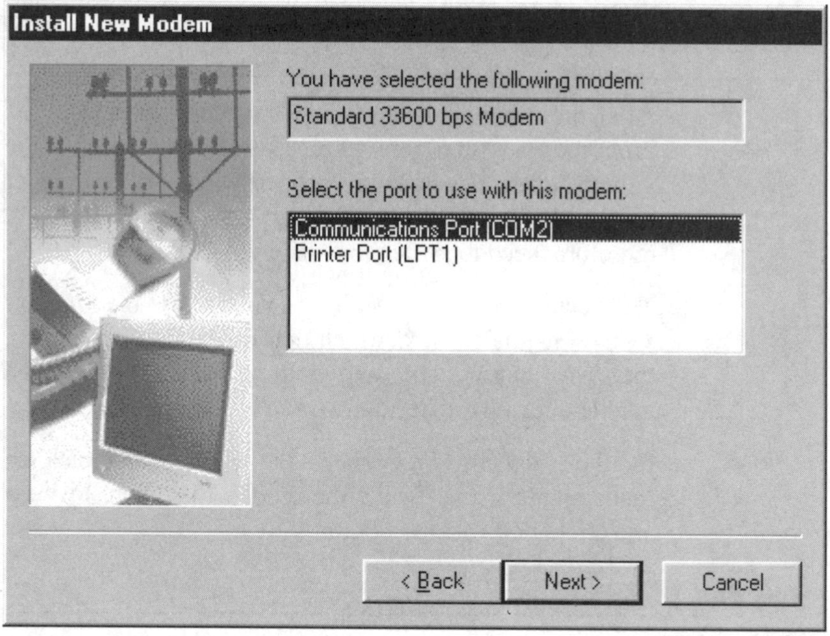

Install New Modem

You have selected the following modem:

Standard 33600 bps Modem

Select the port to use with this modem:

Communications Port (COM2)
Printer Port (LPT1)

< Back   Next >   Cancel

Fig. 11.3:   Connecting the modem

Setup CD-ROM

Insert your *Windows* CD-ROM if you do not keep the *Windows 98* setup on your hard drive. When you confirm with *Next*, Windows will install the driver for you.

If you install a modem for the first time on your computer, you have to decide whether to use *pulse* or *tone dialing* and you must enter the area code into the appropriate text box in the *Location Information* dialog. Exit the modem installation by clicking the *Next* and then the *Finish* button. Your modem will now be listed and usable by Windows.

Choosing Properties for the Modem

After the installation of the modem, you can change the properties anytime you like. The 'fine-tuning' of the system often depends on properties such as transfer speed. Maybe you want to connect other peripherals and, therefore, need to switch to a different COM port.

To execute such adjustments you need to use the *Modems Properties* dialog box, which you can access by clicking the *Start* button, choosing *Settings/Control Panel* and double-clicking on the *Modems* icon.

Modems icon

In the *Modems Properties* dialog box all installed modems are listed. Select the modem you want to view and click the *Properties* button.

Selecting Port and Speed

A dialog box with two tab pages appears. The *General* tab page provides information about the serial port used by the modem and the maximum speed.

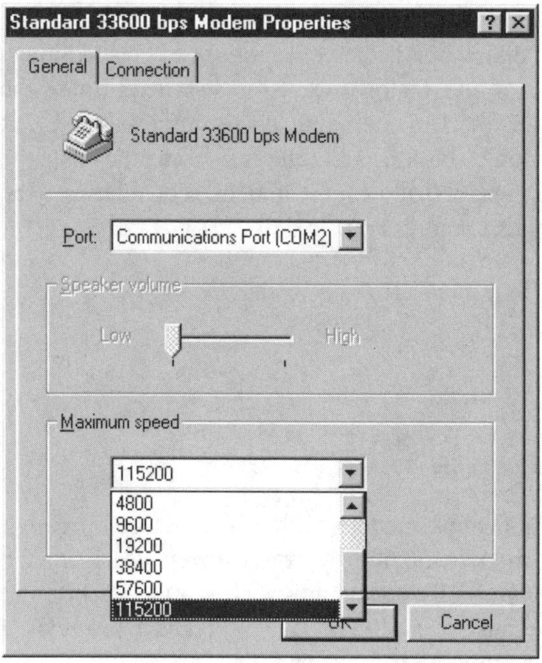

Standard 33600 bps Modem Properties

General | Connection

Standard 33600 bps Modem

Port: Communications Port (COM2) ▼

Speaker volume

Low ▬ High

Maximum speed

115200 ▼

| 4800 |
| 9600 |
| 19200 |
| 38400 |
| 57600 |
| 115200 |

Cancel

Fig. 11.4:   Checking the properties of an installed modem

If the modem is now connected to a different serial port, open the *Port* drop-down list and choose the correct port from the list. In the *Speaker volume* group box you can adjust the volume of the speaker in the modem, if available. Just place the slider at a suitable position anywhere between *Low* and *High*.

Tip!

With the standard modem drivers, some of the described features cannot be adjusted. For example, the built-in speaker cannot always be accessed and appears disabled as shown in Figure 11.4. However, the most important settings are possible with this type, too.

One of the most important settings in the *Modem Properties* dialog box is the *maximum speed,* located in the lower part of the dialog box. This list determines the speed of the modem including data compression. Click the drop-down button and choose from the list the maximum speed of your modem considering the available data compression.

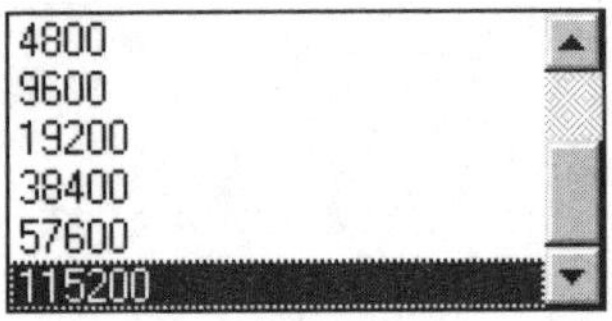

4800	▲
9600	
19200	
38400	
57600	
115200	▼

Fig. 11.5: Selecting the maximum speed with data compression

Data compression

With a 33,600 bps modem with *V.42* data compression and for a modern 56,000 bps modem, choose from the *Maximum Speed* list the highest entry, *115,200* bits per second, because the *V.42* data compression provides a compression ratio of as much as 4:1.

Transfer rate

Only for older modems that have a transfer rate of 14,400 bps and *V.42* data compression, should you select the entry *57,600* in the *Maximum Speed* drop-down list. Subsequently, exit both dialog boxes with *OK* and *Close*. Close the *Control Panel* also. Further adjustments of the modem settings will be discussed in the following sections.

Connection Settings for the Modem

A modem converts digital data into analog pulses, which can be transferred through the telephone line. The receiver modem reconverts the analog stream back into digital data.

Setting the connection

The way in which data are transferred and verified depends on the particular purpose of the modem. Some online applications require a modification of the default connection settings.

To change the settings, select the *Settings* item in the *Start* menu and, in the overlapping menu, the *Control Panel* command. In the *Control Panel* double-click the modem icon. The *Modems Properties* dialog box lists all installed modems.

Select the modem whose settings you want to modify and click the *Properties* button. In the dialog box which appears, activate the *Connection* tab page. Here, under *Connection Preferences*, you can determine the number of data bits and stop bits as well as the parity.

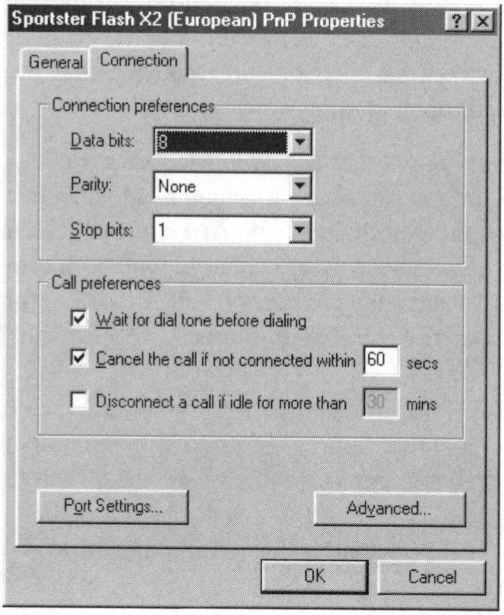

Fig. 11.6: Setting the connection preferences for the modem

Parity test

The parity test under *Windows 98* in the *Parity* box provides the entries *None, Odd, Even, Mark* and *Space*. Most online services, mail boxes or Internet Service Providers require the default settings of the *Dial-Up Networking*, which consists of 8 data bits, parity off and 1 stop-bit.

In the online world, this default is often referred to as *8,N,1*, where the N stands for none, that is, no parity test.

So the *Windows 98* default settings are perfect for normal use. However, some E-mail applications can run into problems here. If all the other modem settings seem to be correct and still no connection can be established, or you receive only cryptic data in *HyperTerminal*, the reason can be that the settings in this box are incorrect.

Wait for dial tone

If your modem is properly connected and refuses to dial, clear the *Wait for dial tone before dialing* check box. This problem sometimes occurs with modems that are particularly jittery upon dialing.

Check the *Cancel the call if not connected within* check box and type in the number of seconds after which *Windows 98* should stop dialing. The *Disconnect a call if idle for more than* check box can save you a lot of money, as it will interrupt a connection that is inactive for more than the specified number of minutes.

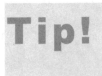

With the *Install New Modem* wizard you can create several entries for the same modem and name them differently. For each entry, you can select different settings. Then you do not need to change the settings each time you use a special online service that requires different settings.

Setting the Error Control and Data Flow Control for Your Modem

The way in which data are transferred, the data flow control or the manner in which the data should be compressed again, depends on the use of the modem. Some online applications require changes in the settings, such as disabling data compression.

Modem icon

To change the advanced settings, in the *Start* menu select the *Settings* item and in the overlapping menu the *Control Panel* command. In the *Control Panel* double-click the modem icon. The *Modems Properties* dialog box lists all installed modems.

Advanced settings

Select the modem whose settings you want to change and click the *Properties* button. When the properties dialog box pops up, activate the *Connection* tab. On the *Connection* tab page, click the *Advanced* button to bring up the *Advanced Connection Settings* dialog box shown in Figure 11.7.

Internet connection

For an Internet connection that uses *Dial-Up Networking* to connect to an Internet Service Provider, select the *Hardware(RTS/CTS)* radio button in the *Use flow control* option group.

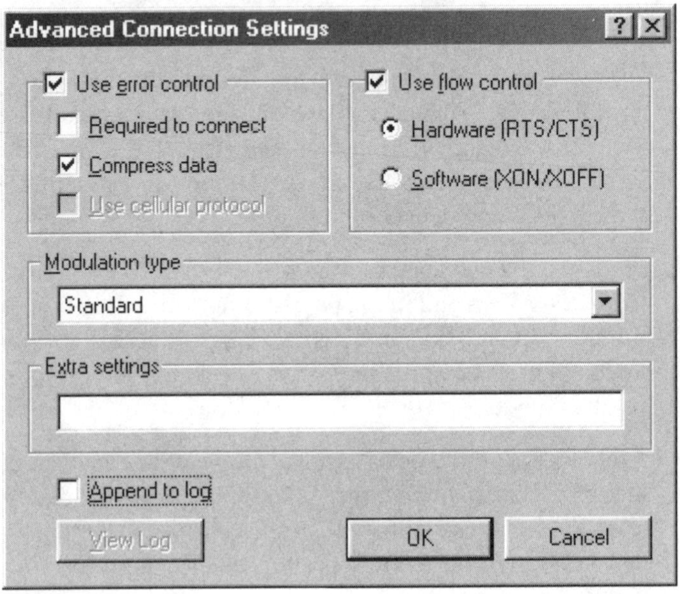

Advanced Connection Settings   ？ ✕

☑ Use error control
   ☐ Required to connect
   ☑ Compress data
   ☐ Use cellular protocol

☑ Use flow control
   ⦿ Hardware (RTS/CTS)
   ○ Software (XON/XOFF)

Modulation type
   Standard   ▼

Extra settings
   [   ]

☐ Append to log

   View Log   OK   Cancel

Fig. 11.7:   Changing the *Advanced Connection Settings* dialog box

Handshaking

This has to do with the communication between your modem and your PC. This is also known as *Handshaking*. With the *Hardware (RTS/CTS)* option, the task of handling messages that automatically pause and restart the data flow during a transfer is given to the modem. The *Software (XON/XOFF)* is rarely needed. The above mentioned task is, in this case, fulfilled by the communication software.

Far more important are the check boxes in the *Use error control* option group. Since most online services work with their own manufacturer-specific error controls, incorrect settings in this option group sometimes lead to problems. The *Compress data* check box enables the modem data compression and the *Required to connect* check box forces this particular setting.

Use cellular
protocol

With *Use cellular protocol* you specify the usage of the protocol for cellular phones when connecting to such devices. These entries only have an effect if they are supported by the modem. After your changes confirm with *OK* to return to the *Modem Properties* dialog box and close the dialog box by clicking the *OK* button. Then close the *Modems Properties* dialog box and the *Control Panel*.

Tip!

With Internet access using *Dial-Up Networking*, it is best to inquire with the providers as to what the respective permitted options are.

Configuring the Settings for a Serial Port

After the correct installation and configuration of the modem, nothing should disrupt the communication anymore. If your computer has problems connecting or your ultra high-speed modem is not performing up to the mark, then you may need some of the tips from the next section.

COM-Ports

Since you always connect a modem to one of the COM-ports of the computer, it is time to have a look at the settings of the port. However, the configuration for the ports is well hidden on your system. Select on the *Start* menu the *Settings* item, and in the overlapping menu the *Control Panel* command. In the *Control Panel* double-click the modem icon.

Select the modem you are using and click *Properties*. In the *Modem Properties* dialog box activate the *Connection* tab. Click the *Port Settings* button to display the dialog box shown in Figure 11.8.

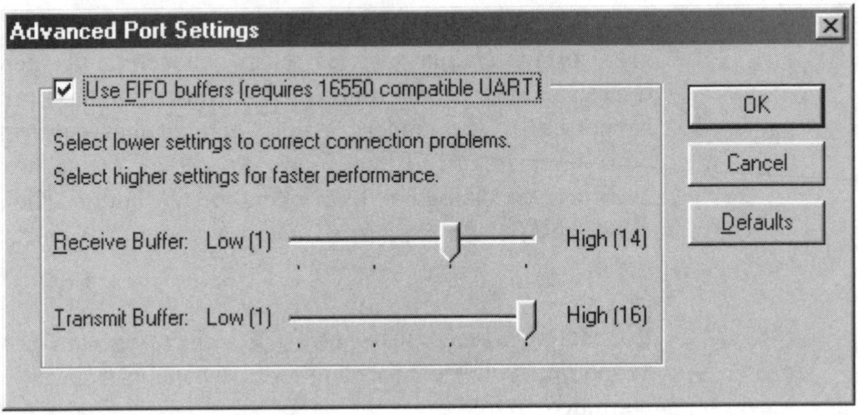

Advanced Port Settings

☑ Use FIFO buffers (requires 16550 compatible UART)

Select lower settings to correct connection problems.
Select higher settings for faster performance.

Receive Buffer: Low (1) ————————————— High (14)

Transmit Buffer: Low (1) ————————————— High (16)

OK

Cancel

Defaults

Fig. 11.8:   Settings for FIFO-buffered serial interfaces

If you have a Pentium PC, check whether the *Use FIFO buffers* check box is selected.

UART Chip

This concerns the *UART* Chip, a communication building block in the layout of the interface electronics. The *UART* Chip is also responsible for parity checking. Only with the help of this buffer chip can the high transfer rates of the 33,600 or 56,000 modems be truly reached. If you have a 486 processor, be sure to read the next section carefully.

Transmit buffer slider

If you are continuously having problems with your modem, and you can eliminate a bad line or a wrong number from the list of possible causes, try pulling the *Transmit Buffer* slider to the left, to a lower position and then try dialing again.

Receive buffer slider

If you have trouble with a high-speed modem and you are sure it is neither the online service or the Internet, nor the quality of the line, then slide the *Receive Buffer* to the right, to a higher position and try dialing again.

Testing Serial Ports

Windows 98 not only helps you with the installation and configuration of a modem, but the operating system has a feature for easily testing the devices connected to the serial ports as well. In this way, even before you connect for the first time, you can trace any possible modem malfunctions and configuration problems.

Diagnostics of the interface

For the serial port diagnostics you need to open the *Control Panel*. From the *Control Panel* double-click the *Modems* icon.

In the *Modems Properties* dialog box activate the *Diagnostics* tab. All COM ports and the connected devices are listed. Click the *Driver* button to view details on the driver for the selected device.

Details button

Select the *COM* port to which your modem is attached and click the *More Info* button. Your modem has to be switched on and connected in order to do this. A message box informs you that the modem is being queried for information. Subsequently the *More Info* dialog box gives you a long list of information about the modem and the port. This list is particularly important if you are using an older 486 PC.

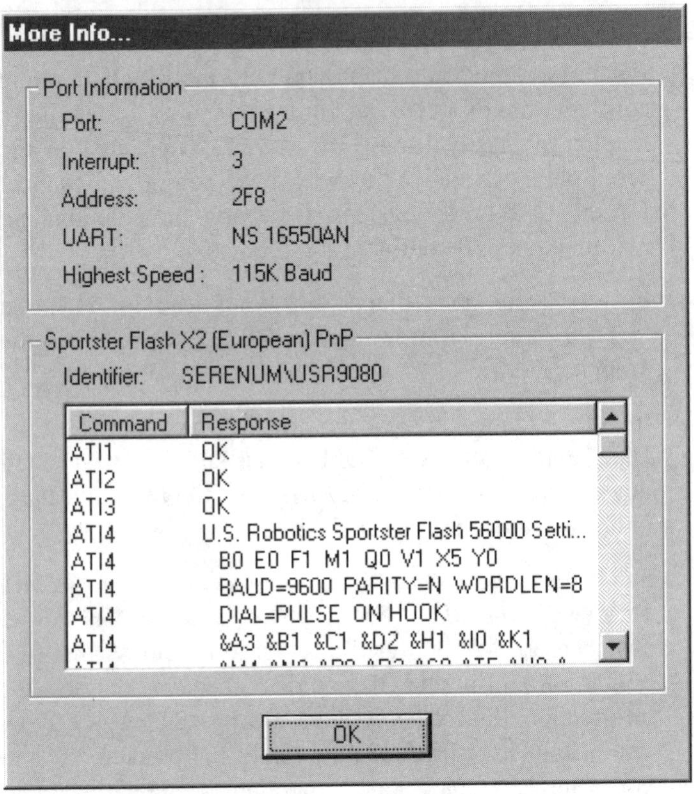

More Info...

Port Information
Port:	COM2
Interrupt:	3
Address:	2F8
UART:	NS 16550AN
Highest Speed :	115K Baud

Sportster Flash X2 (European) PnP

Identifier: SERENUM\USR9080

Command	Response
ATI1	OK
ATI2	OK
ATI3	OK
ATI4	U.S. Robotics Sportster Flash 56000 Setti...
ATI4	B0 E0 F1 M1 Q0 V1 X5 Y0
ATI4	BAUD=9600 PARITY=N WORDLEN=8
ATI4	DIAL=PULSE ON HOOK
ATI4	&A3 &B1 &C1 &D2 &H1 &I0 &K1
ATI4	&M4 &N0 &P0 &R2 &S0 &TF &U0 &

OK

Fig. 11.9:   Result of the modem and interface diagnostics

Port Information

In the *Port Information* box you will see information about the interrupt, the address and, more importantly, the type of *UART* chip used. If the steering chip of the (*UART*) interface is the *8250* chip, then, on this system, no transfer rates faster than 14,400 bps are possible.

UART chip

The *UART* Chip (*Universal Asynchronous Transmitter*) is the heart of the serial port interface and is responsible for the creation of the required signals. The old *8250* version of this chip cannot match the data transfer rate of more modern modems.

Today's standard in all new Pentium computers is a serial interface that works with the powerful *UART 16550* chip (in the diagnostics, this is listed as *NS 16550AN)*. The *UART 16550* chip provides an integrated buffer memory (*FIFO*, First In, First Out) which makes transfer rates of up to 115,200 bps possible.

Setting the Dialing Properties for the Modem

Before using your modem to access the Internet or other online services, you should set the dialing properties for your location. This is particularly important for modems connected to a private branch exchange.

As you already know from using the phone, you do not get a line without an area code.

To configure the dialing properties, from the *Start* menu select the *Settings* item and in the overlapping menu choose the *Control Panel* command. In the *Control Panel* double-click the modem icon.

Dialing Properties

In the *Modems Properties* dialog box click the *General* tab and click the *Dialing Properties* button. The *Dialing Properties* dialog box shown in Figure 11.10 appears.

In this dialog box, click the *New* button and click *OK*. Type into the *I am dialing from* dialog box your location or any name which identifies where you are. Into the box under this, enter your country name and area code. This entry enables *Windows 98* to distinguish between local calls and long-distance calls, so that it can automatically omit unnecessary area codes and international codes.

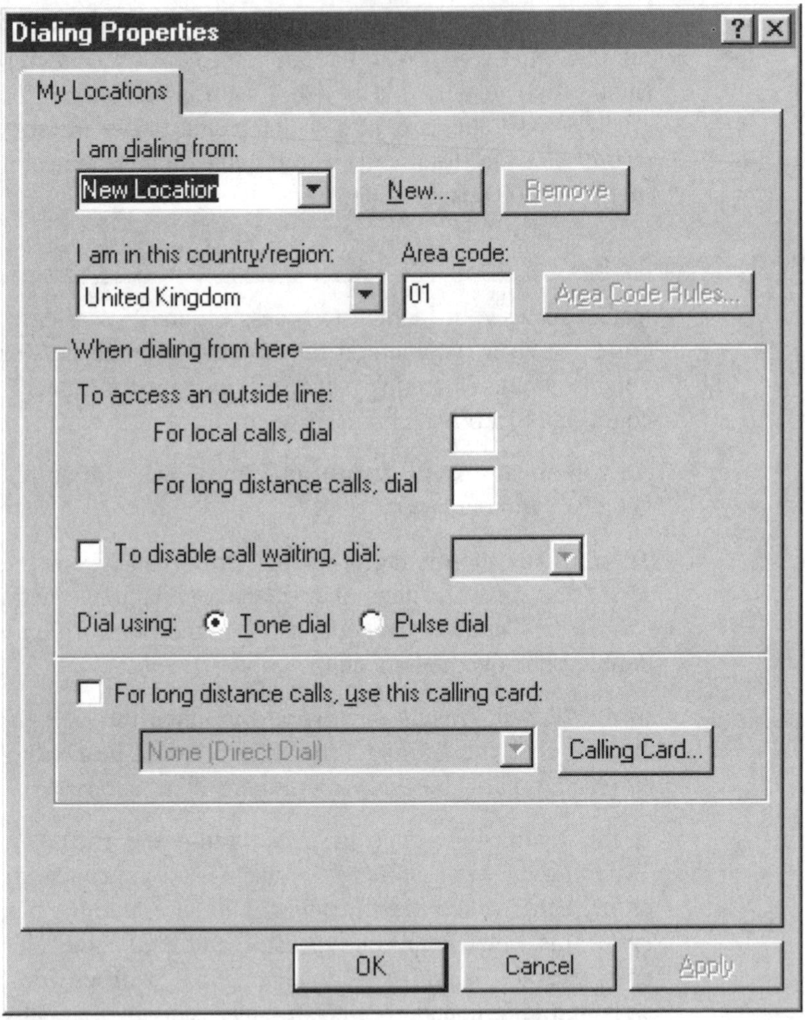

Fig. 11.10:   Setting the dialing properties

Entering the area
code

If your modem is connected to a private branch exchange, in the *When dialing from here* group box, enter the number to dial *for local calls* and if necessary, the number to dial *for long distance calls* into the respective text boxes.

If you work with a notebook computer, you can define different locations with different dialing properties. Just click the *New* button again and repeat the procedure with the different parameters.

In this way you can, later on, simply select the name of the location from where you are connecting and all the properties will be automatically set for you.

Setting the Dialing Mode for Your Modem

Before you use the modem you also need to specify the dialing mode according to your telephone line.

Dialing properties
To do so, in the *Start* menu, select the *Settings* item and in the overlapping menu, choose the *Control Panel* command. In the *Control Panel*, double-click the modem icon. In the *Modems Properties* dialog box, click the *Dialing Properties* button. The dialog box displayed in Figure 11.11 appears.

Two dialing modes
You will not be able to connect to a number with the incorrect dialing mode. Two dialing modes are still common. The pulse dial mode is quite old and outdated, and it can be recognized by the puttering sound it makes and the long dialing time.

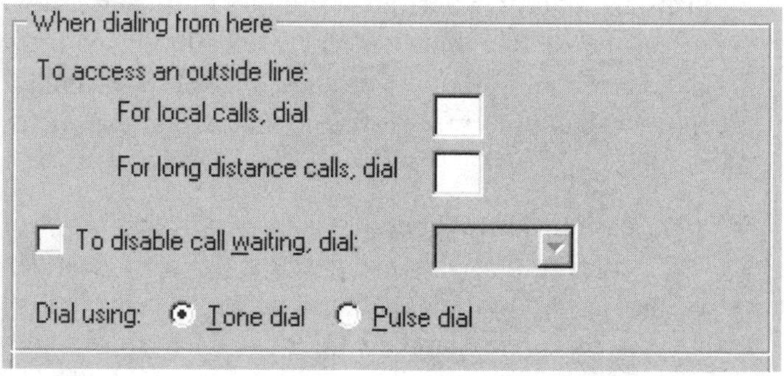

Fig. 11.11:   The faster Tone dial radio button

Pulse dial

If you work in an area where the phone system still operates using pulse, choose the *Pulse dial* radio button.

Tone dial

The modern digital multifrequency dialing mode is recognizable by the different tones that accompany this faster dialing method. Choose the *Tone dial* radio button and close the dialog box by clicking the *OK* button.

Tip!

If you do not know whether you can use the digital tone dial mode, call up your telephone company to find out. You can also switch over to the new mode with your normal telephone and your fax machine.

Installing and Configuring an ISDN adapter

As an alternative to a modem you can also use an ISDN card. For this, however, you will require a digital ISDN connection, since an ISDN card cannot operate with an analog line.

ISDN telephone network

The digital *ISDN* telephone network (*Integrated Services Digital Network*) transfers telephone calls, faxes and computer data.

With ISDN, data transfer rates of 64,000 bits per second (bps) per telephone line can be reached. Since every ISDN connection offers two lines, called B channels, ISDN is capable of transferring phone calls as well as data.

You are assigned three numbers and two lines with your ISDN connection. It is now possible to receive a fax while having a chat on the phone or while being online on the Internet. The Standard ISDN connection provides the following features:

- ISDN connection with two lines and three numbers

- Up to 8 ISDN devices per connection

- Transfer rate of 64,000 bps per channel

Prices

Prices change rapidly, as with all new technology... It would be better if you inquire about the latest prices yourself.

ISDN telephones

To actually make a call, you also need an ISDN telephone or a private branch exchange to connect the analog devices such as phones, faxes or modems. To connect the computer to the digital line you also need an additional device. This is the ISDN adapter which usually comes in the form of an internal card. You will need a vacant PCI or ISA slot in your computer, depending on which type of ISDN card you've purchased.

External ISDN adapters

There are also external ISDN adapters in the form of stand-alone units. These can be connected to the PC through a serial port. For now we will deal only with the less expensive internal version. We also assume that you have already inserted the card into a free slot in your system.

Plug and play or not

Ideally, the bootup of your computer is automatically followed by the setup routine for the ISDN card and the installation wizard leads you through all the necessary configurations. For the non-Plug and Play compliant ISDN adapters, the configuration is, of course, more complicated. Your computer has to address every hardware component separately from other components.

Configuring the ISDN Adapter

Therefore, during its setup, each component reserves an address range so that it can talk to the *Central Processing Unit (CPU)*. For the computer-literate user this is known as the *I/O Address* (*Input/Output*). Additionally, the route of the electronic messages is controlled by the *Interrupt Request*, or *IRQ*.

The manufacturers of the various PC components are now trying to use interrupts and addresses that are not yet used by other types of components. ISDN typically creates conflicts here, for example with an existing sound card on your system. To avoid such conflicts check the default settings of your ISDN card.

IRQ 5

A sound card usually uses the IRQ 5. This can be altered in the sound card setup; however, it seems simpler to change the default for the new ISDN card. If you set both cards on IRQ 5, one of the cards will not work at all. If *Windows 98* changes the IRQ for the sound card, you probably will not have any sound on DOS-based games. Therefore, it would be better to change the settings for the ISDN card.

Add New Hardware Wizard

Most ISDN cards can be installed by *Windows 98* with the help of the *Add New Hardware Wizard*. Ideally, once you've inserted the card into its slot in the PC, this wizard starts as soon as you boot the PC. But sometimes you have to start the wizard manually.

If the *Add New Hardware Wizard* starts the setup of the ISDN card automatically, click the *Next* button in the first dialog box. You can manually kickstart the *Add New Hardware Wizard* by double-clicking the *Add New Hardware* icon in the *Control Panel*.

Clicking the *Next* button again will start the search for Plug and Play devices. If Plug and Play devices were found and the ISDN card is listed in the next dialog box, click the *Yes, the device is in the list* radio button, highlight the entry in the *Devices* list and click the *Next* button.

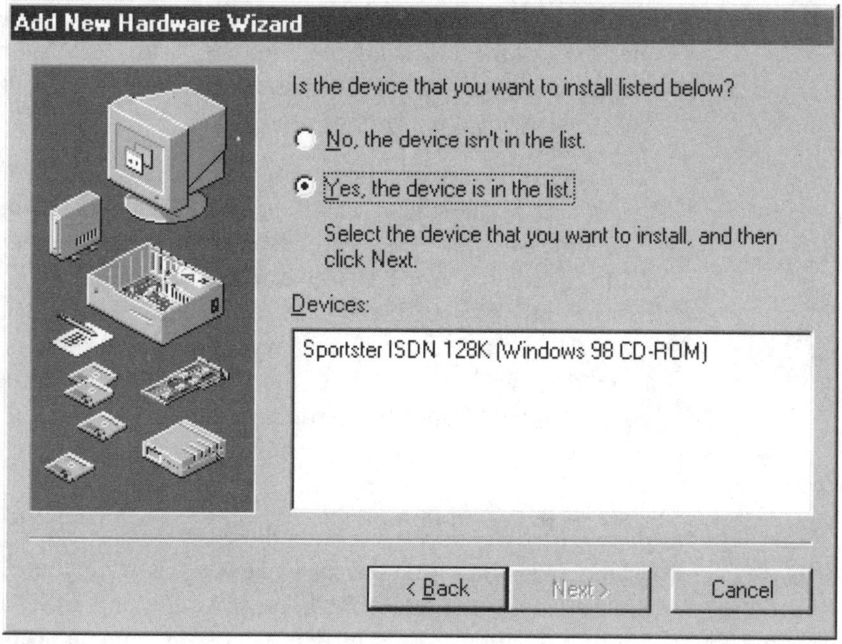

Fig. 11.12: Installing an ISDN adapter with the Wizard

If the ISDN adapter is not in the list, select the *No, the device isn't in the list* radio button and click the *Next* button. Choose the *No, I want to select the hardware from a list* option and click the *Next* button again.

Select the *Other devices* entry in the *Hardware types* list box and again click the *Next* button. Now choose the manufacturer and model of your ISDN card.

If the ISDN adapter is not listed here either, click the *Have Disk* button. Insert the driver disk supplied with your ISDN card and confirm with *OK*. Choose your ISDN model in the next window and again click the *OK* button. Click *Next* and *Finish* and the new hardware will be installed. You may need to insert the *Windows 98* Setup CD ROM at some point in this process.

Restart

Remove the installation disk from the drive and confirm a message asking to restart the computer with *Yes*. After the computer restarts, the PC will recognize the card, but the card is not yet ready to be used.

To check the configuration, you can open the *Control Panel* and double-click the *System* icon. To see this icon, you sometimes have to scroll down in the *Control Panel* folder window. On the *Device Manager* tab page search for the entry of your ISDN card. If the entry is preceded by a yellow question mark or a red exclamation point or is marked with a red cross, then there is a hardware conflict. Read Chapter 8 on troubleshooting to see how to solve it.

Installation of the CAPI Communication Driver

CAPI driver

Along with the correct ISDN adapter you have found, you have to install the *CAPI* driver software for the ISDN card. This driver is used by *Windows 98* to communicate with the ISDN card. The CAPI driver is a standardized driver used by all ISDN applications to address all ISDN devices. Because hardware differs, the manufacturer has to take care to supply the right CAPI driver. You therefore have to install this driver from the disk shipped with the ISDN card.

For *Windows 98* you always need a CAPI 2.0 driver. There are two standards for CAPI drivers. Both are up-to-date versions for different modes of communication. You need the CAPI 1.1 standard for *Windows 3.x* and all older 16-bit ISDN applications.

CAPI 2.0 is required by all 32-bit ISDN applications under *Windows 98*. So, if you have to choose between the two standards, go in for the CAPI 2.0 or the 'dual' CAPI standard. Such drivers offer both CAPI standards, 1.1 and

Tip! 2.0. With a dual CAPI you can avoid many problems with different versions of ISDN software right from the start.

Also, always install the latest version of the necessary CAPI-driver. For the first try, you can use the driver shipped with your ISDN adapter. Updates are usually provided via FTP servers of your ISDN adapter manufacturer.

Start the CAPI installation program by following the instructions in your ISDN adapter manual as well as any other on-screen instructions. For Internet access you only need the CAPI communication module; however in most cases it cannot be installed separately.

ISDN-applications In most cases the ISDN applications are installed along with the CAPI driver. To effectively use all the ISDN features such as the fax, answering machine, File-Transfer or the integrated modem emulation, you need the software that comes along with the adapter. We will not go into more detail at this point.

Tip! If you want to use your ISDN card only for Internet access and not for features like the fax, answering machine, File-Transfer or the integrated modem emulation, all you need is the CAPI driver, while for the other features you will need specific software.

Installing and Configuring Dial-up Networking

At this point in space and time we can welcome back the modem users again. All further steps for configuring the Internet are the same, whether you are using a modem or ISDN.

Checking the installation

Dial-Up Networking is used for Internet access as well as in other online applications under *Windows 98*. The first thing you have to check is whether this application has already been installed on your computer. Open the *Start* menu and move over the items *Programs, Accessories* and then *Communications*. If you find the *Dial-Up Networking* item in this program group, you can skip the rest of this section and go straight to the one that follows.

Web browser

If this item is missing, you have to install this online control center of *Windows 98*. In addition, to access the various services of the Internet, you will need certain software. For the WWW (World Wide Web) you will need to use a web browser such as *Microsoft Internet Explorer*, which is integrated into *Windows 98*.

Now let us start the installation of the *Dial-Up Networking* for Internet access. Choose *Start/Settings* and in the overlapping menu choose the *Control Panel* entry. Double-click the *Add/Remove Programs* icon and then activate the *Windows Setup* tab page.

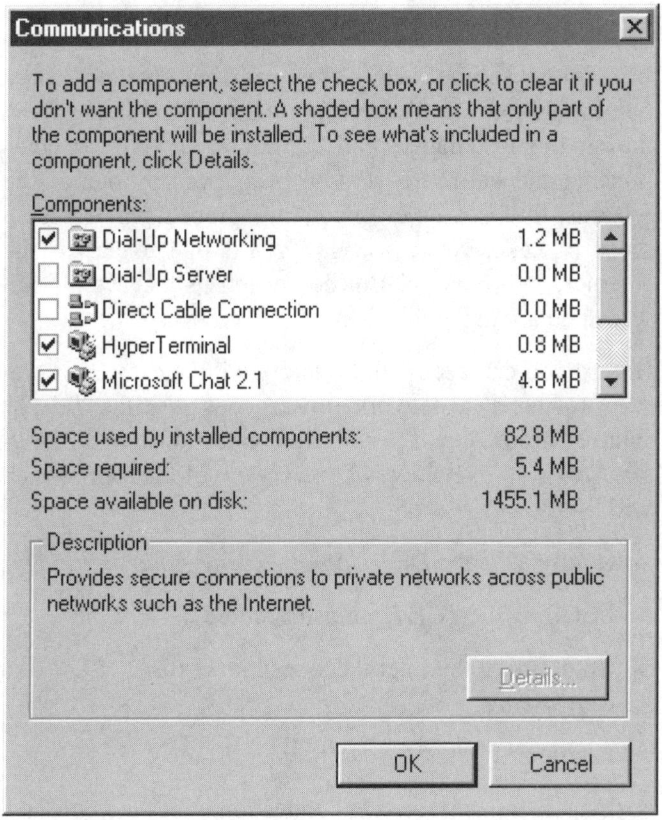

Communications ☒

To add a component, select the check box, or click to clear it if you don't want the component. A shaded box means that only part of the component will be installed. To see what's included in a component, click Details.

Components:

☑ 🖳 Dial-Up Networking	1.2 MB	▲
☐ 🖳 Dial-Up Server	0.0 MB	
☐ 🖳 Direct Cable Connection	0.0 MB	
☑ 📞 HyperTerminal	0.8 MB	
☑ 📞 Microsoft Chat 2.1	4.8 MB	▼

Space used by installed components:	82.8 MB
Space required:	5.4 MB
Space available on disk:	1455.1 MB

┌─ Description ──────────────────────────────────┐
Provides secure connections to private networks across public networks such as the Internet.

                                           Details...
└──┘

                              OK   Cancel

Fig. 11.13:   The add/remove Software / Windows Setup / Communications dialog

Select the *Communications* item in the *Components* list and click the *Details* button. Select the check box next to the *Dial-Up Networking* entry and confirm with *OK*. If necessary, insert the *Windows 98* setup CD-ROM and click *OK* again. After rebooting the PC the *Dial-Up Networking* will be available.

Configuring the Dial-up Networking Adapter

In the meantime, you are probably feeling more comfortable now with working under *Windows 98*. Even during the installation and configuration of new components and hardware, you are supported by one of the wizards. In this way, even complex procedures become a piece of cake. Now, you say you'd like to access the Internet? No problem! But do not tell us that we did not warn you about the following:

Overview

Before you can access the Internet with *Windows 98* you have to install a network driver, configure the *TCP/IP* Internet protocol and install the connection icon in *Dial-Up Networking*. Below is an overview of the steps which will follow:

- Configuring the *Dial-Up Networking Adapter*

- Installing the *TCP/IP* transfer protocol

- Configuring the Internet connection with *Dial-Up Networking*

- Configuring the *TCP/IP* Internet-Protocol

- Establishing an Internet connection with the *Dial-Up Networking*

- Automating the Internet connection

Tip!

If you plan to access the Internet via a provider such as *CompuServe* or *Amrrica Online,* all these configuration steps are unnecessary. The online services offer an all-in-one package which enables you to surf the Net without the above configurations. These packages are already partly contained in *Windows 98* if you have installed the *Online Services* program group.

By following the procedure below you will be able to access the Internet using *Dial-Up Networking* in *Windows 98*. If you find it too complicated, we strongly recommend that you get an Internet all-in-one package from one of the big national providers such as *CompuServe* or *America Online*. You can then spare yourself the following complex installation to obtain Internet access.

You should only work with *Windows 98* and *Dial-Up Networking* if your Internet provider does not provide the software, or if you have to pay extra for it as is the case with certain local providers.

Tip! If your provider offers you its own Internet access software, you should use it. The software of the *America Online, CompuServe, The Microsoft Network, Prodigy, and AT&T* providers is shipped with *Windows 98* and accessible via the *Online Services* program group. Start the setup programs by choosing the respective icons. The use of these services has to be paid for after a certain trial period.

After the installation of *Dial-Up Networking* you have to install and configure the *Dial-Up Adapter*, a special network driver.

Network icon

This step has to be taken even if *Dial-Up Networking* was already installed on the system. Open the *Control Panel* and call up the *Network* dialog box with a double click on the *Network* icon.

Entry Dial-up adapter

Here you will see all installed network components. If you see the *Dial-Up Adapter* item, then skip this section. Otherwise, click on the *Add* button in the *Network* dialog box. In the dialog box that appears, choose *Adapter* and click the *Add* button again.

In the *Manufacturers* list box (Figure 11.14), select the *Microsoft* item and choose the *Dial-Up Adapter* entry in the *Network Adapters* list box. You may need to insert the *Windows 98* setup CD-ROM at this point. Close the dialog box by clicking the *OK* button.

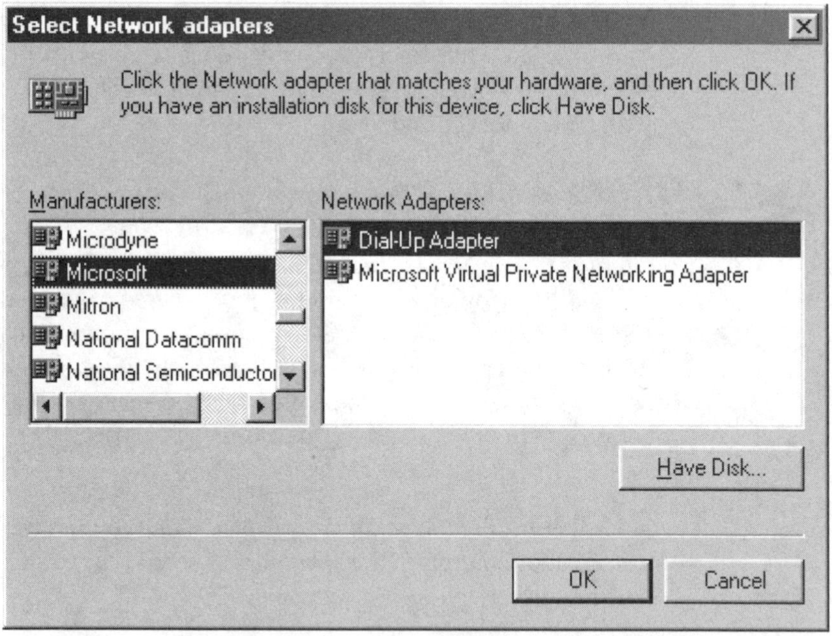

Fig. 11.14:   Installing the Dial-up Networking Adapter

The driver will be installed and will appear in the list in the *Network* dialog box. Keep the dialog box open and configure the necessary *protocol*.

Installing the TCP/IP Network Protocol for Internet Access

Once you have installed the *Dial-Up Adapter* you will have to install the *TCP/IP* network protocol. To do so, activate the *Configuration* tab page in the *Network* dialog box (*Control Panel/Network*). Click the *Add* button and choose the *Protocol* entry in the *Select Network Component Type* dialog box. Click the *Add* button again.

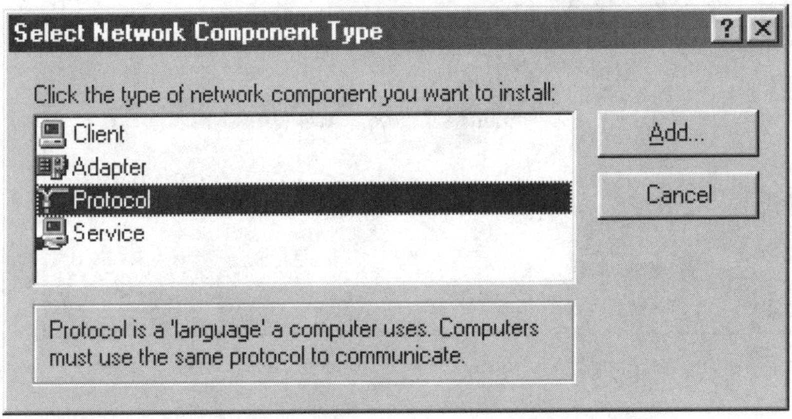

Select Network Component Type

Click the type of network component you want to install:

- Client
- Adapter
- Protocol
- Service

Add...

Cancel

Protocol is a 'language' a computer uses. Computers must use the same protocol to communicate.

Fig. 11.15: Installing a new protocol

In the *Manufacturers* list box, select the *Microsoft* entry and select the *TCP/IP item* in the *Network Protocols* list. Close the dialog box by clicking the *OK* button.

You may have to use the scroll bars to view the *TCP/IP* entry. On network computers, *Windows 98* also installs the *TCP/IP* protocol for the network card.

If such is the case, then in the *Network* dialog box select the entry *TCP/IP >Network card name* and click the *Remove* button to delete the entry. Install only the protocols which are absolutely necessary and remove all other entries.

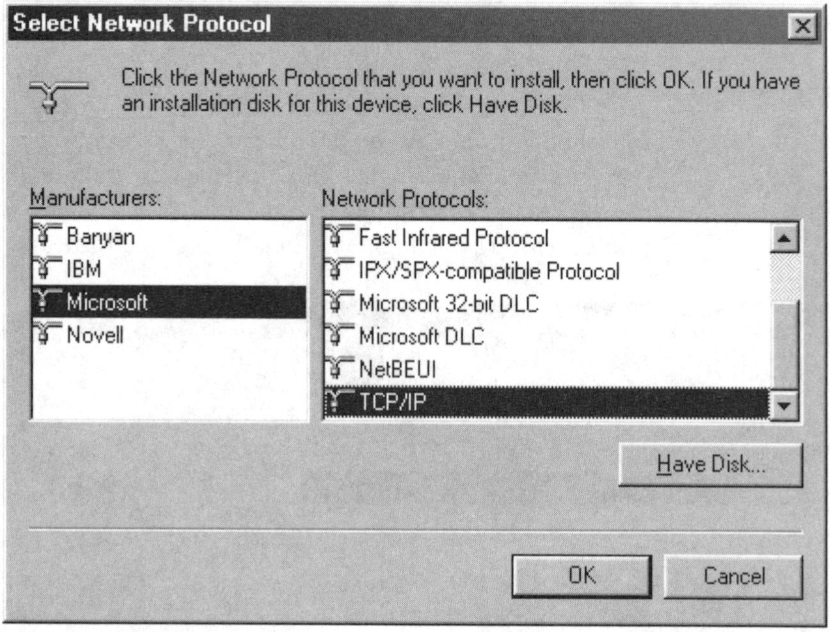

Select Network Protocol   ☒

Click the Network Protocol that you want to install, then click OK. If you have an installation disk for this device, click Have Disk.

Manufacturers: Network Protocols:

Banyan   Fast Infrared Protocol
IBM   IPX/SPX-compatible Protocol
Microsoft   Microsoft 32-bit DLC
Novell   Microsoft DLC
                                  NetBEUI
                                  TCP/IP

                                              Have Disk...

                              OK   Cancel

Fig. 11.16:   Choosing the TCP/IP protocol for Internet access

If you want to set identical *TCP/IP* properties for all connections in *Dial-Up Networking*, go on reading the following section and learn how to configure the Internet protocol with the information of the provider. If you want to define different protocol settings for different connections, just skip the next section.

Configuring the TCP/IP Internet Protocol Globally

In this section we will describe the configuration of the *TCP/IP* transfer protocol for all connections of *Dial-Up Networking*. Now the whole thing gets a little tricky, because in order to configure *TCP/IP* you need to have quite a lot of knowledge about network addresses and network-related technical terms.

Configuration of
the Internet
protocol

Before you can start configuring the Internet protocol you need a contract with an Internet Service Provider who offers you access to the Internet. This can either be charged monthly or by connection time. Before you configure the protocol, make sure that you have the following data from your provider:

■ The name of the *Host* and/or the *Domain* to which you are connected

■ The *IP address* of your own computer, if this cannot be obtained automatically

■ The *Subnet Mask*
(for stand alone systems this is *255.255.255.0*)

■ The *IP address* of the *Gateway*
through which the data is transferred

■ The *IP address* of the *DNS server*,
which finds out the Internet addresses for you

■ The type of protocol
(*PPP, CSLIP* or *SLIP*)

■ The user ID and the password for your internet connection

■ The phone number to dial for the provider

■ The names of a mail server and a news server

The data which you will actually need depends on your provider. Find this out before you go any further. To configure *TCP/IP*, the respective information has to be entered on various tab pages. Missing entries will make it impossible to establish a connection with the server.

Configuration

To configure the Internet protocol, you need to use the *Network* dialog box in the *Control Panel*. On the *Configuration* tab page, select the *TCP/IP Adapter* entry (*TCP/IP->Dial-Up*, if it exists) and click the *Properties* button. Read the message shown in Figure 11.17 and proceed only if you really want to change the properties globally for all new connections.

TCP/IP Properties Information   ☒

ⓘ You have asked to change TCP/IP properties for a dial-up adapter. In most cases, these properties are unique to the specific network which you are calling. For this reason, it is better to set TCP/IP properties in each connection icon which calls a network. Otherwise, properties set for the adapter will override the per-connection settings.

Connection icons can be found in the Dial-Up Networking folder under Start Accessories. Right click an icon to see its properties sheet; select Server Type, and then TCP/IP settings.

Fig. 11.17:   Warning before displaying the TCP/IP settings

Confirm the message with *OK* and on the *IP Address* tab page, select the *Specify an IP address* radio button and type the information from your provider into the respective text box. Then enter the information for the *Subnet Mask*. For a private Internet configuration or a configuration on a stand-alone system, the *Subnet Mask* will always be 255.255.255.0. If the *IP address* can be allotted dynamically by the provider, select the *Obtain an IP address automatically* radio button instead.

WINS
Configuration

Change to the *WINS Configuration* tab page and check that the *Enable WINS Resolution* is deselected. If so, select the *Use DHCP for WINS Resolution* radio button, so that you can get the required information from a server.

With the incorrect *WINS Configuration* settings the Internet access will not work properly and you may get strange error messages.

Tip! If later on you get messages concerning *DHCP*, answer the question whether these messages should be displayed in future with a decisive click on the *No* button.

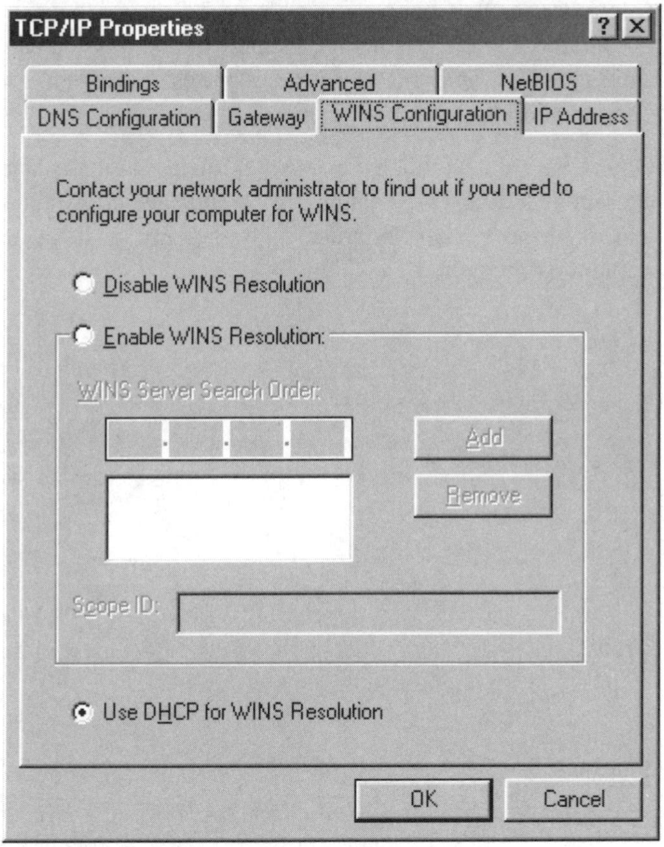

Fig. 11.18: DHCP settings for the TCP/IP protocol

Gateway tab page

Switch to the *Gateway* tab page and enter the *Internet Protocol* (*IP*)number for the gateway of the transit network of your provider into the *New gateway* text box.

Some providers require you to access the Internet through such a gateway. The gateway organizes the routing of data packets.

DNS configuration

The next step in the procedure is to activate the *DNS Configuration* tab page. If necessary, select the *Enable DNS* radio button. With this option your computer can automatically find out the IP addresses based on an internet address.

Otherwise you would have to enter them manually for each connection. *DNS* stands for *Domain Name System*, and it differentiates Internet addresses by a host or domain name.

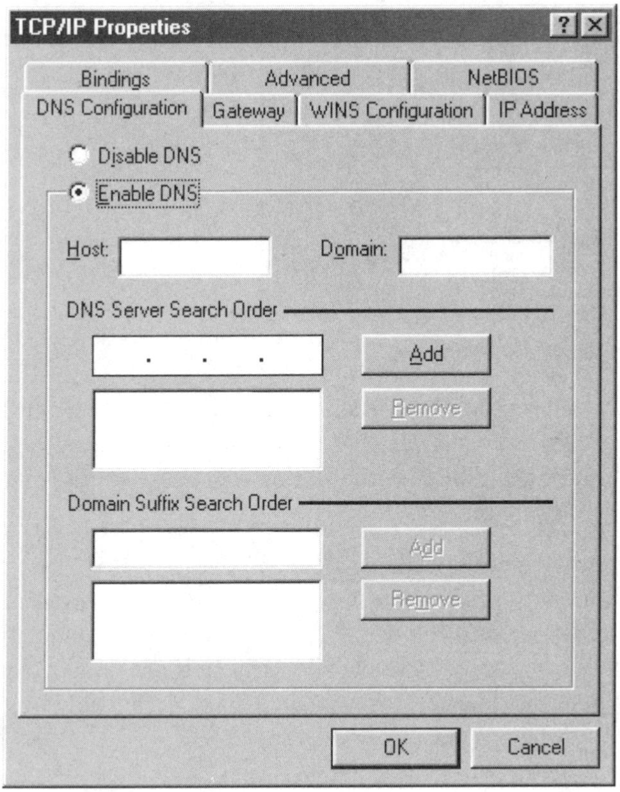

Fig. 11.19: Enter the host name and domain address for the Domain Name System

In the *DNS Server Search Order* box enter the IP addresses you got for the *Domain Name System* from your provider, and click the *Add* button next to it.

Normally, only one *DNS Server* can be used, and therefore, you usually do not have to worry about the other text boxes.

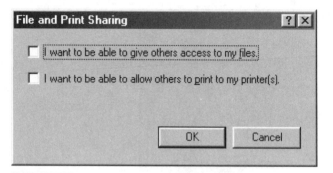

Clearing the File and Print Sharing

After entering all data necessary for your provider, close the *TCP/IP Properties* dialog box by clicking the *OK* button. Back in the *Network* dialog box click the *File and Print Sharing* button.

Disable sharing

Be sure to uncheck the two check boxes labelled *I want to be able to give others access to my files* and *I want to be able to allow others to print to my printer(s)*. Otherwise every Internet user can intrude into your computer and access your data. This is probably not exactly what you want.

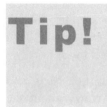

If you work with the default method, meaning a single configuration for every connection icon of the *Dial-Up Networking*, the previous step can be skipped, since *Windows 98* will then remind you to disable the access before going online.

Installing the Internet connection with Dial-up Networking

We can now begin with the installation of Internet connections under *Windows 98*. In this section we will describe how to set up *Dial-Up Networking* for Internet access.

So here, finally, we come to the discussion on connecting to the server of your *Internet Service Provider*. Prior to this step, all the necessary driver and protocols have to be installed.

Dial-Up
Networking

To install the Internet access you need to open the *Dial-Up Networking* folder. You can either open *My Computer* and click the *Dial-Up Networking* icon, or you can open the folder by clicking on the *Start* button and choosing *Programs/Accessories/Communications*.

Then select the *Dial-Up Networking* item. If you've selected this icon for the first time, the *Welcome to Dial-Up Networking* dialog box appears. Here you have to click the *Next* button. Otherwise, double-click the *Make New Connection* icon in the *Dial-Up Network* folder.

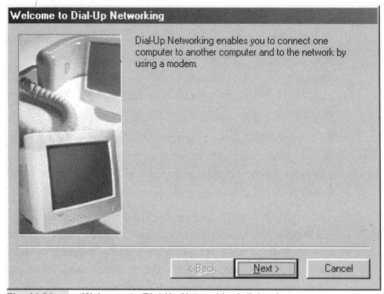

Fig. 11.21:   'Welcome to Dial-Up Networking' dialog box

Fig. 11.22:   The folder 'Dial-UP Networking'

In the first text box enter a name for the connection, for example 'Internet access'. In the drop-down list at the bottom of the dialog box, choose the modem you want to use for the connection.

Tip! With the *Configure* button you can activate the *Modem Properties* dialog box and change the parameters of your modem if necessary.

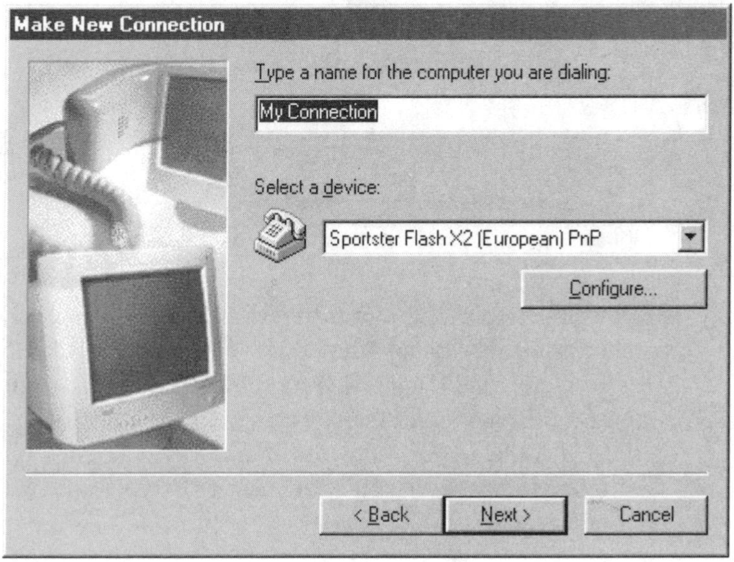

Make New Connection

Type a name for the computer you are dialing:

My Connection

Select a device:

Sportster Flash X2 (European) PnP

Configure...

< Back | Next > | Cancel

Fig. 11.23: Make New Connection Wizard to install a new connection

Entering phone numbers

In the *Make New Connection* dialog box, click the *Next* button. Enter the phone number and area code of the server of your Internet provider in the next window. Confirm with *Next*.

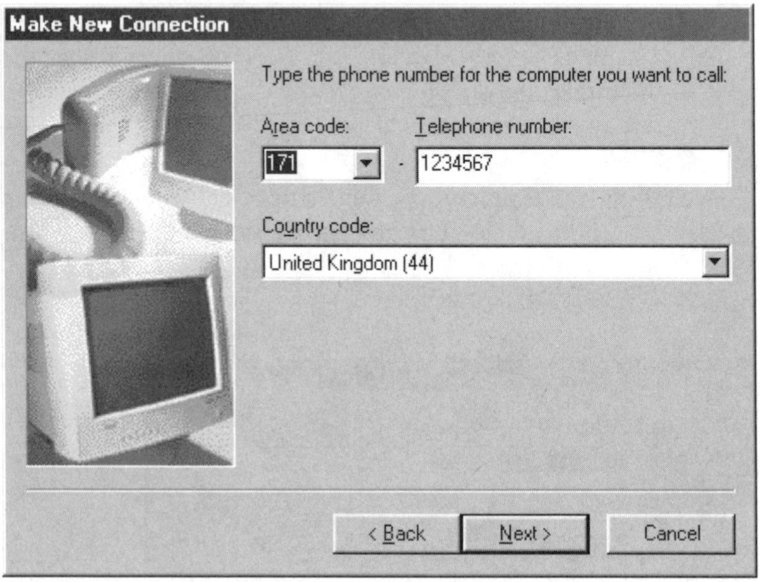

Make New Connection

Type the phone number for the computer you want to call:

Area code: Telephone number:

[171] ▼ - [1234567]

Country code:

[United Kingdom (44)] ▼

< Back | Next > | Cancel

Fig. 11.24:   Entering the phone number of the server

New icon

In the last step of the wizard you can once again check and/or change the name of your new connection. Click the *Finish* button and the *Make New Connection Wizard* will create a new icon with the name of the connection in the *Dial-Up Networking* folder. In future, a double click on the icon will connect you to the server of your Internet Service Provider.

Setting properties

Prior to connecting, you have to set the properties of the server connection. Right-click the icon of the new connection and, in the shortcut menu, choose the *Properties* command.

Activate the *Server Types* tab page. To select the necessary dial-up protocol, open the *Type of Dial-Up Server* list (Figure 11.25) and choose the required dial-up protocol (*PPP, SLIP* or *NRN*, etc.).

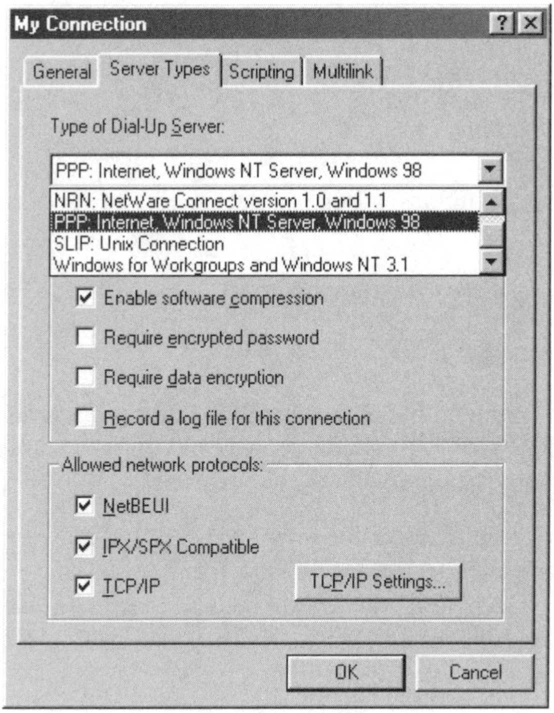

Fig. 11.25:   Setting the server type

In addition to the already installed *TCP/IP* Internet protocol, an Internet connection through the modem and the phone line requires another protocol which is this dial-up protocol.

Diverting protocols

There is a kind of war going on concerning dial-up protocols among the various providers. With some providers you can choose which protocol to use. Anyway, that does not really concern us here, and we just use the protocol that our provider recommends.

Internet dial-up protocols

On the Internet, the following three dial-up protocols for modem connections are in use:

- *PPP (Point-To-Point Protocol)*

- *SLIP (Serial Line Internet Protocol)*

- *CSLIP (Compressed SLIP)*

Intranet dial-up protocols

With company Intranets, other protocols can be used as well:

- *NRN (NetWare Connection Novell)*

- *Windows for Workgroups and Windows NT 3.1*

PPP dial-up protocol

The most common dial-up protocol for Internet access is the modern *PPP* protocol, which is automatically installed with *Dial-Up Networking*.

Use this dial-up protocol for Internet access and network connections under *Windows NT* and *Windows 98*. If you need the older *SLIP* or *CSLIP* protocol, choose the respective entry from the list.

TCP/IP-Settings

If you have not configured the *TCP/IP* settings globally for all *Dial-Up Networking* connections (as described above), then click the *TCP/IP Settings* button now. In the *TCP/IP Settings* dialog box, you have to enter the IP address and/or the address of the server.

IP-Address

Choose the *Specify an IP address* radio button and subsequently enter the Internet provider data if it is necessary for the connection. Otherwise, choose the *Server assigned IP address* radio button since it is the *Windows 98* default.

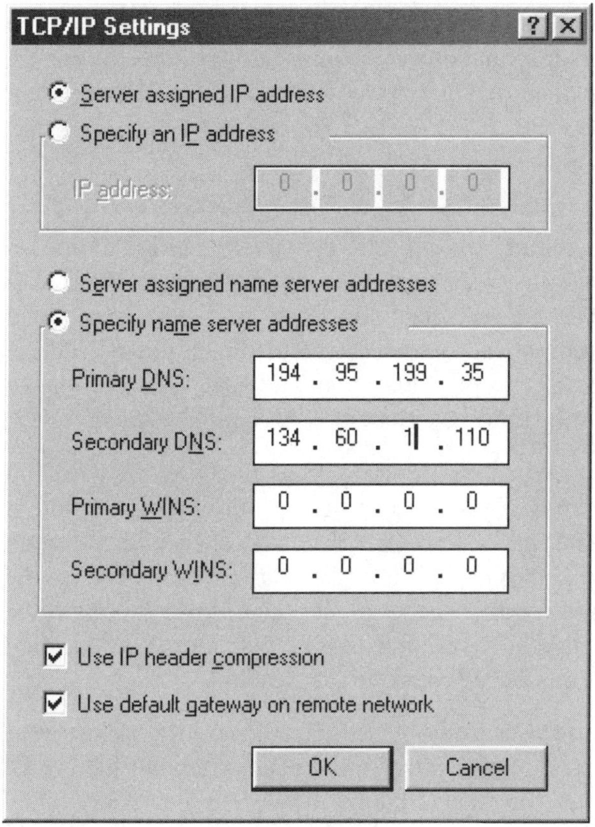

Fig. 11.26:   Entering the server's DNS

Server DNS

Activate the *Specify name server addresses* radio button and in the *Primary DNS* text box enter the name of the server in the form *XXX.XXX.XXX.XXX*, where the *X*'s are numbers. With invalid entries, you will get an error message. Enter the secondary DNS server address into the *secondary DNS* text box, and proceed in the same manner.

Close the dialog box by clicking the *OK* button. If no further information is required, close the *[name of connection]* dialog box as well. Proceed with the next section.

Automating the Dial-up Procedure with a Script

In this section we will talk about automating the dial-up connection process. Some online services such as *CompuServe* ask for more than just your name and password when you dial in. To automate this procedure, you need a *script* which you can easily create with the help of the built-in script editor in *Windows 98*.

Before we call up the script program and create a dial-up script, move over the icon of your Internet connection in the *Dial-Up Networking* folder and click with the right mouse button. In the shortcut menu, choose the *Properties* command. Activate the *Scripting* tab. On the *Scripting* tab page, make sure that the *Start terminal screen minimized* check box is cleared.

Ready made script file

If you have a ready made script file from your provider with the *SCP* file extension, copy it onto your hard drive and click the *Browse* button. Change to the folder of the . *SCP* file, select it and click the *Open* button. The file will then be displayed in the *File name* text box. Close the *[name of connection]* dialog box by clicking the *OK* button.

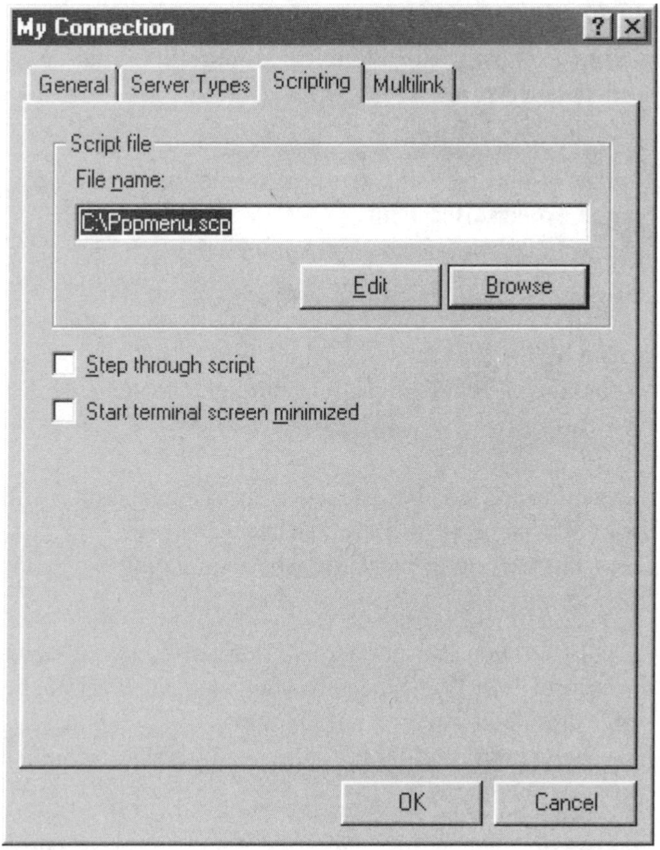

Fig. 11.27:   Using an existing dial-up script

Example scripts   If no script file has been provided, you need not give up
hope, since you can make one yourself. Click the *Browse*
button on the *Script* tab page. Change to *C:\Program
Files\Accessories*, in order to use one of the *SCP* files
examples, depending on which dial-up protocol you have.

- *PPPMENU.SCP*
  for *PPP* hosts, with a terminal window after dial-up,
  that expects user input

- *SLIPMENU.SCP*
  for *SLIP* hosts, with a terminal window after dial-up,
  that expects user input

- *SLIP.SCP*
  for *SLIP* hosts, that expects user input

- *CIS.SCP*
  for *CompuServe* connections through *Dial-Up
  Networking*

Notepad

Select the desired file and click the *Open* button. The
script file name is displayed in the *File name* text box.
Click the *Edit* button and *Notepad*, containing the script
file contents, will be opened (Figure 11.28).

In *Notepad*, you can now create the dial-up script using
the information from your provider. Several lines of the
script are already there and additional comments describing the various sections are preceded by a semicolon.

In a script, all of the required commands that are awaiting
your input, such as the login prompt and password entry,
can be placed in one file.

This happens in such a way that the results are sent
automatically, so a script can automate the whole login
procedure.

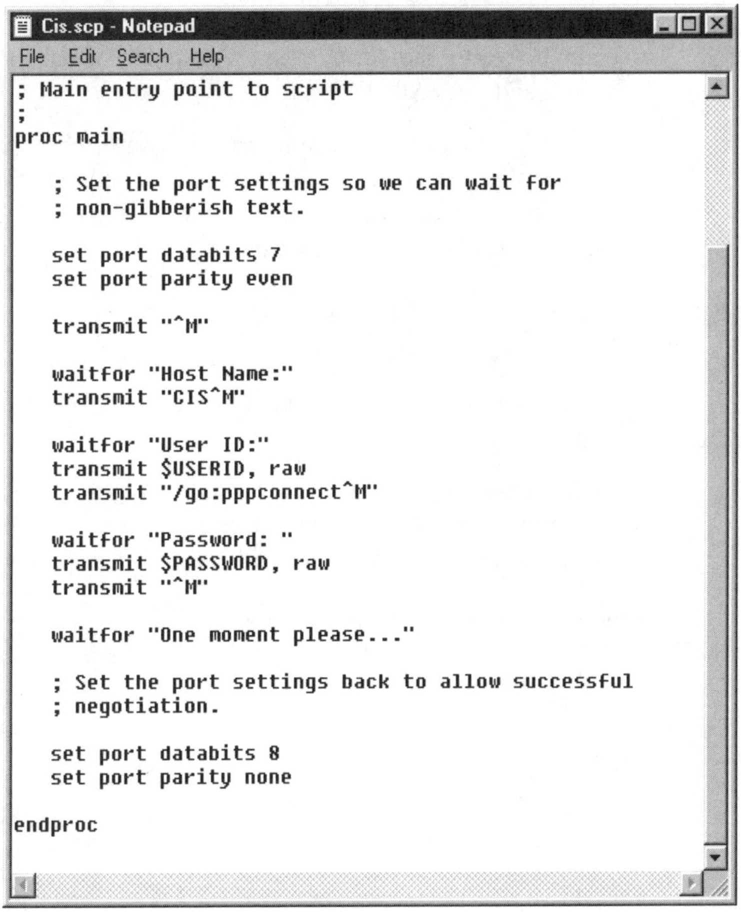

```
Cis.scp - Notepad                                    _ □ ×
File  Edit  Search  Help
; Main entry point to script
;
proc main

    ; Set the port settings so we can wait for
    ; non-gibberish text.

    set port databits 7
    set port parity even

    transmit "^M"

    waitfor "Host Name:"
    transmit "CIS^M"

    waitfor "User ID:"
    transmit $USERID, raw
    transmit "/go:pppconnect^M"

    waitfor "Password: "
    transmit $PASSWORD, raw
    transmit "^M"

    waitfor "One moment please..."

    ; Set the port settings back to allow successful
    ; negotiation.

    set port databits 8
    set port parity none

endproc
```

Fig. 11.28:   Editing a script in Notepad

Script-syntax

In principle, a script starts with the line *proc main* and needs to end with the line *end proc*. In between are all the required script commands in the form of a series of *waitfor-* and *transmit* commands. *Waitfor* waits for a message from the server and *transmit* sends certain information to the server.

Saving the script

Do not enter your user identification and your password in plain text into the script. Use instead the variables *$USERID* and *$PASSWORD*.

When you have entered all commands, choose *File/Save*, and close *Notepad* with *File/Exit*. Close the properties dialog box by clicking the *OK* button and try the dial-up settings as described in the next section.

Using Dial-Up Networking to Access the Internet

Welcome to the last step in configuring *Windows 98* for Internet access! Believe it or not, the dream has almost come true.

We will establish contact with alien intelligence, that is, if there is any, in the Web... You will need to use *Dial-Up Networking* and the icon you created for your connection.

Using the connection icon

Double-click the connection icon in the *Dial-Up Networking* folder to start the first access. The *Connect To* dialog box appears.

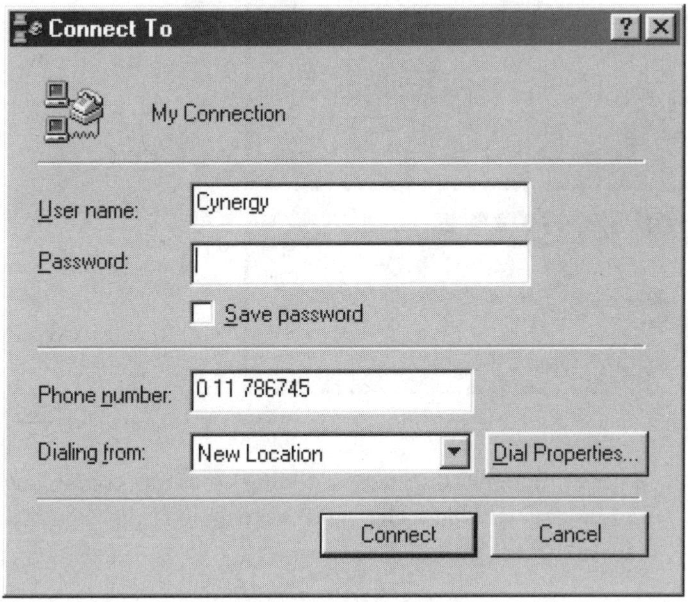

Fig. 11.29: The *Connect To* dialog box

Enter the user name and the password for your Internet access through the server of your provider. If necessary you can check the phone number in the dialog box and using the *Dial Properties* button, you can edit the dialing mode and the area codes.

Connect Button

Click the *Connect* button to begin dialing. The dialing procedure is indicated in a dialog box. When the connection is established, a terminal window appears in which the Internet server prompts you for your name and password.

Enter the required information. Confirm the displayed IP address with a mouse click.

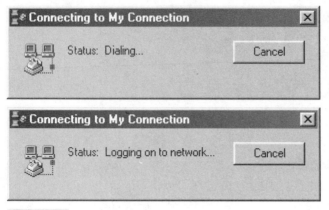

The first dial-up ... and logging on

With a modem, the actual dialing and the connecting phases are audible. The next step is logging onto the network of the provider.

When the connection is established the *Connecting to...*dialog box is minimized to an icon on the taskbar, just left of the clock. A double-click on the icon shows the current connection status. (Figure 11.31).

Fig. 11.31: The connection status

The current connection is displayed in the dialog box with the current transfer rate and the number of sent and received bytes. Now start the appropriate software to access the various Internet services, for example the *Microsoft Internet Explorer*. Double-click the *Internet Explorer* icon on the *Windows 98* desktop.

Active connection

Fig. 11.32:   In the Internet, here is the home page of The Corporation of London

Internet Explorer displays the *Microsoft* Home Page by default. More about navigating the WWW and the handling of the Web browser will appear in the following sections.

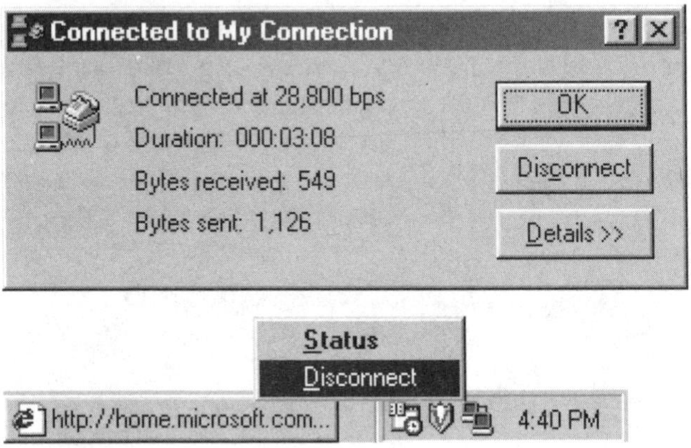

Fig. 11.33:   Disconnecting from an online session

Disconnecting

To disconnect the current connection, you can do one of two things: you can double-click on the connection icon on the taskbar to the left of the clock. The *Connected to* dialog box appears (Figure 11.31). Click the *Disconnect* button. (Figure 11.33, top).

Shortcut menu

Another way of disconnecting is to right-click on the connection icon and choose the *Disconnect* command from the shortcut menu (Figure 11.33, bottom). The connection will be terminated, although *Internet Explorer* will remain open in offline mode.

Configuring Internet Access with the Internet Connection Wizard.

In the previous sections you have manually installed the Internet access step by step. In this section we will show you how to perform the same procedure with the help of the *Internet Connection Wizard*.

You have several ways of calling up the *Internet Connection Wizard*. One way is to double-click the *Connect to the Internet* icon on the desktop. Another method is start the program with *Start/Programs* and

Internet Explorer. Choose *View/Internet Options* in *Internet Explorer* and activate the *Connection* tab page, then click the *Connect* button.

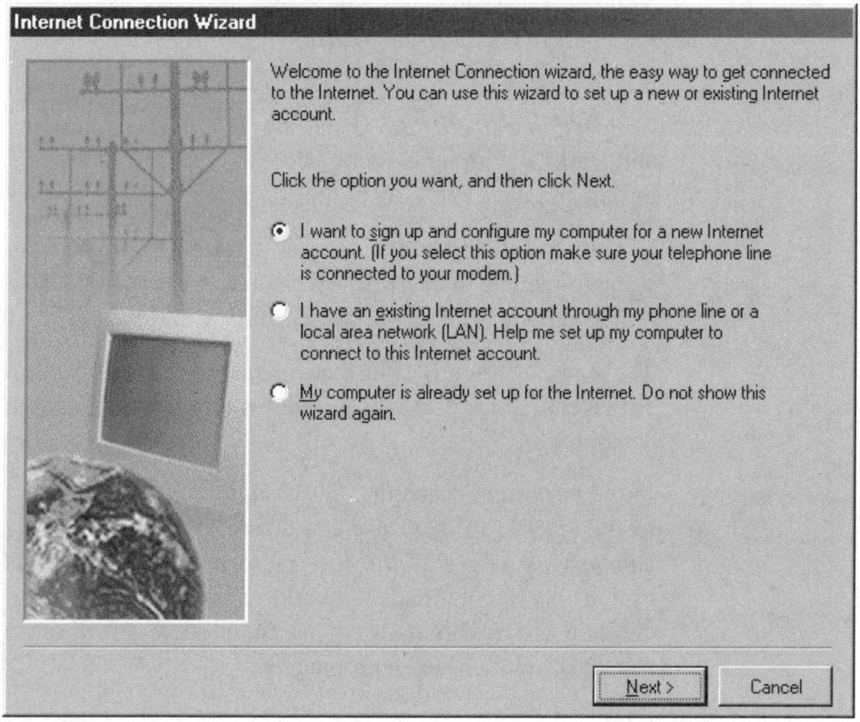

Internet Connection Wizard

Welcome to the Internet Connection wizard, the easy way to get connected to the Internet. You can use this wizard to set up a new or existing Internet account.

Click the option you want, and then click Next.

○ I want to sign up and configure my computer for a new Internet account. (If you select this option make sure your telephone line is connected to your modem.)

○ I have an existing Internet account through my phone line or a local area network (LAN). Help me set up my computer to connect to this Internet account.

○ My computer is already set up for the Internet. Do not show this wizard again.

[Next >] [Cancel]

Fig. 11.34: Configuring Internet access with the help of the Wizard

Internet
Connection Wizard

Either way you get the on-screen *Internet Connection Wizard.* In the first dialog box, determine whether you want to configure the Internet applications of *Windows 98* in such a way that an existing Internet connection is used, or if you want to sign up and configure your computer for a new Internet account.

Sign up...

With this option, your modem dials into the *Microsoft Referral Service*. On the basis of your area code it will present a list of Internet providers in your region.

You can select one and gain access to it with the help of the *Internet Connection Wizard*.

Existing account

For the moment we will deal only with the *Internet Connection Wizard* and installing *Windows 98* Internet applications with an existing account. Choose the second option and click the *Next* button.

Internet provider or online service

In the second step of the wizard, determine whether you want to use an Internet provider or local network, or an online service such as *Amerca Online* or *CompuServe*.

These providers will offer their own software in any case, so we can concentrate on the first option here. Click the *Next* button.

Choosing the modem

In the next step, determine how *Windows 98* will connect to the Internet. If you use a modem, always choose the *Connect using my phone line* radio button. The second option is for internal networks in companies. After clicking the *Next* button, choose the modem you want to use and click the *Next* button again.

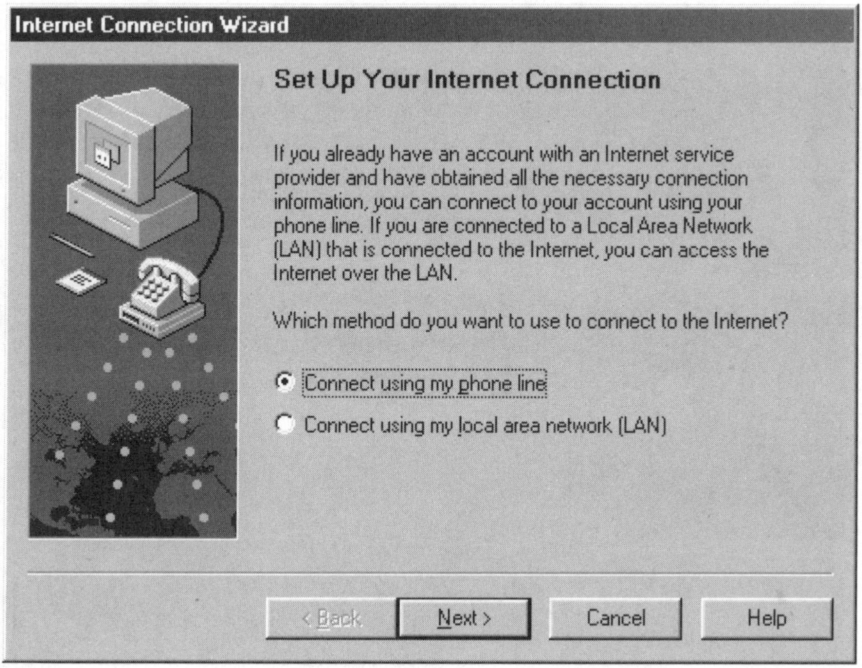

Fig. 11.35:   Internet access with modem or with a local area network (LAN)

Dial-Up

Networking

The next step offers you the choice between using an existing *Dial-Up Networking* connection and creating a new *Dial-Up Networking* connection.

If you decide to create a new connection, please read the section on *Dial-Up Networking*; otherwise use one of the connections listed in the lower list box and click the *Next* button.

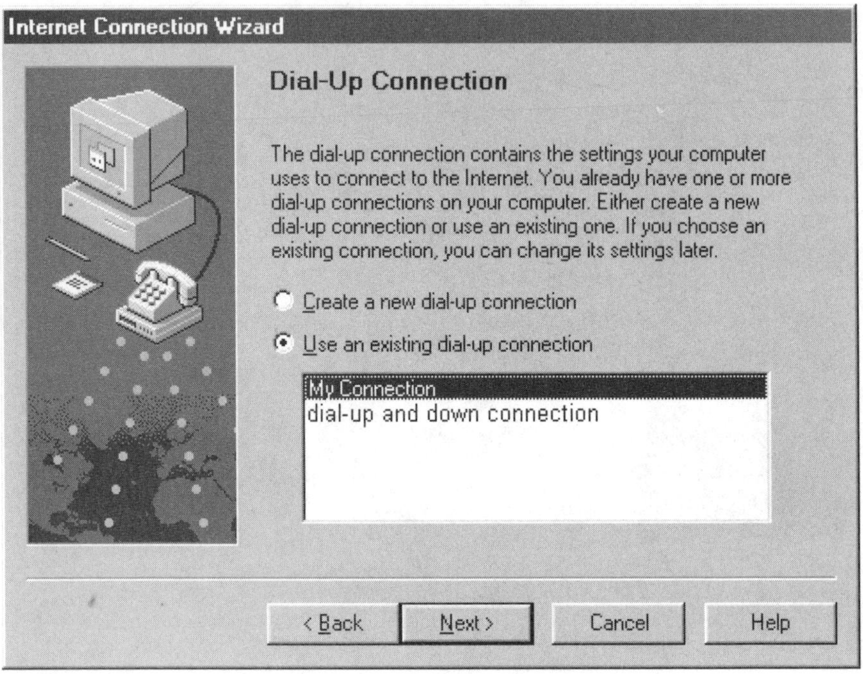

Fig. 11.36: Using an existing Dial-Up Networking connection

Internet Mail
account

Choose *No* when prompted to change the selected connection and click the *Next* button. In the next steps you can install a mail account and a news account. To install it now, you need to have your own account already. If you do not, then click *No* and *Next*.

If you choose *Yes*, you can choose an account for the respective services. Confirm the necessary steps with *Next*. Subsequently, confirm the import of the settings step.

Internet Connection Wizard

Confirm Settings Import

The Internet Connection Wizard detected the following settings:

Your name:	Harold Morgan
E-mail address:	hmorgan@CompuServe.com
Outgoing mail server:	mail.compuserver.com
Incoming mail server:	mail.compuserve.com
Account name:	hmorgan

Do you wish to change these settings?

○ Change settings

◉ Accept settings

< Back	Next >	Cancel	Help

Fig. 11.37:   Using an existing Internet Mail account

Unless you are importing an existing account, all information (E-mail address, mail server name, etc.) will be requested item by item. Keep the data ready. Proceed in the same way with the installation of an *Internet News Account* (for discussion groups and forums, called *Newsgroups*) and the installation of an *Internet directory service* account that provides access to an address book which contains information on other Internet users. At the end of the configuration, click the *Finish* button. Now all Internet applications are configured.

Working with Microsoft Internet Explorer

After the manual installation of the *Dial-Up Networking* or after going through the procedure with the *Wizard*, you can use the built-in *Microsoft Internet Explorer* anytime you want to browse the World Wide Web (WWW), the information service of the Internet.

Internet Explorer

Fig. 11.38:   Internet Explorer goes online

Establishing a connection

Establish the Internet connection. As soon as the connection to the provider is established, you can start the *Microsoft Internet Explorer* or switch to the pre-started *Microsoft Internet Explorer* by clicking the respective icon on the taskbar.

Microsoft Internet Explorer will then display the default start page. In *Windows 98*, if you click a button that is linked to the Internet, the *Microsoft Internet Explorer* starts automatically and displays the dialog box of the *Dial-Up Connection*, where you can get online with a click on the *Connect* button.

World Wide Web

The *World Wide Web (WWW)* is the name for the world's largest information system and is a part of the Internet. The WWW is, without a doubt, the most frequented Internet service. Often it is thought to be synonymous with the whole Internet, which is seen as a gigantic network of computers all over the world connected by the telephone network.

HTML

Hypertext Markup Language (*HTML*) is the basis of all displayed information on the WWW. In HTML, every element in a Web page, be it a picture or text, can function as a pointer, which leads to other elements in the page or to entirely different pages. Such pointers are called *Links* and should be easily recognizable, usually because of their different color.

Browser

To get the information from the WWW onto your screen, you need a browser such as the *Microsoft Internet Explorer*. Only by using a browser is it possible to display information from Web servers and, therefore, be able to navigate in the Web.

Now let's come down to reality. After establishing the connection to your Internet provider through *Dial-Up Networking,* start *Microsoft Internet Explorer* by double-clicking its icon 🌐 on the desktop. If you have used the *Internet Connection Wizard,* you can double-click on the icon straightaway. You should get the dialog box shown in Figure 11.38 where you can be connected with a click

Home Page

on the *Connect* button. The *Internet Explorer* starts with the default start page.

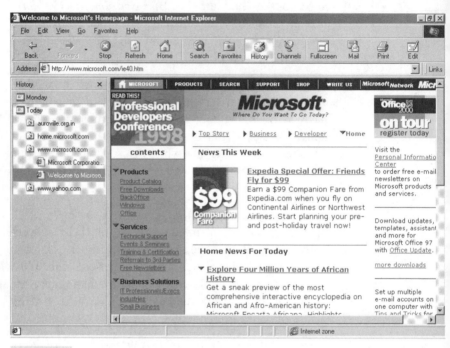

Fig. 11.39:   The Microsoft Internet Explorer

To learn about *Internet Explorer* and its functions, you had better disconnect from your provider's server, otherwise, you will waste precious connection time. We will work offline.

Fig. 11.40:   Disconnecting...

Disconnecting

To disconnect the active connection, double-click the connection icon on the taskbar just left of the clock, and choose *Disconnect* in the dialog box which appears (Figure 11.33, top).

Tip!

To disconnect you can right-click the connection icon 🖳 on the taskbar and choose *Disconnect* from the shortcut menu (Figure11.40). The connection is then terminated, but *Microsoft Internet Explorer* remains open in offline mode and displays the last accessed Web page.

The Controls of Internet Explorer

The Web browser window always displays three sections. The top section contains a title bar with the title of the current document, a menu bar, the *URL* (the Web address) in the *Address* bar and an icon that is animated while accessing information. The middle section displays the contents of the required document, and can be scrolled up and down using the scroll bar. In the bottom section you will see a status bar for messages concerning the connection and the remaining download time.

The Home Page is the Web page that is automatically loaded when the browser is launched. Here you can either specify your own page or an *URL* from the Web.

Title bar

As in all *Windows 98* applications, the title bar in *Microsoft Internet Explorer* is at the top edge of the application window. In *Internet Explorer,* it contains the title of the current page in addition to the *Microsoft Internet Explorer* text.

URL

The *URL* (*Uniform Resource Locator*) is the address of a Web site and is displayed in the *Address* bar as well as in the status bar. Known *URLs* can be entered directly into the *Address* bar. When you point at a link, the destination URL is also displayed in the status bar.

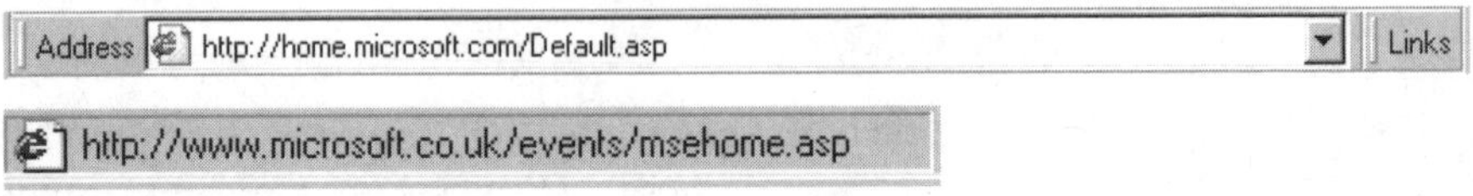

Address http://home.microsoft.com/Default.asp ▼ Links

http://www.microsoft.co.uk/events/msehome.asp

Fig. 11.41: The address bar (top) and the status bar

WWW addresses

All WWW addresses are constructed in the same way: The general syntax for an *URL* is:

protocol://service.host address/path/file name.

With *http* you specify the transfer protocol *HyperText Transfer Protocol*. '*www*' stands for the *World Wide Web* Internet service. The paths never contain spaces.

Menu bar

The menu bar is located directly below the title bar. The available *Internet Explorer* menu items are listed here. A click on a menu opens the menu. Below the menu bar, you will find the *Standard Buttons* toolbar to navigate the Web. This toolbar contains thirteen buttons to navigate the WWW.

Fig. 11.42: The *Internet Explorer* toolbar

Explorer bars

With these buttons you have quick mouse-based access to often-used commands. In the next section you will find an overview of the functions of the various buttons. Greyed buttons are currently not available. The *View* menu manages the display of the various bars, such as the status bar, the *Standard Buttons* toolbar and the *Explorer* bars. The bar can be moved with the 'handle' ▌ at the left of each bar.

Here a list of the most important *Internet Explorer* buttons:

Button	Name	Function
Back	*Back*	Back to the last displayed document
Forward	*Forward*	Forward reverses the action of the Back button
Stop	*Stop*	Cancels the downloading of a page
Refresh	*Refresh*	Loads the current page again
Home	*Home*	Back to the default Home page, which is shown at startup
Search	*Search*	Searches Web sites with the default search engine for the WWW
Favorites	*Favorites*	Saves and recalls interesting *URL* addresses
History	*History*	Splits the window in two; the left pane shows sites already visited
Channels	*Channels*	Splits the window in two; the left pane shows preset *channels*
Mail	*E-mail*	To read, write and send E-mail
Print	*Print*	Prints the current document on the default printer
Edit	*Edit*	Opens the application with which the current file is associated

With the left mouse button, you can drag the *Links* toolbar to underneath the *Address* bar if you want to display further links that lead to *Microsoft* products, to Hotmail or to the Channel Guide, among other things.

| Links | Best of the Web | Channel Guide | Customize Links | Free HotMail | Internet Start | Microsoft | Windows Update |

Fig. 11.43:   The *Links* toolbar

Best of the Web

This toolbar can be used for quick access to frequently used documents, such as the Best of the Web [Best of the Web].

The status bar displays information about the current status of a requested document. A lock icon indicate whether or not you are currently connected to a secure server. Watch out for this icon during all sensitive data transactions such as a mail order via credit cards.

Navigating the Web with Internet Explorer

We will now take a look at how to work online with *Internet Explorer*, so you will need to establish a connection with the Internet. Get online by clicking the *Microsoft* button [Microsoft] on the *Links* toolbar. If the connection is configured in *Dial-Up Networking,* you will get the *Dial-Up Connection* dialog box. Click the *Connect* button.

Dialing status dialog box

During the process of establishing a connection with the server of your provider, which will be audible when using a modem, the *Connecting To* dialog box will be displayed. Once the connection has been established, the required page will be displayed:

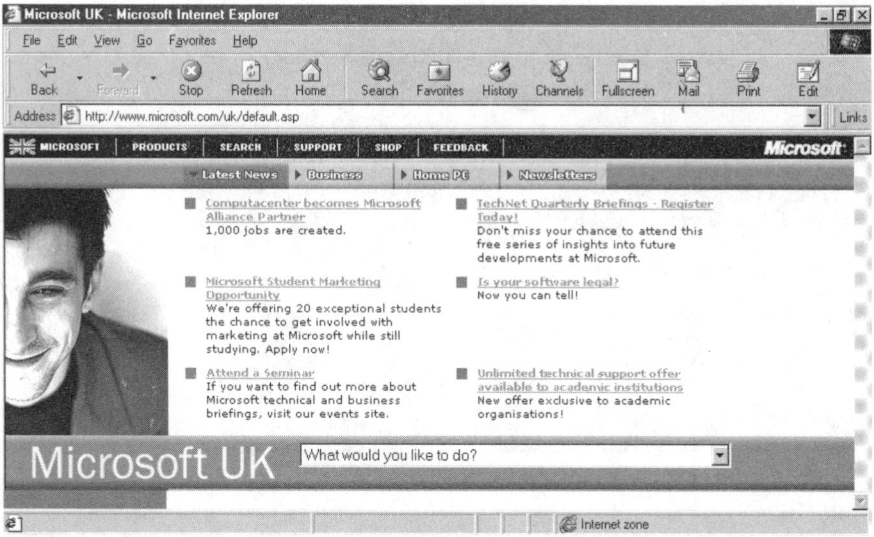

Fig. 11.44: Online in the Microsoft Home Page

Since the Internet is one of today's fastest developing and rapidly changing medias, you should consider the links and references given in this section as examples only. You may not find them at all, or find them with a different appearance or others instead.

Activating a link

Move over the ▦ SUPPORT *link* and click once. Observe the information shown in the status bar. The *support* page of *Microsoft* will be displayed. Click on the *Support Online* link ▦ Support Online in the support page to open the list, then choose the link *All in one,* to change to this Web site.

Open the drop-down list and choose the entry for *Word for Windows 6.0,* enter *update* into the text box below. Click the *Go* button 🟢.

Once the page is displayed, point to one of the underlined links, and click it to display the next page. Because you are now sending information to the Internet Zone, *Internet Explorer* displays a warning message which you should confirm with *Yes*.

Security Alert   ☒

You are about to send information to the Internet zone. It might be possible for other people to see what you are sending. Do you want to continue?

☐ In the future do not show the warning for this zone.

[Yes]   [No]

Fig. 11.45:   Security warning in the 'Internet Zone'

Forward and back

The results of your search will be displayed. Read the information and just try out some other links. To return to the previous page click the *Back* button . To jump to the next page after going back, click the *Forward* button .

Stop button

If the transfer of a page is taking too much time, you can interrupt the download with the *Stop* button . The *Refresh* button will reload the current page. With the *Home* button you can always change to the default home page.

Tip!

Before you go online with *Microsoft Internet Explorer*, start the Internet access software from your provider. If you are connecting with *Dial-Up Networking*, enter your user identification and password into the dialog box and click the *Connect* button. As soon as the connection is established, *Internet Explorer* will display the default Home page.

Tip!

Web sites are being continuously updated and it is therefore not feasible to give more detailed information about Web sites in a book. You can use the power of the WWW to get the latest accessories and Tips & Tricks for *Windows 98,* or to get free software, graphics, sounds, video clips, icons, games, screen-savers and tons of other things as well. And, you'd better get yourself a bigger hard drive soon too...

Virus scanner

Be aware that any time you download there is a certain danger: the data you download could contain a computer virus. You are in any case warned before you download any data that it might contain a virus. After downloading a file you can check it with a virus scanner before you open it.

By default graphics are displayed in steps: first the text description appears, then a placeholder with the name of the graphic, and then the graphic files one after the other. In this way you do not have to wait until the whole procedure is completed to know what the page is about.

Entering Web Addresses in the Internet Explorer

To enter a known Web address (*URL*) click into the *Address* bar of *Internet Explorer*. Overwrite the selected address with a complete address. If you do not know any *URLs* right now, try the following *URL* for the Home page of *Microsoft* in the U.K.:

▪ *http://www.microsoft.com/uk*

Press the *Enter* key ⏎ to confirm the entry and to start the search for the site.

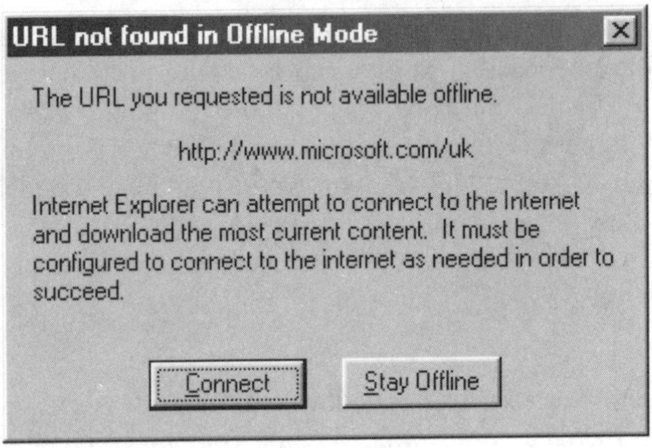

Fig. 11.46:   'URL not found in Offline Mode'

If you are currenly offline, the dialog box shown in Figure 11.46 may appear. Click the *Connect* button. Then the *Dial-up Connection* dialog box is displayed. You may have to enter your user identification and your password. Click the *Connect* button again. You will then land up on the *Microsoft* Home Page. Click the ▣**SUPPORT** button to change to the *Support page* of *Microsoft*.

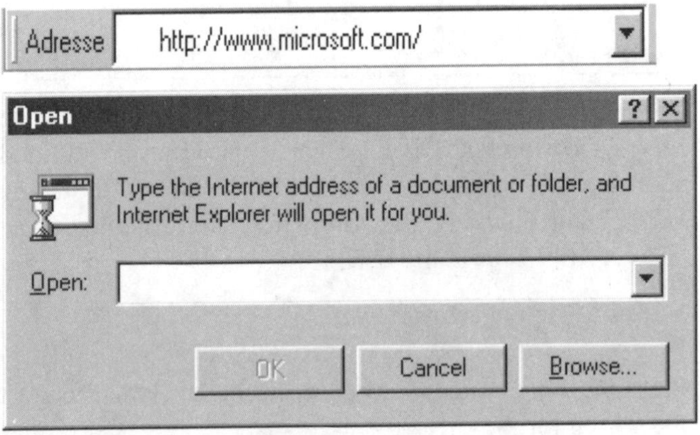

Fig. 11.47:   Entering addresses directly or with the *Open* dialog box

Now choose *File/Open*, and in the dialog box enter the *URL* again:

■ *http://www.microsoft.com/uk*

AutoComplete

Observe the display in the *Address* bar. Press the *Enter* key ⏎ as soon as *Internet Explorer* has automatically completed the rest of address, which it remembers from the previous entry. Again, the *Microsoft* Home Page is displayed.

Another way of opening Web sites that you have already visited is to use the drop-down list of the *Address* box. Open the *History* list by clicking the drop-down button ▼, and choose one of the entries with the mouse.

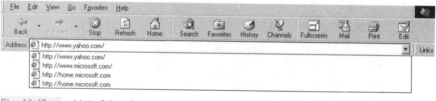

Fig. 11.48:   List of the sites last visited

Working with Links on Web Pages

Now jump to the *Microsoft* Home page once again with a click on the *Home* button 🏠. If your browser is configured for a different home page, you can use the *http://www.microsoft.com/uk* entry in the history list to jump to this page.

Colored text

On the web page that will be displayed you will see different kinds of links, appearing as text in another color, for example: ■ **Attend a Seminar**. All these regions are called *hyperlinks*, or *links* for short. Move over various areas of the page and observe the shape of the mouse pointer and the text displayed in the status bar.

Hand cursor

When you move over a link (for example blue or underlined blue text, a button, a graphic, etc.) the mouse pointer becomes a hand. In the status bar the *URL* of the linked object is displayed.

Links can be found in buttons, graphics or any other object on the page. Click on the *Support* **SUPPORT** link. You will jump to the *Support page* of *Microsoft*. There, click the *Support Online* **Support Online** link.

Link to other

Resources

This link opens a list. Click the link *All in one*, and the Web page changes. Choose an entry in the *Products* link, enter a keyword to search and click the *Go* **GO** link.

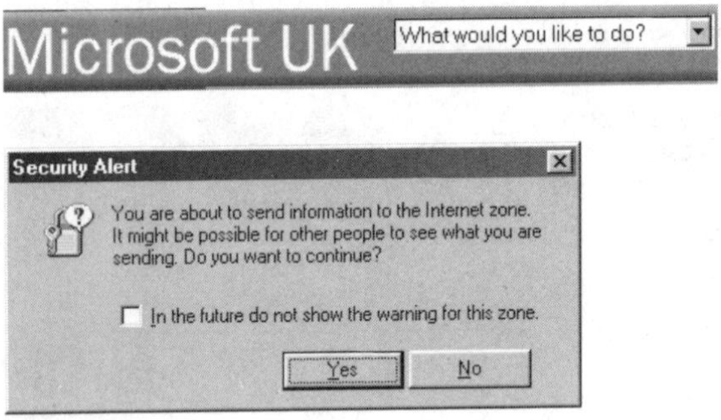

Fig. 11.49: Links obtain information or change to other resources

Since you are now changing to the Internet zone (i.e. You are going to upload certain information), *Internet Explorer* gives you a warning message. Click the *Yes* button. Click a link on the new page, like the underlined text ■ **Attend a Seminar**, to show a different document.

Tip!

With the *Support* [SUPPORT] link, you can go from the *Microsoft* Home page, for example, to a Web page with links on various accessories that you can download free of charge. Here you could get the latest version of *Internet Explorer* or add-ons and viewers for various *Microsoft* programs. A viewer is a program that lets you view files, such as *Word* documents or *Excel* worksheets without having installed *Word* or *Excel*.

Violet links

Internet Explorer remembers which hyperlinks you have already activated and displays them in a different color (by default, violet).

The *Clickable Maps* are graphics, pictures, lists or tables that are linked. You will find them when you move over them and the mouse pointer changes into a hand.

If you move over a link, the *URL* of the respective document or service will be displayed in the status bar. To activate this link click with the left mouse button.

Configuring Internet Explorer

To configure your Web browser, first disconnect from the server. Right-click the connection icon 🖳 on the taskbar, just left of the clock. In the shortcut menu choose *Disconnect*. The connection is terminated but *Internet Explorer* stays open offline and displays the last accessed Web page.

Changing the start page

To change the default home page, choose *Internet Options* from the *View* menu. In the *Home page* option group on the *General* tab page, you can click the *Use Blank* button to start with an empty Web page.

Individual home page

You can also, of course, enter an address of your choice into the *Address* text box. Be careful with the syntax and do not forget to type *http://www* too, otherwise all you will get is an error message. Confirm by clicking *Apply*.

---Home page---

You can change which page to use for your home page.

Address: http://home.microsoft.com/Default.asp

[Use Current]   [Use Default]   [Use Blank]

Fig. 11.50:   User defined Home page

Home page

The start page is also called the *Home page* and it is the document which is loaded automatically whenever the *Internet Explorer* is started, provided that another address is not already entered. With the *Home* button  you can jump back to this starting point anytime you like.

Own Home page

Home pages usually provide a graphically enriched presentation of data on the Internet. Every Internet user can, in principle, create his/her own Home page and upload it onto the Web. It ultimately depends only upon the provider, because he has to reserve the hard disk space for it on the server. With the *FrontPage Express* program in *Windows 98*, you can create your own Home page (*Start/Programs/Internet Explorer/FrontPage Express*).

Tip!

In the *Home page* option group a click on the *Use Default* button is enough to restore the original *Microsoft* Home page *(http://www. Microsoft .com/)*.

Any Internet address is called a *Uniform Resource Locator (URL)* in WWW terminology. A *URL* address always follows the syntax: *protocol://host address/path/ filename*, like: *http://www.microsoft.com/uk/default.asp*.

In this example, *www.microsoft.com* is the host address, while *http://* is the transfer protocol, short for *HyperText Transfer Protocol*. *'www.'* stands for the *World Wide Web* Internet service. *microsoft.com* is the name of the server. Further, attached paths (for example */uk*) can be entered, and you can also specify a particular document (for example *default.asp*).

Setting program
colors

To set the program colors, choose *Views/Internet Options*. Click the *Colors* button on the *General* tab page. If you prefer other color combinations than the *Windows 98* default, clear the *Use Windows colors* check box. Open the color palettes for elements like *Text* or *Visited* links, choose a color and confirm by clicking the *OK* button.

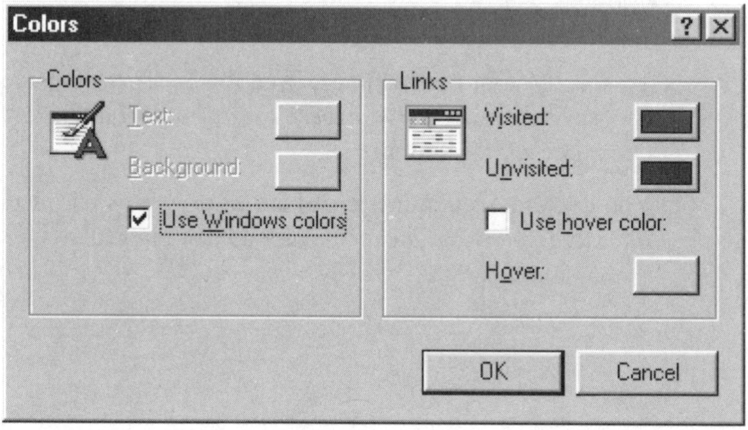

Fig. 11.51: Assigning colors in Internet Explorer

Fonts

To assign fonts, choose *Views/Internet options*. Click the *Fonts* button on the *General* tab page.

Open the various font lists and choose the font you want.

In the *Font size* drop-down box you can roughly select a font size. Close the dialog box by clicking the *OK* button.

 The font you choose in the *Fonts* dialog box has no effect on the loading speed of *Internet Explorer*. The browser simply converts the *HTML* documents using the user-defined font. This procedure is local, meaning that it happens only on your system.

Security tab page

Change to the *Security* tab page. From the *Zone* drop-down list, choose a zone for which you want to change the security.

Select the required security level by choosing the *High* radio button, for example. Read the explanations underneath the respective radio buttons to find out what kind of security is offered.

Active Web
contents

To specify your own settings, from the *Security* tab page choose the *Custom (for expert users)* radio button and click the *Settings* button.

You can then determine what kind of programs and data *Internet Explorer* will execute or load automatically.

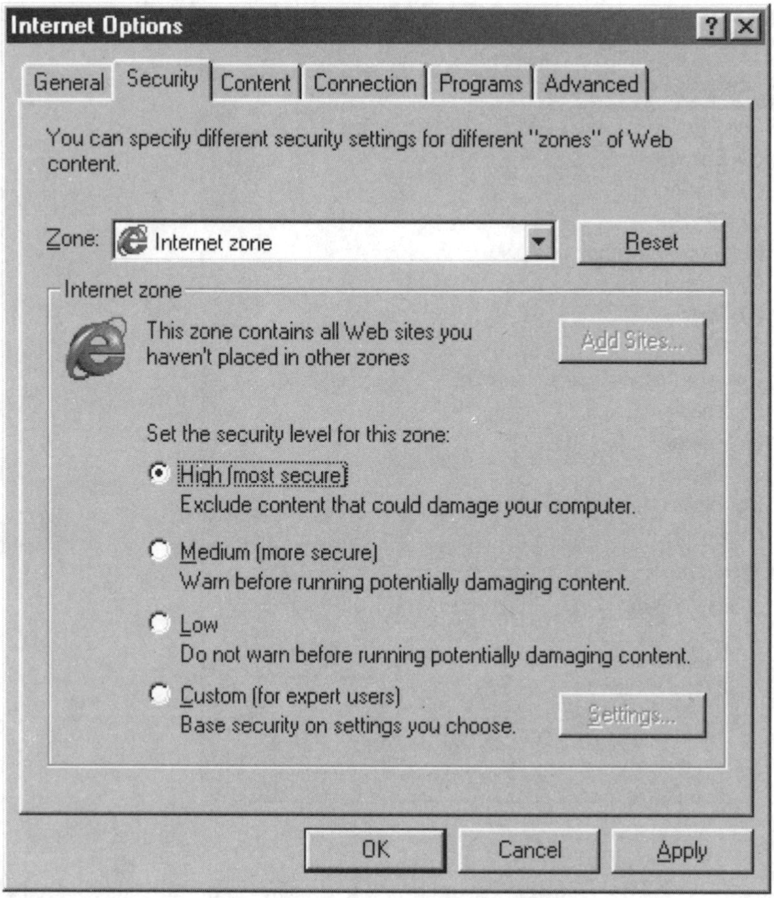

Fig. 11.52: Setting the high security level for the Internet Explorer

By default, the transfer of active contents such as videos, sounds and animated text is allowed. The various *ActiveX Controls* and *JavaScript* programs are responsible for loading and executing animations, sound and three-dimensional graphics. This will improve the presentation but decrease the security. Confirm your changes with *OK*.

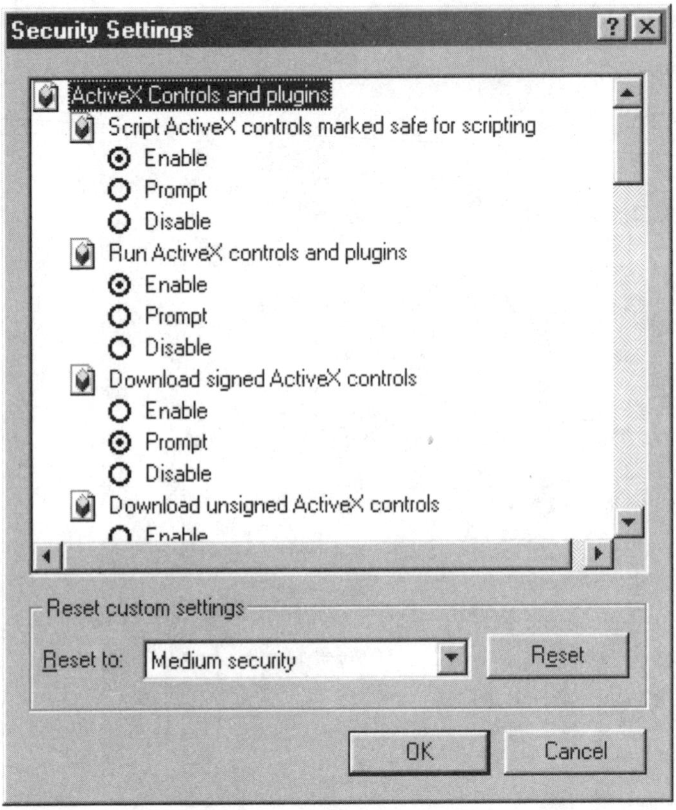

Fig. 11.53:   Adjusting security settings for Internet Explorer

History option
group

The *History* group box on the *General* tab page can be used to control that folder. You can specify how many days at a time *History* should keep track of your Internet activities. The *Clear History* button will do just that, clear the *History* folder.

Saving and Recalling Interesting Web Sites as Favorites

Internet Explorer provides the *Favorites* feature, allowing you to save the most interesting Web locations. You can save visited sites and recall them later on quickly and conveniently.

Display an interesting site

Let us try this out. Load, for example, the *Microsoft* Home page at *http://www.microsoft.com/uk*. Click the *Support* SUPPORT link. On the *Support* page of *Microsoft* click the *Support Online* ▶ Support Online link. In the list click the *All in one* link. On the Web page that appears thereafter, choose an entry from the *Products* drop-down list, enter a keyword and click the GO button.

Add to favorites

To save the support page that now appears as a *Favorite*, choose the *Add to Favorites* command from the *Favorites* menu or the shortcut menu. You can overwrite the proposed name in the *Name* box with, for example, *Microsoft Support UK*, and click the *OK* button to store the current page in the *Favorites* menu.

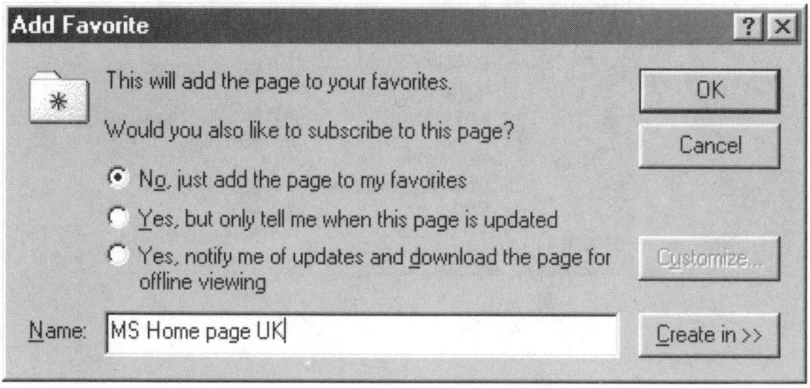

Fig. 11.54: Creating a 'Favorite'

Favorite-folder

Links

You can then change to other WWW sites and save more *Favorites*. To go back to a saved *Favorite*, click the *Favorites* button. The *Internet Explorer* window will be divided into two. In the left pane, you will see a list of *Favorites* and *Favorites* folders. By default, new

Favorites are added at the bottom of the list. Click one of these *Favorites* in order to go to that Web site. Open the folder *Links* and test one of the *Favorites* stored there.

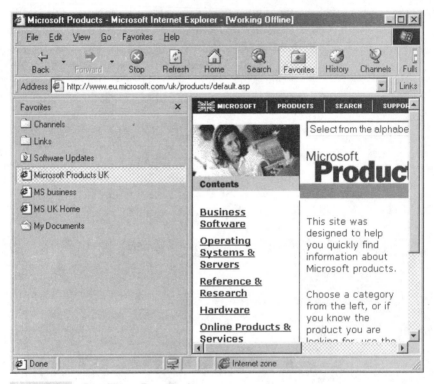

Fig. 11.55:   Recalling a *Favorite* site

Tip! By default, new *Favorites* are listed at the bottom of the *Favorites* list. You can also store favorites in existing folders. To do so, click the *Create in* button in the *Add Favorite* dialog box. Select the destination in the list and confirm with *OK*. You can also click the *New Folder* button to create a new folder.

Favorites menu   The *Favorites* feature saves you the trouble of entering long and often difficult *URL* addresses. After clicking the *Favorites* button, the left pane of *Internet Explorer* displays the *Favorite* entries. If you now click an entry, *Internet Explorer* transfers the address from the *Favorites* folder into the *Address* bar and tries to establish a connection. Alternatively, you can also choose an item from the *Favorites* menu.

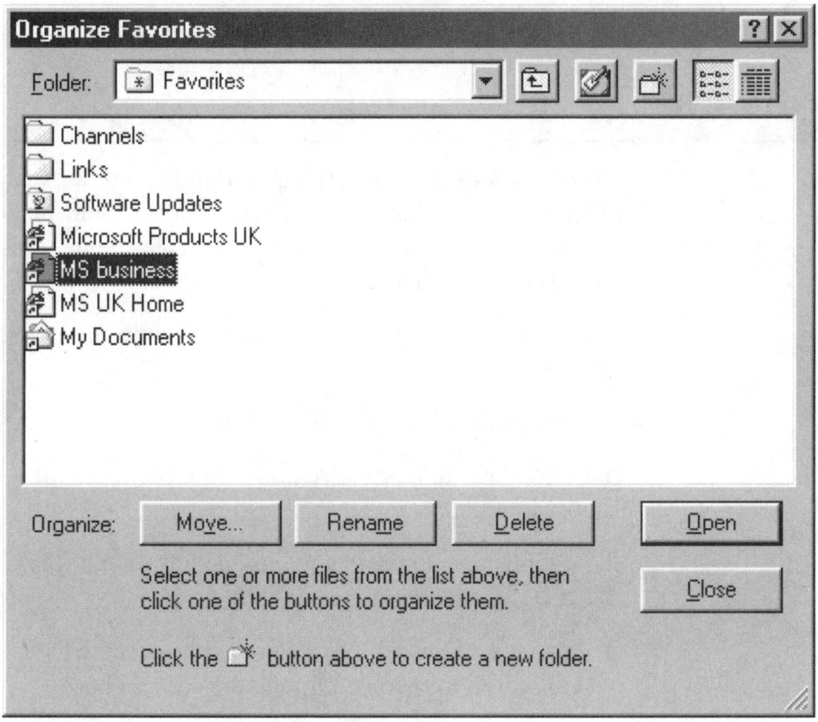

Fig. 11.56:   Organizing Favorites

Favorites can be reorganized at any time. To do so, choose the *Organize Favorites* command from the *Favorites* menu. Open the desired folder and select the respective item from the list. Then use one of the

available commands, either *Move, Rename,* or *Delete.*
Click on *Close* to close the dialog box.

Tip! Selected files can be renamed in the *Organize Favorites* dialog box by clicking on the name, and then clicking again. Just overwrite highlighted text. To finish renaming the entry press the *Enter* key ⏎.

Working with Microsoft Outlook Express

Microsoft Outlook Express is the program that comes with *Windows 98* and helps you organize all electronic messages, in addition to facilitating the electronic communications with other people.

Overview

You can use *Microsoft Outlook Express* for the following tasks:

▦ To read, write and organize E-mails

▦ To read, write and organize news from Newsgroups on the Internet

▦ To establish a connection and use data from the *World Wide Web* or other online services

▦ To manage addresses, i.e., to store and organize them and to search for people through the address book

Online access

For most of the above mentioned features your computer either has to be part of a network or has to have access to the Internet. The E-mail and News features additionally require an Internet mail account and an Internet news account respectively.

Outlook Express

Outlook Express can send and receive electronic messages from the office, from home and while on the road. You can view messages before you actually open them, you can use electronic signatures, among other things.

Address book

Of course you can also use *Microsoft Outlook Express* without online access. In this case, the software is useful for organizing personal and business data such as addresses with the help of the *Address Book*. In the *Address Book* you can keep your personal and business contacts up-to-date. *Outlook Express* has its own search to conveniently find data.

Starting and Configuring Microsoft Outlook Express

In this section you will become acquainted with the application window of *Outlook Express*. Start *Microsoft Outlook Express* using one of the following methods:

Desktop

- Double-click the *Outlook Express* icon on the Desktop

Taskbar

- Click the *Launch Outlook Express* button on the taskbar

- Launch *Outlook Express* by clicking the *Start* button and choosing *Programs/Internet Explorer* and choosing *Outlook Express* from the overlapping menu

Stand-alone unit

Depending on the configuration of the program, *Microsoft Outlook Express* starts with or without any messages. Usually you will get something resembling the picture in Figure 11.57.

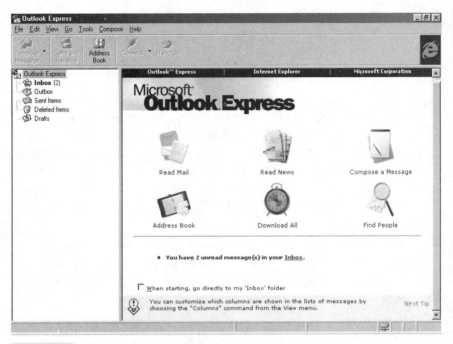

Fig. 11.57: The application window of Microsoft Outlook Express

Connecting and Working Offline

You will get the above *Outlook Express* window only with fully installed Internet access. If information about mail and news servers is missing, the respective dialog boxes will appear.

Establish a
connection

Microsoft Outlook Express needs to know before starting whether or not a *Dial-Up Networking* connection should be established. Therefore, the dialog box shown in Figure 11.58 will appear, wherein you can choose from the *Select the connection you would like to dial* drop-down list a connection in the *Dial-Up Networking* folder. Click the *OK* button to get the *Dial-up Connection* dialog box and choose *Connect*.

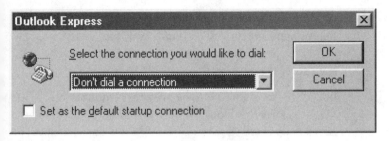

Fig. 11.58:   Asking for a connection at the start of Outlook Express

Start offline

However, if you want to start *Microsoft Outlook Express* offline, choose from the *Select the connection you would like to dial* drop-down list the *Don't dial a connection* entry and confirm with *OK*. Now you will be connected to your Internet service only when it's needed, for instance when you want to send and receive mail or when you want to get the news. If you select the *Set as the default startup connection* check box, this dialog box will not reappear.

Tip!

You should configure your mail and news servers before you launch *Microsoft Outlook Express* for the first time. It is simple to do this with the *Internet Connection Wizard* that you learned about earlier on. The exact procedure for the mail and news configuration depends on your online service. All required information for the configuration of the mail and news services can be obtained from your Internet Service Provider.

Organizing Electronic Messages with Outlook Express

With *Outlook Express* you can display all kinds of electronic messages in one folder, regardless of whether you receive them as faxes, as E-mail from online services such as *The Microsoft Network, CompuServe* or *America Online,* or as Internet mail from the WWW (World Wide Web).

529

Fax-software

If you want to use *Windows 98* to send faxes, you need a fax/modem or an ISDN card and the respective fax software, since *Windows 98* does not come along with such software.

Starting Outlook Express

In order to start *Outlook Express*, double-click the *Outlook Express* icon 🖳 on the desktop or click the *Launch Outlook Express* button 🖳 on the taskbar. The first time *Outlook Express* starts, it will be in offline mode. Select from the *Select the connection you would like to dial* drop-down list the *Don't dial a connection* entry and confirm with *OK*.

Inbox folder

To view the list of received messages, click the *Inbox* 🖳 **Inbox** item in the left pane of *Outlook Express*. All available messages are displayed in the right window pane. Alternatively, you can click the *Read Mail* 🖳 button to reach the inbox.

Reading messages

You can also follow these steps without Internet access, because *Microsoft* provides some 'messages' with *Outlook Express*. If you want to read a message. just click the respective entry in the right window pane. *Outlook Express* displays the message in the lower part of the window. Just above it, you get information about the sender, the date received and the subject.

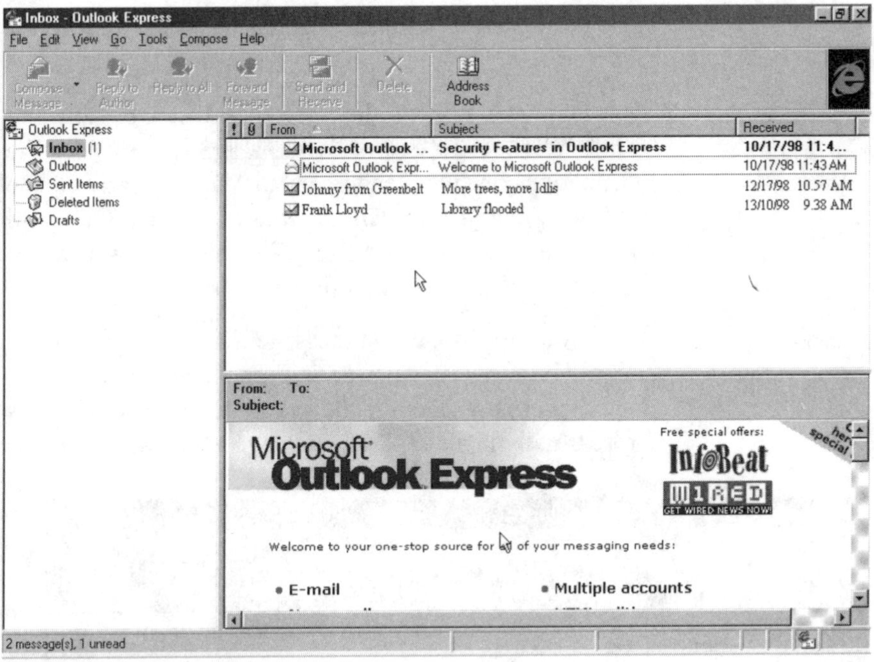

Fig. 11.59: Viewing the inbox with Outlook Express

Sample messages

Enlarge the *Outlook Express* window if necessary or use the scroll bars to read the message. Sample messages that come with every *Windows 98* computer include:

- *Welcome to Microsoft Outlook Express*

- *Security Features in Outlook Express*

Unread messages

Outlook Express displays all unread messages in the right window pane with the closed envelope icon ✉. Messages which have been read but not deleted are indicated by an open envelope icon ✉.

Sort messages

You can decide the way in which the messages in the right pane are to be sorted at any time. Click the *Subject* column heading to sort all messages by their subject, or click the *Received* column heading to sort messages by date received.

Outlook Express Help

You can open one of the messages listed by clicking ☑ Microsoft Outlook ... Welcome to Microsoft Outlook Express Check the information on the sender in the upper part of the window. Enlarge the *Outlook* window or use the scroll bars to read the whole message. This message is a part of the *Outlook Express* Help too.

Separate window

If you want to display the message in a separate window and if you want to answer it immediately via E-mail, double-click on one of the message entries. *Outlook Express* will open a separate message window.

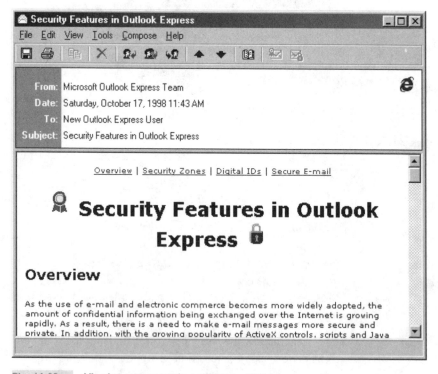

Fig. 11.60: Viewing messages in a separate window

By clicking the appropriate button on the toolbar in the message window you can answer the mail. The message heading is displayed in the title bar of the message window.

Answering Electronic Mail

Reply to author

Click the *Reply to Author* button 🖳 on the toolbar to automatically transfer the sender's information into the *RE:...*window.

Delete the unnecessary parts of the source message and type your reply. Then click the *Send* button 🖃 Send. Now *Microsoft Outlook Express* will try to establish an online connection. Confirm the *Dial-up Connection* dialog box with a click on the *Connect* button to send the message.

In order to view a list of messages that still have to be sent, click on the *Outbox* folder in the left pane of *Outlook*. Here all electronic messages that are written or created but not yet sent are stored. The sending procedure can be configured so that you can make good use of cheaper telephone rates. To do this, choose *Tools/ Options*.

Tip!

To sort information in the inbox or the outbox, click the column heading of the respective column. If you want to view information about the messages, choose *View/ Columns*, select the column name in the *Available Columns* list and click the *Add* button. After clicking the *OK* button the additional columns will appear.

Buttons

You can use *Outlook Express* to create and send your own electronic messages (E-mails). To organize the messages and faxes, it is best to use the toolbar of the message window. *Outlook Express* displays a message window after you double-click on an entry in the inbox.

These buttons are also available in the *New Message* window which can be accessed by pressing [Ctrl]+[N] or choosing *Compose/New message* from the *Outlook Express* window.The list below describes the functions of the buttons in the *Microsoft Outlook Express* message window:

Button	Name	Function
	*Save this message*	Saves the current E-mail in any folder
	*Print*	Prints the displayed message on the default printer
	*Copy*	Copies the selected text of the current message to the clipboard
	*Delete*	Deletes the current message or the selected text without further confirmation
	*Reply to Author*	Prepares a reply message to the author of the current message
	*Reply All*	Sends the message to the sender and all other original receivers
	*Forward*	Forwards the message to other receivers of your choice
	*Previous*	Opens the previous message in the inbox
	*Next*	Opens the next message in the inbox
	*Address Book*	Opens the address book

Fig. 11.61: Some buttons on the message window toolbar

Creating an E-mail with Outlook Express

Start *Outlook Express* offline. If a dialog box appears first, then choose from the *Select the connection you would like to dial* drop-down list the entry *Don't dial a connection* and click the *OK* button. On the toolbar click the *Compose Message* button.

Enter mail address   In the *New Message* window enter an E-mail address into the *To:* text box or click the *Select recipients from a list* button 🔠 just left of the *To:* text box in order to display the *Select Recipients* dialog box.

Fig. 11.62: The window for creating a new message

Subject

Next to *Cc* you will find the *Select carbon copy recipients from a list* button. Here you can enter or select an existing E-mail address to which a copy of your message should be sent. In *Subject* you can type in a title for the message. In the text box at the bottom of the window, you can then compose your message.

It is better not to format messages using the buttons on the toolbar. Such messages will be sent by *Outlook Express*, but they will arrive as an *HTML* document and not as plain text. Not every E-mail application on the receiver's side can display such formatted messages. Basically this is only possible with real *Internet Mail* which is displayed in a Web browser. Also refrain from using any kind of special characters.

Sending E-mail with Outlook Express

Send button

To send a message, choose the *Send Message* command in the *File* menu. Alternatively, you can also press the [Ctrl]+[S] key combination or click the *Send Message* button when using the default mail server. The mail will now be transferred to the *Outbox* folder.

Online-
connection

Outlook Express then tries to establish an online connection to your Internet service. Confirm the *Dial-up Connection* dialog box with a click on the *Connect* button to send the mail right away.

A copy of the message will be stored in the *Sent Items* folder. If you are working offline, the message is just copied into the *Outbox*. In that case, establish a connection and send the mail. Otherwise, your mail will remain in the *Outbox* and will be sent only when you are next connected or the next time you start up *Outlook Express*.

If you want to send files with *Outlook Express*, choose *File Attachment* from the *Insert* menu or click the *Insert File* button 📎.

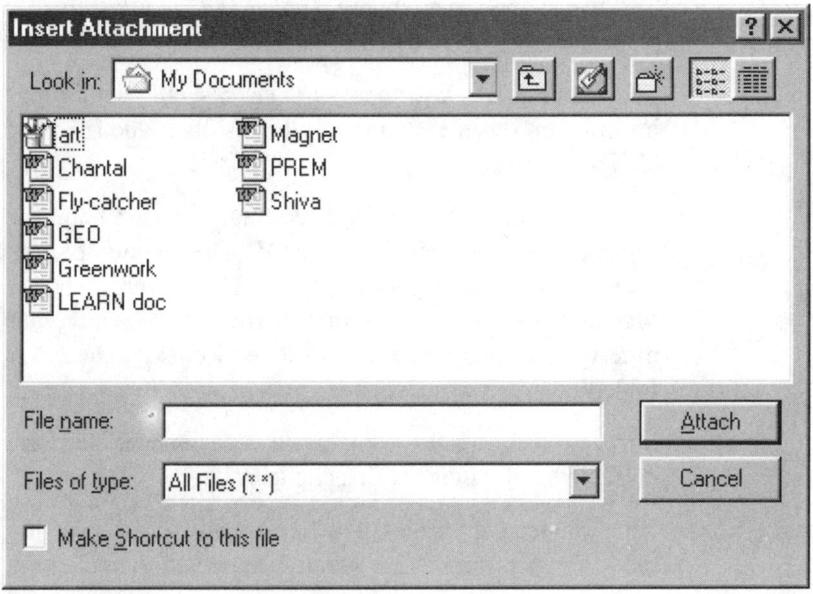

Fig. 11.63:   Attaching a file to an E-mail

Insert attachment   Change to the required folder and select the respective file in the *Insert Attachment* dialog box. If you always send files as attachments, and do not check the *Make shortcut to this file* check box, then everything should run smoothly.

Receiving E-mail with Outlook Express

Receiving mail is really easy too. Just start *Outlook Express* with a double-click on the *Outlook Express* 📧 icon, or click the *Launch Outlook Express* 📧 button on the taskbar. Start *Outlook Express* in online mode, that is, with a connection to the Internet. You can do this by choosing the entry for your *Dial-Up Networking* connection from the *Select the connection you would like to dial* drop-down list. Close the dialog box by clicking the *OK* button.

Send and receive

To receive messages choose *Tools/Send and Receive* or press the ⌈Ctrl⌉+⌈M⌉ key combination.

Inbox folder

The command *Download All* checks all configured information services and stores the results in the *Inbox* of *Outlook Express*.

News server

Here the online connection to the Internet is used and the respective news areas are checked. The online services take care of storing your E-mail or News with a special Mail and News server. Disconnect after downloading your messages, and read the E-mail offline by clicking the *Inbox* folder in the left window pane.

Files as attachment

If received messages contain file attachments they are displayed in the *Inbox* with a clip icon ⏚.

Messages received

You can read messages you have received by selecting the *Inbox* icon in the left window pane and then clicking on the message in the right window.

To reply, double-click on the message to open it in a new window together with the sender information. By clicking the *Reply to Author* button ⏚, the information about the sender will be automatically copied into the *Re:* Reply window.

Using the Address Book

With *Windows 98*, you can also organize addresses, fax and phone numbers, business contacts and E-mail addresses. However, the command to launch *Address Book* cannot be found in the *Start* menu.

Address Book

This is because the *Address Book* is an integral part of *Outlook Express*.

Entering Addresses into the Address Book

Microsoft Office
Suite

The entries in *Address Book* can be used in other applications too. You can look into the *Address Book* from any program in the *Microsoft Office Suite*, such as *Microsoft Word*, and transfer addresses from there.

To enter addresses into the *Address Book,* first start *Microsoft Outlook Express* with a double-click on the *Outlook Express* ![icon] icon, or click the *Launch Outlook Express* ![button] button on the taskbar. Start *Outlook Express* offline, without a live connection to the Internet.

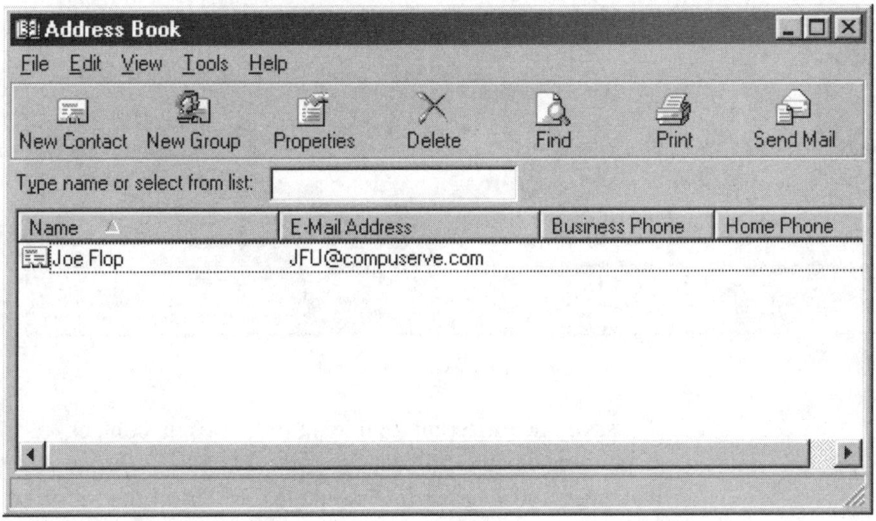

Fig. 11.64:   The Address Book

New contact

Start the *Address Book* by clicking the *Address Book* button ![icon] on the toolbar. The *Address Book* is probably still empty. Enter new contacts with the *File/New Contact* command or by clicking on the *New Contact* button ![icon].

A dialog box with a number of tab pages pops up. Enter data into all the text boxes on the *Personal* tab page.

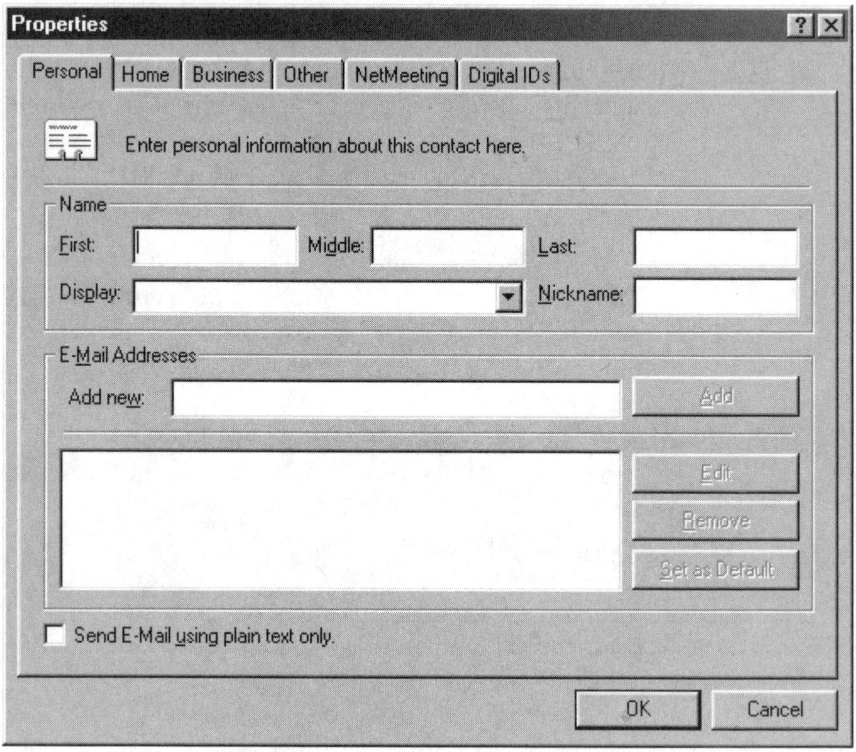

Fig. 11.65: Entering new contacts into Address Book

To save the different online numbers of a contact, use, depending on the contact type, the *Home, Business, Net-Meeting*, and *Digital IDs* tab pages. Enter all the required information on the various tab pages.

When you click the *OK* button the dialog box will close and the new contact is now a part of the *Address Book*.

Tip!

In the *New Mail* window, if you click on the *Address Book* button 📧 next to the *To, Cc* or *Bcc:*, the *Address Book* will always appear. You can then transfer an entry into the address line of the mail or enter a new address into the *Address Book* with a click on the *New Contact* button. A selected entry can be edited by clicking the *Properties* button.

Organizing Addresses in Address Book

In order to organize your addresses you always have to begin by starting *Microsoft Outlook Express*. Then bring up the *Address Book* by clicking on the *Address Book* icon 📖 on the toolbar, or by using the Ctrl+⇧+B key combination.

Details on the entry

The *Address Book* is a simple and convenient method of organizing postal addresses, fax numbers, phone numbers and E-mail addresses of people and companies on a small scale. You can get details on the displayed entries in the form of a *ScreenTip* by moving over the respective entry and waiting for a moment.

File/ Properties

With a double-click on the entry or by selecting the address and choosing *File/Properties*, you get all available tab pages in the *Properties* dialog box. Alternatively, the *Properties* button 📖 can be clicked if the address has been selected.

The information on the various tab pages can be overwritten and added to at any time. Confirm an entry by clicking the *OK* button and the changes will be saved.

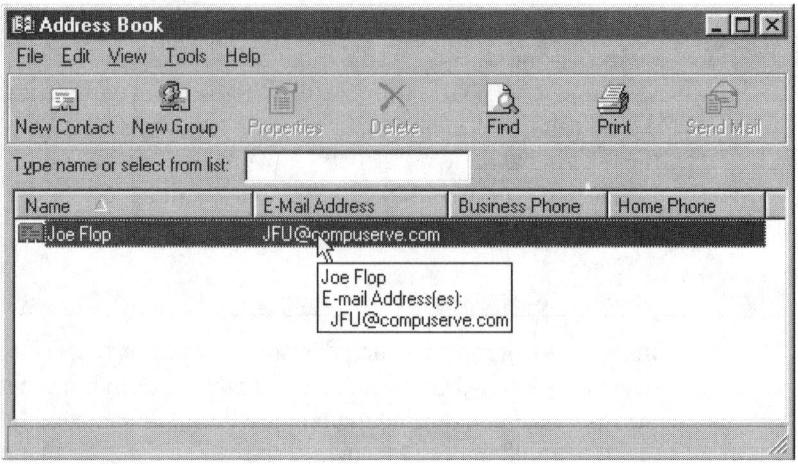

Fig. 11.66: Displaying additional information on selected entries

Deleting entries

To remove entries that you do not need anymore, select the entry and click the *Delete* button ⊠ or choose *File/Delete*. If you confirm the message that appears with *Yes,* then the entry will be deleted from the *Address Book*. If you have a lot of entries in the *Address Book,* you will appreciate the *Find* feature, which can be accessed by clicking on the *Find* button or choosing the *Edit/Find* command. The key combination for this is Ctrl+F. You can also click the *Find People* icon on the right window of the *Microsoft Outlook Express* main page to start the search function.

Finding addresses

Enter the desired name or a part of it into the respective text box and click the *Find Now* button.

Display matches

In the enlarged *Find People* dialog box all results are listed, as this is the case with all *Windows 98* search functions. If no entries are found, you will get the message, '*There are no entries in the Address Book that match your search criteria*'. Click the *OK* button and try again.

Tip! You do not have to search for the name of a person, you might remember just a part of the E-mail address or the street name. Just type it into the respective text box and *Find People* will find it for you.

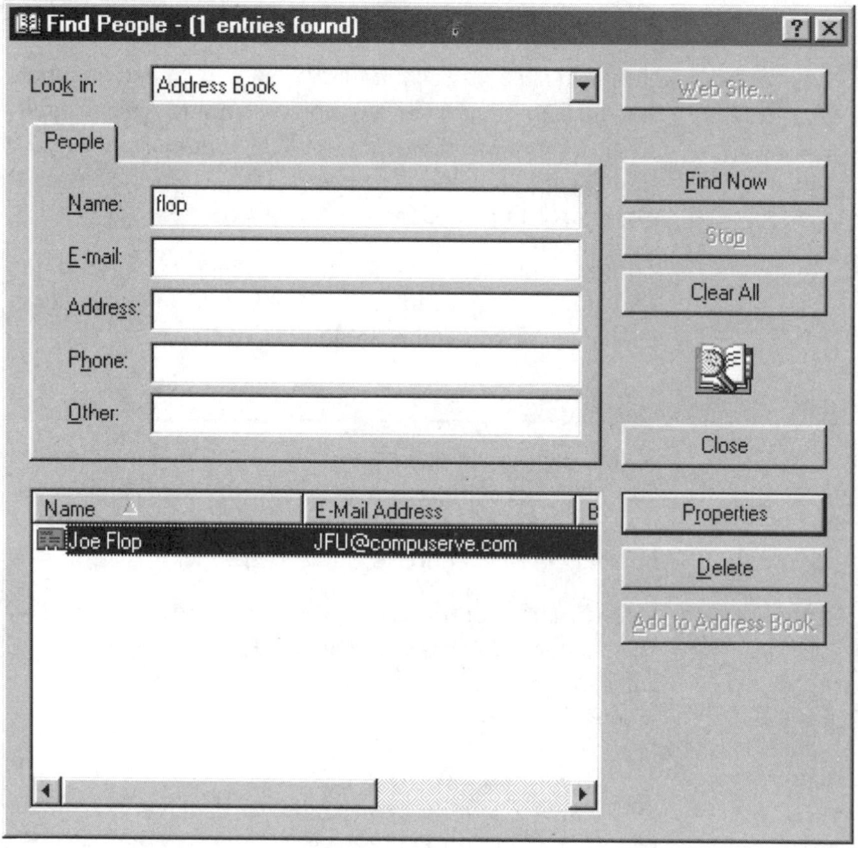

| **Find People - (1 entries found)** | ? X |

Look in: Address Book ▼ | Web Site...

| People |

Name: flop | Find Now

E-mail: | Stop

Address: | Clear All

Phone: |

Other: | Close

Name △	E-Mail Address	B	Properties
Joe Flop	JFU@compuserve.com		Delete
			Add to Address Book

Fig. 11.67:   Executing a search in Find People

Online search   The properties of the people that were found can be displayed by double-clicking on the result, or by first selecting the result and then clicking on the *Properties* button. With the *Find People*, feature you can also search for a particular person in an online database of E-mail addresses. Open the *Look in* list and select one of the available E-mail databases. Click the *Find Now* button to go online with *Dial-Up Networking*.

The Phone Dialer

You can also use *Windows 98* to dial phone numbers provided your modem has voice support. After establishing a connection you can either communicate via the sound card in your computer and a connected microphone or via the modem and headphone.

To dial a phone number in *Windows 98,* choose the *Phone Dialer* application. It not only looks like a modern telephone, it works like one too.

Dialing Numbers with Phone Dialer

In this section we will show you how to dial numbers. In the next section you learn how to store and recall numbers. Then you will be able to dial long phone numbers in their entirety with a single click.

Open *Start/Programs/Accessories/Communications* and choose the *Phone Dialer* application. To dial directly, enter the number into the text box or click the respective numbers on the key pad.

Separator for the
area code

To separate the area code from the rest of the number, you are allowed to use separators such as '-'. *Phone Dialer* will then just ignore them when dialing. Subsequently click the *Dial* button.

Windows will display the *Dialing* dialog box which gives information about the most important dialing properties and the status. If *Phone Dialer* cannot establish a connection, you will get a message box informing you of the same.

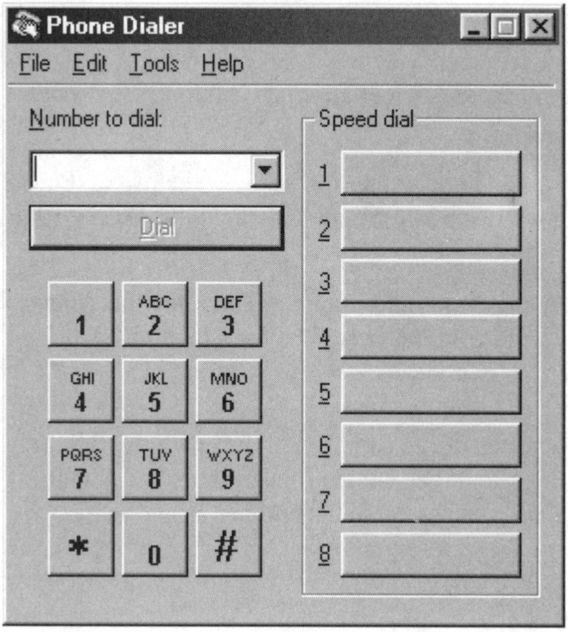

Fig. 11.68:   Dialing with Phone Dialer

Disconnecting

After establishing a connection, you can use the voice function of your modem and communicate via sound card and microphone or via the microphone on the modem.

To close the connection, click the *Hang Up* button in the *Dialing* dialog box. To configure the dialing properties either click the *Change Options* button or you use the *Telephony* option in the *Control Panel*.

Storing Frequently Used Phone Numbers in Phone Dialer

The *Phone Dialer* in *Windows 98* can be used for direct dialing. However, the application can also be used to store important phone numbers and later recall them with a single click on a button.

Storing phone
numbers

Launch *Phone Dialer*. If you want to enter and store a number in the speed dialing list, choose the *Edit/Speed Dial* command and select an empty button in the option group on top.

You can also click, in the application window of *Phone Dialer*, directly on an empty button in the *Speed Dial* option group.

Now enter the *name* and *phone number* for the connection. The name you put in will be used later as a label on the speed dial button. Click the *Save* button.

If you do not want to enter the number with the key pad, you can also use the buttons of the simulated phone of *Phone Dialer* and assemble the number using the mouse.

Programming and editing Speed Dial

Edit speed dial

To edit a number, choose the *Edit/Speed Dial* command again and select, in the *Edit Speed Dial* dialog box, the button you want to modify. Enter a new name and number into the respective text boxes. Click the *Save* button.

Deleting numbers

The same dialog box can be used to delete phone numbers. Just delete the name and the number and click the *Save* button. The label and functionality of the button will be removed.

To use a *Speed Dial* number, click the respective button. *Windows 98* displays the *Dialing* dialog box which shows the most important dialing properties and the status. If *Phone Dialer* cannot establish a connection, you will get an error message box informing you of this.

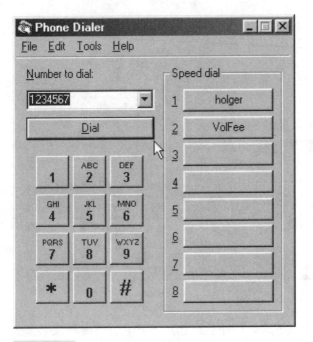

Fig. 11.70: Dialing a selected speed dial

Hang up button   To disconnect, click the *Hang Up* button in the *Dialing* dialog box. Close the *Phone Dialer* with *File/Exit*.

12. Paint

The *Windows 98* drawing program Paint enables you to conveniently draw up your own pixel graphics. To create a drawing use the basic geometric shapes, out of which forms proceed to grow. Of course you could also choose to draw your lines free-hand or employ the spray can.

You will read about how to copy, move or delete selected areas of a picture in Paint and about how you can create colored objects, overwrite them and use the *Zoom* tool. Further themes in this chapter include the stretching and skewing of parts of images and the creation of an independent background image in Paint.

Drawing with Paint

In this section we will introduce in detail the different drawing options available.

Tool Box

To get into the drawing program move through *Start/ Programs/Accessories* and choose *Paint*. The drawing tools used in *Paint* are contained in the *Tool Box* on the left border of the window.

ScreenTip

The function of most drawing tools is described either by name or button labels. To find out the name of a tool, leave the mouse pointer over the tool button for about a second until a *ScreenTip* appears containing this information.

Selecting a
drawing tool

To select a drawing tool, just click on the appropriate button. Paint will provide additional information in the status bar about the meaning or function of the tool selected.

If the *Tool Box* does not appear on your screen, you can go to the *View* menu to display it.

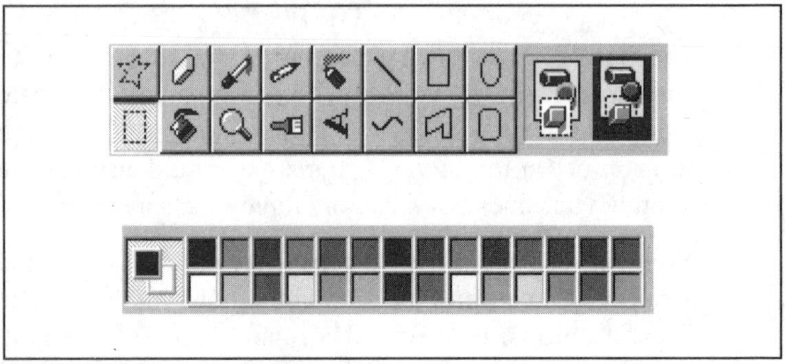

Fig. 12.1:   The *Tool Box* (turned 90°) and the Paint Color Box

Rectangles and ellipses

Using the *Rectangle* button ▣ you can draw rectangles and squares, while with the *Ellipse* button ◯ you can draw circles and ellipses. Using other buttons you can draw rectangles with rounded corners, lines and curves as well as polygons. But now let's move on to drawing with Paint.

Drawing

Select a tool before you start drawing. Point onto the drawing area and click and hold down the mouse button. Drag the mouse until the object reaches the desired size and shape.

Squares and circles

As soon as you release the mouse button, the object is created. If you want squares or circles instead of rectangles and ellipses, you must also hold down the ⬙ key on the keyboard while you draw.

Outlines

With the default setting, the tools only give you outlines. To create a filled object with an outline, or an object without an outline, select the corresponding option in the *Tool Box Options*.

This box is displayed below the *Tool Box* buttons after a tool has been selected. Select a tool and choose the line thickness or fill mode from the *Tool Box Options* using the mouse.

Drawing straight lines

In order to draw straight lines use the *Line* button ◥. By selecting the tool, the options for the line tool will appear automatically in the *Tool Box Options* area. From here you can select the thickness of the line. Start the beginning of the line by pressing the mouse button and draw the line while holding the mouse button down. For horizontal lines, vertical lines, or lines at 45 degree increments, keep the ⬚ key pressed at the same time.

Free-form lines can be drawn in whatever shape you want using the *Pencil* tool ✎. Vertical or horizontal lines can be obtained by holding down the ⬚ key. To draw lines with a different thickness use the *Brush* button ▮, and select the thickness from the options under the *Tool Box*.

Drawing curved lines

Using the *Curve* button ⟨ you can draw curved lines. For simple curves press and hold down the mouse button at the point where the curve should start and drag the mouse to the end point of the curve. Then release the mouse button. Now move the mouse to somewhere near the line and press and hold down the mouse button to pull the line into a curve. You can determine the curve by moving the mouse. Click once more on the drawing page, and the curve will be drawn.

Polygons can be drawn using the *Polygon* button ▱. In the *Tool Box Options* you can determine whether you only want outlined or solid polygons. Click and hold down the mouse button at the starting point of the first line in the polygon.

Closing polygons

Draw the first line by dragging the mouse to the end position of the line and releasing the mouse button. Press and hold down the mouse button once again and proceed to draw the next line. The end of each line is marked by releasing the mouse button.

To complete the polygon click onto the point of origin again. An alternative way to close a polygon is to double-click at the end of the last line. Paint then draws a straight line between the position of the cursor and the point of origin.

Sprayed free-form lines

Colored spots in the form of dots are made by using the *Airbrush* button. By holding down the mouse button you create the effect of sprayed free-form lines. Select the spray size from the available options. The color-density depends on how quickly the mouse is moved over the area.

Inserting text

In order to label elements in a drawing, use the *Text* button A. Click on the position where you want to place the text and a text frame with the *Fonts* toolbar will appear. It is also possible to draw the frame in the desired size right from the start.

Type your text into the frame. To format the text use the buttons on the *Text* toolbar (accessible via *Text Toolbar* on the *View* menu). If you make a mistake while entering your text press the ← key. For longer texts press the ↵ key at the end of a sentence.

Bold, italic or underlined

When the text reaches the right side of the text frame, *Paint* automatically wraps the text onto the next line. You should select the font and text style (*Bold, Italic* or *Underlined*) from the *Text* toolbar while the text frame is visible.

Tip!

Clicking outside the text frame or selecting another tool button fixes the text so it cannot be changed. Drawing mistakes can be corrected using *Edit/Undo*. You can save at any stage in the execution of the drawing by selecting *File/Save*. This way, when you make a mistake, you can reload the last saved version.

Selecting Color for Outlines or Filling

By default, Paint generally draws only black outlines and fills objects in black. However, if you wish to use a different color, you can select the color before drawing the object. It is also possible to fill previously drawn closed objects with a color.

Color Box

To select a color before you draw, use the *Color Box*. This is located just above the status bar and contains 28 colors. To the left of the colors the current *foreground color* and *background color* are displayed.

The current foreground color is displayed in the foreground box. This is the color used to draw lines or outlines of geometric shapes. The foreground color is used for anything drawn using the left mouse button. The background box displays the current background color.

Foreground and background color

You can draw or fill objects with the background color using the right mouse button. To select a color, simply click on the color swatch. Click the left mouse button to define the foreground color, and press the right mouse button to set the background color.

Fig 12.2: *Fill With Color* tool (upper left), *Tool Box Options* and *Color Box* (below)

| Right mouse button | New colors only affect newly drawn objects. Objects drawn with the left mouse button are always filled in with the current background color, while the outlines are shown in the foreground color. If you use the right mouse button to draw you will invert these colors, i.e., the outlines will appear in the background color and the objects will be filled in with the foreground color. |

| Subsequent coloring | To subsequently color shapes or closed outlines already drawn in Paint, use the *Fill With Color* tool 🖾. Click on the *Fill With Color* button 🖾 and select the foreground color by clicking with the left mouse button on any color in the *Color Box*. |

| Fill With Color | Point into a closed object on the drawing page and click. The current color will fill the shape. To color the object with the background color use the *Fill With Color* tool 🖾 and use the right mouse button instead. |

Using Paint to Select, Copy, Move and Delete

Even if an object is needed more than once in a Paint picture, it still needs to be drawn only once. Then it can be copied as many times as required.

Location	The location of a drawn object is not fixed. A free-standing object that is already drawn can be moved around to any location within the drawing page at any time. If you have drawn an item that is not up to your satisfaction, you can delete it whenever you like.
Selecting objects	For any of the above mentioned procedures, select the object in question. Optimally, the object should be a free-standing item on the drawing page, so that it does not affect the elements of the drawing under it.
Selection tools	Paint offers two special tools for the selection of items in a drawing. The *Free-Form Select* button ▨ is located right at the top of the *Tool Box*. This allows you to select parts of a picture in several ways.
Free-Form Select button	Using the *Free-Form Select* button ▨ you can select a free-form area within the picture. To do this, hold down the mouse button and draw a line around the item to be selected. When you release the mouse button, the line becomes a selection rectangle that encloses the item. However, the free-form line you have drawn still defines the outline of the selected area.
Select button	You can select a rectangular area by using the *Select* tool ▨. Press and hold down the mouse button down while drawing the selection rectangle. Elements or items of a drawing that have been selected· using the *Free-Form Select* button ▨ or the *Select* button ▨ always have dotted outlines (see Figure 12.3, left). The selected object can now be moved anywhere in the *Paint* drawing area with the mouse button held down.
Moving a selection	Moving a selection by default happens on an opaque background. Select *Draw Opaque* in the *Image* menu for the background of the selected object to become transparent, and to make all elements with the current background color transparent.

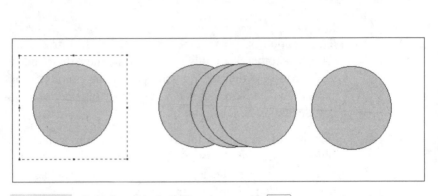

Fig 12.3:   Selecting objects (left) and copy with `Ctrl`

Deleting objects

To delete the selected object or the selected drawing area, press the `Del` key. Should the selection be located within another drawn object, you will be left with an empty either rectangular or free-form area that will have the color of the background (by default, *White*).

Cancelling selection

A selection can be cancelled at any time by clicking anywhere on the drawing area outside the selected rectangle. On every selection frame, you have eight resize handles that enable you to skew or stretch, enlarge or reduce the selection by clicking and dragging the mouse over one of them.

Copying objects

Selected objects can be copied onto the clipboard by using *Edit/Copy* or with `Ctrl`+`C`. An alternative is to select the *Copy* command from the context menu. Using *Edit/Paste* or the key combination `Ctrl`+`V`, objects can be pasted any number of times into *Paint* or any other Windows application.

Insertion point

In *Paint* the insertion point is always in the upper-left corner. The inserted element is automatically contained within a selection frame by which it can be dragged. If you press the `Ctrl` key during the drag, you produce a copy of the selection, leaving the original unchanged.

Cutting objects

Using the *Cut* command on the *Edit* menu, the context menu, or the key combination ⌈Ctrl⌋+⌊X⌋, a selected area can be removed from *Paint* and stored in the clipboard. From there it can be inserted any number of times.

Tip!

Pressing the ⌊⇧⌋ key while you are moving a selection causes the selection to be copied uninterruptedly. This process is known as dragging and creates an interesting looking effect with the selected object copying itself in a trail which follows the movement of the mouse.

Drawing Opaque or Using Insert in Paint

In Paint, drawn objects can be moved to any part of the drawing area. Any element of a Paint drawing that is repeatedly used can be drawn just once and then copied any number of times.

Draw Opaque

The inserted copies can be relocated anywhere within the drawing area. In the Paint default opaque drawing mode, the selection will completely cover the image beneath it. (see Figure 12.4, right). This may not always be you want. To turn off the opaque mode, select *Draw Opaque* from the *Image* menu.

Transparent mode

In this mode of Paint, any area of the selected rectangle that is drawn in the current background color will remain visible beneath the moved object.

Free-form selection

Select the desired section from the drawing. Using the *Free-Form Select* ⊡ you can select portions of the picture by drawing a free-form line. To achieve this, keep the mouse button pressed down as you move around the object. Upon releasing the button, the line encloses the object and appears in the form of a dotted rectangle.

The selection is still defined by the free-form line, it just appears rectangular.

Select tool

Using the *Select* tool ▣ you can select rectangular areas in a picture. Keeping the mouse button pressed, you can move the selection to its new location (Figure.12.4, left).

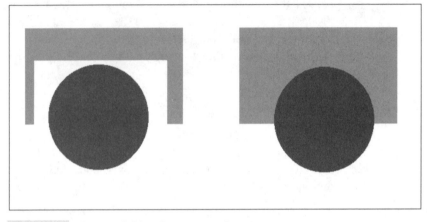

Opaque (left) and transparent inserts

Elements of a drawing that have been selected with the *Select* button ▣ are outlined by a rectangular selection frame. When you move the selection, the place where the object originally was is filled in with the background color.

New background color

If you select a new background color and move the selection, the original location of the selection will now be colored in the new background color.

Tip!

The *Opaque Drawing* command also affects objects inserted from the clipboard using *Edit/Paste* or the Ctrl+V key combination.

Zooming in and out in Paint

Every Paint object consists of individual pixels. Corrections in Paint are made by deleting or overwriting these pixels.

Precision select pointer

Sometimes it is quite difficult to find the exact start- or end-point of a new object with the precision select pointer.

If you wish to work with a greater level of precision, you will have to zoom into the picture. Paint, with a maximum zoom-in of 800 per cent, enables you to do this very well indeed.

Zoom command

To enlarge your drawing, select *Zoom* from the *View* menu. The submenu displays a variety of zoom options from which to choose.

Large Size command

The *Large Size* command enlarges the view by 400 per cent. You can use *Custom Zoom* for a custom zoom per cent. In the *Custom Zoom* dialog box you have five options to choose from ranging between 100 and 800 per cent.

New zoom sizing

Select one of the available radio buttons in the *Zoom to* option group with a mouse click and confirm your selection by clicking on *OK*. The new zoom percentage will be implemented.

Fig. 12.5:   Selecting the Zoom factor and options of the magnifying glass(below)

Tip!

A more direct way of enlarging the view is by using the *Magnifier* button . Select the button and a frame appears on the drawing area which indicates the section that to be enlarged. Move the frame to the desired area and click to enlarge it. The zoom factor of the *Magnifier* can be selected in the *Tool Box Options*.

Working pixel
by pixel

Detailed work can be done most effectively under zoom factors between *600% (6 x* in the *Tool Box Options* of the *Magnifier* tool) and *800%* (*8 x*). To work with pixel-level precision, use the *Pencil* button .

Normal size

To return to a 1:1 view, select *View/Zoom* and from the submenu click *Normal Size*, or if the magnifier is selected, click on *1 x* in the *Tool Box Options*.

Selecting Picture Size in Paint

Every time you open Paint through *Programs/Accessories* on the *Start* menu you are offered a new empty drawing area. You can draw anywhere on the white surface. If you enlarge the Paint application window using the *Maximize* button, the drawing area will occupy the whole screen.

Drawing area

As you can see, the drawing area extends to the frame of the *Paint* application window. In reality the drawing area is even larger, which can be recognized by the scroll bars.

Unnecessary
memory

If you only draw a small object, the greater part of the drawing area remains empty. So far so good. However, saving such a picture may be a problem. As Paint saves the entire drawing area, you will be taking up unnecessary disk space. Apart from that, the small object cannot be isolated from the large image if you want to insert it into another Windows application, such as the programs of the Microsoft Office Suite.

Full size
insertion

In that case, the Paint file is inserted in its full size (including the white area). This effect however, can be eliminated by defining the picture size in Paint. To do this, select the *Attributes* command from the *Image* menu, or press the Ctrl+E key combination.

Attributes
dialog box

In the *Attributes* dialog box, Paint displays the current size of the picture in the current measurement unit. The unit of measurement should be set to *Pixels*. The default values correspond exactly to the resolution with which you are working.

On a VGA display, that would be equivalent to 640 x 480 pixels, at a resolution of 1024 x 768. These values would appear in the *Width* and *Height* text boxes.

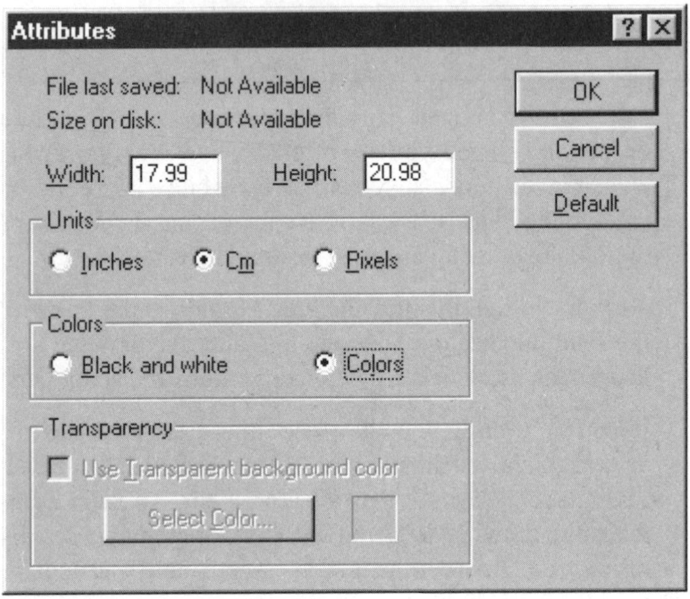

Attributes `?` `X`

File last saved: Not Available
Size on disk: Not Available

Width: `17.99`   Height: `20.98`

OK

Cancel

Default

Units
○ Inches   ⊙ Cm   ○ Pixels

Colors
○ Black and white   ⊙ Colors

Transparency
☐ Use Transparent background color
Select Color...

Fig. 12.6:   Changing picture-size in Paint through *Image/Attributes*

Width and *Height*
text boxes

To determine the new size of the picture in pixels, select the *Pixels* radio button in the *Units* option group box, and enter the desired values in the *Width* and *Height* text boxes. Then confirm with *OK*. Should you prefer to define the area in centimeters, select the *Cm* radio button instead, and enter your values in centimeters in the *Width* and *Height* text boxes before clicking *OK*.

Should you insert an image from the clipboard that is larger than the defined drawing area, you will get a message box which you must confirm with *Yes*, otherwise the picture will be chopped to the size of the drawing area.

Special Effects in Paint

Images you have drawn yourself, as well as other pictures opened in *Paint,* can be flipped, rotated, skewed or stretched. The same applies to selected areas.

Flipping and Rotating Selected Areas

The rotation of objects or selected picture areas is always effected in fixed gradients of 90, 180 or 270 degrees. The picture or selected element of an image is always rotated around an imaginary vertical or horizontal center-line.

Selecting
picture area

Selection areas should be defined before implementing the *Flip* or *Rotate* commands, since otherwise the command will affect the entire picture. Use the *Free-Form Select* tool 🔲 or the *Select* tool 🔲 from the *Tool Box* to select only certain elements in a drawing to be rotated or inverted.

Free-Form Select

Using the *Free-Form Select*, select any area of the drawing in the shape of a free-form line. To do this, keep the mouse button pressed as you draw the line around the object in question. Upon releasing the mouse button, the line will take the shape of a closed rectangle. The selection itself, however, is still defined by the free-form outline drawn by hand. Using the *Select* tool 🔲 with the mouse button pressed enables you to make rectangular selections of picture areas.

Flip and Rotate
dialog box

Next, select the *Flip/Rotate* command either from the *Image* menu or from the context menu. Alternatively, you can also make the *Flip and Rotate* dialog box appear by using the Ctrl+R key combination.

Flipping horizontal or vertical

To flip a picture or parts of a picture from left to right, select the *Flip horizontal* radio button, and confirm with *OK*. Supposing you want to have a picture upside-down, select the *Flip vertical* radio button and confirm with *OK*.

Flip and Rotate ? ✕

Flip or rotate
- ⦿ Flip horizontal
- ○ Flip vertical
- ○ Rotate by angle
  - ⦿ 90°
  - ○ 180°
  - ○ 270°

[OK]
[Cancel]

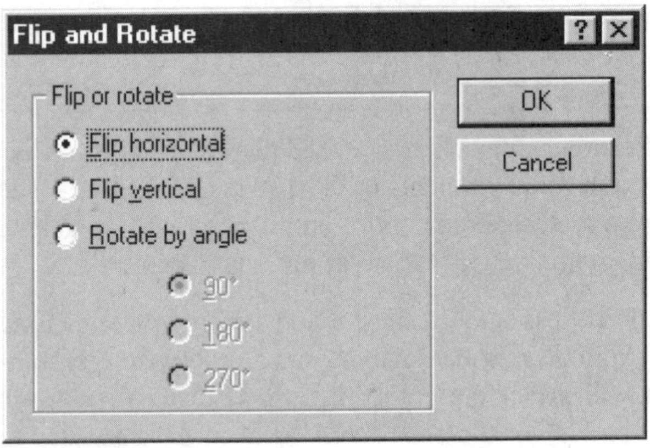

Fig. 12.7:   Flipping pictures vertically or horizontally

Degrees set by default

In order to rotate parts of pictures or entire images by a predetermined setting, select the *Flip/Rotate* command on the *Image* menu or on the shortcut menu. As an alternative, you can also press the Ctrl+R key combination.

Select the *Rotate by angle* option, and then click on one of the radio buttons presented, either *90, 180* or *270* degrees. Confirm with *OK* to perform the rotation.

Stretching and Skewing Pictures in Paint

Pictures you created yourself, images opened in Paint, and selected areas can be stretched and skewed using the image manipulation functions. Stretched objects will become either longer or narrower, or taller or narrower.

Skewing a selected area or picture, however, will tilt it to the left or right, or upward or downward.

Stretch and skew

Before you activate the *Stretch/Skew* command, make sure that you have selected the desired area of the picture. Otherwise the command will affect the entire image.

If only certain elements need to be stretched or skewed, use either the *Free-Form Select* 🔲 or *Select* 🔲 tools in the *Tool Box* to select these areas.

Selection tools

You can select any picture area using the *Free-Form Select* 🔲 by drawing a free-form line. Keep the mouse button pressed while you draw a line around the object to be selected.

Upon releasing the mouse button, the selection will appear as a rectangle fully enclosing the line you drew. The selected area, however, is still defined by the drawn line. Using the *Select* 🔲 tool, you can select rectangular areas of a picture.

Stretch/Skew command

Next, from the *Image* menu or the context menu, select the *Stretch/Skew* command. As an alternative, you can press the Ctrl+W key combination to call up the *Stretch and Skew* dialog box.

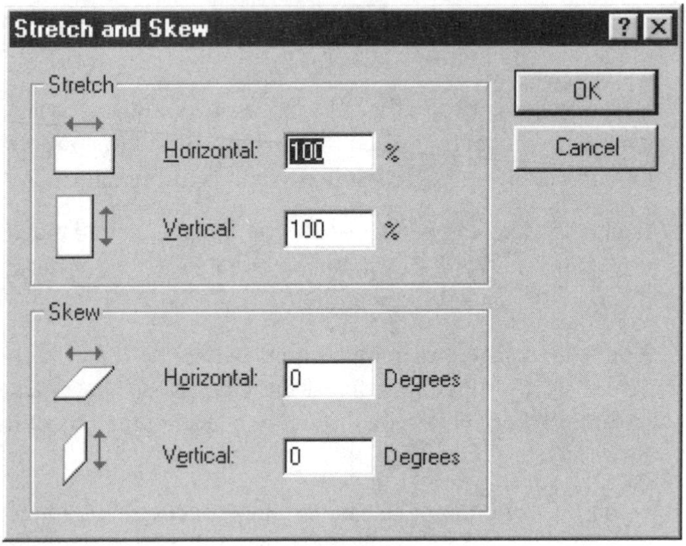

Fig. 12.8:   Objects can be stretched or skewed

Horizontal option

To stretch the selected area or the entire picture horizontally, click on the *Horizontal* text box in the *Stretch* group box, and enter the required percentage. Numbers less than 100% decrease the size, while numbers greater than 100% increase the size. Confirm with *OK*.

Vertical option

However, should you wish to stretch the selected area or the entire picture vertically, click on the *Vertical* text box in the *Stretch* group box and specify the appropriate percentage. Numbers less than 100 decrease the size while numbers greater than 100 increase the size. Confirm with *OK*.

Tilting parts
of a picture

If you want to skew a selected area or the entire picture, select the *Stretch/Skew* command from the *Image* menu, or from the context menu.

Alternatively, you can also use the ⌈Ctrl⌋+⌈W⌋ key combination to call up the *Stretch and Skew* dialog box. To skew the selected area or the entire picture to the right, click on *Horizontal* text box in the *Skew* group box and specify the number of degrees. Positive numbers skew the object to the right.

Negative numbers Negative numbers skew the selection or image to the left. Once you have entered the required value, confirm the command with *OK*. To skew the selected area or the entire picture vertically, click on the *Vertical* text box in the *Skew* group box and specify the number of degrees. Positive numbers skew the image upward. Negative numbers skew the selection downward. To perform the skewing, click *OK*.

Tip! There are eight resize handles on every selection frame. By keeping the mouse button depressed, you can use the pointer over a resize handle to stretch the selection, or increase or decrease the size manually.

Opening, Saving and Printing Paint Drawings

Not only can you produce and save your own drawings in Paint, but you can also open already existing bitmap images. The opened picture can then be edited and saved again. This is also useful when you want to insert a selection from an image into another program.

Opening Drawings in Paint

To open a bitmap in Paint, select the *Open* command from the *File* menu. By default, the *My Documents* folder is displayed up in the *Open* dialog box, and the *Files of type* drop-down box is set to *Bitmap Files (*.bmp)*.

Bitmap files

If you do not have any of your own bitmaps, switch to the Windows folder and use the scroll bar to scroll through the background images available. Windows 98 marks image files with the ▓ icon.

Selecting from list box

Suppose you have images, stored on a CD-ROM, you want to view in Paint. Click the drop-down button of the *Look in* box and move to the drive and folder that contain the desired files. Select a bitmap and click on the *Open* button. As an alternative, a file in the *Open* dialog box can also be opened with a double click or, after selecting it, by pressing the ⏎ key.

Various graphic formats

Images can be stored in many graphic formats. Paint supports three of the most common picture formats. Images in other formats can be opened with the *Imaging* application. This must, however, be explicitly installed first, and then it can be accessed through *Programs/Accessories*.

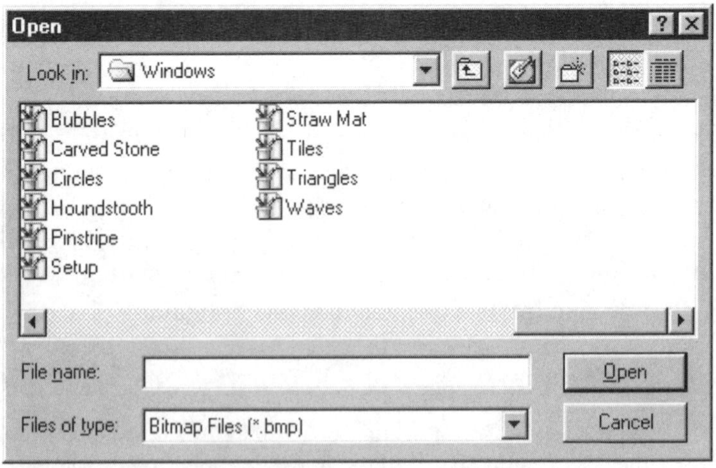

Fig. 12.9:   Opening bitmap files in Paint

Bitmap files

file type

The first format in the *Files of type* drop-down box is *Paint's* preferred and default format. The Windows file type *Bitmap Files* uses the file extension *BMP*. The default background pictures of the desktop are stored in this format.

GIF-format

Secondly, we have the *Graphics Interchange Format (GIF)* Internet format, which you find presently on many Websites and which was developed by the online service *CompuServe* for the purpose of graphic data transfer. The other compressed pixel format available that is also used on the Internet is called *JPEG*. The file extension for this is *JPG*.

Tip!

Officially Paint can only open and save pictures in these formats. There's a little trick, however, that you can use to open the widespread picture format *TIF* (*Tagged Image Format*). From the *Open* dialog box, select the *All files* entry from the *Files of type* drop-down box. Find and select a *TIF* file and click *Open*. The picture is then opened in Paint.

Saving a Selected Area of a Paint Drawing

If you draw only a small object in Paint, the greater part of the drawing area remains white. In the process of saving this white area is also saved pixel by pixel, since Paint always saves the entire drawing area.

Unnecessary

memory

The drawbacks to this are, firstly, that it occupies unnecessary memory, and secondly, you cannot take the object alone and insert it into another Windows application, for example as a logo in a letter created with WordPad.

Insert/Object

command

Should you proceed to insert such a file using *Insert/Object* into another program, the Paint file in its full size, white area and all, would be inserted. To avoid this, you could define the picture area in Paint, but you could also use a special method so as to save only selected areas of a picture.

Save a selection

To do this, draw the graphic which you want to save separately in any part of the Paint drawing area. Of course you can also open an already existing picture from which you want to save a selected area under a separate name.

Selecting an area

Select the desired area of the picture. Do this by selecting *View/Zoom/Custom...*, or use the *Magnifier* button 🔍 to obtain an enlarged picture which can be selected more easily with pixel accuracy. To save the selection, choose *Edit/Copy To*. Change to the target drive and folder, and give the selection a name in the *File name* text box. You can enter the color intensity (if necessary) of the picture in the drop-down box titled *Save as type*. Paint will then save only the selection, without the surrounding drawing area.

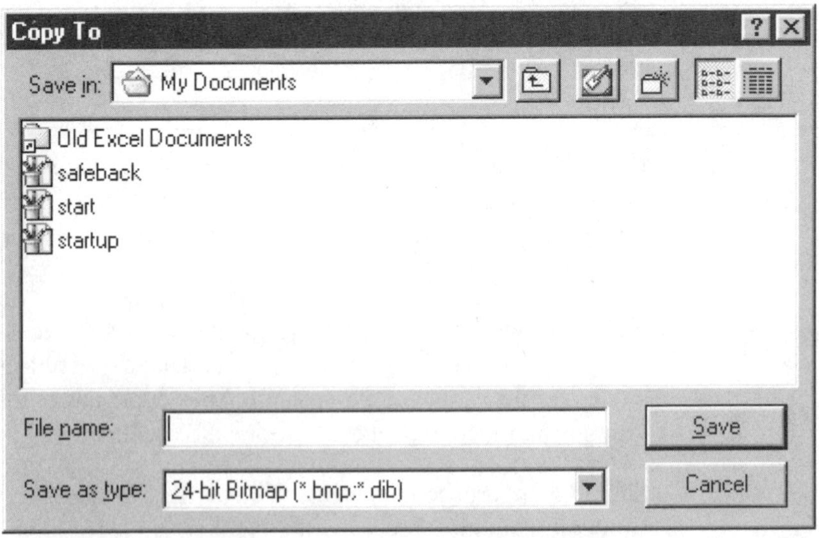

Fig. 12.10:   Saving selected objects with the *Copy to* command

> **Tip!** If you want to insert a selection from Paint into another application, the selection can be sent to the clipboard and inserted at the cursor position using *Edit/Insert*. This way you do not need to save it first.

Saving Drawings in *Paint*

Save As
dialog box

In order to save your own pictures or altered files in Paint, go to the *File* menu, and select the *Save As* command.

In the *Save As* dialog box enter a name of not more than 255 characters in the *File name* text box.

File names can contain upper and lower case letters/characters as well as spaces. Use the *Save in* drop-down box to switch to the target drive and target folder.

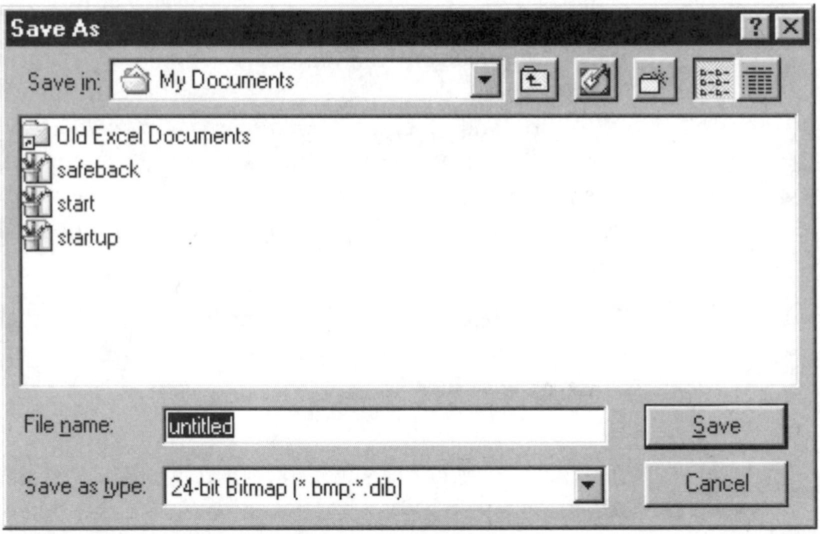

Fig. 12.11:   Saving a Paint drawing as a bitmap file

Specifying file type

Now simply specify the file type in the *Save as type* drop-down box. Using the *Save as type* drop-down box you can specify the image format of the file, as well as the color depth of the picture. In the case of pictures you have drawn yourself without custom color palettes, it is recommended to use the *256 Color Bitmap (*.bmp)* entry.

Color depth

This color depth is sufficient in most cases and saves a lot of memory. Color photographs or edited areas of high resolution images, however, should be saved under *24-bit Bitmap (*.bmp)*.

If you want to save pictures for the Internet, for instance for your personal homepage, you should use one of the compressed picture file types, *JPEG (JPG)* or *Graphics Interchange Format (GIF)*. To save the picture, click the *Save* button.

Tip!

By default, Paint saves bitmap images under *24-bit Bitmap* (which corresponds to 16.8 million colors), but it can also save with a color depth of 8, 4 and 2 bits. This corresponds to 256, 16 and 2 colors (*Monochrome Bitmap*). The number of colors directly defines the amount of memory needed. You can also save Paint drawings in the widespread *TIF*-format. To do so, simply enter '.*TIF*' after the file name.

JPEG (JPG) and *GIF* images can be displayed in Internet Explorer, or inserted into FrontPage Express for the composition of Web sites.

Tip!

After the first save, use the command *File/Save* or the convenient Ctrl+S key combination for further intermediate saving. Save any changes made during the editing of a Paint image. The already existing file will always be overwritten by the newer version.

Printing Drawings from *Paint*

Printing drawing

Drawings that you have created with Paint can be printed at any time. To do this, you need a printer attached to your computer and installed under *Windows 98*. Read the relevant section in Chapter 8 to find out more.

To print a drawing in Paint, select the *Print* command from the *File* menu to call up the *Print* dialog box. The printing process is identical in all Windows applications. If you have several printers attached to your computer, the *Name* drop-down box will display the default printer set in the *Printers* folder.

Setting the printer

Open the *Name* drop-down box in the *Printer* options group and select the printer you wish to use. A color printer is recommended for making printouts from Paint.

Setting the print range

In the *Print range* options group you can set the pictures to be printed. The option *All*, which is set by default, will print the entire contents of the picture.

Should you activate *Pages,* only the pages between the values entered in the *from* and *to* text boxes will be printed. Unfortunately, Paint does not display a preview of the distribution of a large drawing over several pages.

Print   ? ✕

Printer

Name: HP LaserJet 4L ▼   Properties

Status: Ready
Type: HP LaserJet 4L
Where: LPT1:
Comment: ☐ Print to file

Print range

◉ All

○ Pages   from: 1   to:

○ Selection

Copies

Number of copies: 1

☐ Collate

OK   Cancel

Fig. 12.12:   The *Print* dialog box

Setting number of copies

In the *Copies* option group, you can enter the number of copies to be printed into the *Number of copies* spin box. If your printer supports the collate function, select the *Collate* check box. Begin the printing process with *OK*.

Graphics tab page

As long as you print from the Paint drawing program, the settings on the *Graphics* tab page in the *Properties* dialog box of your printer are used. These settings can also be obtained through the *Print* dialog box by clicking on the *Properties* button.

To do this, click *Properties* in the *Printer* group box. That will open the *[Printer] Properties* dialog box.

Switch from the *Paper* tab to the *Graphics* tab page, which will appear similar to the *Windows 98* printer driver illustration in Figure 12.13.

Modifying properties for graphics printing

Tip!

If you have not installed a *Windows 98* printer driver, the tab page may have a completely different set-up. Should you encounter printing problems, choose the *Use raster graphics* radio button on the *Graphics* tab page.

Dithering

Most *Windows 98* printer drivers allow you to choose from different types of dithering such as *None, Coarse, Fine, Line art* and *Error diffusion*.

Error diffusion

The *Error diffusion* option provides a highly sophisticated printing result, even with a laser printer. Ultimately, it is by trial and error that you can find out what works best. The *Intensity* slider allows you to regulate the brightness of the printout. Confirm the changes by clicking the *OK* button.

Creating a Background Picture for the Desktop with Paint

Every drawing that you make with the Paint drawing program that is shipped with Windows can be used as a background image for the desktop. You may already have tried out the packaged background pictures, which offer you a variety of shapes and images, none of which can compare to one of your own pictures, of course.

Save a background picture

Before you save a background picture for the desktop, you must allow your imagination to run free and create a drawing in *Paint*. To do this click the *Start* button and then choose *Programs/Accessories/Paint*. Use the above-mentioned tools to create your very own desktop picture.

Setting attributes

Should you wish to draw only a small picture, use the *Image/Attributes* command to readjust the size of the drawing space.

Tip!

By default, Paint sets the picture size at the number of pixels of your screen resolution, for example 1024 x 768 pixels. But Paint cannot display the entire drawing area in one go. Should you wish to produce a picture that fills the entire screen, remember to use the scroll bar to scroll to the hidden parts of the picture.

File name

Once you have completed the picture, save it by selecting *File/Save*. Go to a folder of your choice (for example *My Documents*), and enter any file name you choose for it in the *File name* text box. Then click *Save*. You can now place the background picture on the desktop.

Set As Wallpaper command

To do this, go to the *File* menu and select the *Set As Wallpaper (Centered)* command. If you have only drawn a very small picture, then select *Set As Wallpaper (Tiled)* instead. The tiled effect is only visible if the picture is smaller than the desktop.

Minimize all windows

Now click the right mouse button on the taskbar and select the *Minimize All Windows* entry in the shortcut menu. View the desktop which now contains your picture as a background. Then close down Paint if you are satisfied by right-clicking on the Paint button and selecting *Close* from the context menu.

Tip!

If you do not like the picture you made as a background for the desktop, you can remove it. To do so, go to the *Control Panel*, double-click on the *Display* icon and choose *(None)* in the *Wallpaper* group box on the *Background* tab page.

Working with the Clipboard Application

The Clipboard serves as an intermediary for data exchange between applications. In *Windows 98* you can also use the Clipboard to copy or paste objects between folders. The clipboard is essentially an invisible buffer memory, the contents of which are lost when the computer is turned off. The Clipboard is one of the most important Windows features and is available on every computer.

Clipboard

The *Copy*, *Cut* and *Paste* commands are always available to you irrespective of the installation. This section, however, deals with the Clipboard application which you can use to view the contents of the memory buffer.

This Windows component is not installed by default, but you can install it later on.

Before you proceed with the following instructions, you should check to see if the Clipboard program is already available on your PC. You can do this by selecting *Start/Programs/Accessories* and opening the *System Tools* program group.

If the Clipboard has been installed, the Clipboard program icon will appear somewhere on the *System Tools* menu. If this is not the case, proceed as follows.

Installing the *Clipboard* Application

In the *Start* menu, select the *Settings* command and click on *Control Panel* in the submenu. This calls up the *Control Panel* folder. Double-click the *Add/Remove Programs* icon, and in the *Add/Remove Programs Properties* dialog box, switch to the *Windows Setup* tab page.

Using the scroll bar move to the *System Tools* item in the *Components* list box. Click on the *System Tools* entry, and click the *Details* button.

Components list

Once again use the scroll bar to move through the *Components* list box. Now click on the check box to the left of the *Clipboard Viewer* item.

Fig. 12.14: Installing the Clipboard application

Insert your *Windows 98* Setup CD-ROM into the CD-ROM drive and click *OK*. The data will be copied. Next, close the *Control Panel*.

Viewing the Clipboard

Starting
Clipboard

To call up the Clipboard program, select *Start/Programs/ Accessories* and open the *System Tools* program group. Click on the *Clipboard* item on the *System Tools* menu. The Clipboard application window appears.

Fig. 12.15:   Viewing the contents of the *Clipboard*

Bitmap of Windows
Desktop

Now just press the [PrtScr] key to copy the contents of your display onto the clipboard. In the Clipboard application window, you will see a bitmap of your Windows desktop. Using the [Alt]+[PrtScr] you take a snapshot of the active window on the *Windows 98* desktop.

The Clipboard can also be used for copying folders and files. In this case, the Clipboard program displays the path as text.

13. Word processing with Windows 98 and Office 97

In this chapter, we will discuss word processing in *Windows 98*. A simple word processing program is included in the *Windows 98* accessories. For basic word processing, the functions offered by WordPad are usually sufficient, considering that the methods for entering, selecting, copying and pasting text are the same as those used in the professional programs of the *Microsoft Office Suite*.

Now you know why we have given this chapter the heading 'Word processing with *Windows 98* and *Office 97*'. Should you be working with *Windows 98*, without an additional word processing program, then read the corresponding sections to learn about the different program functions.

Tip!

Suppose you already have the Microsoft Office 97 Suite installed on your computer: you can directly use the Microsoft Word word processing program for your correspondence. If there are any differences with Word-Pad, these will be summarized at the end of a section in a *Tip* such as this one.

Entering text

Do not expect this to be a typing lesson. We regret being unable to help you press the right keys!

Entering text

In this section we will tell you about certain things you should be aware of while entering text into a word processing program such as WordPad or Microsoft Word.

This will enable you to avoid making the mistakes which beginners usually make.

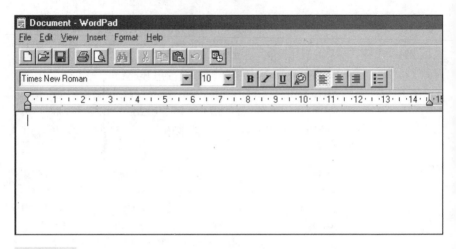

Fig. 13.1: In WordPad the text cursor blinks in the upper left corner

After you start WordPad the text cursor will blink in the upper left corner of the working area. When entering text in WordPad, start by exercizing care with the *Enter* key.

On the computer keyboard this key looks like this: ⏎. And unlike on a typewriter, you should not press the ⏎ key at the end of each line in WordPad. Word processing programs such as WordPad or Word employ an automatic *word wrap*.

Automatic
word wrap

Whenever you come to the end of a line, WordPad automatically moves the text which no longer fits on that line to the next line. This way you can enter your entire letter without having to use the ⏎ key once.

Paragraphs management

Press the ⏎ only when you want to end a so-called paragraph. WordPad deals with text by paragraphs. These paragraphs can be formatted or entered independently of one another. This is why you should enter text belonging to one paragraph without any line breaks. You will soon realize how convenient this method of text insertion really is. For one thing, you do not have to pay attention to the line endings, and for another, word processing is simplified by paragraph management.

Example

If , for example, you were to write a letter and press the ⏎ key at the end of every line, and then decide to increase the font size from the original 10 point to 14 point, what you would get is a completely disrupted text. The same thing would occur if you changed the font style or the margin. Due to the fixed paragraphs created by pressing the *Enter* key, WordPad and even Word 97 cannot automatically join the lines. If you refrain from making paragraphs, WordPad and Word 97 can automatically wrap the lines and readjust the text.

***Word* tab page**

You can activate the automatic word wrap feature in WordPad. To do so, select the *Options* command from the *View* menu. In the *Options* dialog box activate the *Word* tab page. This corresponds to the default format set by WordPad. This format is also used in the Microsoft Word 95 (Version 6.0) that preceded Word 97.

Wrap to ruler

In the *Word wrap* option group, turn on the automatic word wrap by selecting the *Wrap to ruler* radio button. Confirm by clicking *OK*.

> **Tip!**
>
> Microsoft Word 97 uses a new file format. This format is called *Word Document* and employs the file extension *DOC*. It can only be read by Microsoft Word 97. However, Word 97 can easily read all WordPad formats. To save a Microsoft Word 97 document for use with WordPad, use the *Word 6.0/95* file type. Microsoft Word 97 will then save the document in *RTF* (Rich Text Format) which can be read by WordPad.

Controlling the Text Cursor

In text boxes and in the word processing programs, the mouse pointer changes shape whenever you point at text. This mouse pointer has the form of a vertical beam I. The pointer shape is also called a *text cursor* or *insertion cursor*.

Text cursor

As you are entering text into WordPad another object moves along with your entry, the *text cursor*. This marks the position of your current entry point, and normally corresponds to the location at which you are typing in your text. The mouse pointer can be in a completely different location at this time.

Text cursor is important

The position of the text cursor always decides where changes to the text or additional text insertion will take place, regardless of where your mouse pointer is located. The location of the insertion cursor can be determined by several methods.

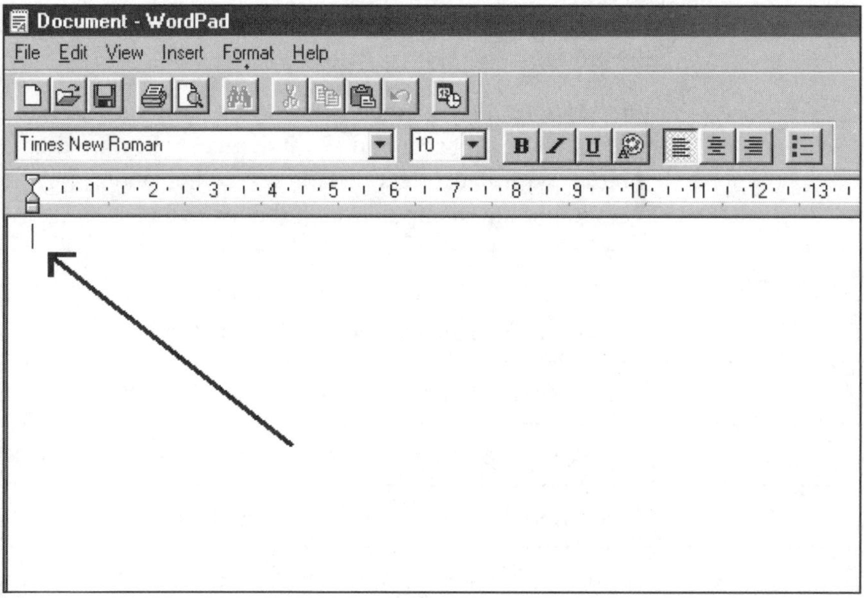

Fig. 13.2: The text cursor in a WordPad-document

Locating the text cursor

The most convenient way of locating the text cursor is with the mouse. To do this, simply point with the mouse at the exact location in the text where you want to place the insertion cursor, and then click the mouse button. The text cursor will then begin blinking at this location.

Scroll bar

To move to a text passage which is not displayed on-screen, use the scroll bar(s) or the [PgUp] and [PgDn] keys. When you have found the part you are looking for, simply click the mouse at the desired position to place the text cursor there. You can then proceed to make changes to the text or to add new text at this place.

Keyboard control

As you are using your hands on the keyboard anyway when working with a word processing program, this input device is often more convenient for changing the position of the text cursor. Especially beginners find it easier to manipulate the text cursor with the keyboard than with the mouse.

Key combinations

Furthermore, this method allows you to avoid the constant switching back and forth between keyboard and mouse. WordPad offers certain key combinations for the most important manipulation of the text cursor.

Key combination	Description
← →	to move one character to the right or to the left
↑ ↓	to move one line up or down
Home	to position the text cursor at the beginning of a line
End	to position the text cursor at the end of a line
Ctrl + Home	to position the text cursor at the beginning of the text
Ctrl + End	to position the text cursor at the end of the document
Ctrl + →	to jump to the beginning of the next word
Ctrl + ←	to jump to the beginning of the previous word
Ctrl + PgUp	to jump to the first line on the screen
Ctrl + PgDn	to jump to the last line on the screen

Fig. 13.3:   Key combinations for the manipulation of the text cursor

Tip!
Memorizing these key combinations will greatly facilitate your work in WordPad. The keyboard shortcuts also work in Microsoft Word 97, in the text boxes of dialog boxes, as well as in the Notepad. Microsoft Word 97 additionally offers a wide range of key combinations. Use the *Office Assistant* to view the additional key combinations available under Microsoft Word.

Selecting Text

Before activating any commands in WordPad or Microsoft Word, the text passage to be modified has to be selected. Most formatting can only be applied to selected text. If no text has been selected, the chosen commands will only apply to new text. To format parts of an existing document, first select them.

Selecting text

There are several ways to do this.

Selecting with the Mouse

To select with the mouse, point the cursor on the first character of the passage to be selected. Press down the mouse button and drag the cursor to the right until you reach the end of the area to be selected. Then release the mouse button.

Black bar

The selection will be displayed with a black background. In general, if you point to any part of a word with the cursor and then move to the right or the left, WordPad and Word 97 automatically selects it.

Deactivate
Automatic word selection

However, if you just want to select single characters within a word, turn off the automatic word selection. To do this, go to the *View* menu in WordPad, and select the *Options* command.

Activate the *Options* tab page and clear the *Automatic word selection* check box with a mouse click. Confirm by clicking on *OK*. You can then select individual characters in a word.

To do the same thing in Word 97, however, select *Tools/Options* and deactivate the *When selecting, automatically select entire word* check box on the *Edit* tab page.

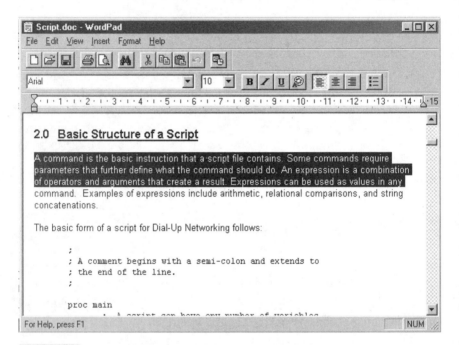

/Fig. 13.4: Selecting text in WordPad

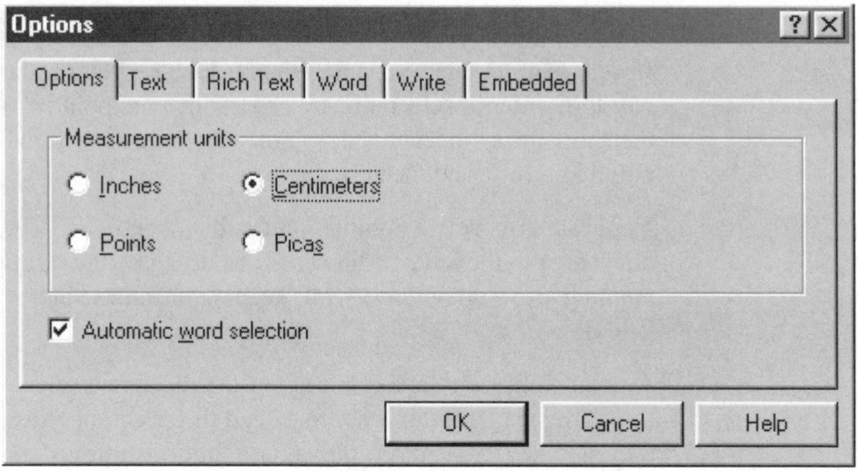

Fig. 13.5:   Activating and deactivating *Automatic word selection* (WordPad)

Selecting entire
lines

The *Automatic word selection* works both forwards and backwards. With the mouse it is easy to select entire lines, paragraphs or even pages. Should the cursor reach the upper or lower end of the WordPad screen, the window contents will automatically be scrolled line by line.

Selecting with the Mouse and Keyboard

Press the
⬆ key

To use a keyboard and mouse combination to select text, click in front of the first character of the passage to be selected. Hold down the ⬆ key and click on the last character of the text to be selected. Now release the ⬆ key.

Several pages

The combined selection using the keyboard and mouse combination can be used over several pages. To do so, use the scroll bar box in between to scroll down to the end of the text you wish to select.

Selecting with Multiple Clicks

Scroll bar

If you want to select a word, simply double-click on the word. In order to select a line of text, move the pointer to the left of the line until the pointer changes to a right-pointing arrow, and then click.

You can also select multiple lines by clicking on the blank area to the left of a line and then dragging the right-pointing arrow up or down while keeping the mouse button held down.

Double click

A double click on the left margin of the document selects an entire paragraph. In order to extend the selection, press the ⬚ key and move the mouse pointer upward or downward.

Selecting Text Using Menu Commands

Select all

Press the Ctrl+A key combination, which corresponds to the *Edit/Select All* command to select the entire document in WordPad.

Selecting Text Using Key Combinations

Key combinations

When you are working in word processing programs, it is sometimes more convenient to select text using keyboard shortcuts, since your hands are already resting on the keyboard. Using the keyboard you can often control the text cursor better than with the mouse. The most important key combinations for selecting text using the keyboard are listed in the table below.

Keyboard shortcuts	Description
⇧ + ← or →	Selects one character at a time to the left or the right
⇧ + ↑ or ↓	Selects one line at a time moving up or down
⇧ + Home	Selects from where the cursor is to the beginning of the line
⇧ + End	Selects from where the cursor is to the end of the line
⇧ + Ctrl + Home	Selects from where the cursor is up to the beginning of the document
⇧ + Ctrl + End	Selects from where the cursor is up to the end of the text
⇧ + Ctrl + →	Extends selection to include the next word
⇧ + Ctrl + ←	Extends selection to include the previous word
⇧ + Ctrl + PgUp	Extends selection from where the cursor is up to the first line on the screen
⇧ + Ctrl + PgDn	Extends selection from where the cursor is up to the last line on the screen

Fig. 13.6: Key combinations for selection

Tip! Memorizing these key combinations will greatly facilitate your work in WordPad. By the way, these keyboard shortcuts also work in NotePad. Microsoft Word offers an additional variety of key combinations. Use the *Office Assistant* to get an overview of the keyboard shortcuts available in Microsoft Word 97.

Turning off the Entire Word Selection in Microsoft Word

In order to turn off the automatic selection of entire words in Microsoft Word, select the *Options* command from the *Tools* menu, and activate the *Edit* tab page.

In the *Editing options* group box, clear the *When selecting, automatically select entire word* check box and confirm with *OK*.

From then on, you will be able to select individual characters with your mouse. In order to select an entire word, point to where the word starts, press down the mouse button and drag the cursor to the end of the last character to be selected.

Tip! The automatic word selection feature can temporarily be deactivated by using the ⎀+Ctrl key combination while selecting text.

Correcting Typing Errors

In the beginning, you are probably going to make some mistakes when you start typing text in WordPad. This is where the advantages of owning a computer start to become evident.

Correcting errors

A word processing program provides very convenient ways of correcting errors. The following section describes the various possibilities at your disposal to do this.

If you mistype some text, there are several ways in which you can correct your error. We will show you the most important ways. You can then use the appropriate method as you go along.

Deleting Characters to the Left or Right of the Text Cursor

Correcting typing errors

Mistyped characters to the left of the text cursor can be deleted one by one using the ← key. You can then enter the correct characters.

Typing errors to the right of the text cursor can be deleted in the same way using the Del key. You can then proceed to type in the new text.

Activating the Overwrite or Insert Mode

To replace longer character sequences to the right of the text cursor, press the Ins key. Now you have switched from the default *Insert* mode to the *Overtype* mode.

Replace character sequences

As you enter text, each new character you type will replace the character to the right of the text cursor. Press the Ins key again to reactivate the *Insert* mode.

Deleting and Overtyping Selections

Pressing the
[Del] key

You can also select mistakes and delete the text using the [Del] key, and then enter the new text. You can also overwrite a selection directly by simply typing in the new text.

Copy, Cut and Paste

Moving text
passages

To move text passages in WordPad or Microsoft Word, use the clipboard. To do so, select the text you wish to move. There are several ways you can work with the clipboard.

Copying selected
text areas

To copy selected text areas – without removing them from their original position – to the clipboard, select *Edit/Copy*. You can also click the *Copy* button 🖺 on the toolbar or use the [Ctrl]+[C] keyboard shortcut.

Deleting text

However, if you select the *Edit/Cut* command, the selected text will be deleted from the document, and copied to the clipboard. To do this, you can also use the *Cut* button ✂ on the toolbar, or the [Ctrl]+[X] key combination.

Inserting text

Copies from the clipboard can be inserted at other locations in the WordPad document (as well as into other applications such as those in the Microsoft Office Suite). Place the text cursor at the position where the text is to be inserted, and from the *Edit* menu, select the *Paste* command.

Alternatives

As an alternative you can also click the *Paste* button 🖺, or use the [Ctrl]+[V] key combination.

This procedure can be repeated as often as required, either in different places in the same document or in entirely different programs.

Clipboard

Note: a text copied to the clipboard or a text that is cut will be overwritten by another copy to the clipboard, and will be deleted when the computer is shut down.

Tip!

The *Copy, Cut* and *Paste* commands can also be accessed by calling up the shortcut menu with a right click of the mouse. Select the desired text passage, right-click the mouse, and choose one of the commands such as *Copy* or *Cut*. Then click with the text cursor at the position where the text is to be inserted, and select the *Paste* command from the context menu.

Text Formatting

If you are writing a letter in WordPad or Microsoft Word, these word processing programs use the *Times New Roman* font in the 10 point font size by default.

That does not have to stay like that, however. Every character in WordPad or Microsoft Word can be formatted in any of the fonts and font sizes available.

Font Formatting and Sizing

Select from the existing text characters or passages, or – using Ctrl+A – the entire text. Then, from the WordPad *Format* menu choose the *Font* command to call up the *Font* dialog box as shown in Figure 13.7.

Font style and
Size list boxes

The font style and the font size you are now using are given in the *Font style* and *Size* text boxes. You can see a preview of the settings in the *Sample* box. All available fonts are displayed in the *Font style* list box.

TrueType fonts

Scalable *TrueType* fonts are represented by a **T** icon in front of the font name. Select the new font from the *Font* list box with a click. If necessary, use the scroll bar to scroll through the list of installed fonts.

Changing font size

To change the font size, select a new value, measured in *points*, from the *Size* list box. Finally, confirm all selections with a click on *OK*.

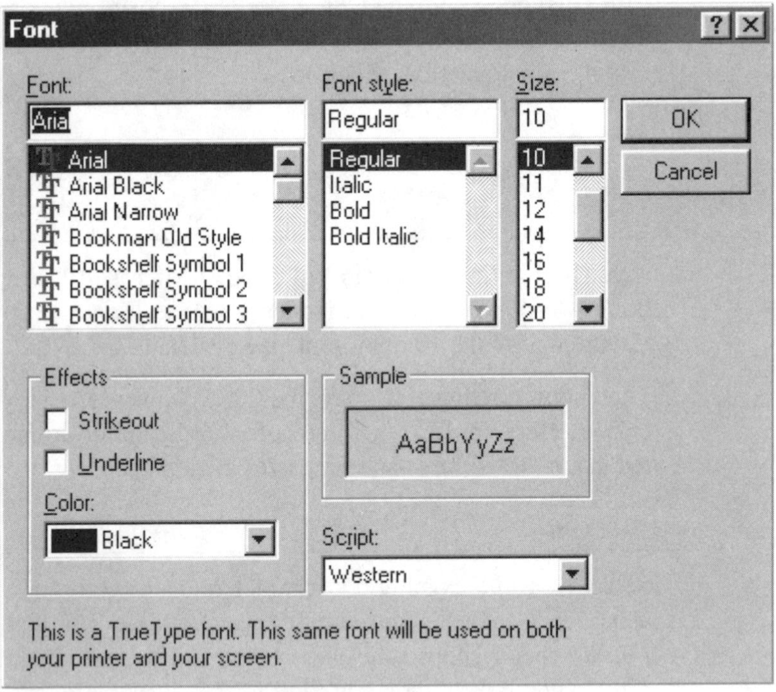

Fig. 13.7:   The *Font* dialog box in WordPad

Font drop-down box

A faster way to format text is by using the *Font* drop-down box Times New Roman and the *Font Size* drop-down box displayed in the *Format* bar that you can hide or show using the *View* menu.

Open the drop-down boxes and select the required entries. The font size can also be typed in directly and confirmed by pressing the ⏎ key.

Shortcut menu The font style and size, however, can also be entered prior to or during the text entry, and will remains valid as long as you do not enter a different formatting. The *Font* command is also accessible in the shortcut menu, provided that you right-click after having selected a text area.

Tip!

For font formatting in Microsoft Word 97, select the *Font* command in the *Format* menu. In the *Font* dialog box, the current font and font size are displayed in the *Font* and *Size* drop-down boxes. You can see what the text will look like in the *Preview* box.

A faster way to format text is by using the *Font* drop-down box Times New Roman ▾ and the *Font Size* drop-down box 10 ▾ displayed on the *Format Bar* that you can hide or show through the *View* menu. The maximum value possible for the *Font size* is 1638 points, which corresponds to a letter height of 58 cm!

Formatting Characters using Bold, Italic or Underline

In the section above we showed you how you can specify the font and size in WordPad. Now we will show you how to format text passages, single characters, or the entire text in bold, italic or underline. But first, the text whose appearance you want to change using font style formatting needs to be selected.

Text styles The *Bold, Italic* and *Underline* text styles can be specified using the *Font* command on the *Format* menu. At the end of this section, you will see how you can set the styles by using buttons. If you want to format a text passage in bold, then first select the desired text.

Font style format

Next, from the *Format* menu, select the *Font* command. In the *Font* dialog box, select the *Bold* item in the *Font style* list. You can also format selected characters in *Italic* and *Bold Italic*. Likewise, bold or italic text can be formatted in the *Regular* font style.

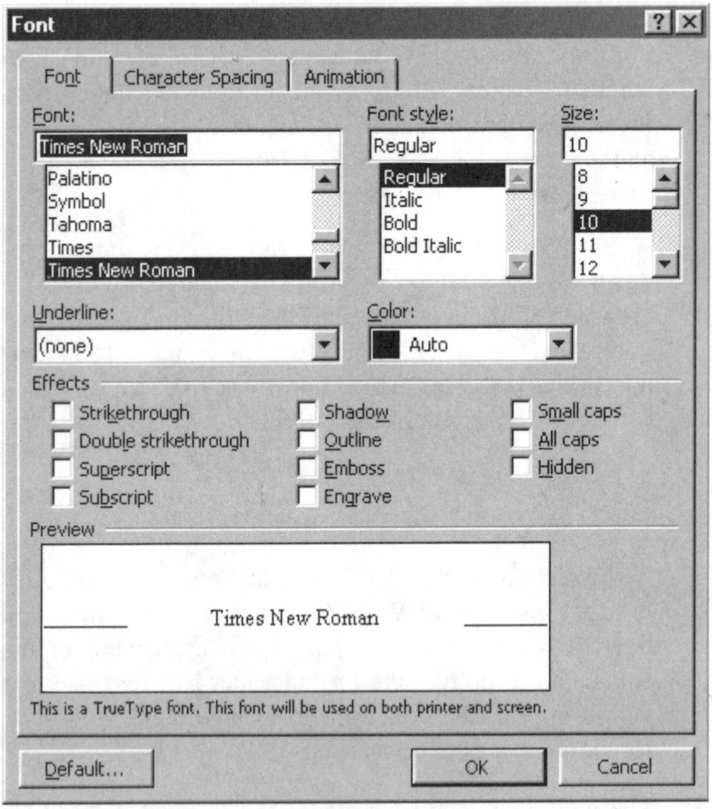

Fig. 13.8   The *Font* dialog box in Microsoft Word 97

Preview

In the sample box, you will get a *Preview* of the current formatting. You can specify the *Strikethrough* and *Underline* attributes in the *Effects* option box, by selecting or clearing the corresponding check boxes.

Next, click *OK* to implement the formatting of the selection. A faster way to work is by using the buttons on the WordPad *Format Bar*.

Fig. 13.9: The *Format Bar* (WordPad, top) and the Word 97-*Formatting* toolbar

View/Format Bar

You can hide or show this toolbar by using the *View/Format Bar* command. To format text passages in bold, click on the *Bold* button **B** . The *Italic* button *I* slants selected characters, and with the *Underline* button u you can underline the selected text. For more complicated formatting, call up the *Format/Font* dialog box.

The *Color* drop-down box

Click on the *Color* drop-down box to open a color palette, from which you can select the color for the text. A faster way to call up the color palette is by using the *Color* button 🖉 on the *Format Bar*.

Key combinations

Keyboard fans are not left in the lurch here either. The key combination for italic is Ctrl+I and to underline selected text, simply press the Ctrl+U keys. Likewise, text can be made bold by pressing the Ctrl+B keys.

The way the text is displayed on-screen is also the way it will appear on the printed document, irrespective of the printer installed. This is known as *WYSIWYG* and stands for *What you see is what you get.*

Tip!

In order to specify the font styles, select the *Font* command from the *Format* menu in Microsoft Word. In the *Font* dialog box (see Figure 13.8) the current font style is selected. A preview is displayed in the so-called *Preview* box. Use the entries, *Regular, Italic, Bold,* and *Bold Italic* to determine the font style.

You can work more quickly using the buttons on the *Formatting* toolbar. To format text in bold, click on the *Bold* button **B**. The *Italic* button *I* slants selected text, and you can underline text with a single line using the *Underline* button **U**. For more complicated formatting – such as a double underline – call up the *Format/Font* dialog box. In order to put a strike through text passages, use the *Strikethrough* check box in the *Effects* group.

Those who prefer to work on the keyboard can use the key combination Ctrl+B for *Bold*, and for italic they can use the Ctrl+I key combination. For a single underline, the Ctrl+U combination is used.

Setting Text Alignment

Paragraph

Both WordPad and Word 97 work, like any other word processing program does, with paragraphs. A paragraph is always created when you press the *Enter* key ⏎. When you are typing in text, all characters you type will belong to the same paragraph until the ⏎ key is pressed again.

If you make extra spaces by pressing the ⏎ key, these will still be treated as paragraphs, empty ones perhaps, but even so they will have an impact on the way the text is displayed.

Paragraph Formatting

You can change the appearance of a paragraph, which includes whatever text occurs in between the last and the next time you press the *Enter* key ⏎. Paragraphs can be changed or rearranged by using the *Alignment, Spacing* and *Indentation* of lines.

Format for paragraph

Every paragraph in WordPad can be formatted differently. Using *Paragraph* formatting, you can easily contrast selected text passages one from another or make them stand out visually. Paragraph formatting can be implemented by opening the *Format* menu and choosing the *Paragraph* command, or by using the buttons on the *Format Bar*. If this toolbar is not be visible in the window, it can be activated from the *View* menu by selecting the *Format Bar* command.

Cursor in the paragraph

First type in or load a text in WordPad. To set the text alignment of a paragraph, position the cursor in the paragraph, or select several paragraphs if necessary.

Setting Text Alignment

Format/Paragraph

Next, select the *Format/Paragraph* command. Open the *Alignment* drop-down box. The following entries – *Left, Centered,* and *Right* – are available. The default entry is always *Left*. What does *Alignment* signify?

Left alignment

The lines in a paragraph are always aligned to a margin, or to the center of the page. If you want to align the lines of one or several paragraphs to the left margin, select the *Left* entry under *Alignment* in the *Paragraph* dialog box.

As this is already set by default, this step is really quite unnecessary.

The *Paragraph* dialog box in WordPad

Right alignment

If you want to align the lines to the right margin, select the *Right* entry in the *Alignment* drop-down list in the *Paragraph* dialog box. To align lines along an imaginary centre line down the middle of the page, select the *Center* entry from *Alignment* drop-down list in the *Paragraph* dialog box. Centered alignments are often used for headings, while normal text is usually left aligned. The right margin alignment is used for entering the date or such things as bill numbers in documents.

Buttons

A faster way to specify an *Alignment* for one or several selected paragraphs is by using the *Align Left* ≣, *Center* ≣ and *Align Right* ≣ buttons on the *Format Bar*. As an alternative, you can select the *Paragraph* command from the shortcut menu, provided the cursor is located in the appropriate paragraph.

Tip! There are several ways of setting text alignment in Word 97. If you want to work with a dialog box, select the *Paragraph* command from the *Format* menu. Open the *Alignment* drop-down list.

Tip! Select one of the available entries, either *Left, Right, Centered* or *Justified*. To align the text to both the left and the right margins, such as has been done in this book, use the *Justified* option from the *Alignment* drop-down list. Confirm the *Paragraph* dialog box by clicking *OK* or press ⏎ to activate the setting.

A faster way to align one or several selected paragraphs is by using the *Align Left* ▤, *Center* ▤, *Align Right* ▤, and the *Justify* ▤ buttons on the *Formatting* toolbar. As an alternative, you can select the *Paragraph* command from the shortcut menu, provided the cursor is in the correct paragraph.

If you prefer working with the keyboard in Microsoft Word 97, use the following shortcuts: *Align Left*: Ctrl+L, *Align Right*: Ctrl+R, *Center*: Ctrl+E, and *Justify*: Ctrl+J.

Setting Text Indentation

The *indentation* of a paragraph can also be set in the WordPad *Paragraph* dialog box. In order to indent an entire paragraph to the right, enter the value in centimetres into the *Left* text box.

If, on the other hand, you enter a value into the *Right* text box, the lines will be indented to the left, i.e., away from the right margin.

Left and right indent

If the paragraph should be indented both from the right and the left, enter your values in both text boxes. If you only want to indent the first line of a paragraph, enter the value in centimeters into the *First line* text box. You can also combine this setting with a left indent.

Tip!

In Microsoft Word 97, it is possible not only to indent paragraphs from the left and the right margins, but the first line, when indented, can eventually play an important role too. For example, in newspaper columns the so-called *First line Indentation* is used for the separation of paragraphs. Another variation of this is the *Hanging Indentation*, which leaves the first line unchanged and indents the rest of the paragraph.

In Microsoft Word select the *Paragraph* command from the *Format* menu, and activate the *Indents and Spacing* tab page. Enter into the *Right* or *Left* boxes in the *Indentation* option group the appropriate values in centimeters, or modify the current settings using the spin buttons.

The *First line* option in the *Special* drop down list indents the first line by the value indicated in the *By* box. The *Hanging* option, however, only indents the following lines by the value indicated in the *By* box.

You can increase left indents by 1.25 cm at a time using the *Increase Indent* button on the *Formatting* toolbar. The *Decrease Indent* button moves indented text to the left in steps of 1.25 cm.

Text with Tabs

During the creation of documents you may need to create columns, for example when making lists, product surveys, invoices or small chart-like listings.

Tabs

One way of doing this that is common to both WordPad or Microsoft Word is by using the so-called tab stops or tabs.

Setting Tabs

Tabs are essentially jump marks in the document, that you can set yourself. The text cursor jumps to these tab stops as soon as you press the ⎄ key. If you press the ⎄ key again, the text cursor jumps to the next tab stop. Since the tabs are spaced at fixed intervals, it is a convenient way of setting up charts or lists in which the text needs to be aligned in columns.

Default tab stops

By default the tab spacing in WordPad is set at 1.25 cm. Thus, every time the ⎄ key is pressed, the text cursor jumps to the right by 1.25 cm. Default tabs stops are displayed on the ruler as light grey lines. If the ruler is hidden, you can display it with *View/Ruler*.

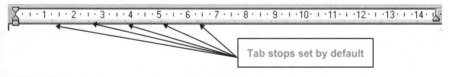

Fig. 13.11:   Tab stops set by default on the ruler

Press the
⎄ key

If you enter text and then press the ⎄ key, the text cursor jumps to the right. Then enter further text and press the ⎄ key again. If you repeat this process in the next line, the text will be positioned in the same column. Default tabs can be replaced by custom tabs stops anytime.

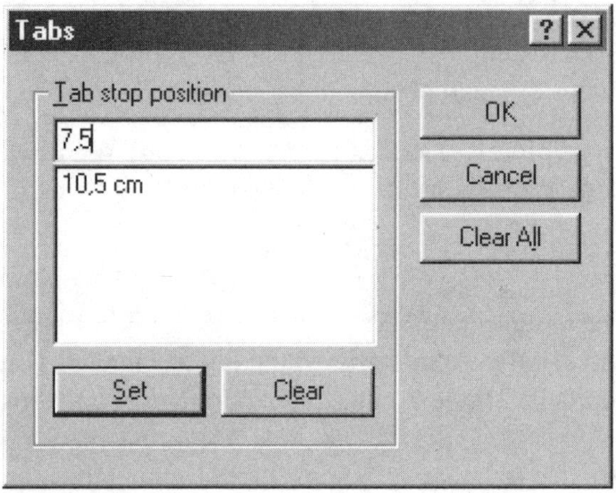

Fig. 13.12:   The *Tabs* dialog box in WordPad

Tabs dialog box

If you want to replace them with your own settings, select the paragraphs to which the settings should apply, and select *Format/Tabs*. In the *Tabs* dialog box enter the value in centimeters for the first tab in the upper text box, and click on the *Set* button. The new tab stop position will appear in the *Tab stop position* list box.

Aligning text

Repeat this procedure for all required tabs. Confirm with a click on *OK* to close the dialog box and set the tabs. Then proceed to enter your text and align it by pressing the ⬚ key.

Clearing tabs

Tabs that are not required any longer can be removed from the *Tabs* dialog box, which is accessible from the *Format* menu. To do so, select the tab that you want to clear in the *Tab stop position* list box, and click on the *Clear* button. To delete all custom tabs, click on the *Clear All* button. Confirm with *OK* and the tabs will be cleared.

Tab stops on
the ruler

Custom tabs are also indicated on the ruler. For this, WordPad uses a small 'L' at the position of the tab. But the ruler can do more than that. Tabs can conveniently be set by visual approximation.

Just point the mouse at the desired position on the ruler and set a tab with a mouse click. Custom tabs can be moved to other positions on the ruler by dragging them with the mouse button pressed.

Dragging a tab
out of the ruler

Dragging a tab out of the ruler and then releasing the mouse button will delete the tab. During the time you are moving a tab, WordPad indicates its position by a dotted line on the workspace.

Tip!

To set tabs in Microsoft Word, select the paragraph to which the settings will be applied, and choose *Format/ Tabs*. In the *Tabs* dialog box enter the value in centimeters for the first tab in the *Tab stop position* text box. Then click on the *Set* button. The new tab position appears in the list box under *Tab stop position*.

You can clear tabs which are no longer required using the *Format/Tabs* dialog box. To do so, select the tab to be cleared from the *Tab stop position* list box and click on the *Clear* button. To clear all custom tabs, click on the *Clear All* button. Confirm with *OK* to clear the tabs.

Using the ruler, tabs can conveniently be set by sight. To set the tab alignment, click on the [L] button until you get the appropriate alignment from the *Left Tab, Right Tab, Center Tab* or *Decimal Tab* options.

Inserting Numbering of Paragraphs

Business letters often require paragraphs in which appointments or products have to be listed and which need to stand out from the rest of the text. Naturally, you can select such passages manually in WordPad and give them another font or font style, such as *Bold, Italic* or *Underline.*

However, in this section we will show you how you can emphasize listings or important paragraphs with a single mouse-click.

The magic word for this kind of formatting is known as *Bulleting.*

You insert a mark in front of one or several paragraphs to draw the reader's attention to it.

Bullet Style command

To mark one or several paragraphs in WordPad with a bullet in the shape of a small black dot, select the paragraph or paragraphs and choose the *Bullet Style* command from the *Format* menu or from the shortcut menu by accessing it with a right mouse click.

Bullets button

A faster way is to click on the *Bullets* button on the *Format* bar.

WordPad slightly indents the bulleted paragraph automatically. If the paragraph contains several lines the following lines will also be indented to maintain the alignment.

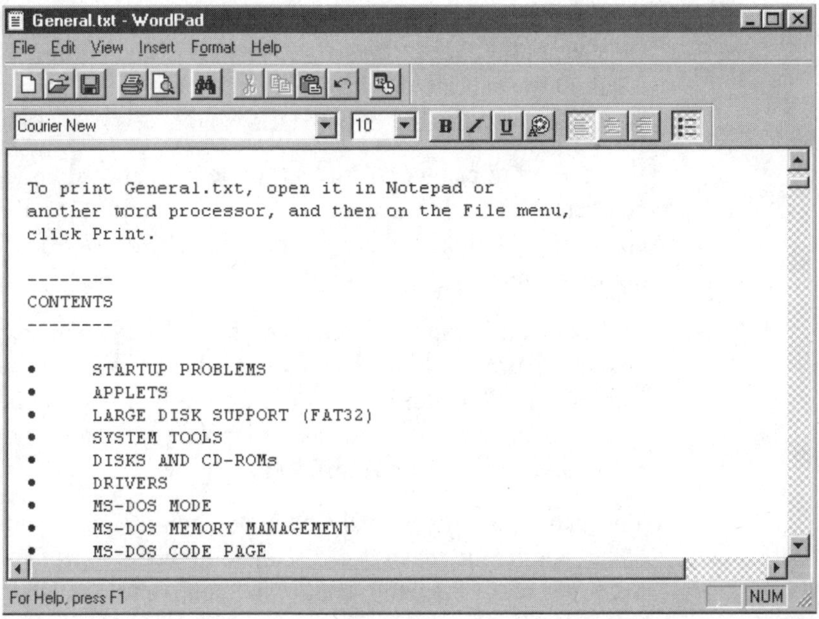

```
General.txt - WordPad                                    _ □ ×
File  Edit  View  Insert  Format  Help

 □ 🖻 🖫  🖨 🖳  🏭  🖫 🖺 🖺 ⌐  🖳

Courier New              ▼  10  ▼   B  𝑰  U  🖉  🖩 🖩 🖩   🖽

 To print General.txt, open it in Notepad or            ▲
 another word processor, and then on the File menu,
 click Print.


 --------
 CONTENTS
 --------

   •     STARTUP PROBLEMS
   •     APPLETS
   •     LARGE DISK SUPPORT (FAT32)
   •     SYSTEM TOOLS
   •     DISKS AND CD-ROMs
   •     DRIVERS
   •     MS-DOS MODE
   •     MS-DOS MEMORY MANAGEMENT
   •     MS-DOS CODE PAGE                                ▼
 ◄                                                    ►

For Help, press F1                                  NUM
```

Fig. 13.13:   Bulletted paragraphs in WordPad

Removing bullets   To remove bullets, select the bulleted paragraphs and click once more on the *Bullets* button 🖽.

Tip!   To bullet one or several paragraphs in Word, select the *Bullets and Numbering* command from the *Format* menu or the shortcut menu. Once you have made your changes, confirm by clicking *OK*. A faster way is by clicking the *Bullets* button on the displayed *Formatting* toolbar.

Supposing you want to use something besides a black dot for your bullet. Select *Format/Bullets and Numbering* and click on the sample displayed in one of the eight sample boxes that contains the bullet you wish to use.

If you want to change the indent or view additional bullet characters, click on the *Customize...* button, and select the appropriate bullet character from the *Bullet character* option group box.

The indentation can be entered into the *Bullet position* text box in centimeters, and increased or decreased with the spin buttons. An additional indent for the first line can be specified in the *Text position* group box. Click *OK* to close the dialog box and confirm the setting.

You can also automatically number paragraphs, lists or other specified items in Word. To add numbers in front of lists, first select the paragraph(s) that you want to number. On the *Formatting* toolbar, click on the *Numbering* button ☰. Word automatically inserts a numbering scheme beginning with the number '1'. To add new numbered paragraphs at the end of the list, simply press the ⏎ key.

To clear numbering from a paragraph, first select it, and then click on the *Numbering* button ☰ on the *Formatting* toolbar. Word clears either all the numbers or those of selected paragraphs only. The numbering for the following paragraphs will automatically be adjusted.

Inserting the Date in Documents

Someone who regularly uses a word processing program for the daily correspondence usually needs to enter the current date into a document several times a day. Of course you can simply type in the date on the keyboard.

Automatic date

But then, why not let your computer and the word processing program do it for you? This has two advantages: first, you can select the most suitable format from a selection of date formats, and second, you will always be sure to have the current date in the letter. In this way a certain amount of human error can be avoided.

Condition

The precondition for having the correct date in WordPad documents is of course having the correct system date in Windows 98.

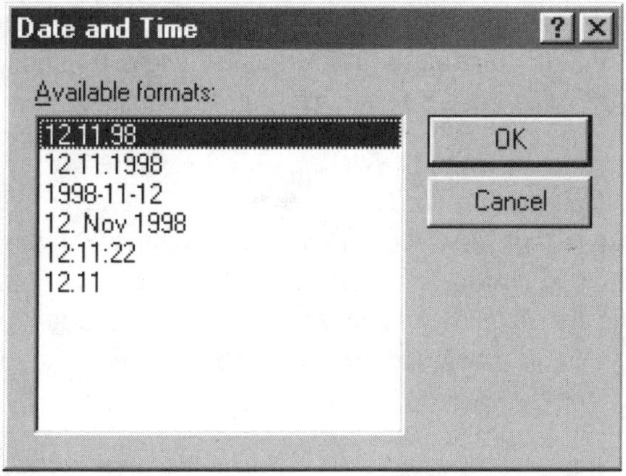

Fig. 13.14:   Entering the date and time in WordPad

Date and time
command

To insert the date into a WordPad document, place the text cursor at the point where it should be inserted. Next, select the *Date and Time* command from the *Insert* menu.

Available date
formats

In the *Date and Time* dialog box, select one of the formats available in the list. To do this, you can use the scroll bar if need be to scroll to the formats which are not immediately visible. The selected date format will be entered into the document with a click on *OK*.

Date and time button

A quicker way of working is to use the *Date/Time* button on the toolbar. If the toolbar is hidden, you can call it up by selecting *View/Toolbar*. Click on the *Date/Time* button to call up the *Date and Time* dialog box.

Time formats

At the end of the *Available formats* list in the *Date and Time* dialog box, you will find time formats with which you can also insert the system time.

Tip!

In Microsoft Word you can also insert a date that is automatically updated. To do so, place the text cursor at the required position. Then, from the *Insert* menu select the *Date and Time* command. In the *Date and Time* dialog box select one of the available formats in the *Available formats* list.

Check the *Update automatically* check box. The selected date format is then inserted into the document after you click on the *OK* button or by pressing the ↵ key. If you click inside the date, you will see a shaded background, by which you can recognize the date as an inserted field.

Tip!

In the *Date and Time* dialog box, a selected date format can be set as the default date format by clicking on the *Default* button and then confirming the message which appears by clicking *Yes*.

Finding and Replacing Text

With the search function integrated into WordPad, words spread out over the entire text can be searched for and found. If you want to replace certain terms with others, you can use the *Replace* function.

Searching for Text

Should you want to search for specific terms, single characters or a group of words in WordPad, select the *Find* command from the *Edit* menu. As an alternative you can also click the *Find* button  or press the Ctrl+F key combination.

Find dialog box

You can then enter the text you want to search for in the *Find* dialog box. If you select the *Match whole word only* check box, WordPad searches for the entire word that you have entered, and words containing prefixes or suffixes are ignored.

Upper and lower case

If you select the *Match case* check box, WordPad will search for an exact match, including the specified upper and lower case letters.

Find	? X
Find what: memory	Find Next
☐ Match whole word only	Cancel
☐ Match case	

Fig. 13.15:   The *Find* dialog box

Begin the find process

Enter the text to be searched for into the *Find what* text box, and begin the search with a click on the *Find Next* button. WordPad will select the first instance of the search term it finds in the document.

Click again on the *Find Next* button to search for the next occurrence of the word. You can close the dialog box and continue the search using *Edit/Find Next*, or by pressing the F3 key.

WordPad always begins the search at the point where the text cursor is, or at the beginning of a selection and moves down through the text. When it reaches the end of the document, the search automatically continues from the beginning of the text.

Basically, the entire text will be searched every time, irrespective of where in the text the *Find* function is started. If you have selected a word prior to choosing the *Find* command, WordPad places this word in the *Find what* text box.

In order to be able to alter a matching search word when the *Find* dialog box is open, simply click into the selected area in the document. At the end of the search you will get a message that can be closed with *OK*. The *Find* dialog box can be closed by clicking on the *Cancel* button, or the *Close* button ☒ on the title bar.

Tip! Search for text in Microsoft Word 97 by selecting the *Find* command from the *Edit* menu. As an alternative you can also use the ⌊Ctrl⌋+⌊F⌋ key combination. Enter the text to be searched for into the *Find what* text box in the *Find and Replace* dialog box. Then initiate the search process by clicking on *Find Next*. To find whole words only, click on the *More* button in the *Find and Replace* dialog box. Then select the *Find whole words only* check box. With this option, prefixes and suffixes or other word parts are ignored. If you select the *Match case* check box, the search will look for an exact match of characters, including upper and lower case specifications. If the *Use wildcards* check box is selected, Word will search for placeholders, special characters or special search operators from the *Special* list. If the *Use wildcards* check box is cleared, all characters in the *Find what* text box will be treated as normal text. After you close the *Find and Replace* dialog box, the search can be resumed using *Edit/Find* or the ⌊Ctrl⌋+⌊F⌋ key combination.

Replacing Text

If you want to replace certain characters, words or character and word combinations with other ones, select the *Replace* command from the *Edit* menu.

The key combination for the *Replace* command is [Ctrl]+[H] and calls up the *Replace* tab card on the *Find and Replace* dialog box.

Enter the text you want to search for into the *Find what* text box, and in the *Replace with* text box enter the replacement text.

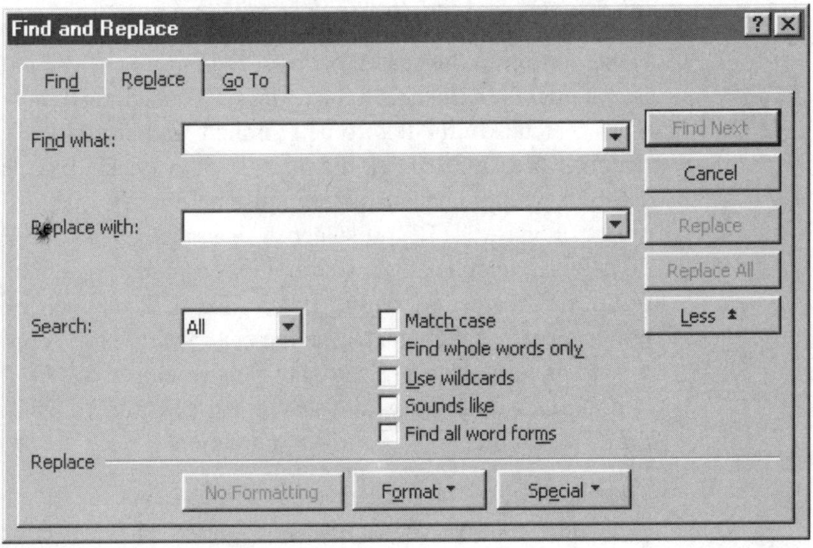

Fig. 13.16: The *Find and Replace* dialog box (Word 97)

Configuration

Configure the search using the *Find whole words only* and *Match case* check boxes. Begin the search with the *Find Next* button. A click on *Replace* will replace the first matching text it finds with the replacement text. The search will then continue automatically.

Replace

You have to click on the *Replace* button every time you want to replace the search word. If you want to replace every instance of the searched for element, click on *Replace All* instead. You can close the dialog box by clicking on the *Close* button ☒ in the title bar.

Tip!

If you want to replace certain characters, words or character and word combinations with others in Microsoft Word, choose the *Replace* command from the *Edit* menu. The shortcut for the *Replace* command is Ctrl+H and it calls up the *Find and Replace* dialog box. Enter the text to be searched for into the *Find what* text box, and the replacement text into the *Replace with* text box.

Tip!

Next, configure the search process. If you select the *Find whole words only* check box, *Word* only finds whole word matches in the text to be searched, and partial word matches are ignored. If the *Match case* check box is selected, words and characters must be exactly matched during the search. If you select the *Use wildcards* check box, *Word* searches for place holders, special characters or special search operators. If the *Use wildcards* check box is cleared, all characters in the *Find what* text box are treated as normal text. Even after you've closed the *Find and Replace* dialog box, the search can be resumed using *Edit/Find* or the Ctrl+F key combination.

The check boxes have no influence whatsoever on the replacement process. Word always replaces an occurrence with the exact text entered into the *Replace with* text box. Begin the search with the *Find Next* button. One click on the *Replace* button replaces the first occurrence with the replacement text, and the search is then automatically resumed. Click the *Replace* button whenever the search term recurs. Click the *Replace All* button to instantly replace all findings.

Reviewing and Printing a Document

WordPad is not exactly an ideal example of a layout view for displaying a complete letter. During the editing, neither the margins nor the entire page are shown on the screen. Of course you can use the scroll bar to scroll from the beginning to the end of the document if you want to preview the page layout before printing. But the right kind of preview is not available.

Previewing the Document in the Print Preview

The best way to have an overview of the document you wish to print is by using the *Print Preview*, which can present one or two full pages of a document at a time.

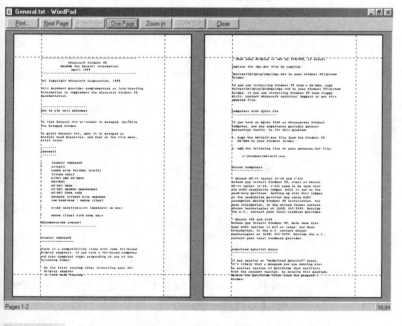

Fig. 13.17:   A document in the WordPad Print Preview

Print preview

To do this, select the *Print Preview* command from the *File* menu, or click the *Print Preview* button 🔍 on the toolbar. WordPad presents the document in a way similar to the one shown in Figure 13.17. You can then get a pretty good idea of how the page will look. If necessary, you can enlarge the *Print Preview* window.

Enlarging

Point to the document and click once with the 🔍 cursor for the first enlargement level, and a second time for the next greater enlargement. Another click with the magnifier cursor 🔍 reduces the size of the document back to its smallest size.

Scrolling through pages

To view a document containing several pages, use the *Next Page* and *Prev Page* buttons to scroll backward and forward through the document. If you want to view two pages simultaneously, click on *Two Page*. The *Print* command will call up the *Print* dialog box, where you will need to click *OK* to start the printing process.

Text cannot be edited in the *Print Preview* window. To edit text, click on *Close* and change, if necessary, the line spacing. Then preview the text once again.

The Microsoft Word *Print Preview* presents the page layout of a document on-screen exactly as it will appear in print. Depending on the view options selected, the page border can be viewed as well as the margins.

To call up the print preview, select the *Print Preview* command from the *File* menu, or click the *Print Preview* button 🔍 on the *Standard* toolbar. The key combination to switch to the *Print Preview* mode is Ctrl+F2.

Point into the document and click the magnifier cursor 🔍 once to enlarge the view. A further click with the magnifier cursor 🔍 reduces the size of the document to it original size. Click on the *Multiple Pages* button ⊞

Tip!

and, keeping the mouse button pressed down, select the number of pages to be displayed from the palette that appears. To switch to a single page display, click on the *One Page* button 🔲.

Setting Page Formatting and Margins

If you are setting up a new document in WordPad, the Windows word processing program uses certain default settings for the paper size, the formatting and the blank margins. But this does not have to remain as it is. All the settings mentioned can be modified in the *Page Setup* dialog box (see Figure 13.18), which can be activated by selecting the *Page Setup* command from the *File* menu.

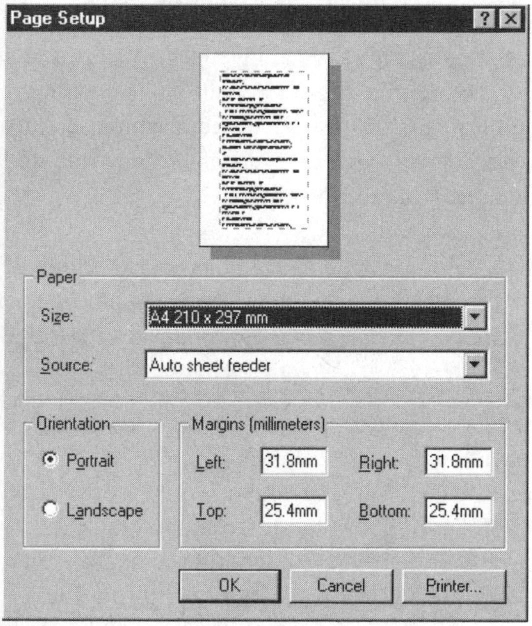

Page Setup   ? ✕

Paper

Si_z_e: A4 210 x 297 mm ▼

_S_ource: Auto sheet feeder ▼

Orientation

⦿ P_o_rtrait

◯ L_a_ndscape

Margins (millimeters)

_L_eft: 31.8mm   _R_ight: 31.8mm

_T_op: 25.4mm   _B_ottom: 25.4mm

[OK]   [Cancel]   [_P_rinter...]

Fig. 13.18:   The *Page Setup* dialog box in WordPad

Setting margins

To set the margins of a document, use the *Margins* group box. Double-click on the *Left, Right, Top* or *Bottom* text boxes, depending on the values to be changed, and over-write the entry with new values in millimeters. Above the options, you are given a preview of the changes you have made in a miniature page.

Portrait

Landscape

If you want to change the page orientation, use the *Orientation* options group, and click on one of the two radio buttons, either *Portrait* or *Landscape*.

Paper size

In the *Size* drop-down list the default *Letter 8 ½ x 11 in* setting can be changed to *A4*, executive or legal sizes. From the *Source* drop-down list, you can set which tray of your printer contains the selected paper size. The entries available in the drop-down boxes depend on the printer. After making modifications, confirm with *OK*.

New line wrap

Ideally, you should change the settings for the margins and the paper size before you begin to create your document. The page setting can also be set for text which already exists; however, it will undergo a different line wrap and may, therefore, need to be reformatted.

Tip!

To set the page layout, paper dimensions and margins in Word 97, use the *Page Setup* dialog box, which can be accessed by opening the *File* menu and choosing the *Page Setup* command.

To set the margins, use the text boxes on the left side of the *Margins* tab page. Double-click on the *Top, Bottom, Left* or *Right* text boxes depending on which values need to be changed, and enter the new values in centimeters by over-writing the current ones. If you are working with pages that face each other, you can define the extra margin in the so-called *Gutter* text box after selecting the *Mirror margins* check box.

Tip!

If you want to change the paper orientation, activate the *Paper Size* tab page and from the *Orientation* option group select one of the two given options given there, either *Portrait* or *Landscape*. You can change the paper size using the *Paper Size* drop-down box. The *Custom size* entry enables you to define custom paper sizes using the *Width* and *Height* text boxes.

You can choose the tray of your printer that contains the selected paper size on the *Paper Source* tab page. The entries in the drop-down box depend on your printer. In addition, you can set a different paper source for the first page in the *First page* list box, and for the following pages from the *Other pages* list box.

The *Layout* tab page allows you to define headers and footers. Should you want to fix all the different changes made on various tab pages in the *Page Setup* dialog box as the new default settings, simply click on the *Default* button and choose *Yes* in the message box which appears.

Printing a Document

Every document created with WordPad or Microsoft Word can obviously be printed, otherwise, using a word processing program on PC would not make much sense. However, there is no harm in taking a look at the WordPad *Print Preview* before you start printing.

Print preview

To do this, click on the *Print Preview* button 🔍 on the toolbar, or select *File/Print Preview*. Click the *Print* button there to call up the *Print* dialog box.

File/Print

The printing process, by the way, is identical in all Windows applications. To print a document in WordPad, select the *Print* command from the *File* menu to call up the *Print* dialog box.

Default printer

If you have several printers attached to your computer, the *Name* drop-down box always displays the *default printer* installed in the *Printers* folder. If necessary, open the *Name* drop-down box in the *Printer* group box and select the printer you wish to use for the printing.

Print range options group

In the *Print Range* options group, specify the particular pages or the part you want to print. The default setting is *All,* which prints all the pages in the document. However, if you select the *Pages* radio button, only the pages specified between the values in the *From* and *To* text boxes will be printed. In this manner, long documents can be printed in manageable sections. Selected portions of documents can be printed using the *Selection* radio button.

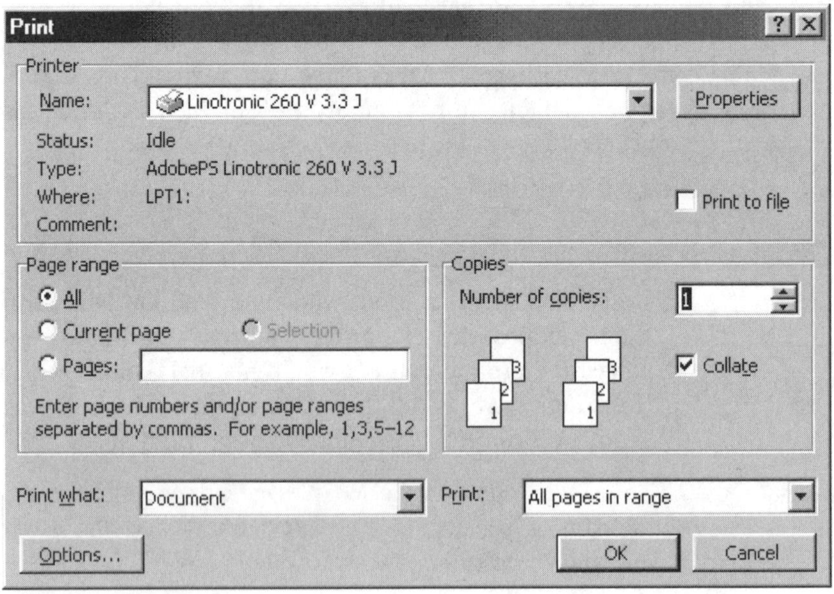

Fig. 13.19: The *Print* dialog box

Copies options group

In the *Number of copies* text box in the *Copies* options group, enter the number of copies to be printed. Select the *Collate* check box if your printer is capable of sorting. Finally, begin the printing process with *OK*.

Print button

A faster way to print documents using the default settings in the *Print* dialog box is with the *Print* button 🖶 on the toolbar. If the toolbar is not visible, it can be displayed via the *View* menu.

Tip!

Now about printing documents in Microsoft Word 97: to print a document from the *Normal* or the *Page Layout* view in *Word*, select *File/Print* to call up the *Print* dialog box. Without modifying the default settings, simply press ↵, or click on the *OK* button.

If you have several printers attached to your computer, the display in the *Name* drop-down box of the *Print* options group will always show the *default printer* installed in the *Printers* folder. If necessary, open the *Name* drop-down box and select the printer you wish to use. You can specify which portions of the document are to be printed in the *Page Range* options box.

In the *Copies* options group, enter the number of copies into the *Number of copies* text box. Select the *Collate* check box if your printer is capable of sorting. Next, begin the printing process with *OK*. A faster way of printing is to click the *Print* button 🖶 on the *Standard* toolbar.

Saving and Opening Documents

If you are creating text documents on a computer using WordPad or Microsoft Word, you will surely want to save them for a future point in time. Only documents which have been saved can be reopened, printed or edited if necessary, for further use. In this section, you will learn about how to save and open documents in WordPad, and where you need to pay attention.

Saving Documents

If you want to store a document on the hard disk, select the *Save* command from the *File* menu. The *Save As* dialog box automatically appears if you are saving your document for the first time. This is recognizable by the *Document – WordPad* description in the title bar.

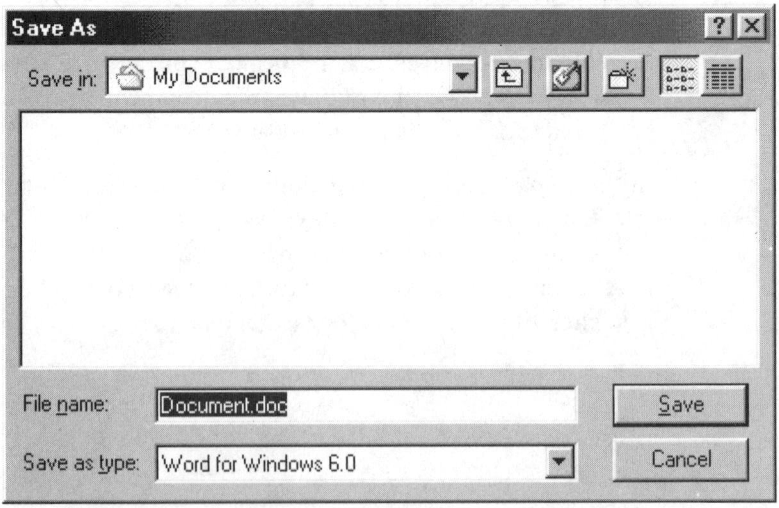

Fig. 13.20:   The *Save As* dialog box

File Name text box	A default name has already been placed in the *File name* text box. Overwrite the selection with a valid file name that can contain up to 255 characters, including spaces and other special characters as well as upper and lower case letters.
The last used folder	Using the drop-down box and the list box, switch to the folder in which you want to store the document. WordPad will display the last used folder the next time you save. Click the *Save* button to save the document on the hard disk.
File format	By default, WordPad uses the file format of Word. The files are given the *DOC* file extension. In the *Save as type* drop-down box in the *Save As* dialog box, this is indicated as *Word for Windows 6.0*. You also have the option to save your WordPad texts in other formats.

Tip!

If you want to save a document created in *Word* on the hard disk, select the *Save* command from the *File* menu. A faster way to do the same is by clicking on the *Save* button 🔲 displayed on the *Standard* toolbar.

By default, Word uses the Word Document file format. The files are given the *DOC* file extension. This file format is different from the earlier Word versions. You can open files created in WordPad or Word 95 (6.0 version) directly in Word 97. All data and formatting that you have created in WordPad or Word 95 is supported. Further information about this will be given in the following section.

Setting File Format and File Options in WordPad

By default, all documents that you save with WordPad are given the Word for Windows 6.0 file type and the *DOC* file extension. This is also the document format of the Microsoft Word 95 (version 6) word processing program. But in WordPad, files can also be saved or loaded in other formats. To do this, the settings must be specified separately for each document format.

Options
dialog box

To do this, start WordPad by choosing the WordPad item from *Start/Programs/Accessories*. Then select the *Options* command from the *View* menu. In the *Options* dialog box, you can select settings from four different kinds of text formats. The options affect the word wrap and the toolbars displayed.

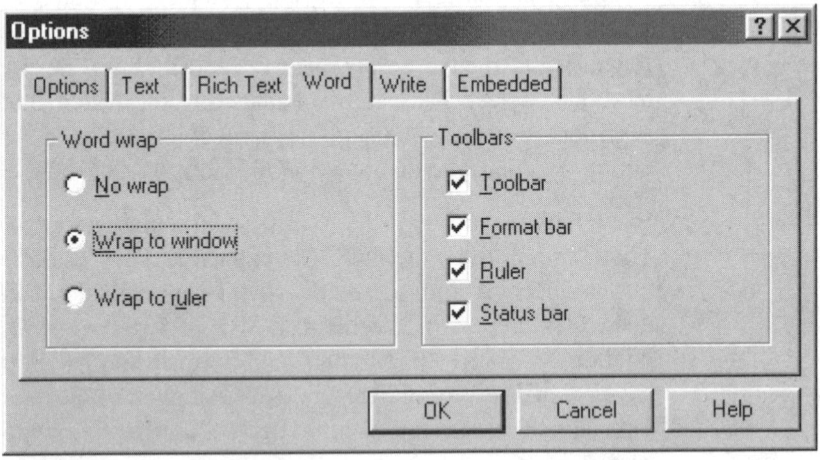

Fig. 13.21:   Setting *Options* in WordPad

Let's begin with the Word tab page that corresponds to the default format of WordPad, and therefore to the Microsoft Word 95 format (Version 6.0).

Setting
line wrap

In order to wrap the lines at the right margin, set the automatic line wrap using the *Wrap to ruler* radio button in the *Word wrap* group box. Select all the check boxes in the *Toolbars* group box in order to show the *Toolbar, Format bar* and *Status bar*, as well as the *Ruler*. Then switch to the next tab page and enter the same settings. Of course, you are only to use the options for text formatting that you would also use in WordPad.

Different text
formats

WordPad texts can be saved, irrespective of the original formatting, in different text formats. However, this only makes sense if you want to use documents in applications that are unable to recognize the *Word for Windows 6.0* format.

Save as type
drop-down box

Select *File/Save As* and open the *Save as type* drop-down box. You will get a list containing all possible formats. The format you select will depend on your requirement. Select the *Text Document* entry if you want to use a WordPad document in an application which is unable to load or convert the *Word for Windows 6.0* format. The text is given the *.TXT* file extension and is saved without formatting.

Text document –
MS-DOS Format

Should you want to use a WordPad text in an MS-DOS program, select the *Text Document – MS-DOS Format* item. The document will then contain the *.TXT* extension. All formattings will be removed, and the text will be saved in the *MS-DOS ASCII* character set. Select *Unicode Text Document* if this character set is to be used.

RTF Format

Should you want to use a formatted WordPad document in another word processing program that is unable to load the Word for Windows 6.0, select the *Rich Text Format (RTF)* file format. You can convert a WordPad document to another file format at any time. To do so, open the document in question and save it in the format of your choice. The original file remains in the Word for Windows 6.0 format. Not all WordPad formatting can be saved in every other document format.

Tip! By default, all texts saved in Word are provided with the *Word Document (*.doc)* file type, and the *DOC* file extension. However, this is not the document format of the previous version Microsoft Word 95 (Version 6). This format can only be read by Microsoft Word 97. Nevertheless, Word 97 enables you to save or display documents in other formats. Select *File/Save As* and open the *Save as type* drop-down box. You are presented with a list of all the file formats available. The format you choose will depend on your requirement. In order for Word 97 documents to be readable in WordPad or Word 95(Version 6), save them in the Word 95 format (Version 6). To do this, click on the Word 6.0/95 entry, in the *Save as type* drop-down list. This entry corresponds to the *RTF* format *(Rich Text Format)* that is supported by WordPad.

Opening Documents

To open an already saved document file, select the *Open* command from the *File* menu. In the *Open* dialog box, switch to the source drive or the folder in which the document has been stored.

Choosing a file name

Enter the name of the file you wish to open into the *File name* text box, or use the mouse to select one of the files listed in the list box above it. Next, click the *Open* button. WordPad will then load the selected file. In the *Open* dialog box, the *Files of type* drop-down box lists document formats other than the Word for Windows 6.0 (*.doc) format.

Supported
formats

WordPad is able to open documents in the following formats:

- *Text Documents (*.txt)*

- *Text Documents - MS-DOS Format (*.txt)*

- *Rich Text Format (*.rtf)*

- *Windows Write (*.wri)*

- *Unicode Text Documents (*.txt)*

Windows-Write
file type

The *Windows Write (*.wri)* file type corresponds to the file format of the *Write* program, which belonged to the earlier Windows 3.x. Select this file format to open files that have been written in older Windows versions and Write. WordPad is able to read Write documents, but unable to save this format.

DOC file
extension

The *DOC* file extension is only associated with WordPad as long as you have not installed the Microsoft Office Suite. Otherwise, the file type is associated with Microsoft Word.

DOC files

DOC files can be opened in folders of *My Computer* with a double click on the document icon 📄 or on the accompanying file name.

However, if you have Word 97 installed on your computer, Windows 98 will start the much more versatile Microsoft Word 97 program instead of WordPad.

To open a document in Microsoft Word 97, select the *Open* command from the *File* menu. In the *Open* dialog box, use the *Look in* drop-down list to find the folder containing the files you wish to open. The subfolders of the folder shown in the drop-down box are displayed in the large list box.

Double-click on one of the folders to open it. The files contained therein are displayed with the file name and the document icon. Recently used Word documents can also be opened from the *Document* menu in the Windows 98 *Start* menu.

Further alternatives are offered by *My Computer* and the Windows Explorer. In these Windows applications you can browse through folders and double-click on a Word document icon to open it.

Another alternative is offered by the *Microsoft Office Shortcut Bar*, using the *New Office Document* and *Open Office Document* buttons, through which new or existing office documents can be created or opened for editing.

Viewing Text and System Files with Notepad

Windows 98 already contains a word processing program. If you have additionally installed the Microsoft Office Suite, you have a professional word processing program, Microsoft Word, at your disposal.

Word processor

Aside from this there is also a text editor called *NotePad* that only opens short unformatted files.

Unformatted files are indicated by the *Text File* file type and carry the *TXT* file extension. Similar files can also be opened in *MS-DOS* since they have no formatting whatsoever, such as bold, italic or underline.

WordPad or Microsoft Word

Anyone having acquired some experience with WordPad or Microsoft Word will point out here that these programs are also able to open and save *Text Files,* and they are absolutely right. But the Notepad only comes in handy when small text files, system files or so-called initialization files need to be viewed and modified.

Advantage of notepad

The advantage of Notepad is that the program is quick to start, the capacity is completely adequate for this purpose, and mistakes cannot occur while saving (see Tip).

Programs/ Accessories

To start *Notepad*, click the *Start* button, select *Programs/ Accessories* and click on the *Notepad* item. In Notepad, select *File/Open* and open the *(C:)* drive. Double-click on the *Windows* folder. Using the scroll bar, scroll to the right to view documents not shown.

Information file

The files displayed are information files on Windows 98, the contents of which are often evident from the description.

Open button

Finally click the *Open* button. Using the scroll bar, scroll through the text file. As an example, let's open a system file. Select *File/Open,* and open the *C:\Windows* folder. Then type *'win.ini'* into the *File name* text box, and click *Open* to load the file.

Notepad with a system file and the *Find* function open

Find what?

Since the file concerned could be a very long one, select the *Search/Find* command. Type *'fonts'* into the *Find what* text box.

Keep clicking the *Find Next* button, until the *[FontSubstitutes]* entry is found. Then click the *Cancel* button to hide the *Find* window. Look at additional information in *Win.ini*, and finally select *File/Exit* to exit Notepad.

System information

At every Windows startup certain files containing system information are automatically read. These files are called initialization files, because they contain data by which certain basic settings can be controlled. One such basic setting is information about what devices are attached to the PC, and where the corresponding driver files are to be found.

Initialization files Initialization files can be recognized by their *INI* extensions. The *Win.ini* file saved your settings in previous Windows versions, and still exists for compatibility reasons. Windows 95/98 applications save this information in the *Registry*.

Even the *System.ini* file only contains technical information regarding older hardware, such as the names and paths for the driver files of these devices. *INI-*, *TXT* as well as *BAT-* and *SYS* files can all be opened in the Notepad.

Tip! If you try to open large text files in Notepad you will get a message asking you whether you want to open the file in WordPad. If you confirm this and change a system or *INI* file, you must always remember to specify the *Text Document* file type and use the original name.

Glossary

Background application

An application which runs but is not active. All background applications are displayed as buttons in the taskbar.

Clipboard

Temporary storage space, which receives data that is either cut from a document with the *Edit/Cut* command or the *Cut* button, or copied with the *Edit/Copy* command or the *Copy* button. You can insert this data at another position within the document or into another document using the *Edit/Paste* command or the *Paste* button.

Command buttons

Control elements in dialog boxes. A button or command button is a rectangular box with a label.

Context-Sensitive help

Part of the Windows help which gives an explanation about an unknown window element, such as an item in a dialog box.

Control Panel

Folder containing icons with which all the basic settings for the connected hardware components, like mouse, printer, keyboard, screen, as well as installed software, can be customized.

Defragmenting

Data of a file is not always stored in one location but is often distributed among different sectors of the hard disk. In this case the file is fragmented. A fragmented file slows down the hard disk access.

Desktop

The control center of Windows. The desktop is displayed after the startup. It contains standard icons for *My Computer* and the *Recycle Bin*. Additionally, personal shortcut icons for files and programs can be placed there.

Details

The view that displays information in addition to the file or folder name in *Explorer*, *My Computer*, or in the search function. This view shows the size, type, and the last date of modification of an object.

Drag

Moving an element across the screen, by selecting it with the mouse pointer and pulling it while holding down the left mouse button. Release the mouse button at the target location. In this way icons can be moved on the desktop or within or between folders.

Drag-and-Drop

Method of copying or moving data using the mouse.

DriveSpace

System utility that can compress small drives (up to 850 Mbytes). On a compressed drive, the data is saved in such a way that the disk space required is cut approximately in half.

Explorer

Program to maintain and organize folders and files. With *Explorer* you can copy and move, delete, create, rename, and create links to files and folders.

HyperTerminal

> Communications program (*Programs/Accessories/Communication*) which you can use to establish, via a modem, a connection to other computers, a mail box, or an information service.

Maximize

> Increasing the size of a window to full screen, which is the maximum size under Windows. This process is called maximizing.

Menu

> Horizontal bar below the title bar, which contains the labels of the menus.

Microsoft Backup

> Program to backup files. *Microsoft Backup* is used mostly to backup large amounts of data.

Microsoft Outlook Express

> Application to maintain and organize faxes and mail of any kind. *Outlook Express* contains folders for incoming and outgoing mail, as well as for deleted or sent objects.

Minimize

> Windows can be minimized using the system menu, a button in the title bar or the shortcut menu. A minimized window is displayed as a button on the taskbar.

Modem

> Device which transforms digital information from the computer into audio signals, which can be transmitted via telephone lines.

MS DOS Prompt

> Window to enter MS-DOS commands under *Windows 98*

My Computer

Specific folder to maintain and organize the computer, its disk drives, hard disk(s), CD-ROM drive, connected printer(s) etc. *My Computer* is right below the desktop in the object hierarchy of Windows.

NotePad

Program to open, read, browse and modify unformatted text files. *Windows 98* comes with *NotePad* to edit INI files and other system files.

Paint

Graphics program that comes with Windows, which creates and modifies bitmap files.

Phone Dialer

Program which allows you to save and automatically dial phone numbers.

Print Preview

WordPad view, which allows you to check one or more pages of a document before printing. The print preview shows the document exactly as it will be printed.

QuickView

File viewer, which allows you to view the contents of files from the search function, *Explorer* or *My Computer* without having to open the program associated with the file.

Recycle Bin

Special folder in which deleted data is stored. Data deleted by the user is temporarily stored here, before being finally deleted.

Restore

The term *Restore* is used by Windows in three different areas. The *Restore* command button in the title bar restores a maximized window to its original size. The *Recycle Bin* will restore previously deleted files with this command. *Microsoft Backup* restores damaged or deleted files from the backed-up data.

ScanDisk

System program which you can use to check drives for errors and automatically correct those that are found.

Scroll bar

Window elements at the edge of a window which are always shown if not all the contents of the window can be displayed.

Send to

Command which sends files and folders to floppy disks, or to printers and fax functions, or even to the mail service of *Outlook Express*.

Shortcut

A shortcut establishes a connection to an object, which is saved in another location. You can use shortcuts, for example, to start programs or files directly from the desktop.

StartUp

Program group whose documents and programs are automatically opened when starting Windows. The folder can be viewed in the object hierarchy of *Explorer* from *Windows/Start Menu/Programs/StartUp*.

Startup disk

Since the computer needs an operating system to function, it cannot be used if Windows is damaged. To be able to start your computer in such a case, you have to make a startup disk, onto which Windows will copy all the files needed for the Windows startup.

System Menu Icon

The icon in the upper-left corner of the title bar of every window. It contains commands to move, change the size of and close a window.

Target folder

The folder into which you want to copy or move one or more files.

Taskbar

Windows element at the bottom of the desktop. Enables you to switch between different running applications, called 'tasks'. The taskbar displays buttons of running programs.

WordPad

Word processor. You can start it with *Start/Programs/Accessories/WordPad*. *WordPad* contains functions to edit and format text. In addition, it contains a page preview function and the possibility to embed objects from other programs. You can choose in which format *WordPad* should save the documents. In the standard setting *WordPad,* will save in the *Word for Windows 6.0* format.